American Space/American Place

American Space/American Place

Geographies of the Contemporary United States

EDITED BY

John A. Agnew and Jonathan M. Smith

Edinburgh University Press

© editorial matter and organization John A. Agnew and
    Jonathan M. Smith, 2002
© the chapters the various contributors, 2002

Transferred to digital print 2009

Edinburgh University Press Ltd
22 George Square, Edinburgh EH8 9LF

Typeset in Goudy Old Style and Gill Sans Light
by Pioneer Associates, Perthshire, and
printed and bound in Great Britain by
CPI Antony Rowe, Chippenham and Eastbourne

A CIP record for this book is available from the British Library

ISBN 0 7486 1317 X (hardback)
ISBN 0 7486 1318 8 (paperback)

Contents

CONCLUSION

Preface

In 1941 American magazine magnate Henry Luce wrote and published *The American Century*, a patriotic essay stating what would soon become the popular view of the nation's destiny. His immediate purpose was to urge American entry into the Second World War, an adventure then opposed by about 80 percent of the American population, but his ultimate goal was to change the way Americans understood their place in the world. America's participation in the war was to be simply the first step toward taking its proper role in world affairs, toward assuming its full responsibilities and entitlements as global hegemon. Expressing what would become the standard interpretation of American history between 1918 and 1941, Luce wrote:

> In the field of national policy, the fundamental problem with America has been, and is, that whereas their nation became in the 20th Century the most powerful and most vital nation in the world, nevertheless Americans were unable to accommodate themselves spiritually and practically to that fact. Hence they have failed to play their part as a world power – a failure which has had disastrous consequences for themselves and for all mankind. (Luce 1941: 22–3)

The disaster for all mankind was the rise of expansionist totalitarian states and the global war that necessarily resulted. The disaster for Americans was a spiritual malaise brought on by their indecision. Americans did not know what to do, Luce contended, because they would not decide what to do; they dreaded the future because they lacked the will to shape the future into something more to their liking.

Luce's essay called for completion of the half-accomplished fact of American hegemony, with ensuing benefit to the world and the United States. America's gift to the world was to have four parts. It would guarantee free trade, and thereby promote prosperity. It would train the world's technocrats, and thereby promote progress. It would distribute aid, and thereby alleviate want. It would promulgate the ideals of liberty and democracy, and thereby ennoble mankind. In return for these gifts, it would recover the sense of unique purpose and mission that is necessary to American national identity.

A half century later it seemed that much in this vision had become reality, and that "a truly American internationalism" had become for many Americans and non-Americans "as natural . . . as the airplane or the radio" (Luce 1941: 26). Americans did accommodate themselves, spiritually and practically, to playing the part of a world power, shaping the "world-environment" to their own advantage and, many believed, the advantage of others (Luce 1941: 24). The popular mood in many quarters of the United States was, indeed, triumphal at century's end, with the collapse of the USSR (1989), the swift victory in the Gulf War (1991), and the long economic boom and technological revolution of the 1990s following one another in quick succession. The twentieth century appeared to have been the American Century after all, or, as more than a few ebullient observers insisted, the First American Century. In 1989 then president George Bush spoke of a New World Order that differed hardly at all from the "vital international economy" and "international moral order" championed by Luce (Luce 1941: 25).

This spectacle of America's triumph had at the same time, for many observers, a curiously unreal and evanescent quality. It seemed impermanent, like so many of the buildings springing up beside American expressway interchanges. It seemed illusory, like so many of the public personalities and synthetic experiences booming in the electronic media. More than a few writers noted its resemblance to a theme park. But above all else, it seemed inflated. Historian John Lukacs has taught us that inflation is not limited to the money supply, but can occur to the supply of anything when that supply increases more rapidly than the supply of other things to which it had traditionally stood in some sort of significant relation (Lukacs 1970). There is no denying that this is often desirable, as when improved productivity leads to inflation in the supply of food, health, education, and useful consumer goods, to reduced prices and wider distribution of such goods. But such inflation is also confusing because these goods no longer mean what they once meant as symbols of status or indicators of individual and collective achievement. Less desirable but no less confusing is inflation in the supplies of symbolic goods such as high marks for students, titles and degrees, encomiums, and the language (hyperbole), which was vigorous in the late twentieth-century United States. To take but one example, it was difficult to judge just where American education stood after the vast inflation of high school graduates, from 25 percent of the population in 1940 to 82 percent in 1996.

Skepticism over the apparent successes of the American Century was in many cases legitimated and amplified by a critical attitude that originated in radical political movements of the 1960s and subsequently spread to the universities and the media. These institutions popularized the critical attitude, particularly among the rising generation, and abetted the decline in public trust in authority. The terrorist attacks of 11 September 2001 encouraged both a sense of the limits of American power and a rallying around the flag.

Skepticism and a critical attitude explain only part of the outlook of those who doubted whether the United States had ended the century in an unequivocally triumphant position. There were also unsettling changes in the nation itself. Deep, disruptive, and highly controversial changes were underway in social structure (especially the family), culture (especially attitudes toward sex and work), and the economy (especially deindustrialization and the shift to finance and service-sector employment). Although they were concerned by different aspects of these changes, and drew from them very different lessons, critics on both the left and right publicly worried over their implications. It was in this mixed atmosphere of triumph and trepidation that this book was originally conceived, as a geographical analysis of the United States at the end of the American Century and the beginning of a century that awaits its name. Recent changes in the actual geography of the United States have been momentous, but they are in most cases background to these essays, not the substance. Thus you will not find chapters on mass suburbanization, the urbanization of the intermontane West, or the settlement patterns of recent immigrants, important and interesting as these matters are. What you will find are essays that describe the ways in which geography has affected the way that Americans understand themselves and the part they are to play in world affairs. The goal in this book is to approach changes in actual geography by way of changes in imagined geography, by way of changes in the American geographical imagination.

Being the work of many hands, this book is not uniform in its assumptions or its conclusions, but there is agreement that Americans are, in various ways and for various reasons, working toward a new understanding of their place in the world. They are accommodating

themselves spiritually and practically to some new facts. Despite similarities between the so-called New World Order and the American
Century, Americans seem increasingly to understand that the future
that Luce challenged Americans to imagine in 1941 is now largely past.
If, as he claimed, Americans require a unique sense of purpose and
mission in order to maintain their national identity, they must in coming years invent a new, post-hegemonic purpose and mission. Without
this the foundational belief in American exceptionalism will be unsustainable and American space must, in the American geographical imagination, become but another national space on a globe covered with
equally significant national spaces.

Just as Americans are coming to a new understanding of American
space, so they are coming to a new understanding of what it means
to be an American place. The ongoing diversification of the nation –
demographically, culturally, and economically – demands continuous
enlargement of the range of types of places admittedly American.
Thus just as the meaning of American space is growing less clear and
distinct, so too is the meaning of American place. This further tests
the national identity, which has long rested on belief in archetypal
American places (Meinig 1979). Therefore the question at the heart of
this book might be said to be a question as to the meaning of the
adjective American, what it signifies or whether, as deconstructionists
claim, it signifies anything at all (and therefore nothing whatsoever).
The contributors to this book cannot begin to answer this question,
but they do make clear that any answer will depend, to a degree not
widely appreciated, on the emerging geography of the United States,
both real and imagined. For even if the twenty-first century turns out
to be in some significant sense "American," it will take its name and
character from an America that Luce and his generation would scarcely
recognize.

References

Luce, Henry (1941), *The American Century*, New York: Farrar & Rinehart, Inc.
Lukacs, John (1970), *The Passing of the Modern Age*, New York: Harper and Row.
Meinig, D. W. (1979), "Symbolic Landscapes: Models of American Community,"
    in Meinig (ed.), *The Interpretation of Ordinary Landscapes*, New York: Oxford
    University Press, pp. 164–92.

The authors

Paul C. Adams is Assistant Professor of Geography at the University of Texas at Austin. He has published articles in *Political Geography, Urban Geography, Geographical Review,* and *Annals of the Association of American Geographers*. He was co-editor of a special issue of *Geographical Review,* and co-editor of *Textures of Place: Exploring Humanist Geographies*. His research is dedicated to the intersection between communication theory and geography.

John A. Agnew is Professor and Chair, Department of Geography, UCLA (University of California, Los Angeles). From 1975 until 1996 he taught at Syracuse University in New York. He is the author or co-author of numerous publications on political geography, geopolitics, and international political economy. His books include *Place and Politics* (1987), *The United States in the World Economy* (1987), *The Geography of the World Economy* (1989), *Mastering Space* (1995), and *Place and Politics in Modern Italy* (2002).

James S. Duncan teaches geography at Cambridge University and is a Fellow of Emmanuel College. He is a cultural geographer who specializes in the interpretation of landscapes in North America and South Asia.

Benjamin Forest earned a doctorate in geography at UCLA in 1997 and held positions at the American Bar Foundation and the University of Illinois at Chicago before joining the Department of Geography at Dartmouth College in 1998. His research concerns the geographic, political and legal construction of racial, ethnic, national, and sexual identity.

Andrew E. G. Jonas is an urban political geographer, with degrees from Durham and Ohio State Universities. He taught in Massachusetts and California before returning to the United Kingdom where he is currently Reader in Geography at the University of Hull. For the past ten years, he has been part of project studying habitat conservation planning in southern California. He is co-editor of the *Urban Growth Machine: Critical Perspectives Two Decades Later* (1999).

Janet E. Kodras is Professor of Geography at Florida State University. Her research investigates material and discursive practices of capital, the state, and civil society that generate and perpetuate income disparities, poverty, and hunger in the United States and abroad. Her purpose is to identify how forces funneling from the global, national, and regional scales intersect with class, race, and gender relations in the local social order to produce place-specific forms and experiences of deprivation.

David R. Lambert received his BA in Geography from Cambridge University, UK. He began doctoral research in 1998, exploring white settler identities in Barbados during the final decades of slavery. He has also taught on historical and contemporary urbanism. In 2001, he began a research fellowship at Emmanuel College, Cambridge.

Jonathan M. Smith is an associate professor in the Department of Geography at Texas A&M University. A cultural geographer with particular interests in the history of geographic ideas and the interpretation of cultural landscapes, he is co-editor of several books and the journal *Philosophy and Geography*.

David L. Rigby is Professor of Geography at the University of California, Los Angeles. His undergraduate degree in geography is from Salford University in the United Kingdom and his doctoral research in geography was conducted at McMaster University. His research interests include regional uneven development, political economy, and evolutionary economic dynamics.

Joanne P. Sharp is a lecturer in geography at the University of Glasgow. Her research interests lie in cultural and political geography. She has written *Condensing the Cold War: Reader's Digest and American Identity, 1922–1994* (2001), on the role of the media in constructing United States political culture.

CHAPTER 1

Introduction

John A. Agnew

Around the world, and also to its residents, the United States can often appear as boringly homogeneous: the homeland and experimental space of such American icons and instruments of global sameness as Coca-Cola, McDonald's, and Motel 6. Yet the United States is also a huge country with a wide variety of physical characteristics – from the Great Lakes and the Rocky Mountains to the Mississippi River and the deserts of the Southwest – and with a complex settlement history involving a multitude of ethnic groups from all over the world. The political boundaries that define it have evolved in complex ways down the years as a result of conquest, negotiation, and historical accident, but the moment of its political founding in the 1770s continues to dominate the way its politics and culture are organized even today. For a self-defined "new nation," founded from scratch in the throes of rebellion against British colonial rule, American popular culture has remained remarkably attached to a set of ideals about political sovereignty, social equality, and national identity which originates in the late eighteenth century. This is in spite of the fact that these ideals have faced enormous pressures from the evolving world economy and from changing expectations within the United States about what they mean. This book is about the interplay between these ideals and the North American setting in which they have played out. What has this got to do with geography?

Geography is the study of how the physical environment, the spatial organization of powerful institutions (the governments of nation-states, businesses, etc.) and the lived experience and ideas of groups of people interact and give rise to geographical, which is to say place-to-place, differences in landscapes and ways of life. Typically, the physical environment – the lay of the land, the enveloping climate, the indigenous soils and vegetation – has been given precedence in regional geographies that describe parts of the world such as the United States or Western Europe. This does not reflect the opinion of most contemporary geographers, who see the impact of the physical environment as indirect and largely mediated through cultural practices and the economy. Regional texts, however, have been slow in following suit: recounting the official stories of the world-regional spaces they hope to describe, they rarely contradict or criticize the sociopolitical ideals associated with them, or consider how these ideals work out in practice. This is because regional geographies have been resolutely apolitical, avoiding any hint of explicit "bias" in measuring the empirical character of places against the political and social claims of the powerful institutions governing the spaces in which the places are located. As a result they end up implicitly endorsing official stories by not examining them explicitly and critically.

This book offers a regional geography of the contemporary United States from a different and, we hope, challenging and revealing perspective. This perspective derives from the tension between the conventional image of American space with a nationally sanctioned story of its origin and function, and the United States as a place (or set of places) which develops and changes in relation not only to the framing of that national story but also to local and global influences which bypass or undermine its bureaucratic and ideological imperatives. The authors contrast the sociopolitical ideals used to portray the United States as a special country – in particular, its official renderings of political identity, national sovereignty, and social equality – and the contemporary condition of the country as a whole and its various geographical parts – regions, metropolitan areas, central cities, etc. The official portrait of the United States, conveyed in American classrooms and in mainstream politics, is of a liberal society with a respect for private property and a commitment to liberty and equality for all; its limited government – divided institutionally between congress, presidency, and supreme court, and geographically through the federal system and territorial political representation – guarantees the nation's values, provides security against its foreign enemies, and sets a political-economic example to the rest of the world.

The United States was indeed the first modern democratic republic. The Constitution and the institutions it gave rise to were designed to chart a new political course away from caste-ridden and decadent Europe, against which the American revolutionaries explicitly compared their experiment in building a nation-state from the very beginning. Many in the European elites were and have remained largely dismissive of the American experiment. Most, though, have failed to examine it on its own terms, as an exercise in political organization of space, and have preferred to make supercilious claims about its cultural vulgarity, compared to posh and sophisticated European drawing-room culture, its lack of a sense of history, when starting from scratch was what it has been all about, and its competitive individualism, compared to Europe's typically much more stratified access to wealth and power. European commentators on the United States from the very serious German philosopher Hegel in the early nineteenth century to the witty French sociologist Baudrillard in the 1970s have all tended, we believe, to miss the point. Even when seen geographically, America is presented as a culturally-deprived geometrical space in contrast to the rich place-laden Europe (e.g. Le Lannou 1977).

Our approach focuses on how the national space of the United States is politically stabilized and homogenized through a dominant story, and how this story is then widely accepted as a true account of the ways things operate, irrespective of empirical observation to the contrary. When overlain with such a national narrative, geography in its sense of place-to-place differences is reduced to the residual, to curiosities of architecture, for example, or folk life, and marginalized intellectually as unimportant. In a society that is widely seen by intellectuals and politicians as uniform and nationalized, with little, if any, internal variation (except perhaps some racial, gender, and class differences that we are all working at removing), geography is also likely to be seen as marginal and unimportant. This approach could be taken to any region of the world (to India or the countries of Europe, for example) where powerful official stories seek to overwhelm what closer observation reveals as much more complicated. The undoubted success of the United States as a political-economic and cultural enterprise over the long term should not blind us to the limitations of the official story. Place differences not only "remain," as, for example, in the continuing cultural distinctiveness of the South, or in the differences between economic opportunities in major metropolitan areas and the small towns of the rural Great Plains and Appalachia, but also are newly created. One has only to contrast areas of high-tech industrial development, as California's Silicon Valley, with the decaying heavy-industry districts of the Great Lakes region.

All countries have "gaps" between the spatial claims implicit in their self-declared ideals and the empirical geography of their places. The American case is unusual, however, in that its founding documents, the Declaration of Independence and the United States Constitution, are usually taken to enshrine an ideology of individual success and personal improvement – often labeled in the twentieth century as the "American Dream" – which provides a public standard by which Americans and others can at any time compare actuality with ideal. The title of the book attempts to capture the contrast by pairing an idealized American space with the "lived reality" of the United States as a set of places. The word "American" typically describes the United States of America. Though potentially applicable to anyone from the so-called New World, the United States has now effectively monopolized the word.

In using the official story of the United States as a standard of comparison for examining its geography after two hundred years of political independence, we have not set out to engage in lambasting it as a "failed society." In many respects the United States has been a fantastically successful enterprise, serving as a magnet for immigrants, encouraging intellectual endeavor and managerial entrepreneurship, and vastly influencing culture, economics, and politics well beyond its shores. It is the tension between the United States as modern, rational, administrative space, on the one hand, and the United States as a rich, differentiated, uneven, human place, on the other hand, that serves as our way of bringing together the official national story with the distinctive diversity of the country. The chapters address many of the dimensions of this tension in the related contexts of the natural environment (Part I), of the political and economic (Part II) and the cultural (Part III). What has happened and is happening in any of these contexts cannot be adequately understood without consideration of the American ethos of the country's "exceptionalism" or singularity as expressed in its commitment to a secure and homogeneous national space.

Space and place

Terrestrial space is often understood in the social sciences as the plane on which events take place at particular locations. It is general as opposed to the particularity of place (e.g. Tuan 1977). Space is also understood as commanded or controlled, whereas place is lived or experienced (e.g. Harvey 1989). Space is the abstraction of places into a grid or coordinate system as if the observer is "outside it" or looking down at the world from above (e.g. Sack 1997: 86). It must be admitted that space and place are sometimes not distinguished at all, but viewed as synonymous (e.g. Shields 1991), and some writers dismiss place as an obfuscating term without analytic merit (e.g. Soja 1996: 40). As a pair of terms, however, space and place do seem to offer an extra something that use of just one or the other would not. Drawing together elements of accounts by Yi-Fu Tuan, Robert Sack, and David Harvey, we see a tension between the two terms that arises from their distinctiveness. Space signifies a field of practice or area in which a group or organization (such as a state) operates, held together in popular consciousness by a map-image and a narrative or story that represents it as a meaningful whole. Place represents the encounter of people with other people and things in space. It refers to how everyday life is inscribed in space and takes on meaning for specified groups of people and organizations. Space can be considered as "top-down," defined by powerful actors imposing their control and stories on others. Place can be considered as "bottom-up," representing the outlooks and actions of more typical folk. Places tend to be localized when associated with the familiar, with being "at home." But they can also be larger areas, depending upon patterns of activities, network connections, and the projection of feelings of attachment, comfort, and belonging.

The most typical modern approach to space is to divide it into national spaces or territories. This division recognizes the central significance in our time of national states as primary units of political, economic, and cultural organization. Of course, there is nothing inevitable about this. Today, in fact, this territorial division of the world is increasingly challenged by networks of power (associated with transnational business) emanating from and linking together major world cities. In the past, centralized empires, territorial states, nomadic groups, and other distinctive types of politico-geographical organization prevailed over large parts of the world, or coexisted in close proximity. In this book we are concerned with a particular state-space, that of the United States. It is the dominant-popular story of the creation of that space which serves as the narrative which gives the United States its meaning as a political entity. This is more than just an "ideology," in the sense of a story that dupes unwitting residents of the American space into accepting the rightness of their residence and how they and others came to be there. It is, rather, an interpretation that defines the American space as a meaningful area in which to be located.

At the same time, the United States is also a "big" place and a congeries of smaller places. People identify with parts of it, and with all of
it; citizens act in interests that they derive from where they live, and
from the way they understand how local factors relate to the wider
territorial polity of which they are part; workers and ethnic groups
mobilize in favor of this or that goal or policy depending on where they
work or reside and how influential they are in that place (often a function of their density); businesses invest and disinvest in different places
depending on their degree of commitment to localities and to their
pursuit of higher rates of return in a better "business climate." States,
capitalists, and other powerful actors try to convert place into space, a
set of similar and therefore interchangeable locations, so as to better
fulfill their goals, be they military, economic, or social (see Chapters 6
and 10). That they often fail to do so is testament to their own diverse
objectives and the everyday acts of opposition and indifference of
ordinary people. The relative distinctiveness of places can decline in
the face of pressures for sameness, as when supermarket chains, motel
chains, fast-food restaurants reproduce the same images from coast-to-
coast. The contemporary American landscape is often lamented in
these terms, and for a subsequent decline in attachment to local places
(see Chapters 9 and 10). But places are not simply remnants in the
present of a fading past, as much of the celebration of place in recent
writing on literature might lead one to believe (Leuchtenburg 2000).
Place is neither just the *genius loci*, the spirit of local places, that the
ancient Romans identified, nor simply the attachment to particular ones,
that generations of poets have evoked. It is also the spaces of everyday
life that continue to be formed and reformed in a technologically and
economically shrinking world. Our point is that the United States is
not yet a geographical pinhead in which place no longer matters, and
there are both persisting and new place variations within it to which
we hope to draw attention.

Lineaments of American space

Although it contains many different physical environments, the
American space is often presented as uniform, the product of the same
settlement process, political ideals, and laws. The American "national
psyche" has always been understood as bound up with America's peculiar geographical origins and development: separated and protected

from Europe by the Atlantic, spreading inexorably from coast to coast during a century of frontier settlement and incorporation, founded by refugees from Europe who believed that individual conscience and effort were the twin conditions for social order, celebrating the possibility of upward social mobility overcoming social inequality through effort, luck, or migration, and bringing together distinctive societies scattered along the eastern seaboard into one ever more "perfect union." This national narrative encouraged Americans to see themselves as inhabitants of a *new* world that was destined to triumph over older polities (native tribal societies, the monarchical empires of France and Spain), and to see themselves as persons transformed by this occupation into "new men," persons with unprecedented capacity for civic virtue, economic achievement, and cultural tolerance. Recalling this story is not only useful to those who "make it" in America, adding themselves as examples into the national narrative of why it is possible, but it also secures a fixed past into which new generations can fit themselves.

The privileging of the revolutionary origin of America as a clean break with the past in 1776 has been particularly important in allowing many different groups and individuals to relate to the official story because it suggests potential for present and future inclusion as opposed to an actual history of exclusion, discrimination, and domination. The Revolution is held up as a prime example of America's unique capacity to make a fresh start. The persistence of the collective memory of an idealized American space depends on this perceived capacity for reinvention (Chapters 2, 7, 8, and 9). Such reinventions can include recognition of demands by previously excluded ethnic groups, regions, or oppositional movements. Witness the rewriting of school history textbooks in response to pressure from the formerly excluded, so that some cowboys now are African-American and women pioneers are celebrated for settling the West. From this point of view, the United States is exceptional primarily in the degree to which its history can be rewritten without altering the basic script.

This collective psyche had older roots. From the first European encounter with the New World, through the American Revolution and into the nineteenth century, the vast, unexplored, and, in European eyes, unorganized space of America excited the dream of making a new start for humanity (see Chapter 2). Of course, Europeans saw themselves as the humanity that needed the new start. With few notable exceptions, such as the so-called "civilized tribes" of the Iroquois or Cherokee, existing inhabitants were dismissed initially as civilizational and, later, racial inferiors. An image prevailed of North America as a pristine wilderness, available for European "development" and wasted on the current population who did not know how to exploit its riches successfully. If "nature" and peoples without an idea of material progress were on one side of the frontier, "history," in the sense of people making something of themselves, was on the other (see Chapters 2, 3, and 4). The geographical accretion of territory to the United States in the nineteenth century has long given credibility to the idea of a foreordained or God-given expansion into North America at the expense of all other claims to it (Figure 1.1).

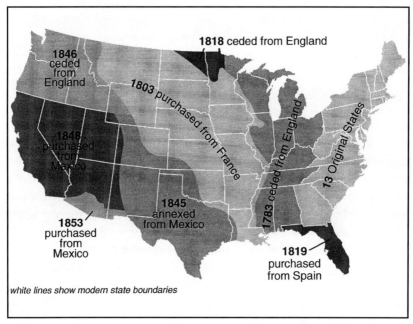

Figure 1.1 The continental expansion of the United States showing the dates at which the "political frontier" of the country was extended into the interior.

The Americans who founded the United States were heirs to this European attitude, rather than the originators of a novel American outlook (Shapiro 1997). What they did was to push it in two new directions. The first was an insistence "on American divergence from fixed patterns of historical development" (McGerr 1991: 1057). This was the idea that America, unlike other nations, was exempt from the "laws of history" that the German philosopher Hegel in the 1820s declared that all nations were subject to. In other words, America did not have to undergo the wrenching transition to modernity that other nations burdened down by feudal and aristocratic pasts had to. It was born already modern, without the class animosities, entrenched poverty, and lack of individual opportunity that afflicted Europe. Individuals could make themselves, even in the face of an encroaching society (Zuckerman 1977). There was just enough everyday empirical evidence to the founding generation of American Independence of the country's unique social features – the lack of a feudal aristocracy, for example – that they took them as self-evident. Though obviously contestable and contested down the years, the image of exemption from the trials of history has underwritten the very possibility of a clean geographical slate upon which the ideals of America could be inscribed (Chapters 4 and 9).

A second direction in which the novelty of American experience has been pushed has been that of American "national superiority" (McGerr 1991: 1097). This came later than the first. Only in the after-math of the Revolution did America take on the role as exemplar to the world (Greene 1993: 208), although certain colonial societies such as puritan New England clearly wished to be an exemplary "City on a Hill" or "New Jerusalem." Even then, the sense of American superiority involved the relatively benign hope of the relevance of the American experiment in making similar political institutions for others elsewhere. Only as time wore on did the ideas of America "as a redeemer nation and of Americans as a chosen people" (Greene 1993: 208) take strong hold. Perhaps only in the decades after the Second World War, owing then more to external challenge from the Soviet Union's alternative "utopia" than to any domestic source, was benign hope converted into smug conceit. The exemplary character of America and the assumption of American superiority encouraged active export of American values beyond the territorial limits of the United States into the world at large. This reminds us of the global significance of American self-images, which, when combined with American economic and military power, have had the capacity to make over large parts of the world in an American image (see Chapter 4).

It is to the political institutions created during the American Revo-lution and the sentiments they represent that American exceptionalism is usually most directly traced. The genius of the American Constitution of 1789 lay in tying powerful central government to instruments for flexible geographical expansion into the continental interior. Unlike the British colonial system that since 1763 had restricted settlement beyond the Appalachian Mountains, and the short-lived Confederation of former colonies, republican government was tied to an ever-expanding system in which a growing population could find its own space without competing for control over that already occupied along the Atlantic seaboard. Yet, at the same time that it represented a common national framework, and fears of democratic excess were harbored by the coastal elite, the Constitution also worked to frustrate the concentration of political power. The division of powers between the states and the central government and the separation of powers at the center between the Congress, the presidency, and the Supreme Court, was an attempt to create a system of "pure" territorial representation in which the votes of individuals for elective offices were non-cumulative and aggregated together in single-member districts on the basis of equality between individuals and districts. A presumption of equality of political treatment across the American space underpinned both the American federation and the expansive nationhood it facilitated, though many parts of the continental interior initially, Washington, DC, and some geographical entities acquired later (such as Puerto Rico) have been defined as "territories" without all of the rights of full state and federal membership.

In the eyes of important commentators, the political *equality* between Americans has been especially important in setting republican America apart from the Britain that its leaders had revolted against. The aristocratic French traveler Tocqueville's book *Democracy in America*, for example, written in the 1830s, is often used to justify the view that political equality is the defining characteristic of the United States. The writings of the Founding Fathers, such as Madison, Hamilton, and Jefferson, and others, are alluded to in making the case for the first example in modern history of successfully starting a new nation from scratch based on the ideas of a few prescient individuals. The commitment to equality under law is seen as central to this process. After all, it was the seeming arbitrariness of British law after 1763 that had turned so many establishment Americans into revolutionaries. George Washington and the other leaders were hardly the wretched of the earth. What they resented was not so much British rule in the abstract as major shifts in government fiscal and settlement policies without consultation with those most affected. Be that as it may, there was an undeniable populist element to the American revolution that fueled the rhetoric of its leaders. The idea of the Revolution as a new birth or regeneration "forced a dialogue between speaker and hearer that disregarded social position and local setting" (Stout 1977: 527).

The second fundamental dimension of the American space involves the geographical limits or boundaries to the governmental system. After Independence the American claim to *sovereignty* rested on both British precedent of control over coastal lands and upon right to occupy as a consequence of conquest, or purchase from other European empires, lands in the interior. Very quickly the claim became continent-wide, reflecting a mix of both the imperial-military logic of the British and the more recent commercial-colonial imperatives of the settlers themselves (Webb 1977). So, a peculiar feature of American sovereignty was maintenance of claims that extended well beyond the territory that Americans actually occupied. Failing to gain all the territory they wanted at the Paris Peace Conference of 1783 that recognized American Independence, the new rulers came up with a rationale for gaining it later.

> By leaps of logic peculiar to American thinking, nationalism and "natural rights" were extended to include territorial rights to the North American continent: a nation conceived in liberty had a right to a homeland; in order to enjoy that liberty the people must feel secure; in order to feel secure and to enjoy the freedom to develop their territory in accordance with the "immense designs of the Deity" they must have control of all areas strategic to their homeland. (Meinig 1986: 416–17)

The balance of federalism might seem at first to contradict the third dimension of the idealized American space, that of an American national *identity*. Indeed, for many years this was a central problem, particularly in managing the South and in establishing conditions of admission to the Union of newly-settled territories with Southern attitudes towards slavery. Nationalism and federalism, however, proved ultimately complementary in incorporating under one flag such a large and potentially centrifugal set of people and areas. The common interest in expansion, resistance to British attempts at reconquest in the

War of 1812 (as Americans saw it), and a basic patriotism resulting from widespread, if uneven, mobilization against British rule militated in favor of a sense of common Americanness. Until the end of the Civil War this proved to be a rather more plural than singular national identity in which local or state identities coexisted with the national one. National identity was less easily wrested from the continent than was the territory to which the identity applied (this volume Chapters 4, 5, and 8).

Turning space into place

The image of spatial uniformity is constantly compromised by persistent and emergent regional differences between places, differences that result from shifting relations between these places and other places within and outside the United States. The pressures have been several. Federation was a patchwork solution to the problem of keeping together a set of regional societies whose interests might otherwise diverge, due to an emerging "geographical morphology" that jointly worked against both equality and common identity. Furthermore, though unified to expand continentally and protect themselves against common imperial foes (such as the British and Spanish), the former colonies remained part of an Atlantic World with respect to trade and economic development. American sovereignty, therefore, was also compromised by the need to sustain external connections, not least those with the erstwhile imperial power, Britain, a source of both markets and investment throughout the nineteenth century. The fact that the federal government was new and had to establish its functions and legitimacy, whereas the states had only to start from where the old colonial governments left off, meant that sovereignty was effectively split between the two levels.

The simplest difference between the new states was in relative area and population size, ranging at the time of Independence from Pennsylvania to Rhode Island and from Virginia to Delaware, respectively, although down the years growth rates and expansion in the number of states have radically changed the ranking of states by area and population size. Relative population growth and the addition of new states profoundly affected the pattern of political representation in the federal government, particularly in elections to the United States House and for the presidency. Each state, irrespective of size, sends two senators to the United States Senate. From an early stage the elites of regional groupings of states with similar historical beginnings, economies, and social structures (e.g. slave-owning South, mercantile New England, commercial agricultural Middle States) were exceedingly concerned about the shifting balance of power between these groupings, or "sections" as they came to be called. At the same time, the states maintained a degree of power and influence over their populations that was much superior to that exercised by the federal government. Some states, such as Virginia, had a higher degree of internal social and political homogeneity than did others, such as New Jersey. If today the federal government has achieved much greater power relative to the states, largely as a result of pressure from social movements and businesses operating nationwide, and if regional economies (such as the Southern cotton economy) are much reduced in significance relative to a variegated local pattern, there are still important regional, state-to-state, and rural-urban differences that represent the continuation, in new geographical forms, of the uneven development that characterized the United States at its outset.

Even as the United States came into being as a political entity, a national economic-communication structure was evolving, and this national "geographical morphology" worked to differentiate American space. Donald Meinig (1986) proposes a heuristic model to illustrate the essential elements of this morphology of early America (around 1800) (Figure 1.2). This framework too, like the idea of regional societies, is historically specific to early America, but the basic morphology has had persisting influence. Even as the United States expanded continentally, the city-regions of the Northeast achieved a grip on national development that they only began to lose in the last thirty years of the twentieth century as the United States economy integrated more fully into a globalizing world economy. New York City and Philadelphia were quickly national rather than state or regional centers. They thrived on interaction with provincial centers and internal hinterlands, and served as entrepôts linking into the wider transatlantic economy. A "nuclear area" including New York and Philadelphia gave way rapidly to a "core region," with such important regional centers as Baltimore and Boston. Beyond this was a "domain" of areas linked directly (in the North) and indirectly (in the South) into the national road, and later, canal, and railroad networks. Finally, at greatest distance from the core was the frontier region or "sphere," exerting a powerful imaginative political pull but as yet weakly incorporated into the economic-communication structure of the new nation. This huge and expanding zone presented serious economic and political problems. The lack of ready communication across the Appalachian Mountains and the orientation of the main rivers and lakes to the north (the St. Lawrence) and south (the Mississippi) made for difficult connections, particularly to the Northeast core. The new lands added stimulus to the conflict between North and South, as the question of the extension of slavery finally boiled up into secession and civil war. Not surprisingly, the sense of belonging to a national, local, or regional enterprise varied enormously between the various types of place. There was nothing inherent in the vast new country to produce an integrated nation. Relative power or capacity to affect economic and political decisions also paralleled this geographical morphology of core, domain, and sphere.

Socially, culturally, and economically the United States remained tied into the Atlantic World (Agnew 1987). Ethnic, religious, and intellectual ties to Europe, particularly to Britain, remained strong. There had been, after all, considerable support for American Independence among elements of the British intelligentsia. Economically, although the United States embarked on an independent course, it was at first hesitating. Only after 1815, and largely at the behest of representatives from the Northeastern core, did the United States Congress pass a tariff to protect domestic manufacturing industries (Sellers 1991: 75). During the global economic turndown of the 1820s and 1830s the United States economy benefited from British investment escaping poor rates of profit at home. This not only stimulated coal, iron, and railroad development, through railroad construction it also began opening up the "sphere" of continental America to the world economy. By the 1830s, therefore, there were complex transatlantic connections in trade, commodity prices, and capital flows that made the United States economy part of a much larger enterprise (see this volume Chapters 3, 4, and 6). The cotton trade was especially important, directly linking the Southern states where cotton was grown to British and other European markets. This external dependence made the South much more resistant to legislation protecting domestic manufacturing, found mainly in the Northeast, and more open to European influence and opinion. The nature of the cotton economy likewise produced a more conservative, hierarchical, and anti-industrial cultural outlook among the dominant classes in the South than prevailed

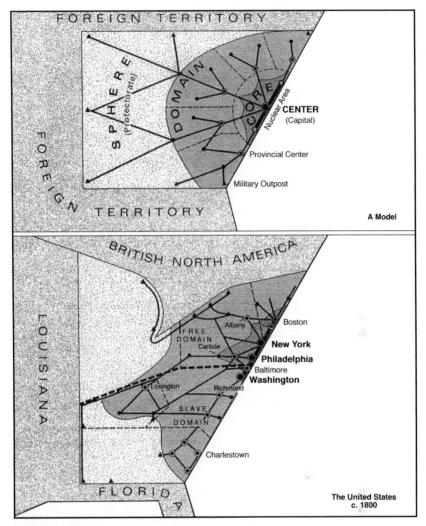

Figure 1.2 Meinig's model of American "geographical morphology" adapted to the United States around 1800. Source: Meinig 1986: Figure 67, 402. Reproduced by permission of Yale University Press.

elsewhere in the country, a perspective with echoes to this day, not just in the South but everywhere whenever the region's representatives achieve influence at the national scale (Genovese 1994).

The actual course of events, then, had consequences for the translation of the available space into a variegated and dynamic American place. First of all, there has been a clear tension between equality and hierarchy. Though the impetus to equality, in particular from back-country or frontier folk, and in the deepest aspirations of the Founders, was real, and to a degree institutionalized, there was at the same time a powerful countervailing force from the aristocratic elements worried about losing out to the masses, nativist groups anxious about their position in the face of immigration, Northeastern city fathers anxious to develop their cities as national centers, Southern planters devoted to slavery, settlers intent on wresting land from its native inhabitants with or without legal niceties, and capitalist industrialists determined either to escape political regulation or to turn it to their advantage (see this volume Chapters 6, 7, 9, and 10).

Second, sovereignty before the Civil War was not neatly vested in the federal government. The states were largely uninhibited in the pursuit of their local identities and interests. Indeed, the Civil War occurred in large part because state control over a specific phenomenon, slavery, was challenged by a federal regime devoted to a national story and a set of economic interests that could no longer find a place for slavery anywhere in the United States. Though the balance obviously changed after the defeat of the Southern Confederacy, with subsequent expansions in the scope of the federal government, most notably in the New Deal of the 1930s and during and after the Second World War, the United States has remained an ambiguous case. Not only can the states pursue a variety of approaches to policy independent of the federal government, but also as a limited and divided entity the federal government has itself never managed to achieve the control over its space that centralized governments elsewhere, as in France or China, for example, have managed to do (Chapter 5). Within the federal government, regional differences are still a significant source of differences of opinion over the scope and direction of United States foreign policy (Trubowitz 1998; Lind 1999). This is not to diminish the central government's actual and potential powers of police surveillance, land ownership, and legal control, only to point out the dangers of treating the United States federal government as something essentially equivalent to the governments of more centralized states. What is clear, however, is that the original loose federation to which the story of America's idealized space makes reference is no more and has not been so for some time.

Finally, national identity remained problematic for many years after the founding of the United States. Not only were many of the country's citizens foreign immigrants with potential loyalties to other countries, groups, and places, but state and local identities also remained strong. The Civil War was crucial in signifying through blood sacrifice the emergence of an American identity that went beyond civic bonds and personal loyalties to parties and politicians. The identity, although deepened, remained exclusive, however. Not only were Native Americans and slaves, and with the abolition of slavery former slaves, long denied full political and legal rights, they were excluded from the heroic roles in national history and from ready definition as "true" Americans. Numerous immigrant groups were to suffer similar, if less long-standing, indignities. Women remained outside the national drama until they, like African-Americans at a later stage, forced themselves into the national political consciousness. All of these shifts in the experience of cultural identity have varied across states and regions, reflecting local cultural and economic differences. Today, the critical question concerns the extent to which the post-Civil War American identity can subsist with multiple other identities of ethnicity, religion, gender, and sexual orientation (see Chapter 8).

Themes of *American Space/American Place*

The book is organized into three sections, moving from the physical-environmental through the political-economic to the social-cultural dimensions of the space/place tension. These sections not only follow the familiar pattern of most regional texts, building from the physical context to the cultural matrix, but they also reflect the historical course of dominant understandings of the American experience. Until the early years of the twentieth century, the physical size and environmental range of the United States were regarded as the pre-eminent features of the American experience, whereas more recently either the American political economy and its mode of governance, or America's social and cultural peculiarities (such as its multiethnic character), have tended to acquire greater significance. Each section, therefore, captures a distinctive part of the tension between an idealized American space and America as an actual place. Before each chapter, a short introduction connects the chapter to the themes of the book. A Conclusion provides a discussion of the themes in light of the material presented in the individual chapters and offers a critical review of the framework for the book laid out in this Introduction.

References

Agnew, J. A. (1987), *The United States in the World Economy: A Regional Geography*, Cambridge: Cambridge University Press.

Genovese, E. D. (1994), *The Southern Tradition: The Achievement and Limitations of an American Conservatism*, Cambridge, MA: Harvard University Press.

Greene, J. P. (1993), *The Intellectual Construction of America: Exceptionalism and Identity from 1492 to 1800*, Chapel Hill: University of North Carolina Press.

Harvey, D. (1989), *The Condition of Postmodernity*, Oxford: Blackwell.

Le Lannou, M. (1977), *Europe, terre promise*, Paris: Editions du Seuil.

Leuchtenberg, W. E. (2000), *American Places: Encounters with History*, New York: Oxford University Press.

Lind, M. (1999), "Civil War by Other Means," *Foreign Affairs*, 78, pp. 123–142.

McGerr, M. (1991), "The Price of the 'New Transnational History,'" *American Historical Review*, 96, pp. 1056–61.

Meinig, D. W. (1986), *The Shaping of America. Volume I: Atlantic America*, New Haven: Yale University Press.

Sack, R. D. (1997), *Homo Geographicus*, Baltimore: Johns Hopkins University Press.

Sellers, C. (1991), *The Market Revolution: Jacksonian America, 1815–1846*, New York: Oxford University Press.

Shapiro, M. J. (1997), *Violent Cartographies: Mapping Cultures of War*, Minneapolis: University of Minnesota Press.

Shields, R. (1991), *Places on the Margin*, London: Routledge.

Soja, E. W. (1996), *Thirdspace*, Oxford: Blackwell.

Stout, H. S. (1977), "Religion, Communication, and the Ideological Origins of the American Revolution," *William and Mary Quarterly*, 34, pp. 519–41.

Trubowitz, P. (1998), *Defining the National Interest*, Chicago: University of Chicago Press.

Tuan, Y.-F. (1977), *Space and Place*, London: Arnold.

Webb, S. S. (1977), "Army and Empire: English Garrison Government in Britain and America, 1569 to 1763," *William and Mary Quarterly*, 34, pp. 1–31.

Zuckerman, M. (1977), "The Fabrication of Identity in Early America," *William and Mary Quarterly*, 34, pp. 183–214.

PART I

Environmental ideals and realities

CHAPTER 2

The place of nature

Jonathan M. Smith

Regional geographies typically begin with a chapter devoted to the physical attributes – relief, climate, soils, etc. – of the larger region or country divided into smaller ones. The logic is that the possibilities and limits of life in a given region are circumscribed by the economic resources provided and physical constraints imposed by the region's natural assets. Over the long span of human history and at a macro-geographical scale there is undoubted truth to this logic. But in the contemporary United States this logic is more than a little misleading. Not only are relatively few people in any region dependent on what resources that region provides, but also economic relations with the natural world now extend, as it were, to the global scale. Many of the resources consumed anywhere in the United States come from some-where else, often well beyond the boundaries of the United States itself. Nature, however, in the sense of the physical environment has not entirely disappeared as a regional reality. If human-environment interaction at a global scale is now largely manipulative and uncon-scious, concerned with the extraction of resources for use at some distance away, at a regional scale it is now largely sensuous and aes-thetic, concerned with the visual pleasures and leisure potential of the region. Cultural geographer Jonathan M. Smith explores how American understandings of nature have shifted historically from a sense of a heroic nature upon which their very difference with where they had come from rested to a sense of an abused nature, a nature that Americans have defiled and misused. Each of these understandings has had associated with it "iconographic landscapes" that represented it to wider audiences – from the majestic Niagara Falls in the former case to the river that caught fire, the Cuyahoga River in Cleveland, Ohio, in the latter one. At the beginning of the twenty-first century, however, even as the idea of an abused nature has persisting strength, the notion of recuperating the environment has also gained in strength, signified by the "restoration" of the Cuyahoga. Particular places, there-fore, carry a heavy load of meaning for the wider American space to which they are thought to relate.

Nature in America is not what it used to be. This is not to say that the observed regularities of the natural order have been suspended, which would be absurd, or to say that natural systems have been deeply altered, which would be truistic, but rather to say that nature no longer means what it once meant. Always a somewhat vague and vagrant category, nature has once again shifted its ground. Many aspects of this change in the meaning of nature fall outside the purview of geography, and of this book, but at least two pertain directly to the geography of the United States at the beginning of the twenty-first century.

The first of these pertains to the scale, or rather scales, at which a typical beginning-of-the-century American experiences nature, which he or she now in all likelihood calls the environment. This experience is now of the environment at two scales, the local and the global, which are so dissimilar that we may usefully speak of two environments. Stated simply, the typical American experiences a local environment, which he largely evaluates in therapeutic terms of aesthetic enjoyment and physical and psychic health, while he simultaneously experiences a global environment, which he largely evaluates in economic terms of profitability and price. This bifurcation is not new, of course, as it is present in some degree wherever long-distance trade operates, but it has at the beginning of the twenty-first century widened throughout the developed world to a point where it is now possible to live in a place without consuming a single local product, excepting, perhaps, the air.

The second change pertains to the places and landscapes that are thought to condense and therefore symbolize the essence of nature. Whatever their form, such places, traditionally described as natural wonders, allow – indeed urge – Americans to experience nature in a refined and highly specialized way. They present nature as a spectacle that one should absorb as sensations, primarily visual, but also as aural, tactile, and olfactory sensations. The symbolic landscape of a natural wonder reduces nature to a source of sensory stimulation: sights, sounds, and smells that excite intellectual, aesthetic, emotional, and in some instances spiritual responses. It presents nature as something one should think about rather than something one should, for instance, eat. Consider the difference between nature as it is presented at the Grand Canyon and nature as it is presented at, say, a pig roast. What a pig roast does that the iconic landscape of the Grand Canyon, properly appreciated, fails to do, is transform nature into food. What the iconic landscape of the Grand Canyon does that a pig roast, properly appreciated, fails to do, is transform nature into an idea.

Because this idea has changed, so have the places and landscapes that Americans turn to when they wish to contemplate this idea. In the last decades of the twentieth century the ideas and icons of what I will call heroic nature began to yield to new ideas and icons of what I will call abused nature. To a growing portion of the population it began to seem that the essential idea – what one really needed to know about nature in America – was no longer incarnated in something like a mighty cataract thundering in the wilderness, but was rather incarnated in something like a waste pipe disgorging industrial effluvium into a turbid and moribund river. This sort of dolorous image of abused nature enjoyed a brief vogue in the late 1960s and early 1970s, but is now recognizable as a transitional icon that conveyed a transitional idea. As the twentieth century drew to its close, the dominant idea seemed to be that nature is a patient; as with so much else in the end-of-the-century United States, nature is a victim of past abuse now in process of recovery under the care of experts.

These two changes in the experience and meaning of nature are, of course, connected, because change in the structure and scale of the spatial networks in which a people finds itself enmeshed leads to change in the hopes and fears, and the insights and illusions, to which that people are prone. These hopes and fears, and insights and illusions, will normally be expressed – reinforced or refuted – in symbolic landscapes.

Superannuation of the natural region

A book on the regional geography of the United States customarily begins with a chapter on the physical environment. This describes the terrain, climate, soils, and vegetation of the country, drawing particular attention to spatial variation in these environmental characteristics. Such a chapter normally culminates in a map of natural regions, territories within which broadly similar physical conditions are found. This custom arose as part of the common belief that study of interactions between humans and their physical environment constitutes "the heart" of geography. Previous generations called this human ecology or the tradition of man–land relations (Brigham 1915; Barrows 1923).

The central premise of this tradition is the reasonable supposition that the environment most germane to any human group is the environment by which that group is immediately surrounded. Geographers argued that the economic opportunities of a human group are limited to the possibilities inherent in the physical characteristics of its circumjacent region (Dryer 1920). Conceding that all human groups have shown great creativity in discovering and exploiting possibilities latent in their local habitats, and that similar physical environments have often given rise to widely differing cultures, ecologies, and economies, geographers nevertheless maintained that a region's economy and culture is almost always in some complex way tied to that region's terrain, climate, soils, and vegetation (James 1959: 35–6). As stated by an early proponent of this view, "the place makes the race and the race progressively remakes the place" (Whitbeck 1926).

This approach had many merits, notably its recognition that there are natural limits to human freedom, and that humans discover and interpret these limits when they exercise their freedom as purposeful work. These environmental limits are not uniform for all of humankind, but in fact vary greatly from region to region and place to place. Each place sets for its inhabitants a unique range of possible activities, a unique gauntlet of risks, and a unique schedule of costs to pursue these activities or minimize these risks. Thus study of natural regions properly served to refute racist arguments for the relative superiority or inferiority of certain human groups, by attributing differences in the rate and direction of their development to the basic inequality of geography. Historian David Landes finds this the central strength of geography's message, and, interestingly, the reason many people prefer to ignore geography. Geography "tells an unpleasant truth, namely, that nature like life is unfair, unequal in its favors; further, that nature's unfairness is not easily remedied . . . The world has never been a level playing field" (Landes 1998: 4, 6). The quality of the earth's surface as human habitation is highly uneven, and although all human groups have shown remarkable ingenuity in making the most of their allotment, this fundamental environmental inequality has contributed to even grosser inequalities of productivity and wealth between human societies. "All human societies contain inventive people," physiologist Jared Diamond writes, "it's just that some environments provide more starting material, and more favorable conditions for utilizing inventions, than do other environments" (Diamond 1997: 408).

The best studies in this tradition have also emphasized work, the long process of acquiring environmental knowledge and accomplishing environmental transformation (Harvey 1984). They made it clear that the unique possibilities offered by a place are never immediately apparent or accessible, but are rather discovered and developed by human ingenuity and labor. It was not, for instance, obvious to observers in 1830 that the Illinois prairie was ideally suited to production of corn and soybeans. This emphasis on discovery and work led regional geographers to realize the extent to which human groups have modified their physical environments, through changes wrought on the land itself and through alterations made in their ways of understanding and representing that landscape (Thomas 1956). The result was appreciation of human dwelling as a multiform process that transforms the natural order into what J. B. Jackson called a "synthetic space" (Jackson 1984: 8). This insight served to denaturalize much of the visible world and reveal its pervasive artificiality. Such disclosure is invariably salutary, if only because it helps to cure what Ortega described as the "radical ingratitude" of modern men and women who are "unaware of the artificial, almost incredible, character of civilization" (Ortega 1932: 63, 89). It also makes it clear that some particular people, or even person, bears responsibility for certain aspects of the visible world, that these attributable aspects did not simply occur as consequences of autonomous natural processes (Samuels 1979).

The historical connection of a region's human population and its environment cannot be gainsaid, and even today it should not be ignored, but in the United States at the beginning of the twenty-first century it must be reconsidered. You and I continue to have our freedom constrained by environmental limits, but ever fewer of these limits are imposed by our local or regional environment. You and I cause work to be done with the environment, but in most instances this work is done by proxy, at a great distance, through the medium of the market. A shortage of timber may prevent me from building a new garage, but I will experience this shortage as exorbitant lumber costs, not as an absence of trees in my vicinity. The limit I face in this instance is a limit in the aggregate supply of lumber drawn from all the lumber-producing regions of the world. Stated simply, growth of the global market economy and declining primary-sector employment have caused an ever-shrinking percentage of the population in any given natural region to be directly dependent for their resources or livelihood on the natural environment of that region (Harvey 1985; Urry 1985). Economic relations with the natural world are increasingly conducted at the global scale.

These changes, and the technological innovations that make them possible, lead Philip Brey to observe that "over the past two centuries, the role of geographical features in the constitution of the identity of places has decreased" (Brey 1998). Historian William Cronon finds this condition implicit in the history of urban-industrial societies, because over the course of their development "the ecological place of production grew ever more remote from the economic point of consumption, making it harder and harder to keep track of the true costs and consequences of any particular product." By effecting this displacement, Cronon concludes, "the geography of capital produced a landscape of obscured connections" (Cronon 1991: 340). Agrarian essayist Wendell Berry claims this decline of a truly local economy, with clear and visible ties to a local environment, causes residents of a place to lose "knowledge of how the place may be lived in and used." The landscape of obscured connections that emerges, "when the urban-industrial economy more and more usurps the local economy," ineluctably leads to a decline in "care" for the local environment (Berry 1990: 166; 1992: 7).

Berry is only partly correct. There are certainly many aspects of local environments in America that a swelling majority of the residents no longer care about, or even understand – periodic drought is an example from my own region – but there are at the same time other aspects about which they have come to care even more deeply. All people continue to depend on the local or regional environment for things like air and water (although for many this is ceasing to be the case with drinking water), which is why air and water quality have become for many people virtually synonymous with environmental quality. Most people also continue to depend on the local environment for recreational opportunities, which is why open space is today an important environmental issue. Relatively few look upon the local environment with the eyes of producers who intend to work that environment; most look with the eyes of consumers who will work with distant environments and simply live and play in the local environment. They are what Robert Kaplan calls "'rooted cosmopolitans,' living in one place but intellectually and professionally inhabiting a larger world" (Kaplan 1998: 327).

Privileged people are, therefore, increasingly able to interact with the natural world in two very different ways, and these two interactions occur at two different scales. Their interaction at the local scale is to a significant degree sensuous, an enjoyment of aesthetic pleasures. These may include enjoyment of beautiful and unlittered vistas, the

Figure 2.1 Therapeutic places. The use and meaning of the local environment has changed as Americans have become increasingly dependent on global markets for resources and commodities. The local environment is today far less likely to be viewed as a source of material resources that can support the economy, and far more likely to be seen as a source of aesthetic, emotional, and physiologic resources that can support the physical and psychic well-being of residents. Beautified and sanitized, such environments may be thought of as therapeutic places. Modern American suburbs like that depicted here are a common sort of therapeutic place. Exclusive resorts and spas where lavish consumption is surrounded by pristine nature offer an even more poignant example. (*Photograph by the author.*)

sound of singing birds, the smell of damp earth or cut grass, the feel of sunshine or a bracing wind against one's skin. A capacity to yield just this sort of aesthetic pleasure is today what we largely mean by the phrase amenity environment. In addition to aesthetic responses, the local environment is cared for as the cause of physiological responses, as a source of chemical compounds found in local air, water, and soil. These aesthetic and physiological responses are tied to a place; their continued quality depends on protection and preservation of that place. Because such places are manipulated to ensure physical health and a sense of psychological well-being, we may well refer to them as therapeutic places (Lasch 1978).

Environmental interaction at the second, global scale is essentially manipulative and acquisitive. It entails alteration of natural patterns and processes, extraction of valued resources, and discharge of refuse and wastes. Unlike local interactions, these interactions occur across an extensive space and their continued operation depends on continued access to that space.

It is not difficult to visualize one's immediate place, since this is by its very definition that which one experiences. The difficulty is to theorize one's immediate place, to see the phenomena it presents as manifestations of larger environmental and social processes (Entrikin 1991). I see a cloud over my house, but it requires considerable theoretical knowledge to see that cloud as part of a climatic process that covers a large territory, endures for a long time, and includes any number of invisible physical and chemical components. When we succeed in such theorizing from the particular to the general, it is often because we have been trained in the sciences, in this case physical geography. What is perhaps equally difficult is to exercise our imagination in the other direction, from the general to the particular; for instance to visualize the distant environments to which we are tied by Cronon's obscured connections. These environments are by their very nature those which we do not experience, or experience only indirectly and partially in the form of commodities. We may understand them in theory, in terms of general notions like the market, consumption, capitalism, and the environment, but only through imaginative effort can we see such incorporeal abstractions in the guise of an immediate, tangible place. When we succeed in this effort, we create a poetic image, a symbolic landscape that makes possible intuitive comprehension of an otherwise unimaginable reality.

Nature is one of the ideas we use to understand the distant places to which we are obscurely connected by exchange relations. Each one of us understands, however dimly, that every commodity we consume contains material and energy originally extracted from somewhere, but, being uncertain just where that somewhere is, geographically or metaphysically, we are normally content to suppose it located in a vast, murky, and poorly charted region that we call nature. This is a poetic idea, not a theory or a thing. It is primal nature, the mysterious source from which we imagine all blessings (and terrors) flow, not the dissected and servile nature of natural science. If we wish to understand the manner in which Americans have imagined this primal nature, we must therefore advance not by way of scientific analysis, but by way of symbol and myth, by examination of what Schama describes as "poetic forms by which such mysteries [are] intricately symbolized" (Schama 1995: 257).

Figure 2.2 Symbolic landscapes. A symbolic landscape is commonly supposed to condense and clarify a meaning that is elsewhere found in a diffuse and ambiguous form. A natural wonder such as the Grand Canyon affords the viewer a number of strong sensations that can be transformed, through interpretation, into an idea of nature. This makes it possible to form an intuitive comprehension of something that is otherwise too large, complex, and abstract for immediate apprehension. Properly interpreted, for instance, this particular symbolic landscape impresses one with an intuitive comprehension of the vast dimensions and astonishing duration of natural processes. (*Photograph by the author.*)

The poetics of heroic nature in America

It has been said that there is something we might call a "taste in uni-
verses," a cultivated and considered preference for one model of reality
over all others (Lewis 1964: 222). The same may be said for nature. It
seems that we approach the evidence offered by our senses predisposed
to bend it to our tastes. One might, for instance, have a taste for materialistic nature, and consequently delight in scientific explanations of
complex relations between natural objects and their past and present
conditions. But this requires one to suppress any number of emotional,
aesthetic, and spiritual intuitions. Alternatively, one might have a taste
for romantic nature, and take pleasure in feelings of mystery, beauty,
and wonder aroused by natural objects, all the time carefully ignoring
rational, scientific accounts of these experiences. It is to this sort of
selective sensibility we refer when we speak of the social creation or
cultural construction of nature (Evernden 1992).

The idea of heroic nature is one such construction, and one of
considerable importance in the mythos of America because Americans
have historically been disposed to see themselves as a people defined
in considerable part by unique relations to nature. That these relations
have been, in fact, ambivalent, ambiguous, and diversified by the several
ways in which Americans have worked nature, in no way vitiates the
popular idea first expressed by Crèvecoeur: Americans believe that
they have had the good fortune to inhabit "the state of nature where
man could be brought back to his true nature" (Kazan 1988: 33). The
first Europeans to settle in North America believed that the "wilderness" afforded them a second chance. Free of the historical accretions
of established custom and power that constrained European social life,
the New World opened the possibility of a fresh start. It appeared to
be an actual surviving instance of the "state of nature" that political
theorists claimed preceded the original social contract, and as such
invited a new social contract, a radical reconstitution of the social
order (Miller 1964: 1–15).

It might well have been feared that this new social order would in
time follow its predecessors down the beaten path to artificiality and
decadence, and that despite its unique and auspicious origins American
civilization would wind up much like any other. But Americans have for
the most part denied this. It is, in fact, the very essence of American
exceptionalism to contend that America is unique in both origin and
development. Once again, this confident outlook is grounded in the

idea of nature. As Perry Miller explained, for two centuries American painters, poets and philosophers have "identified the health, the very personality of America with Nature." They have supposed that the United States was "Nature's nation," inoculated against corruption by persistent exposure to nature, in relic wilderness landscapes and ritualized frontiersmanship (Smith 2001). As Miller explained, they believed that "America can progress indefinitely into an expanding future without acquiring sinful delusions of grandeur simply because it is nestled in Nature . . . Because America, beyond all nations, is in perpetual touch with nature, it need not fear the debauchery of the artificial, the urban, the civilized" (Miller 1964: 208, 211).

Figure 2.3 Ritualized frontiersmanship. The birth of the American people in a natural environment is often supposed to have been a propitious event, for it allowed the new nation to develop freely, unencumbered by the artificiality and historical accretions that bedeviled the peoples of Europe. For the American people to retain this advantage, it is also often supposed that they must periodically renew themselves by contact with nature. Ironically, the passage of time has made those who would seek out nature increasingly dependent on technology. Thus this patriotic fisherman is able to experience the nature of Padre Island, TX, only through the technological medium of his pickup truck. (*Photograph by the author.*)

This nature that is understood as the source and sustaining force of American political ideas is a poetic form, idea, image, or device that has often been used to understand the mysteries of American exceptionalism. It is a poetic concept by intuition that is epistemically correlated with the technical concepts by postulation that one finds in rational theories of formal political philosophy (Northrop 1947: 169–90). This is to say that it is a metaphor that conveys analogically a political doctrine that would be otherwise mysterious, either because it is nowhere clearly articulated or because its clear articulation is too long, difficult, and tedious for an ordinary person to comprehend. The poetic form of heroic nature in America has four aspects, each grounded in Americans' actual experience with nature, but also epistemically correlated with popular political philosophy.

To many of the earliest European colonists, American nature appeared uniquely raw, sinister, and forbidding. It elicited from them feelings of fear and revulsion against the menace of a wild nature in which they saw an obdurate impediment to development, a shadowed lair of enemies, and a dangerous invitation to atavism. "What could they see," William Bradford wrote of the Pilgrims in 1630, "but a hideous and desolate wilderness full of wild beasts and wild men?" Little enough, Bradford recorded, so "when they wandered in the desert wilderness . . . their soul was overwhelmed in them" and they subsisted on little more than "the spirit of God and his grace" (Bradford 1951: 68–9). The face of the land has been altered in the three and a half centuries since, and with it the fears and consolations of those who walk it, but the idea endures that American nature is something essentially wild. To the American, a natural scene is properly desert, which is not to say arid but unpeopled, pristine, virgin. Nature is in this view a realm apart, an entity present in some places and absent from others. This is why, I suppose, the modern American pilgrim will drive two thousand miles to gaze on a desolate landscape: it is his *hadj* to the true presence of American nature.

Time diminished the colonists' perils, real and imagined, so that although most Americans continued to view nature as an adversary they must violently subdue, few continued to view it as an adversary before which they must tremble with mortal fear. By the eighteenth century, nature seemed no longer malevolent, simply stubborn, a vast, potent, and yet rather stupid force, like a great dumb ox that might be tricked, goaded, or lashed into doing what men willed. The attitude is captured in this bit of doggerel published in *Atlantic Magazine* in 1866.

> Working early, working late,
> Directing crude and random nature,
> Tis joy to see my small estate
> Grow fairer in the slightest feature.

This nature was crude and random, but not shockingly wild. Moreover, from this vantage American nature appeared providential, indeed uniquely fruitful. In the face of diligent labor it yielded a plentiful abundance (Potter 1954). Thus many Americans have believed that, in addition to being wild, American nature is also something essentially strong, prolific, and bountiful.

In the early nineteenth century, a small but steadily expanding number of Americans began to discover a third aspect to American nature. It was not malign or recalcitrant, but rather soothing, healing, and purifying. Thus they did not shrink from it, or strain to bend it to their will, but rather surrendered to it, rather as a weary man might surrender to a tub of hot and soapy water. They did so in the faith that nature would restore them, make them whole. They believed that wild nature is a potent antidote to the malign and debilitating strains of civilized life and that periodic retreats to wild places are a sovereign form of physical and psychological therapy. In his poem, "Inscription for the Entrance to a Wood" (1817), William Cullen Bryant wrote:

> Stranger, if thou hast learned a truth which needs
> No school of long experience, that the world
> Is full of guilt and misery, and hast seen
> Enough of all its sorrows, crimes and cares,
> To tire thee of it, enter this wild wood
> And view the haunts of Nature. The calm shade
> Shall bring a kindred calm, and the sweet breeze
> That makes the green leaves dance, shall waft a balm
> To thy sick heart. Thou will find nothing here
> Of all that pained thee in the haunts of men,
> And made thee loth thy life.

Ralph Waldo Emerson described the same purifying wood in his essay, *Nature* (1836).

> At the gates of the forest, [he wrote] the surprised man of the world is forced to leave his city estimates of great and small, wise and

foolish. The knapsack of custom falls off his back with the first step he takes into these precincts.

This did not mean that one should necessarily "camp out and eat roots," for we are "men instead of woodchucks," but that we should discern in the objects of nature "a present sanity to expose and cure the insanity of men" (Emerson 1940: 406, 414, 420).

The idea that nature rejuvenates and restores one to the vigor and innocence of youth remains a powerful strain in the idea of American nature. In a famous line from 1961, Wallace Stegner opined that

> something will have gone out of us as a people if we ever let the remaining wilderness be destroyed . . . For an American, insofar as he is new and different at all, is a civilized man who has renewed himself in the wild. (Brower 1961: 97, 98)

More recently, poet Gary Snyder has described the emergence in America and elsewhere of a "new religion" of wild places. "The temples of this movement are the planet's remaining wilderness areas . . . The point" he continues, "is making intimate contact with the wild world" (Snyder 1984: 205). Thus we must add to the idea of pristine and bountiful nature Americans' belief that nature purifies, that it is a cleansing spirit by which one may be, in a sense, baptized. As a tech-nologically-minded writer put it, it is a place in which one is "recharged just like a battery" (Roth 1968: 2: 29).

Today it seems a majority of Americans has come to agree with Henry David Thoreau, that "'nature' is but another name for health" (Thoreau 1968: 395). No doubt much of this change is attributable to successful work with nature, particularly in the rich lands west of the Appalachians, and to removal or elimination of real hazards (Jackson 1953). But, as noted above, the early colonists looked askance at wild nature not only because it was unyielding and a haven for enemies, but also because they feared prolonged exposure to wild nature might arouse beastly propensities and cause them to regress "to the level of the barbarian or, worse, the animal" (Earle 1992: 64). In 1865 the American historian Francis Parkman described this as "that influence of the wilderness which wakens the dormant savage in the breasts of men" (Parkman 1902: 1: 44). The change from a belief that wild nature fosters wild men to a belief that wild nature restores lost innocence grew out of a radical change in the dominant theory of human nature. The contemptible "natural man" of the Bible, "who receivieth not the things of the Spirit of God," was in many minds superseded by the praiseworthy "natural persons old and young" of Walt Whitman's poetry,

> well-shaped, natural, gay,
> Every part able, active, receptive, without shame or
>   the need of shame . . .
> (1 Cor. 2:14; Whitman n.d.: 105, 179)

In 1858 Congregationalist minister Horace Bushnell lashed out against this new school, which wished "to have society organized according to nature," and which grounded its hopes "not in the supernatural redemption of man, but only in a scientific reorganization of society." "All the naturalism of our day begins just here," he explained, "in the denial of this self-evident and every where visible fact, the existence of sin" (Bushnell 1858: 24, 25, 142). Affirmations of original sin and calls for supernatural redemption have not ended, and a persistent strain of political thought, beginning in the Constitution, views the natural man with grave suspicion, yet for nearly two hundred years America has been dominated by "the bright and hopeful view of what man might become and stood a good chance of becoming in his new [American] home" (Curti 1980: 409; Schlesinger, Jr. 1986: 3–22). Much of this optimism has been grounded in a belief that American manners, institutions, and values are more natural than those found elsewhere, that they are the "least infected by ideology" (Kirk 1991: 22). This was certainly the interpretation offered by nineteenth-century American novelists and historians, who routinely contrasted the natural simplicity, candor, and forthright sensibility of Americans with the extravagance, deceit, and befuddled superstitiousness of foreigners (Levin 1959). To this day, many Americans believe that one can become too civilized, and they are inclined to look to nature rather than culture when they desire a guide to true and just action.

Places of heroic nature

If sufficiently popular, a taste in nature will create a landscape that embodies that taste for, as David Lowenthal has famously argued,

"landscapes are formed by landscape tastes" (Lowenthal and Prince
1965). What is more, a landscape created to embody a taste will suggest to those who behold it that the taste is not, after all, simply a taste,
but rather a privileged perspective on reality. The original poetic form
of heroic nature was composed of four elements: wild nature, bountiful
nature, purifying nature, and nature as a guide to true and just action.
These elements were in varying proportions condensed in iconic
landscapes of heroic nature, particular sites where tangible expressions
of these elements were present. We can call these sites original places
of nature in America.

An early example was the Natural Bridge of Virginia. "It is impossible for the emotions arising from the sublime to be felt beyond
what they are here," Thomas Jefferson wrote in 1781. He went on the
describe how the stone arch drew from spectators profound feelings of
wonder, admiration, and the all-important titillation of fear (Jefferson
1944: 197). In the early nineteenth century, the Hudson River Valley
became the most important icon of American nature, whether viewed
directly or as represented by painters of the Hudson River School
(O'Brien 1981). Following construction of the Erie Canal, Niagara Falls
became a sight that was for many the quintessence of nature in the
New World (McGreevy 1994). The western waters of the Ohio and
Mississippi River Valleys afforded yet another iconic landscape, once
steamboat travel had made it possible for indolent and reflective individuals to form an impression of the interminable tangle of riverbank
vegetation (Jakle 1977). By the end of the century the West had yielded
a host of new icons: the Yosemite Valley, the Yellowstone country, and
the Grand Canyon.

Because heroic nature is imagined as something wild, vast, and
tremendous, something by which a human, and perhaps all humanity,
is properly dwarfed, the original places of nature in America were
normally rather grand. This is why the great icons of American nature
are so often freaks and enormities: giant trees, mammoth caves, monumental valleys, grand canyons, big bends. It seemed proper to symbolize
the poetic ideal of heroic American nature in outsized and prodigious
forms. This was recognized by the British traveler Edward Dicey in
1862, when he wrote that "the single grand feature of American
scenery is its vastness; and so for the American mind, sheer size and
simple greatness possess an attraction which we in the old world can
hardly imagine" (Dicey 1971: 206). Such places were awful in the old

Figure 2.4 Heroic nature. Niagara Falls has long been one of the great icons of heroic American nature. It seemed to many to embody the uncontrolled and wild quality of American nature, and yet its surging water also suggested a power in nature that could be harnessed for human good. Beginning in the nineteenth century, Niagara became an important pilgrimage destination for nature lovers who wished to experience something older and more authentic than civilization. Ironically, this symbol of heroic nature was in the twentieth century surrounded by an industrial landscape and the symbol of abused nature, the toxic waste site at Love Canal, became its next door neighbor. (*Photograph by the author.*)

sense of the word: they inspired a feeling of awe. As Charles Dickens described his first impression of Niagara Falls in 1842: "I ... had no idea of shape, or situation, or anything but vague immensity." Still, in time he discovered the conventional poetic significance of the "tremendous spectacle." "I felt how near to my creator I was standing," he wrote, and this proximity aroused in him "peace of mind, tranquillity, calm recollections of the Dead, great thoughts of Eternal Rest and Happiness" (Dickens 1985: 182). The centuries have done little to dull Americans' taste for what Thoreau described as "pure Nature ... vast, drear, and inhuman," nature as Thoreau saw it on Mt. Katahdin, Maine. Clambering down the mountain side, Thoreau reflected that "here was no man's garden ... It was not lawn, nor pasture, nor mead, nor woodland, nor lea, nor arable, nor wasteland. It was the fresh and natural surface of the planet Earth ... Man was not to be associated with it." (Thoreau 1906: 71, 78). These lines express as well as any the persistent American prejudice that true places of nature are places apart, anti-landscapes that should be pristine, unspoiled, and free of human artifacts. A place of nature in America was properly spectacular and pristine, because these qualities convey the wild element in the poetic form of heroic nature.

Americans also imagined nature as a rich, prolific, and perhaps even inexhaustible source of vital energy, and therefore delighted in what Max Lerner described as "illusions of the illimitable" (Lerner 1957: 252). Such sights are sublime in the old sense of that word: they evoke a sense of irresistible cosmic forces. This illusion is today present in the stupendous flood of commodities, but also in images of nature that brook no intimation of an end to this delightful deluge. It is, I suspect, the promise of indefatigable productivity that explains the special exhilaration Americans feel when they gaze (from a safe distance) upon powerful, brawny nature: waterfall, breakers, rivers, floods, extreme weather. This taste for evidence of nature's force was apparent as early as the 1830s, in paintings by the Hudson River school that depict the visible aftermath of natural violence: twisted and shattered trees, jagged clefts in the earth, storm fronts and thunderheads. It was at the heart of the allure of Niagara Falls, which embodied a nature that appeared to many nineteenth-century visitors as "a boundless realm of power opposed to or beyond the realm of human control" (McGreevy 1994: 4). Emerson wrote in his journal "we love force and we care very little how it is exhibited" (Emerson 1911: 262). As Lerner put it, "unlike men of previous ages, it is not salvation [the American] is after, nor virtue, nor saintliness, nor beauty, nor status. He is an amoral man of energy, mastery and power" (Lerner 1957: 63). A place of nature in America was powerful and brawny, because these qualities convey the bountiful element in the poetic form of heroic nature.

Examples of spectacular and pristine nature are often combined with the presence or traces of violent force. Places where this conjunction occurs have very often been regarded as icons that distill and express the essential qualities of heroic American nature. The third element of the original poetry of American nature is that Americans should by right have free access to these places. Nature, particularly when distilled into the form of a natural icon, is a sacrament of which the people must be permitted to partake. This explains why so many natural icons have been preserved as public parks. As Abraham Lincoln wrote when he transferred the Yosemite Valley to the State of California in 1864, this spectacular place, which along with the nearby Calveras Grove had already become an icon of American nature, was to be forever preserved for "public use, resort and recreation" (Schama 1995: 185–201; Huth 1957: 148). A place of nature in America was properly public, because this conveyed the purifying element in the poetic form of heroic nature.

The activities that one should properly pursue in these iconic places of nature reflect the fourth characteristic of the poetics of heroic nature. These must be activities by which one is, symbolically or in fact, uncivilized. When in the presence of symbolic nature, the American expects to move using slow and strenuous forms of transportation, to sit on hard objects and in awkward positions, to suffer rain, insects, and sunburn, to eat simple and in some cases ill-prepared food: in short, he expects to surrender, however briefly, some of his civilized comforts, and to recover, however imperfectly, the vitality, spontaneity, and integrity of Whitman's natural man. These "desperate quests for authentic experience" express the "careful primitivism" that Jackson Lears identified in late-nineteenth-century American culture, and they remain important rituals for a people who count artless simplicity among their primary virtues (Lears 1981: 92, 131). A place of nature in America was properly primitive, because this conveyed the corrective element in the poetic form of heroic nature.

Abused nature

The idea of heroic nature was dominant in the United States until the last decades of the twentieth century, when it began to be shadowed by its twisted child, the idea that nature in America was defiled, abused, and broken. The iconic landscapes of heroic nature remained very popular, but there was growing awareness of the dark side of this popularity, of the fact that many of these sites were being, as it was sometimes said, loved to death. Reports of haze over the Grand Canyon or smog in the Yosemite Valley became, for obvious reasons, particularly poignant and ominous testimonials to a more widespread environmental degradation. The 1989 wreck of the *Exxon Valdez* and consequent oil spill in Alaska's Prince William Sound became a powerful icon of end-of-the-century nature, at least in part because it occurred in Alaska, America's last and greatest preserve of heroic nature. The same shocking irony illuminated the United States' first toxic waste disaster at Love Canal, a symbol of destructive stupidity made all the more poignant by its proximity to Niagara Falls, that great nineteenth-century symbol of inexhaustible nature (McGreevy 1994).

Every famous fiasco of environmental abuse has not occurred at or near the site of an important icon of heroic nature, of course, but when they have they have made clear the relation between the old poetic form of heroic nature and the new poetic form of abused nature. To be appalled by the idea of nature in chains, one must suppose that nature should be wild. To be shocked by the idea of moribund nature degraded to sterile earth and putrescent water, one must suppose that nature should be fecund, budding, and bountiful. To find something amiss in the idea that nature is a toxic hazard to one's health and an ugly insult to one's senses, one must suppose that nature should be invigorating, purifying, and wholesome. Without the legacy of Thoreau, would we have any reason to object to the proposition that "'Nature' is but another name for carcinogen"? To bristle at the suggestion that one might, when confronted with a malignant and noxious environment, simply withdraw behind the seals and filters of a manufactured habitat, one must suppose that nature is preferable to artifice.

The idea that American nature is abused can be traced to the nineteenth century. As Cikovsky has shown, the tree stump is an ambivalent symbol in nineteenth-century American landscape painting (Cikovsky 1979). George Pope Morris's famous poem, "Woodman Spare That Tree," is, if not exactly environmental, a clear protest against senseless destruction (Morris 1860: 64–5). Any number of European travelers to the American frontier lamented wanton destruction of the forests by Americans, who according to Isaac Weld "seemed totally dead to the beauties of nature, and only to admire a spot of ground as it appears to be more or less calculated to enrich the occupier by its produce" (Handy and McKelvey 1940: 7). In 1864 George Perkins Marsh wrote that such actions expressed a universal principle. "Of all organic beings, man alone is to be regarded as essentially a destructive power." Far from directing crude and random nature, Marsh insisted that "man is everywhere a disturbing agent. Wherever he plants his foot the harmonies of nature are turned to discords" (Marsh 1965: 36). Half a century later, Theodore Roosevelt complained that "we turn our rivers and streams into dumping grounds . . . pollute the air . . . destroy the forests, and exterminate fishes, birds, and mammals" (Roosevelt

1913). In the 1930s there was a growing appreciation of the need for conservation of natural resources. As stated in a textbook on the geography of North America, "exploitation characterized our treatment of this country for the past three hundred years. Can we now change and conserve? We'd better. Otherwise our future as a great power must be short" (Smith and Phillips 1942: 24).

The tenor of this debate took an ominous turn in the 1960s, which saw publication of several books that contended that Americans were not only wastefully depleting their natural resources, but were also poisoning their environment. In future, they insisted, the earth might be not only impoverished, but also uninhabitable. Rachel Carson's *Silent Spring* (1962) was the first and most famous of this genre, which argued that attempts to control nature, particularly through the use of chemicals, might very well end up destroying nature. In *Science and Survival* (1966), Barry Commoner presented the thesis that science and technology, far from being the answer to human problems, were rapidly becoming the primary sources of human problems. This idea was reiterated and popularized in Alvin Toffler's *Future Shock* (1970). What made these books considerably more radical than the remonstrations of the conservationists was their decidedly dystopian interpretation of the human condition. Whereas the earlier books saw destruction of nature as an expression of human ignorance, the newer books saw it as an expression of human intelligence. Reason, science, and technology were as likely malefactors as benefactors of human life on the planet.

With its implicit critique of Western values and institutions (including White's [1967] widely trumpeted critique of Christianity), and its dark prophesy of the impending collapse of industrial society, late 1960s environmentalism accorded well with the contemporary anti-war and civil rights movements. This concurrence was not at first recognized by campus radicals, and environmental protection was not listed as an urgent social problem in a 1969 poll of students. Passionate concern for the environment seems instead to have emerged first among scientists, and then as a popular issue promulgated by the mainstream media. The sudden growth of the movement and its social respectability are evident in the number of entries under Environment in the New York Times Index. These rose from nine in 1967 to 115 in 1970. In 1967 *Sports Illustrated* printed an article that called upon schools to inculcate "ecological consciousness" (Boyl 1967: 48). In January of 1970 *Newsweek* ran a multipart story on "The Ravaged Environment," and in December

of that year *National Geographic* did the same under the general heading "Our Ecological Crisis." On the cover of the publication that had,
perhaps more than any other, brought images of heroic nature into
American homes, a western grebe, oil-soaked and doomed, hopelessly
paddled through the fouled waters of an oil slick.

Thus was the environmental crisis born, not the scientific fact of the
crisis, which was of longer standing, but the cultural event and poetic
image. The actual abuse of nature is a subject for another essay, which
would be of necessity scientific; what concerns us here is the rapid diffusion through America of the idea that nature was abused. Like the
poetic form of heroic nature, this was grounded in Americans' actual
experience with nature – the smog that burned their throats, the dead
fish they saw rotting on the beach – but it was also, as before, epistemically correlated with popular political philosophy. The idea of
abused nature became a metaphor that conveyed analogically the political doctrine that revolutionary social change was necessary. As this
idea evolved into its present form of abused-but-recovering nature, this
doctrine was augmented by ideas that this change should be accomplished not by political or economic revolution, but by comprehensive
bureaucratic management and highly sophisticated technologies. Thus
the poetic image of abused nature might be seen as one of the ways in
which many people intuitively grasped what historian John Lukacs
called the passing of the modern age (Lukacs 1970).

The necessity for radical social change was conveyed in the vivid
apocalyptic threats, stated or implicit, that peppered the writing of
early environmental activists. The alarm of the early years is indeed
striking when read from the distance of three decades. In 1968, *New
York Times* editorials prophesied "vast disasters" awaiting technological
society, since it seemed bent on making "the earth an uninhabitable
environment." "Scientific 'progress'," one editor wrote, "may soon
cause the roof to fall in on all mankind" (January 1: 14; March 12: 42;
July 7: iv, 10). Leading scientists were reported to believe that

> the chances of the world celebrating the dawn of New Year's day in
> the year 2000 are far dimmer than at any moment in recorded history;
> the chances of survival are dimmer than in that great cataclysmic
> moment when the great age of glaciers dawned. (Salisbury 1969)

In 1969 United Nations Secretary General Thant gave humanity ten years to save itself from global disaster; even industrialist Henry Ford the second doubted whether humanity could make it to the year 2000. To commemorate its centennial in 1969, the American Museum of Natural History staged a huge exhibit that posed the disquieting question, "Can Man Survive?" Designed to stimulate "emotional engagement," this early example of envirotainment subjected more than three million visitors to "a hammering barrage of visual, aural, and tactile sensations," all designed to leave them with an intuitive understanding that the answer to this question was, at best, uncertain (Smith 1969). Well-informed Americans who placed their trust in the most respectable authorities began the seventh decade of the twentieth century with a clear intuition that something had gone catastrophically wrong with American nature, that this had happened because something had gone catastrophically wrong with America, and that the time had come for an unprecedented change.

Although exceedingly dire, the image of abused nature was remarkably non-ideological. Indeed, it was widely supposed that environmental protection and restoration was a political movement around which all peoples could make common cause. Thus it seemed that it might be far less violent and divisive than the contemporary civil rights and antiwar movements. A *New York Times* editorial extolled the movement as one that "promises at last to unite today's contending generations in a single cause," a cause ultimately more enduring, it claimed, than Black Power or Vietnam (Bendiner 1969). The environmental movement was also extolled as a goad to international cooperation. Princeton Professor Richard A. Falk saw in it the seeds of "transnational consciousness" (Shenker 1969; Falk 1971). The United States and USSR quickly agreed to cooperate in a range of environmental studies. The movement was taken up at once by the United Nations, which celebrated the first Earth Day on March 21, 1971, and hosted the first international Conference on the Human Environment in the summer of the following year. Today, it is clear that few Americans oppose efforts to maintain the quality of the environment, especially their local environment, which they evaluate in therapeutic terms of health and aesthetics. Although many object to the behavior of groups they describe as environmental "extremists," their complaint is always with the extravagance of such groups and the exorbitance of their demands, never with the basic idea that some degree of environmental protection is a good thing.

The third aspect of the new poetic form of abused nature concerns the means by which the apocalypse was averted. The earliest proposals were for simplification, a universal scaling back of production, expectations, and demands. Like Thoreau, its advocates set out to grow rich by making their wants few, which is why we might call them frugal environmentalists. The essence of frugal environmentalism was distilled in the title of E. F. Schumacher's *Small Is Beautiful* (1973), a very popular book that served as a sort of manifesto for this branch of the environmental movement. Frugal environmentalism received early scientific support from reports like *Blueprint for the Future* (1972), in which British scientists called for radical reductions in population, development, and consumption, and the famous *Limits to Growth* (1972), in which computer models were used to show the impossibility of sustained increases in population and production.

Frugal environmentalism was, however, almost immediately attacked from several angles. Business leaders quickly perceived the danger of costly environmental regulation coupled with slack demand. Spokesmen reminded Americans that no-growth proposals were an "upper-income-class baby" that would put an end to social mobility (Wallace 1972). At the 1972 United Nations Conference on the Human Environment, developing nations protested that, while it was very well for prosperous peoples to curb their appetite for natural resources, voluntary frugality had little appeal for peoples long pinched by involuntary frugality. Engineers and scientists objected to the suggestion that science and technology were necessarily destructive. As an alternative to frugal environmentalism, these groups proposed what we might call technocratic environmentalism. As this combined the technical skills of Western science, the financial resources of big business, the unanswerable moral claims of the developing world, and the politically-popular assurance that consumers in the developed world could have a clean environment and a rising standard of living, there is little cause for surprise at its triumph. Technocratic environmentalism views nature as something to be minutely managed by large public agencies using state-of-the-art technology and proven science to operate the system, or what are sometimes called the life-support systems, of "spaceship earth." Its role is that of an engineering department charged to ensure efficient and reliable operation of a large and highly complex machine.

Iconographic landscapes of abused nature

The idea of abused nature is global, but like other elements of global culture it is given a local flavor by the local poetics of nature by which it was preceeded. Thus abused nature in America can only be understood in relation to heroic nature, as its negation or antithesis. In its heroic form, nature is large and humans are small. These are the proportions one finds in a painting by Frederic Church, say. In its abused form, nature is small and humans are large. These are the proportions one finds in the famous images of earth that were returned by the Apollo missions in the early days of the environmental crisis. The blue planet appeared tiny and fragile, an "oasis" suspended in space (Cosgrove 1994). In contrast, the creature that had managed to photograph the blue planet from such a distance, by shooting himself into outer space aboard a rocket ship no less, appeared enormously clever and powerful. Reversing the standard emotional response to heroic nature, it was now to be human works that elicited feelings of awe and nature that elicited feelings of pity. In its heroic form, nature is strong and prolific; in its abused form, nature is vitiated and moribund. This is evident in images of water. Whereas water in nineteenth-century images of heroic nature is typically moving, often implacably, water in late-twentieth-century images of abused nature is typically stagnant, its oily surface animated by nothing but methane bubbles that eructate from the rotting river bed. In its heroic form, nature is something into which humans should plunge for their health; in the abused form all the old swimming holes have been closed by the Board of Health. Humans must be kept out of polluted nature to preserve the health of humans, and kept out of unpolluted nature to preserve the health of nature, for human relations with nature now seem always to entail some taint of malignancy. Finally, in heroic nature it was nature that saved humans from the corruption of artifice, whereas in abused nature it is human artifice, in the form of science and technology, that saves nature from corruption.

In the United States at the end of the twentieth century, iconic places of abused nature began to invert the original poetics of heroic nature in this way. This is evident in the genesis and development of one particular icon of abused nature, the Cuyahoga River in Cleveland, Ohio. As I'm sure nearly every student who took environmental studies courses in the 1970s was told, the Cuyahoga was the river that burned.

As some sticklers have pointed out, this was not strictly true, since what burned on June 22, 1969, was not, in fact, the river, but only a mat of debris and oil that floated on the river, but this quibble misses the point. Poetics is concerned with vivid images, not facts, and what image of nature could be more unnatural than a river in flames?

Thus the first thing to be observed about the iconography of the Cuyahoga River fire is that a river in flames is a poetic concept that conveys to nearly anyone the troubled state of the waterway, and perhaps by extension all waterways. It is not a theoretical concept like, say, eutrophication, which cannot be appreciated without some knowledge of the postulates of biology; it is a poetic concept that analogically conveys an intuitive appreciation that all is not well with the river. This explains why the Cuyahoga River fire became an environmental myth, and why the Cuyahoga River became an icon of American nature, abused American nature. Just as the late nineteenth century thought that the giant trees of the Calveras Grove conveyed an intuitive understanding of American nature in general, so the late twentieth century thought the Cuyahoga River conveyed an intuitive understanding of American nature in general. The manifest qualities of an iconic place are presumed symbolic of conditions prevalent, if not necessarily conspicuous, across a wider space.

The poetic potential of the Cuyahoga River fire was not at first appreciated. Although the *New York Times* had printed articles about the river, which it recognized as one of the nation's most polluted, it did not report the fire. An article on Cuyahoga pollution printed some months after the fire neglected to mention the remarkable event. Even Cleveland's independent radical newspaper of the day, *The Big US*, which was otherwise quick to trumpet evidence of America's short-comings, failed to mention the fire in the issue that appeared the day after it occurred. Its editors appear to have been blind to the poetic potential of the fire because they assumed that the great American iniquity was social injustice, not environmental degradation. Thus the newspaper issue in which one might expect a (highly editorialized) report of the fire to appear contained instead a story of police harassment of "cool people" who were wont to loiter on the sidewalks of a Cleveland counterculture neighborhood. It took the newspaper four months to realize that they were sitting on top of an iconic landscape that was becoming, in the words of a later writer, the "poster child" of the American environmental movement. In October 1969 *The Big US* changed its name to *The Burning River News*. A landscape cannot be appreciated as a popular icon until the doctrines it is presumed to express are themselves popular.

It is clear that the significance of the Cuyahoga River fire increased in the 1970s, along with popular concern over abuse of American nature. It must be noted that this increased significance was not linked to a belief that the actual fire was important in ways that were not at first perceived; no one contended that damage caused by the fire was widespread, lasting, or profound. What was important and significant was the image of the fire, the poetic concept of water bursting into flames, the iconic landscape of a river so degraded that it had begun to act contrary to nature. The fire was an historic event famous not for its impact on the environment, but rather for its impact on popular perception of the environment.

Twenty years after the fire, the Cuyahoga River remained a popular icon of abused nature, but reports had for some years emphasized the river's remarkable, if imperfect, recovery. Fish had returned to the river, albeit far upstream, as had intrepid – perhaps impetuous – swimmers. Marinas had been built on the river's lower stretches and darting pleasure boats consternated the freighters that served remaining river-front factories. An entertainment district known as the Flats had grown up beside the old industrial waterway, along with the Rock-n-Roll Hall of Fame. Credit for these encouraging developments was, of course, given to the technocratic class of scientists and government regulators.

That this post-industrial landscape of leisure and consumption should crop up in the very heart of this place of gritty industry was an irony that could not fail to attract notice. Restoration of the Cuyahoga was emotionally affecting for the same reason degradation of iconic landscapes of heroic nature had been emotionally affecting: manifest changes in an iconic place of nature convey an intuitive understanding of changes underway everywhere. This place of nature was, as always in America, supposed to convey analogically a poetic understanding of the general state of nature throughout American space.

References

Barrows, Harlan H. (1923), "Geography as Human Ecology," *Annals of the Association of American Geographers* 13, pp. 1–14.

Bendiner, Robert (1969), "Man – The Most Endangered Species," *New York Times*, October 20, p. 46.

Berry, Wendell (1981), "The Journey's End," in *Recollected Essays, 1965–1980,* San Francisco: North Point.

Berry, Wendell (1990), *What Are People For?* San Francisco: North Point.

Berry, Wendell (1992), *Sex, Economy, Freedom, and Community: Eight Essays,* New York: Pantheon.

Boyl, Robert H. (1967), "How to Stop the Pillage of America," *Sports Illustrated,* December 11, pp. 40–53.

Bradford, William (1951), "A Hideous and Desolate Wilderness," in Henry Steele Commager (ed), *Living Ideas in America,* New York: Harper and Brothers, pp. 67–9.

Brey, Philip (1998), "Space Shaping Technologies and the Geographical Disembedding of Place," in Andrew Light and Jonathan M. Smith (eds.), *Philosophy and Geography III: Philosophies of Place,* Lanham, MD: Rowman and Littlefield, pp. 239–63.

Brigham, Albert Perry (1915), "Problems of Geographical Influence," *Annals of the Association of American Geographers,* 5, pp. 3–25.

Brower, David (ed.) (1961), *Wilderness: America's Living Heritage,* San Francisco: Sierra Club.

Bushnell, Horace (1858), *Nature and the Supernatural,* New York: Charles Scribner.

Cikovsky, Nicholai Jr. (1979), "The Ravages of the Ax," *Art Bulletin,* 61, pp. 611–26.

Cosgrove, Denis (1994), "Contested Global Visions: One-World, Whole-Earth, and the Apollo Space Photographs," *Annals of the Association of American Geographers,* 84, pp. 270–94.

Cronon, William (1991), *Nature's Metropolis: Chicago and the Great West,* New York: Norton.

Curti, Merle (1980), *Human Nature in American Thought,* Madison: The University of Wisconsin Press.

Diamond, Jared (1997), *Guns, Germs, and Steel: The Fates of Human Societies,* New York: W. W. Norton.

Dicey, Edward (1971), *Spectator of America,* ed. Herbert Mitgang, Chicago: Quadrangle Books.

Dickens, Charles (1985), *American Notes,* New York: St. Martins.

Dryer, Charles Redway (1920), "Genetic Geography: The Development of the Geographic Sense and Concept," *Annals of the Association of American Geographers,* 10, pp. 3–16.

Earle, Carville (1992), *Geographical Inquiry and American Historical Problems,* Stanford, CA: Stanford University Press.

Emerson, Ralph Waldo (1911), *Journals of Ralph Waldo Emerson,* Vol. 5, ed. Edward Waldo Emerson and Waldo E. Forbes, Boston: Houghton Mifflin.

Emerson, Ralph Waldo (1940), "Nature, Essays: Second Series," in *The Selected Writings of Ralph Waldo Emerson,* ed. Brooks Atkinson, New York: Modern Library, pp. 406–21.

Entrikin, J. Nicholas (1991), *The Betweenness of Place: Towards a Geography of Modernity,* Baltimore: Johns Hopkins University Press.

Evernden, Neil (1992), *The Social Creation of Nature,* Baltimore: Johns Hopkins University Press.

Falk, Richard A. (1971), *This Endangered Planet: Prospects and Proposals for Human Survival,* New York: Random House.

Handy, Myrtle M., and Blake McKelvey (1940), "British Travelers to the Genesee Country," *Rochester Historical Society Publication*, 18, pp. 1–73.

Harvey, D. (1985), "The Geopolitics of Capitalism," in D. Gregory and J. Urry (eds.), *Social Relations and Spatial Structures*, New York: St. Martin's Press, pp. 128–63.

Harvey, David (1984), "On the History and Present Condition of Geography: An Historical Materialist Manifesto." *Professional Geographer*, 3, pp. 1–11.

Huth, Hans (1957), *Nature and the American: Three Centuries of Changing Attitudes*, Berkeley: University of California Press.

Jackson, J. B. (1953), "The Westward Moving House," *Landscape*, 2 (3), pp. 8–21.

Jackson, J. B. (1984), *Discovering the Vernacular Landscape*, New Haven: Yale University Press.

Jakle, John (1977), *Images of the Ohio Valley: A Historical Geography of Travel*, New York: Oxford University Press.

James, Preston (1959), *A Geography of Man*, Boston: Ginn and Company.

Jefferson, Thomas (1944), *The Life and Selected Writings of Thomas Jefferson*, ed. Adrienne Kock and William Peden, New York: Modern Library.

Kaplan, Robert D. (1998), *An Empire Wilderness: Travels into America's Future*, New York: Random House.

Kazan, Alfred A. (1988), *A Writer's America: Landscape in Literature*, New York: Alfred A. Knopf.

Kirk, Russell (1991), *Beyond the Dreams of Avarice*, Peru, IL: Sherwood, Sugden and Co.

Landes, David (1998), *The Wealth and Poverty of Nations: Why Some Are so Rich and Some so Poor*, New York: W. W. Norton.

Lasch, Christopher (1978), *The Culture of Narcissism: American Life in an Age of Diminishing Expectations*, New York: W. W. Norton.

Lears, Jackson (1981), *No Place of Grace: Antimodernism and the Transformation of American Culture, 1880–1920*, New York: Pantheon.

Lerner, Max (1957), *America as a Civilization: Life and Thought in the United States Today*, New York: Simon & Schuster.

Levin, David (1959), *History as Romantic Art: Bancroft, Prescott, Motley, and Parkman*, Stanford, CA: Stanford University Press.

Lewis, C. S. (1964), *The Discarded Image*, Cambridge: Cambridge University Press.

Lowenthal, David, and Hugh C. Prince (1965), "English Landscape Tastes," *The Geographical Review*, 55 (2), pp. 186–222.

Lukacs, John (1970), *The Passing of the Modern Age*, New York: Harper and Row.

McGreevy, Patrick V. (1994), *Imagining Niagara: The Meaning and Making of Niagara Falls*, Amherst, MA: University of Massachusetts Press.

Marsh, George Perkins (1965), *Man and Nature*, ed. David Lowenthal, Cambridge, MA: Harvard University Press.

Miller, Perry (1964), *Errand into the Wilderness*, Cambridge: Belknap Press.

Morris, George P. (1860), *Poems*, New York: Charles Scribners.

Northrop, F. S. C. (1947), *The Logic of the Sciences and the Humanities*, New York: Macmillan.

O'Brien, Raymond J. (1981), *American Sublime: Landscape and Scenery of the Lower Hudson Valley*, New York: Columbia University Press.

Ortega y Gasset, Jose (1932), *The Revolt of the Masses*, New York: W. W. Norton.

Parkman, Francis (1880), "The Woman Question Again," *North American Review*, 16, pp. 16–30.

Parkman, Francis (1902), *Pioneers of France in the New World*, 2 vols., Boston: Little Brown.

Penn, William (1937), *Fruits of Solitude*, New York: P. F. Collier.

Potter, David M. (1954), *People of Plenty: Economic Abundance and the American Character*, Chicago: University of Chicago Press.

Roosevelt, Theodore (1913), "Our Vanishing Wildlife," *Outlook*, 25 January.

Roth, Charles E. (1968), "Are You an E.L.C.?" *New York Times*, August 11, 2, p. 29.

Salisburry, Harison E. (1969), "Among Political Thinkers, the World's Doomsday Clock Still Reads 11:52," *New York Times*, January 6, p. 143.

Samuels, Marwyn S. (1979), "The Biography of Landscape: Cause and Culpability," in D. W. Meinig (ed.), *The Interpretation of Ordinary Landscapes*, New York: Oxford University Press, pp. 51–88.

Schama, Simon (1995), *Landscape and Memory*, New York: Alfred Knopf.

Schlesinger, Jr., Arthur M. (1986), *The Cycles of American History*, Boston: Houghton Mifflin.

Schumacher, Ernst Friedrich (1973), *Small Is Beautiful: A Study of Economics as if People Mattered*, London: Blond and Briggs.

Shenker, Israel (1969), "Man's Extinction Held Real Peril," *New York Times*, April 7, p. 10.

Smith, J. Russell, and M. Ogden Phillips (1942), *North America: Its People and the Resources, Development, and Prospects of the Continent as the Home of Man*, New York: Harcourt, Brace and Company.

Smith, Jonathan M. (2001), "Moral Maps and Moral Places in the Works of Francis Parkman," in Paul Adams, Steven Hoelscher, and Karen Till (eds.), *Textures of Place: Exploring Humanist Geographies*, Minneapolis: University of Minnesota Press, pp. 300–16.

Smith, Robert M. (1969), "Museum Uses Psychadelic Lights and Electonic Music to Show That Life Can Be Ugly," *New York Times*, May 19, p. 29.

Snyder, Gary (1984), "Good, Wild, Sacred," in Wes Jackson, Wendell Berry, and Bruce Colman (eds.), *Meeting the Expectations of the Land: Essays in Sustainable Agriculture and Stewardship*, San Francisco: North Point, pp. 195–207.

Thomas, William L. (ed.) (1956), *Man's Role in Changing the Face of the Earth*, Chicago: University of Chicago Press.

Thoreau, Henry David (1906), *The Writing of Henry David Thoreau*, Vol. 3, *The Maine Woods*, Boston: Houghton Mifflin.

Thoreau, Henry David (1968), *The Writings of Henry David Thoreau, Journal*, Vol. 5, ed. Bradford Torrey, New York: A. M. S. Press.

Urry, J. (1985), "Social Relations, Space and Time," in D. Gregory and J. Urry (eds.), *Social Relations and Spatial Structures*, New York: St. Martin's Press, pp. 20–48.

Wallace, Henry C. (1972), "Zero Growth," *Newsweek*, January 24, p. 62.

Whitbeck, R. H. (1926), "Adjustments to Environments in South America: An Interpretation of Influences," *Annals of the Association of American Geographers*, 16, pp. 1–11.

White, Lynn (1967), "The Historical Roots of Our Ecological Crisis," *Science*, 155, pp. 1203–7.

Whitman, Walt (n.d.), *Leaves of Grass*, New York: Modern Library.
Worster, Donald (1990), "Transformations of the Earth: Towards an Agroecological Perspective in History," *The Journal of American History*, 76, pp. 1087–106.

CHAPTER 3

The place of value

Jonathan M. Smith

The American space was never unified economically. This was inevitable. Different places offer very different combinations of assets for the development of this or that economic activity. Places are also never valued for what they offer in perpetuity, simply because what they have to offer is subject to revaluation. The history of American places is recorded in a landscape of places in various states of de- and re-valuation – former mining ghost towns at one extreme and places of current economic boom, such as California's Silicon Valley, at the other. The course of American economic history has been broadly one of transformation from the exploitation of primary resources to intensive manufacturing of various sorts. One aspect of this transformation has been the generally positive attitude of Americans towards technological change. Anxiety and ambition in an individualistic society have undoubtedly given a boost to the pursuit of change. Cultural geographer Jonathan M. Smith uses Lewis Mumford's idea of "technological complex" to investigate the course of the American space-economy over the past two centuries. He moves beyond Mumford, however, in examining the place connections and the human consequences of the various epochs in American technological development. Paying special attention to the recent *biotechnic* epoch (in distinction from previous *eotechnic*, *paleotechnic* and *neotechnic* eras), Smith identifies a set of places that have prospered from new technologies and those that have suffered as a result of their previous "overinvestment" in the previously dominant technological complex. He also shows the impacts of the technological changes on the life chances of the three main classes of contemporary America: the owners of capital, those with human capital (education, technical skills), and those with neither. Smith concludes by pointing out how misleading it is to ascribe to the United States as a whole or even regional portions of it the attributes of very particular "extreme" places associated with new technologies or their absence. This "topographical chauvinism" serves to obscure the tremendous place-to-place variation within the American space: homogenizing the socially and economically heterogeneous.

A simple and uncontentious definition of geography is hard to come by, but it may be safe to say that geography is, at heart, justified and inspired by the conspicuous diversity of the earth's surface. The face of the globe is not uniform, but highly varied; places differ, one from another. One aspect of this difference is that some places are evidently more valuable than others. Economic geographers observe this in the variable price of real estate and the urban morphologies to which it gives rise; historical geographers observe it in the record of migrations, empires, and wars in which, as Semple put it, "the best land . . . falls to the share of the strongest people" (Semple 1911: 113). Whichever way we look, we see that people are willing to pay a very high price for certain places. They will toil to acquire property in a valuable place; they will move a long distance to reside in a valuable place; they will fight, kill, and die to defend or capture a valuable place. One may very well conclude from this that human geography is largely about values.

All philosophy of value begins with human desire, and geographers observe that humans desire, value, and seek to possess places for two general reasons. They value a place because of unusual things, processes, or activities that occur in that place, or because it stands at a strategic point on the way to such a place and is thus necessary for defense, conquest, or trade. By convention these are referred to as site values and situation values. These are, obviously, related, because the value of any particular site depends not only on the properties of that site, but also on the circumjacent situations that make that site secure or vulnerable, accessible or isolated. The value of any particular situation depends entirely on the value of the site to which it serves as a gateway. The value of any particular place is, in other words, never absolute but always dependent on a system of places in which it is but one component. The value of a place also depends on the people who make use of that place. No place is naturally valuable simply because its land is productive, its harbor is deep, or its hills are filled with gold; it becomes valuable only once it falls to the hands of a people who desire and know how to make use of such things as fertile soil, a generous anchorage, or a precious metal. The value of any particular place depends on the culture of those who control it. The value of a valued place is always, in short, relational; among these relations the most important are relations to constituent properties, relations to other places, and relations to the evolving desires and techniques of human inhabitants. Changes in culture will consequently cause change in the geography of value. When popular ambitions change, or when old ambitions are pursued in new ways, once-valued places may loose their luster and cheapen, while places never before appreciated disclose unexpected merits and attractions. One has only to consider how a growing popular desire for a suntan raised the value of seaside property, or how large-scale mechanized farming reduced the value of hill farms. Some places on earth are not simply more valuable than others, but only presently more valuable. The face of the earth is littered with places that once were highly valued but now are sadly depreciated because the site was degraded, the larger spatial system shifted, or the desires and techniques of inhabitants changed. Value therefore has a history as well as a geography, and we may well speak of a historical geography of value. Human geography is very much a matter of values, but these are fugitive values. The remainder of this chapter will attempt to account for this, paying particular attention to the United States.

Animating desires

The United States is a wealthy country because it comprises an interconnected and coordinated system of constituent places, many of which are valuable, and because these places are inhabited by a people who are, for the most part, trained and motivated to recognize, exploit, and preserve these values. Some of these places are valuable because they are the site of useful natural resources, but the present-day importance of such endowments to national prosperity is not great (McRae 1994: 28). The relative significance of primary production has declined steadily since the nineteenth century, and America's farms, forests, fisheries, and mines today directly account for only a small part of the Gross Domestic Product. At the turn of the twentieth century, the most valuable places in the United States are sites of what we might call artificial or technical resources: machines, networks, utilities, and landscapes, along with the knowledgeable and creative people who operate them.

Before turning to an account of the transition from natural to technical resources, and the geography of value to which it has given rise, we must consider the role of American culture in shaping and reshaping the valuable places of the United States. This culture is complex, so no brief account can detail the range of dissenting opinions and contradictory impulses, but it is not entirely fatuous to speak of it as a culture of change. Americans divorce their spouses and sell their

Figure 3.1 A geography of value. The geography of value is evident in the level of investment in the built landscape. This dilapidated commercial structure in Ceres, Virginia, is obviously located in a place of declining value, due to changes in the geography of American agriculture and retailing. A graffito announces the opinion of at least one native that, despite bucolic appearances, local morals have begun to resemble those of Grace Metalious' steamy 1956 novel *Peyton Place*. Demoralization is indeed one defining trait of depreciating places. (*Photograph by the author.*)

houses with ease; they change careers, opinions, and technologies with little complaint; they demolish and rebuild landscapes, vacate and people neighborhoods, dismantle and re-engineer environments with what appears to be positive relish. This penchant for change accounts for the permanently unfinished appearance of much of the United States, and helps explain the extreme transience of its geography of value.

The best geographic evidence for Americans' historical acceptance of change is the extraordinarily rapid spread of Americans into virtually all of the many and varied environments of North America, largely in the span of a single century. Much has been made of the diffidence and hesitation of westering pioneers as they passed from woodland to prairie, and prairie to desert, but these delays, if they in fact occurred, are remarkable only for their brevity. Americans everywhere adapted to new environmental circumstances with peculiar alacrity, and abandoned accustomed places and ways with little apparent misgiving or regret. This strain of opportunism and ready adaptability remains evident in American willingness to embrace technological innovation, institutional reform, new lifestyles, and new landscapes.

Because it is primarily concerned with doing things, American culture may also be described as instrumental. This is not to say that it lacks intrinsic values, for it has always directed ambition toward certain popular images of the good life, but that its true genius has always been discovery of improved means to conventional ends (Joad 1927). Indeed American culture has produced relatively little that is original in the way of ends, but a vast amount that is original in the way of means. Its intrinsic values are for the most part embellished imports; its instrumental values are to a surprising degree homegrown. This statement will no doubt annoy those many Americans who imagine themselves great idealists and dreamers, but Americans are not in fact unusual in what they want, but only in their facility at getting it.

Opportunistic fascination with instrumental values is long-standing in the United States. Benjamin Franklin wrote *Poor Richard's Almanack* (1732), which was one of the best-selling publications of colonial North America, to affirm that purposeful activity is the natural state of healthy humans. Virtually from its inception, the United States was described by European travelers as home to a people peculiarly preoccupied with means and their improvement. A Spanish gentleman passing through upstate New York in 1835 marveled at the many "very simple mechanisms" by which ordinary men increased the efficiency of their labor, and concluded that the American farmer "thinks and contrives" even as he plods behind the plow (Sewart 1940). Twenty-two years later a Russian noted that in the United States "all their efforts are directed at simplifying work," so that "every new mechanical technique, every discovery, is taken into account and applied to the matter at hand" (Schrier and Story 1979: 81, 258). Americans apparently took to heart David Hume's proposition of 1777, that "utility . . . is the sole source of that high regard paid to [virtue]," as well as the "foundation of the chief part of morals" (Hume 1907: 66). At the end of the nineteenth century the once-celebrated agnostic orator Robert Ingersoll contended that every American child "should be taught that useful work is worship and that intelligent labor is the highest form of prayer" (Ingersoll 1912: 149). As Alexis de Tocqueville wrote in 1835, in the United States "useful is never wrong."

Tocqueville went on to offer a sociological explanation for this instrumentalist bent. In a democracy, he observed, social classes are not fixed and all individuals face an uncertain future in which their social status may rise, or fall. Confronted with this prospect, the citizen experiences strong feelings of ambition and anxiety, a desire to advance in the world mixed with fear of slipping to an inferior station. The normal response to this social insecurity, Tocqueville concluded, is steady purposeful activity of the very sort extolled by Franklin (Tocqueville 1966: 497–9, 515–16).

In strongly stratified societies the personal consequences of industry and indolence are, for any given individual, muted by a social structure that retards the movement from one class to another. The incentive to enterprise is weak, as are the penalties against idleness and dissipation. The situation is very different in a weakly stratified or open-class society, such as the United States substantially was and remains for its white population (McMurrer and Sawhill 1998). Here the individual is induced to look upon his attributes and property as instruments, to exercise for personal advantage whatever powers of assiduity and creativity he may have the good fortune to possess, and to curb insofar as he is able his appetites for sloth, waste, and riot (Tocqueville 1966: 596–7). Visiting the United States in 1906, H. G. Wells described the ideal of American middle-class culture as "self realization under equal opportunity," but understood perhaps more clearly than many the cultural consequences of this fluid social order. Wells sensed restless instrumentalism in the

American landscape, which had in it, he wrote, "no sense of accomplishment and finality." Even "the largest, the finest, the tallest [buildings], are so obviously no more than symptoms and promises" of an endless process that passed under the name of "Material Progress" (Wells 1987: 53, 32).

The opportunism, instrumentalism and transience of fluid middle-class society received formal intellectual expression in John Dewey's doctrine of "endless ends." Dewey urged his readers to discard the very idea of a perfect end, particularly the "single all-important end," and to apprehend that the ostensible end of any activity was merely one of many consequences singled out for attention by mental habit. Thus the miser sees in hoarding the "end" of undiminished wealth, but not the consequence of foregone pleasure; the spendthrift sees in expenditure the "end" of satisfied desire, but not the consequence of depleted funds. What is more, Dewey argued that we developed this habit of singling out one consequence of an act and calling it an "end" because this end serves as a means to justify or motivate the act. A man does not run from a tiger because he wishes to live to a ripe old age, it would seem, but rather wishes to live to a ripe old age because it helps him to run from the tiger (Dewey 1922: 143, 232, 229, 285). The doctrine of endless ends helps us understand why Wells perceived no finality in the American landscape, and why the country seems even today to be always developing, but never maturing. Activity is not here undertaken in order to reach a goal, goals are here pursued in order to stimulate activity, particularly the activity of creative destruction that accompanies unfettered social ambition.

Evolving technics

America's geography of value is beaten into shape by millions of self-interested decisions, but it is not amorphic because there is at any given time a geographic pattern to opportunity that is largely determined by the prevailing way of doing things, by the operative technics of the day (Hugill 1993). In 1934 Lewis Mumford used the locution technological complex to describe coherent historical phases characterized by reliance on certain raw materials and energy resources, organization of production along certain lines, and reliance on, and creation of, certain types of mechanical devices and workers (Mumford 1934). At the time he identified three such complexes in the history of the modern West:

the eotechnic, paleotechnic, and neotechnic. The first was an age of wind, wood, and water, of production in small shops by master crafts-men, skilled artisans, and their apprentices. This was succeeded in the nineteenth century by the paleotechnic, an age of iron, coal, and steam engines, of production in great mills and factories that were owned by capitalists and operated by a degraded proletariat. This was in turn succeeded by the neotechnic, an age of internal combustion engines, electricity, alloys, and chemicals. Although factories remained, they were now owned by stockholders, managed by corporate bureaucrats, and operated by organized labor. In a later work Mumford proposed a fourth phase, then only beginning to dawn, which he called the biotechnic (Mumford 1938). In this he foresaw the growth of the applied life sciences and efforts to exercise rational control over living things, including human beings. This has grown into our age of information and images, of staggering growth in the biomedical sciences and far-reaching attempts at social and psychological manipulation, management, and control.

The idea of the technological complex emphasizes the fact that any specific device is a component in a larger system of devices. Just as a universal joint is one component in an automobile, so an automobile is one component in the neotechnic. It makes no sense apart from highways, assembly lines, oil rigs, tract houses, drivers' licenses, and installment plans. And the technological complex includes more than artifacts. It includes suitable social institutions that support and exploit the system of devices, and habits of thought and imagination adapted to the requirements of the technological complex (McLuhan 1964). A technological complex also has a geography, a system of valuable places that together house, organize, segregate, link, and symbolize the other components of the technological system.

Each technological complex has signature machines: the clipper ship, the train, the automobile, the computer; each has a diagnostic landscape: the mercantile city, the mill town, the industrial city with managerial core and circumjacent suburbs, the post-industrial sprawl of mills, research parks, and fitness centers. Change from one technolog-ical complex to another necessitates a thoroughgoing reshaping of the landscape: creation of new places, spaces, structures, and systems, with a simultaneous abandonment, obliteration, or metamorphosis of the relic places, spaces, structures, and systems of the waning technological complex. The value of some places is reduced, a depreciation evident in out-migration, population decline, dilapidation of infrastructure, and demoralization of lingering inhabitants (Lewis 1972). The value of other places appreciates, sometimes with such astonishing suddenness that we call these places boomtowns.

The valuable places of eotechnic America were sailing ship havens, water-powered mill sites, river ports and canal towns. These were components in a larger system of places that served to connect complimentary agricultural regions. In these places the surplus produce of these regions was processed, exchanged, stored, and packed for forwarding to distant markets. Because of their advantageous location within the distribution system, these places were also attractive to artisans and craftsmen who could conveniently cater to merchants and prosperous landholders. Places of value in the eotechnic United States ranged greatly in size and significance, from isolated mill sites on small streams to sizable cities. Thousands of eotechnic places of value emerged along the eastern seaboard before 1850, each in some way combining water-powered processing of an agricultural product (wheat, cotton, wood) with access to a system of natural and artificial waterways over which boats were propelled by muscle, the currents, or wind.

The onset of the paleotechnic complex in the mid-nineteenth century depreciated the value of many eotechnic places, especially those that lacked easy access to the now crucial resources of coal and iron ore. Large eotechnic cities were assured of a continued role in the paleotechnic world, but their neotechnic site values were of diminishing utility. Many smaller eotechnic places, such as isolated mill sites or small canal towns, stagnated or declined as the supporting eotechnic complex of devices, processes and places decayed and collapsed. In the newly valuable places of paleotechnic America, iron ore, coal, and labor were easily assembled. These places were components in a system of places in which heavy industry fabricated producer goods such as agricultural implements, building supplies, and railroad equipment. Their principal energy source was the coal-fired steam engine, their principal transportation steam-powered boats, ships, and trains. The valuable places of paleotechnic America were spread in a broad band from Boston and Baltimore in the east, to Milwaukee and St. Louis in the west: the traditional American manufacturing belt.

Manufacturing remained at the heart of the neotechnic complex that began to emerge at the end of the nineteenth century, although optimal locations were in many cases altered by reliance on new raw materials

Figure 3.2 An eotechnic place of value. Mill sites like this one in Dover, NH, were important eotechnic places of value. Along with shipping havens and canal towns, such places were nodes in a network for the exchange and processing of agricultural products. With the decline of the eotechnic many of the largest mills were updated with steam power. These structures were, however, poorly suited to the electrical machinery of the neotechnic, which favored a horizontal layout, and many were abandoned in the mid-twentieth century. Interestingly, some of these structures, including the one pictured here, have been easily adapted to biotechnic offices, shops, and studios. (*Photograph by the author.*)

and energy sources, and by the development of a flexible transportation system of metaled roads, automobiles, and trucks. Much of this manufacturing was organized as large corporations that were owned by stockholders and run by bureaucrats. Places that attracted corporate headquarters became, consequently, extraordinarily valuable, and their jagged skylines of serried skyscrapers became a powerful icon of neotechnic America. In the early decades of the twentieth century such cities began to spawn circumjacent suburbs to house the various grades of corporate bureaucracy; these bedroom communities were connected to the downtown skyscrapers by automobiles, busses, and electric trains. Centralization of the command function in corporate headquarters was accomplished with an array of communication devices such as the typewriter, telephone, and passenger airplane. New York City was by a very large margin preeminent among neotechnic control centers; most others of national significance were located in what had been major paleotechnic centers: Chicago, Philadelphia, Pittsburgh, Cleveland (Johnson 1982). The value of such places as control centers was not directly tied to industrial resources, however, but rather to information and capital, which we may think of as raw materials of management.

At the end of the twentieth century the landscape of the United States is to outward appearance still largely neotechnic (Relph 1987: 120). City skylines still bristle with "glazed packing crates of corporate bureaucracy" and the automobile is, if anything, more imperious in the demands it places on household budgets and urban space (Stern 1986: 289). Nevertheless it is clear that we have passed into a new technological complex in which people are the key resource. Mumford called this the biotechnic (Rifkin 1998). Taken as a whole, it is an attempt to exert rational control over life, not to the exclusion of human life, even into the highest reaches of human consciousness.

Figure 3.3 (opposite) A neotechnic place of value. The serried skylines of twentieth-century American cities are a powerful icon of neotechnic America. The densely packed cores of the largest cities in the United States became extraordinarily valuable as a site for corporate offices and ancillary functions. The skyscrapers of central Chicago, some of which are shown here, were considered especially remarkable. Some of the more important of these neotechnic places of value have survived and prospered in the biotechnic, but the general rule since the 1960s has been that downtowns have declined. One can today find many small cities in which proud office towers built in the 1920s are wholly abandoned, obsolete hulks in a wasteland of empty parking lots and shuttered stores. (*Photograph by the author.*)

The biotechnic

Selected human beings are the most valuable resource in the biotechnic complex. Emphasis must be placed on the exclusivity of this group, for the biotechnic has bestowed its favors with great partiality. Individuals who possess a recondite talent or skill necessary to operate or improve biotechnic devices or procedures (in computers, electronics, applied biology, medicine, entertainment, the law), today lead lives of unexampled felicity; individuals deficient in such readily negotiable personal assets often find life in the biotechnic mean, shabby, and hard. Although in many instances devoid of talent or skill, the wealthiest Americans have also fared well, profiting from very high rates of return on investments in rapidly growing biotechnic sectors. The result, Kevin Phillips contends, has been "economic redistribution away from the weak or fading midportions of the population and toward the top one percent of Americans, along with educationally or technologically advanced portions of the middle and upper middle classes" (Phillips 1993: 92). The American middle class is today separating into biotech winners and losers.

The prodigious remuneration of selected sports stars, entertainers, artists and lawyers has attracted much attention, as have the eye-popping compensation packages of certain Chief Executive Officers (CEOs), but these celebrated stars are only the most conspicuous beneficiaries of a technological complex that richly rewards exceptional human capital. The concepts of human capital and human resources are not new (Kiker 1968). Adam Smith described human capital this way: "The improved dexterity of a workman may be considered in the same light as a machine or instrument of trade," because it "facilitates and

Figure 3.4 (opposite)   Shop sign at Quincy Market, Boston, MA. In the 1980s many persons who possessed human capital of declining value found themselves unable to afford the cost of lodging, particularly in cities where biotechnic affluence was raising rents. This contributed to a conspicuous rise in what came to be known as "homelessness." Homeless women came to be known as "bag ladies," due to the large plastic garbage bags in which they carried their possessions. Since many of these women were mentally ill, bag ladies and their antics became the butt of much cruel humor. This sign for an upscale bag shop in downtown Boston makes a pun that depends for its humor on the incongruity between biotech winners sporting chic and costly bags and the miserable wretches of the street. Biotechnic affluence and poverty are thus juxtaposed, not to excite concern but for fun. This sort of ruthless irony is by many biotech winners thought to be a sign of clever sophistication. (*Photograph by the author.*)

abridges labor." Improved dexterity, like a labor-saving device, "though it costs a certain expense repays that expense with profit" (Smith 1937: 259–60). Human capital is, in other words, investment made to improve the productivity of workers (Nadler 1970). It is what today's computer jockeys sometimes refer to as "skillz." One must note that the rate of return on investments in human capital will vary widely, however. Dexterity alone is not valuable; only rare dexterity in practices central to the prevailing technological complex. When demand for performance of a task is small, even the deft worker will profit little; when demand is great, in contrast, even the tyro can reap rich rewards. Economic winners are not only good at what they do, they are good at doing what many others cannot do but wish to have done.

The concept of human capital helps us to understand Phillips's "fading midportion of the population." The contemporary United States may be crudely understood as consisting of three classes: those who possess capital, those who possess human capital, and those who possess neither. The middling class that possesses human capital may be further divided into those whose human capital is presently depreciating and those whose human capital is presently appreciating (Phillips's "educationally or technologically advanced portions of the middle and upper middle classes"). Members of the first subgroup are skilled in obsolescent technologies and practices, and will in time join those without capital of any sort if they are unable to lay their hands on appreciating human capital. The necessary downscaling of this group's consumer expectations has caused a great proliferation of discount houses, bargain eateries, low-rent housing, and consumer credit abuse across the length and breadth of the contemporary United States (Phillips 1993: 169–77). Members of the second subgroup, whose human capital is appreciating, have rising expectations; in time some of them will rise to join the true capitalist class. Even those rising to less exalted stations in the biotechnic complex often identify with the very wealthy, through purchase of affordable luxuries and political affiliation (Galbraith 1992). It is this later group of biotech winners who will primarily concern us from this point.

Some writers have called this the "new class," a technical intelligentsia that grew to unprecedented size in the post-war period (Lasch 1991). In 1951 C. Wright Mills called them "the new middle class" of white collar workers whose social position was founded on education rather than property (Mills 1951: 245). In 1969 Theodore Rozak called this same group "technocrats," technical experts who made claims to authority not because they possessed a title (as do aristocrats) or wealth (as do plutocrats) or a popular mandate (as do democrats), but because they possessed "scientific forms of knowledge" (Rozak 1969: 8). In 1967 John Kenneth Galbraith described this same group as the "technostructure," a hierarchical network of individuals "who bring specialized knowledge, talent or expertise to group decision making" and exercise power because, and to the degree that, they possess technical knowledge necessary to achievement of group goals (Galbraith 1967: 71). More recently Robert Reich has described them as "symbolic analysts," workers who solve problems through manipulation of symbols. Their numbers have grown, Reich notes, from 8 percent of the United States work force in 1950 to more than 20 percent today (Reich 1991: 234).

As Mills (and before him Veblen and Saint Simon) noted, most members of this new class draw their power from technical education and knowledge, rather than from traditional sources of social power such as military monopoly (aristocracy), wealth (plutocracy), or mass movements and popular opinion (democracy). They consequently esteem and flaunt accouterments and insignia of learning. (The framed diploma or university window decal is to the technocrat what the sword and escutcheon are to the aristocrat, what the diamond stud and pinky ring are to the plutocrat, and what the title of elected office is to the democrat: a sign of membership in the privileged elite.) They particularly value technical applied knowledge, such as of law, business, engineering, the applied social sciences and medicine, because "success in the technostructure calls for mastery of one or more of the arts associated with planning, technology, and organization" (Galbraith 1967: 368). Creation of the technostructure thus caused enormous growth in the size of American universities, as these are the places in which the most valuable human capital is produced. This surged in the 1960s when the percentage of the population enrolled in institutions of higher learning more than doubled, from 1.7 to 4.2 percent. It also altered the nature of universities, which increasingly trained and certified students for positions in the technostructure (or gave students the mistaken impression they were receiving such training and certification [Kirk 1978]). This led Wendell Berry to somewhere write that, in the closing decades of the twentieth century, American universities had, despite the apparent plethora of programs in their catalogues, reduced their offerings to the single major of upward social mobility.

Work in the technostructure requires discipline as well as knowledge, although this is not always immediately evident in the informal studios and labs that are quintessential biotechnic workplaces. Informality is evident in flexible work schedules and unconventional working hours, casual work attire, highly personalized office space, and a pretense of sometimes spurious equality. The purpose of this, according to Handy, is to foster a culture of consent and collegial cooperation similar to that presumed to exist in universities. The viability of a biotechnic workplace largely depends on the quality of the intelligence, information and ideas there brought together, and a spirit of informal equality is thought conducive to this quality (Handy 1990). Although the biotechnic corporation differs from its neotechnic predecessor in many visible ways, it remains an organization in which people for the most part work with and depend on other people. Thus it is a social context that requires high levels of conformity. This was first exposed by William Whyte in 1956 when he described the "social ethic" of "Organization Man" (Whyte 1956). Then as now, middle-class Americans who aspire to improve their social condition recognize that success depends not only on their own ability and effort, but also on their membership in a successful collective, or what we today might call a winning team. To join such a team one has to possess technical skills and credentials, but one also has to make one's self physically and personally agreeable, and wholeheartedly internalize the goals and values of the team. This is why biotech winners, although often espousing nonconformity and individualism, are in fact so uniform in their beliefs and attitudes, and why they may be said to constitute a coherent professional culture (see Frank 1996).

In the 1980s one segment of this fortunate group of individuals with appreciating human capital came to be known as Yuppies (young urban professionals) or Dinks (double income, no kids), when they came under media scrutiny because of their urbane and sophisticated consumption habits. What is now clear is that the price of many affordable luxuries was at that time falling due to global trade, while the income of workers in certain fortunate sectors of the economy, such as law and banking, was for the same reason rising. The convergence of these trends (along with biotechnic birth control) permitted the Yuppie lifestyle. Widely ridiculed, and even more widely envied and emulated, Yuppies helped to popularize connoisseurship of affordable luxuries, and in so doing left a lasting stamp on late-twentieth-century American culture. This sort of upscale living is now typical, to one degree or another, among a large part of the rising technostructure and forms one of the more conspicuous elements of its professional culture.

Biotechnic technopolises

Highly educated, adept in the use and improvement of cutting-edge technologies, aglow with group-supported self-approval, enjoying compensation adequate to indulge their taste in affordable luxuries, the winners in the biotechnic complex are a conspicuous presence in the turn-of-the-century American scene. They are not only a sociological phenomenon, however, but also a geographical phenomenon. As former Labor Secretary Robert Reich notes, "in the United States *as in no other nation*, symbolic analysts are concentrated in specific geographic pockets where they live, work, and learn with other symbolic analysts" (Reich 1991: 234, my emphasis). These "symbolic-analytic zones" are the new places of value in the biotechnic United States because it is within these zones that one finds the social milieu and information technologies requisite to collective creativity. These zones combine Handy's three elements of an I3 organization: intelligence (in its population), information (in its data retrieval and storage devices), and ideas (in its formal and informal social exchanges) (Handy 1990: 141). Some authors refer to valuable symbolic-analytic zones as technopolises. (The term is useful, if rather tendentious; today's places of rapidly appreciating value are simply technopolises of the biotechnic complex. In the 1830s a water-powered mill town such as Rochester, New York, was an eotechnic technopolis!)

Preer (1992) identifies seven essential elements in a technopolis (or, more accurately, biotechnic technopolis). The first is a world-class university, which serves as a source of ideas, information, and skilled labor (occasional consulting by faculty, applications for full-time work from students). The roles of Stanford and MIT in the growth of Silicon Valley and the I128 Corridor are exemplary. Next to the university there must be a research park where ideas that issue from the university can be commercialized. Commercialization of untested ideas demands high-risk investment, so Preer's third requirement is a ready supply of venture capital. Venture capitalists must have adequate funds to invest, of course, but they must also possess an uncommon mixture of audacity and prudent discrimination if they are to allocate these funds efficiently. Information resources are, therefore, the fourth requirement. These may be present in libraries, data sets, telecommunication links or human experts imported by way of the local airport. Well-informed humans are the fifth requirement: appropriately skilled labor. A technopolis must create and retain, or attract and retain, a large pool of technocrats and symbolic analysts, not only to operate its machines and carry out its procedures, but also to animate and contribute to its sixth necesity: a stimulating social and intellectual milieu. (Less often noted is the need of a technopolis for large numbers of low-skill workers to perform routine maintenance and services.) To attract large numbers of the technical intelligentsia, a technopolis must offer, as a seventh requirement, an attractive quality of life. Cultural events, a mild climate, attractive scenery, an appealing lifestyle: such local amenities make it easier for firms to attract high-tech workers and consequently for an aspiring technopolis to attract high-tech firms.

These are the artificial or technical resources that define a place of value in the biotechnic United States. It should be noted that, with the exception of local amenities (the therapeutic environment mentioned in Chapter 2), none of these are related to natural resources. Technopolises come in many grades, and many center on little more than a technical college or regional medical center, but even to the casual observer they betray a family resemblance, largely due to the common professional culture of their workers. They are newer, shinier, better maintained than other places; their landscapes are daily cleaned and polished by money. Their residents appear (and in fact are) healthier, with better teeth, better skin, better haircuts. They drive newer cars, wear newer, more stylish clothing, inhabit larger, more opulent houses. They speak an expensive and often jargon-ridden language; they raise expensive children with the aid of expensive professionals. These and other indicators of a valuable place repeatedly present themselves to the geographer's discriminating eye (Sauer 1956).

We often speak of the United States as a technologically advanced country, and as a land of opportunity, but these spatial generalizations obscure the degree to which advanced technology and economic opportunity have always been localized. Value is concentrated in particular places, not spread evenly across space. In the biotechnic, most places of value are "semi-urban agglomerations inhabited mainly but not exclusively by white professionals." Elsewhere in the United States, McRae notes, there are forming "large pockets where living standards,

Figure 3.5 Trendy meeting place. San Diego, CA, has every characteristic of a technopolis and consequently has enjoyed remarkable prosperity in the biotechnic era. Sidewalk cafes such as this one in San Diego's Horton Plaza are important settings for the exchange of ideas and the creation of a stimulating milieu. They are also, incidentally, ideal settings for public consumption of the affordable luxuries that are central to the professional culture of the biotechnic. Upscale dining facilities and trendy menus are clear indicators of a place of appreciating value. Where they are absent one can reasonably surmise that biotech winners are also in short supply. (*Photograph by the author.*)

education levels, unemployment and public health will be [in coming decades] more akin to a developing country than an industrial one." Although Americans are accustomed to think of these problems in racial terms, McRae contends that "it is more helpful to see [American economic inequality] in geographic and cultural terms." "Certain regions of the United States . . . have lost their economic function," he writes, "and there are certain cultural attitudes [typically localized] which make it impossible for people who espouse them to contribute anything positive to the economy." Should present trends continue,

McRae, like Phillips, believes that the United States may well evolve into a geographically segregated dual economy of prosperous technopolises surrounded by, and very likely fortified against, large areas in which a much more primitive economy operates (McRae 1994: 209, 214, 216). Like the American middle class, American places appear to be separating into biotech winners and losers.

Journalist Robert Kaplan takes a similar view. He sees the contemporary United States evolving into an archipelago of "suburban pods" where fortunate individuals in possession of appreciating human capital work and enjoy the comforts (and vexations) of a "rushed, cell phone global culture" (Kaplan 1998: 72–3). These pods will not be closely tied to their surrounding hinterlands, as were the valuable places of the eotechnic; nor will they be closely integrated with other industrial centers of their region or the nation as a whole, as were the valuable places of the paleotechnic and neotechnic. They will be points in a global exchange network, with interests, attitudes, and standards of living more closely aligned with other points in the network than with places in the adjacent territory.

Topographical chauvinism

The geography of value is uneven and transient, and the pace of this transience is quickened in an open-class society like that of the United States, where few restraints are placed on social ambition and economic opportunities are swiftly exploited. In time, one must suppose, the biotechnic geography of value will be superseded, although few can venture to guess the shape of its successor. In time, one must suppose, boys will throw stones at the remaining windowpanes of buildings in abandoned research parks and pigeons will roost in the disused dormitories of redundant universities. It is difficult to take such images seriously, I know, but this is only because each one of us is in some degree afflicted with chronological chauvinism, a phrase I've adapted from Owen Barfield. We are inclined to look upon the past with condescension (even with the supreme condescension of nostalgia), and to view the future as little more than a span in which present-day technique will be perfected and more widely deployed. One has only to glance at neotechnic visions of the future to see this. They envision a land of ubiquitous skyscrapers, taller, more numerous, and linked by lofty highways streaming with strangely antiquated automobiles (Canto

1993). The paleotechnic looked forward to a world of steam-powered robots! (Kouwenhoven 1982: 127–45).

Chronological chauvinism is not actually a projection of the present onto the future, but rather a projection of one portion of the present. This partiality is evident in the prognostications of McRae and Kaplan, who seem to suggest that, in future, all of the United States will come to resemble either the most dismal slums or the most affluent suburbs of the present day. Two types of place are taken as prototypes for the entire future. This sort of two-point perspective is preferable to the one-point perspective one normally encounters, which takes one type of place as the prototype of all future places, but it betrays the same fallacy. We may call this topographical chauvinism. Topographical chauvinism is the view that one particular place, or type of place, is the consummation of all the ages, and that future geographic change will consist of perfection and spatial diffusion of this model of human settlement. It was topographical chauvinism that caused neotechnic visionaries to assume that, in future, every place would come to resemble lower Manhattan Island in New York City.

This sort of topographical chauvinism is difficult to avoid, and may in fact be forgiven if we recognize, with Dewey, that these images are not in fact ends, but only means to incite present activity. A more serious type of topographical chauvinism projects the image of one place or type of place over a large and, if truth be told, heterogeneous area, or space. This might be styled contemporary or synchronic topographical chauvinism. This is the prejudice that causes many people to labor under the misapprehension that all, or at least most, of the contemporary United States resembles southern California, or central Iowa, or rural New England (Meinig 1979). Topographical chauvinism projected onto the future takes one place or type of place as a prototype; contemporary topographical chauvinism takes one place or type of place as an archetype.

Perhaps because their meaning and portent appear clearer, extreme places are more readily adopted as prototypes and archetypes. This may be why it appears to some that the United States is, or will shortly become, a set of places that are nothing more than variations on themes already present in what are generally regarded as the best and worst. A dystopian minority discounts the present significance and future viability of the best places; a sanguine majority discounts the present significance and future viability of the worst places. In fact, the topographical chauvinism of the sanguine majority sees all, or at least most, places in the United States reflecting or evolving into biotechnic technopolises. This is understandable, but as geographers we must dispute it, along with all other forms of topographical chauvinism. The face of the globe is not uniform, but highly varied. Places differ, one from another. It is unlikely that this will change.

References

Canto, Christophe (1993), *The History of the Future: Images of the 21st Century*, Paris: Flammarion.

Dewey, John (1922), *Human Nature and Conduct: An Introduction to Social Psychology*, New York: Henry Holt.

Frank, Thomas (1996), "Hip Is Dead," *The Nation*, 262, April 1, p. 16.

Galbraith, John Kenneth (1967), *The New Industrial State*, Boston: Houghton Mifflin.

Galbraith, John Kenneth (1992), *The Culture of Contentment*, Boston: Houghton Mifflin.

Handy, Charles (1990), *The Age of Unreason*, Boston: Harvard Business School Press.

Hugill, Peter (1993), *World Trade since 1431: Geography, Technology, and Capitalism*, Baltimore: Johns Hopkins University Press.

Hume, David (1907), *An Enquiry concerning the Principles of Morals*, Chicago: Open Court.

Ingersoll, Robert (1912), *The Works of Robert G. Ingersoll*, Vol. 4, New York: Dresden.

Joad, C. E. M. (1927), *The Babbitt Warren*, New York: Harper Brothers.

Johnson, R. J. (1982), *The American Urban System: A Geographical Perspective*, New York: St. Martin's Press.

Kaplan, Robert D. (1998), *An Empire Wilderness: Travels into America's Future*, New York: Random House.

Kiker, B. F. (1968), *Human Capital in Retrospect*, Essays in Economics No. 16, Columbia, SC: Bureau of Business and Economic Research, University of South Carolina.

Kirk, Russell (1978), *Decadence and Renewal in Higher Learning: An Episodic History of American University and College since 1953*, South Bend, IN: Gateway.

Kouwenhoven, John A. (1982), *Half a Truth Is Better than None: Some Unsystematic Conjectures about Art, Disorder, and American Experience*, Chicago: University of Chicago Press.

Lasch, Christopher (1991), *The True and Only Heaven: Progress and Its Critics*, New York: W. W. Norton.

Lewis, Peirce F. (1972), "Small Town in Pennsylvania," *Annals of the Association of American Geographers*, 62, pp. 323–51.

McLuhan, Marshall (1964), *Understanding Media: The Extensions of Man*, New York: McGraw Hill.

McMurrer, Daniel P., and Isabel V. Sawhill (1998), *Getting Ahead: Economic and Social Mobility in America*, Washington, DC: Urban Institute Press.

McRae, Hamish (1994), *The World in 2020: Power, Culture and Prosperity*, Boston: Harvard Business School Press.

Meinig, D. W. (1979), "Symbolic Landscapes: Models of American Community," in Meinig (ed.), *The Interpretation of Ordinary Landscapes: Geographical Essays*, New York: Oxford University Press, pp. 164–92.

Mills, C. Wright (1951), *White Collar: The American Middle Classes*, New York: Oxford University Press.

Mumford, Lewis (1934), *Technics and Civilization*, New York: Harcourt, Brace and Company.

Mumford, Lewis (1938), *The Culture of Cities*, New York: Harcourt, Brace, Jovanovich.

Nadler, Leonard (1970), *Developing Human Resources*, Houston, TX: Gulf Publishing.

Phillips, Kevin (1993), *Boiling Point: Democrats, Republicans, and the Decline of Middle-Class Prosperity*, New York: Random House.

Preer, Robert (1992), *The Emergence of Technopolis: Knowledge, Intensive Technologies and Regional Development*, New York: Praeger.

Reich, Robert B. (1991), *The Work of Nations: Preparing Ourselves for 21st Century Capitalism*, New York: Alfred A. Knopf.

Relph, Edward (1987), *The Modern Urban Landscape*, Baltimore: Johns Hopkins University Press.

Rifkin, Jeremy (1998), *The Biotechnic Century: Harnessing the Gene and Remaking the World*, New York: Jeremy Tarcher/Putman.

Rozak, Theodore (1969), *The Making of a Counter Culture: Reflections on the Technocratic Society and Its Youthful Opposition*, New York: Doubleday and Co.

Sauer, Carl Ortwin (1956), "The Education of a Geographer," *Annals of the Association of American Geographers*, 46, pp. 287–99.

Schrier, Arnold, and Joyce Story (trans. and eds.) (1979), *A Russian Looks at America: The Journey of Aleksandr Borisovich Lakier in 1857*, Chicago: University of Chicago Press.

Semple, Ellen Churchill (1911), *Influences of Geographic Environment: On the Basis of Ratzel's System of Anthropogeography*, New York: Henry Holt.

Sewart, Watt (1940), "A Spanish Traveller Visits Rochester," *The Rochester Historical Society Publication*, 18, pp. 106–17.

Smith, Adam (1937), *The Wealth of Nations*, New York: Modern Library.

Stern, Robert A. M. (1986), *Pride of Place: Building the American Dream*, Boston: Houghton Mifflin.

Tocqueville, Alexis de (1966), *Democracy in America*, ed. J. P. Mayer and Max Lerner, trans. George Lawrence, New York: Harper and Row.

Wells, H. G. (1987), *The Future in America*, New York: St. Martins Press.

Whyte, William H. (1956), *The Organization Man*, New York: Simon & Schuster.

PART II

Political and economic dimensions of the American experience

CHAPTER 4

America, frontier nation:
From abstract space to worldly place

John A. Agnew and Joanne P. Sharp

The American "geographical imagination" is often tied to the experience of the expanding frontier that both sets American history apart
from elsewhere (particularly Europe) and serves as the dominant
metaphor for American initiatives inside and outside its national territory. The American understanding of national sovereignty has been
unusual because of the duality of the national geographical imagination. On the one hand, it is about a national space wrested from
an unwilling continent (and its then inhabitants) by people with a
civilizing mission. On the other hand, the national project is without
geographical limits, based on the projection into the rest of the world
of a set of values resulting from the national frontier experience
judged as beneficial to all. America's exceptional history, therefore,
licenses both a spatially-bounded American difference from everyone
else and an expansive evangelical mission to make over the world in
America's image. The political geographers John Agnew and Joanne
Sharp describe the historic vagaries of this dual vision and the impact
that it has had on American relations with the rest of the world. They
see the crisis in the American self-image during the Vietnam War and
as a result of the economic and cultural changes in the late 1960s and
1970s as a crucial watershed in the shattering of the widespread
national consensus about America's place in the world. They consider
how far the present world economy is essentially the product of the
projection of the American identity and interests into the world at
large and investigate whether trends in this world economy, associated
with the term globalization, show signs of undermining the mythic
power of the frontier story. The long-term ambiguity of American
sovereignty, they suggest, may now be eroding popular acceptance of
a singular American identity tied to the frontier experience. They
show that, once the cultural blinkers of the unifying frontier myth
have been removed, we can begin to recognize the richly differentiated
America alluded to in other chapters.

The idea of the "frontier experience" is often identified as the touchstone of what sets the United States apart from other countries. From the outset of colonial settlement on the eastern seaboard of North America, "America" has been seen by the makers of American public culture – political leaders, writers, and educators – as the space where European settlers met an alien environment and by taming and absorbing it created the most powerful polity and plentiful cornucopia yet known to humanity. They created an American space out of what they saw as a pristine wilderness. From school textbooks to Western movies and political speeches, American identity is closely associated with wresting political-economic success out of a difficult environment and imprinting the values of the founders of the United States as the frontier moved westwards. Yet, "America" has also represented a set of universal ideas about political-economic and cultural organization. For example, the geography evoked by the American Declaration of Independence is neither continental nor hemispheric but universal. It is directed to "the earth," the "Laws of Nature and of Nature's God," and to all of "mankind." In this vision, "America" is seen as a model for humanity, a perfect model for any space. So, though exceptional in its own geo-graphical experience, America has also been seen by many, if not most, Americans as a role model for the rest of the world.

Until the 1890s the spatially-bounded sense of America predomi-nated in both domestic politics and foreign-policy making. In particular, America was defined in opposition to Europe. "Europe," George Washington observed in his farewell address of 1796, "has a set of pri-mary interests which to us have none or a very remote relation. Hence she must be engaged in frequent controversies, the causes of which are essentially foreign to our concerns" (in Richardson 1905: vol. 1, 214). The unilateral declaration of what became known as the Monroe Doctrine in 1823 went further, establishing that the European powers represented a different system from that of America against which the newly independent states of Central and South America had to be protected. By the later decades of the nineteenth century, however, the increased wealth and power of the United States, along with one of those periodic downturns in the world economy that have afflicted the entire world since the arrival of a true global economy in the nine-teenth century and the scramble for colonies by the major European countries as a reaction to this, led to a new emphasis on America's global role (Agnew 1987). The hemispheral identity of the United States and the protection of its sovereignty from European challenge gave way to universalist themes and identities concerning race, political maturity, and the civilizing influence of American values. Presidents McKinley and Theodore Roosevelt were the first to see the United States as an agent of global discipline and order based on American experience of its internal development. The internationalism of President Woodrow Wilson marked perhaps the apogee of the vision of America as an inspiration for the rest of the world and set the terms of the twentieth century conflict between those Americans keen on a global crusading role, usually known as "internationalists," and those attached to a spatially limited definition of America, often portrayed as "isolationists."

This chapter will describe the main features of the American geographical imagination as inscribed on a world scale (particularly the practical impact of the frontier idea), consider the influence the practice of an expanding American frontier has had on the globalization of the world economy in the twentieth century, examine the crucial impact of the Cold War with the former Soviet Union (1947–89) on American collective self-understanding, and, finally, survey the joint effects of the crisis at the beginning of the twenty-first century in the American geographical imagination and the workings of the contemporary world economy on the United States itself. The approach will involve an examination of the respective roles of economic, geopolitical, and cultural processes, and the particular convergence of these processes as seen in America's relationship to the world as a whole.

JOHN WAYNE'S AMERICA (by Garry Wills, New York: Simon and Schuster, 1997, pp. 302–3). Reproduced by permission of Simon and Schuster.

Why was Wayne the Number One Movie Star, even as late as 1995? He embodies the American myth. The archetypal American is a displaced person – arrived from a rejected past, breaking into a glorious future, on the move, fearless himself, feared by others, a killer cleansing the world of things that "need killing," loving but not bound down by love, rootless but carrying the Center in himself, a gyroscopic direction-setter, a traveling norm.

Other cultures begin with a fixed and social hearth, a temple, a holy city. American life begins when the enclosure is escaped.

One becomes American by going out. We are a people of depar-
tures, not arrival. To reach one place is simply to catch sight of a
new Beyond. Our basic myth is that of the frontier. Our hero is
the frontiersman. To become urban is to break the spirit of man.
Freedom is out on the plains, under the endless sky. A pent-in
American ceases to be American. In his 1844 lecture on "The
Young American," Emerson said that Americans need the boundless West in order to become themselves.

> The nervous [strong-nerved] rocky West is intruding a new and
> continental element into the national mind, and we shall yet have
> an American genius [ethos] . . . Whatever events in progress
> shall go to disgust men with cities, and infuse into them the
> passion for country life, and country pleasures, will render a
> service to the whole face of this continent, and will further the
> most poetic of all the occupations of real life, the bringing out
> by art [of] the native but hidden graces of the landscape . . . We
> must regard the land as a commanding and increasing power
> on the citizen, the sanative and Americanizing influence, which
> promises to disclose new virtues for ages to come . . .

The "young American" Emerson imagined out on the horizon
had the easy gait and long stride of John Wayne.

The American geographical imagination at a world scale

Spatial orientations are of particular importance to understanding
America, whether this is with respect to foreign policy or to national
identity. It could be argued that a geographical imagination is central
to all national political cultures. Imagining a coherent territorial entity
containing a group of people with a common attachment to that
territory has been crucial in the making of all national states. However,
if all nations are imagined communities, then America is the imagined
community par excellence (Campbell 1992). The space of "America"
was already created in the imaginations of the first European settlers
en route to the "New World" (Dolan 1994) as a space of openness
and possibility. It was not constructed and corrupted by centuries of

history and power struggles as was Europe. Even now, America is a country that is easily seen as both "nowhere" and "pastless," constructed as totally modern and democratic against a European (or some other) Other mired in a despotic history and stratified by the tyranny of aristocracy. The ideology of the American Dream, an ideology which stresses that anyone can be successful given hard work, luck, and unintrusive government, marks out the American historical experience as unique or exceptional. Narratives of the history of America as a country of migrants successfully seeking a better way of life provide practical evidence for this imagination. The enslaved Africans and conquered Indians who made constructing the New World possible are not surprisingly largely absent from this vision except as incidental characters or as barriers to be overcome.

The mindset of limitless possibility was reinforced by the frontier experience of individual social mobility, of the energy of a youthful country in contrast to the social stagnation and economic inequality of "old" Europe. Americans were free to set themselves up in the vast expanse of "empty" land available on the frontier, discounting the presence of natives whose self-evident technological and religious "backwardness" justified the expropriation of their land. All settlers were equal on the frontier, so the myth goes, and those who were successful succeeded due to their own hard work, not through any advantage of birth. Clearly there are historiographical problems with this national myth, not least the violent erasure of other people and their pasts that occurred as part of this geographical movement (see Shapiro 1997). However, the myth has long remained as a powerful aspect of American culture. The initial presumption was that as long as the frontier continued to expand America would flourish. This mindset remained influential beyond the physical expansion of the United States across the continent as "the frontier" was reconfigured around the necessity to expand the "American way" and "American good" beyond American shores, especially in the years following the end of the Second World War when another power (the Soviet Union) offered a competing utopian rendering of political economy. Importantly, the frontier story is not simply an elite construction told to the population at large but one retold and recycled through a variety of cultural forms: most obviously through mass education, but more importantly through the media and in popular culture (Slotkin 1973, 1986, 1992).

The "frontier" character of the American economy – expanding markets for goods and opportunities for individuals beyond previous limits – figures strongly in the American stimulus to contemporary economic globalization. As we shall see, this is itself tied to a particular cultural image: the ethos of the consumer-citizen (Cross 2000). The American position in the Cold War of defending and promulgating this model ran up against the competing Soviet model of the worker-state. The resultant geopolitical order was thus intimately bound up with the expression of American identity. This was spread through ideas of "development," first in such acts as the Marshall Plan to aid the reconstruction of Europe immediately after the Second World War, and then in the modernization of the "Third World" following the elements of a model of American society pushed most strongly during the short presidency of John Kennedy (1961–2).

Recent changes in American culture that have been termed "the end of victory culture" (Engelhardt 1995) signal an erosion of confidence in the idea of an inherent American superiority due to the peculiar geographical experience of frontier expansion and subsequent service as a global role model. This trend, according to Tom Engelhardt, is the result of an increasing mismatch during the Cold War between the United States historical experience of pacifying Indians, on the one hand, and modern technological warfare, on the other. But it is also because the United States has become less distinctive in terms of its self-defined virtues – individual liberty, wealth, and democratic institutions – and more distinctive in respect of its historic vices – impoverishment, violence, and crass vulgarity – than many other countries. The final blow to the self-confident story of inevitable national victory came with the United States military debacle in Vietnam in the years 1968–75. With the end of the Cold War in 1989–91 and the national sense of purpose it provided, the lived space or place "America" has begun to lose its self-evident central material-symbolic position within the world for many Americans as well as for others. The end of the Cold War with the collapse of the Soviet Union can be seen as a victory for the United States but it has also intensified the relative decline of United States victory culture. The removal of the Soviet threat from the global geopolitical stage has led to an undermining of faith in the relevance of the triumphalist element in the American national story. In this construction, evident across the entire political spectrum, if with islands of support for the older outlook still apparent in parts of the South and Midwest, the resolve of the frontier spirit and commitment to a core American identity have been replaced by the disorder of a more fragmented American society, split culturally along axes of gender, ethnicity, economic status, and attitudes to government that are increasingly manifested geographically in local and regional differences of political identity and interest. These place differences in turn have stimulated renewed disagreement over the course of American foreign policy reflecting the renewal of the long-standing tension between globally-oriented internationalists and territorially-oriented isolationists that had faded during the Cold War years.

Frontier nation: the American origins of twentieth-century globalization

The creation of a global economy under American auspices reflects the dominant ideology about the founding of the country and the essence of its national identity and character. Twentieth-century economic globalization has been linked to two important political-economic principles which have been closely associated with the American frontier ethos and its realization first in continental expansion and later in global power (Williams 1969; Agnew 1999). First was the view of the expansion of the marketplace as necessary to national political and social well-being. Second was the idea that economic liberty or independence is by definition the foundation for freedom per se. The American Constitution and early interpretations of it combined these two principles to create a uniquely American version of democratic capitalism. On the one hand the federal government underwrote expansion into the continental interior and stimulated interest in foreign markets for American products but, on the other hand, the federal sub-units (the states) and the division of power between the branches of the federal government (the Congress, the presidency, and the Supreme Court) limited the power of government to regulate private economic activity. The Constitution is open to contrary interpretations on the relative powers of both federal branches and tiers of government (Lynch 1999). Down the years, however, the federal level has expanded its powers much more than any of the Founders, including its greatest advocate, Alexander Hamilton, could have foreseen. At the federal level, and reflecting the essential ambiguity of the Constitution, the Supreme Court has also come to exert great power through its capacity for interpreting the meaning of the founding document.

Each of the political-economic principles can be seen as emerging from stories about American "national character" and the model of citizenship offered by the vision of American exceptionalism. Although Americans celebrate some historic occasions, such as Independence day (the 4th of July), and founding documents, such as the Declaration of Independence and the Constitution, they have not had much history to define themselves by. America has been defined not so much by a common history, as most imagined communities of nationhood seem to have (Anderson 1983). Rather, Americans have defined themselves through a shared geography expressed in the future-facing expansion of the frontier by individual pioneers. The Founding Father, Thomas Jefferson, said he liked "the dreams of the future better than the history of the past."

The expansion of the United States into the interior of North America in the nineteenth century created a land mass and resource base unmatched by other empires save that of Russia (Figure 4.1). Initially geared to agricultural development, the national policy of conquest, settlement, and exploitation gave way after the Civil War (1860–5) to the establishment of an integrated manufacturing economy. The Civil War was a struggle over the economic trajectory of the country as a whole as well as a conflict over the morality of slavery. The victory of the industrial North over the agrarian-slave South ensured the shift of the American economy from an agrarian to a manufacturing base. The South and the West became resource peripheries for the growing manufacturing belt of the Northeast, providing food and raw materials to the factories of the now dominant Northern industrialists and their banker allies (Agnew 1987). A set of important place differences in the nature and level of economic development, as well as in outlooks on the balance between federal and state levels of government and conceptions of the public good, took root during the process of settlement and development of a national economy to challenge the idea of an idealized, abstract American space with little or no internal differentiation between regions, classes, and ethnic groups (see the magisterial survey of the shaping of America beginning with Meinig 1986).

The emerging national economy of the late nineteenth century was based in large part on the growth of the first capitalist consumer economy. American businesses pioneered in advertising and salesmanship as ways of bringing the population into mass markets for

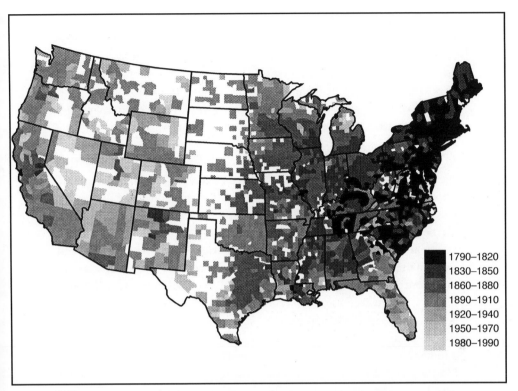

Figure 4.1 The course of the settlement frontier in the continental United States. The geographical expansion of the United States into North America, United States counties by the date the population first reached 10,000. One-quarter of all counties have not yet reached 10,000 residents and probably never will. Many of the counties in a broad swath running through the Great Plains from Canada to Mexico are losing what population they had to low birth rates and high out-migration. The greatest period of settlement of the American West was between 1940 and 1960. From this perspective, the literal settlement frontier had not closed in 1890. Of course, now it was cities and not the small towns and countryside of the West that attracted most of the immigrants. So figuratively, in terms of the image of the frontier as settlement sweeping through hostile countryside, the frontier had closed long before. Source: Forstall 1994.

manufactured goods and processed foodstuffs. Relative to the rest of the world, American growth in manufacturing output was incredible. By 1913 the United States was to account for fully one-third of the world's total industrial production. From the 1870s on much of this growth was managed by large industrial firms and investment banks whose American markets generated less and less profit at ever greater expense. It was in the period 1896–1905, however, that the United

States saw the greatest spate of mergers and business consolidation in its history such that by 1905 around two-thirds of the manufacturing capital of the United States was controlled by 300 corporations with an aggregate capital worth of $7 billion (in 1992 dollars). That the 1890s also saw the peak of a major economic depression with high unemployment and increasing political unrest meant that there was added incentive to look for markets beyond the territorial limits of the United States itself.

It was in the context of the economic downturn of the 1890s that the historian Frederick Jackson Turner (1920) famously wrote of the impact of the frontier on American identity and culture. Celebrating the liberating and invigorating powers of the expanding frontier, Turner feared for the consequences of the "closing of the frontier" when all land was taken and the American urge for growth and movement would consequently cease. Turner envisaged this as an immediate concern. Renewed expansion was required in order to lower unemployment, reintegrate American labor into the American Dream and thus reduce the appeal of subversive politics. The issue of American expansion was not only an economic issue then, given that a moving frontier was the source of America's uniqueness – its Manifest Destiny, as it was first called in the 1840s – and that the United States could only achieve its full potential if it continued to expand. Turner insisted upon the need for an end to American isolationism with the closing of the internal frontier, and for the development of "a vigorous foreign policy... and for the extension of American influence to outlying islands and adjoining countries ..." (Turner 1896: 289).

Turner preached to the already converted. The involvement of American business abroad was both aided and legitimized by the United States Presidents who took office after 1896, the critical year in the shift from an internal to external frontiers. To extend from the Atlantic to the Pacific Ocean had always seemed too geographically neat not to be the product of fate or the hand of Providence. Overseas expansion was seemingly more difficult to justify, particularly when it required open territorial annexation. The United States had itself emerged from colonial revolt so colonizing others required some ratio-nale. It was forthcoming by reference to the values and ideals that America represented. America was sold as an idea. American investors would provide needed capital. American trade would bring sophisti-cated American goods. American reform would bring new institutions and practices and break down barriers of caste and creed. In other words, America would bring progress as attested to by America's own experience of developing a consumerist economy (Rosenberg 1982).

The American approach was only intermittently territorial, and, with the exception of the Spanish-American War of 1898–1900, largely in its immediate vicinity, in the Caribbean and Central America. Otherwise it was resolutely interactional, focused on the possibilities of and proceeds from foreign capital investment. Unlike business in the other industrial capitalist countries, American business favored direct rather than portfolio investment and conventional trade. Economic advantages previously specific to the United States in terms of economic concentration and mass markets, such as the cost effectiveness of large factories and economies of process, product, and market integration, were exported abroad as American firms invested in their subsidiaries. A new pattern of foreign direct investment designed to gain access to foreign markets for large firms was coming into existence under American auspices. American leaders could preach against European territorial colonialism as American businesses created a whole new phenomenon of internationalized production. Unknowingly, these businesses were laying the groundwork for the globalization of production that American governments became the main sponsors of, with the 1930s and 1940s as the only period of retraction since then.

The expansion beyond American shores was never simply economic in motivation. There was a mission, contentious but unmistakable, to spread American values. Pushing American ways of economic and political organization was more than simply a mechanism for increasing consumption of American products. But the mission to spread American values did often lead to the consumption of American products, later epitomized in the global audiences for MTV, the near-universal popularity of Coca-Cola, and global consumption of McDonald's hamburgers. The products represented America to the world at large (Twitchell 1999). The reach into the global arena continued throughout the twentieth century with the exception of the Depression of the 1930s which encouraged a flurry of economic protectionism. This ended with the Second World War which reinforced globalization for a number of reasons. First was the rise of the Soviet Union and the specter of global communism. Soviet communism was seen as antithetical to the United States economically because of its goal of state-led autarkic development, which resisted the expansion of American capitalism.

Furthermore, the expansionism of the USSR threatened to limit the global reach of the American model of democratic capitalism. This appeared to be made all the easier with the collapse of the industrial capitalist world in the wake of war. In order to steel Western Europe against the temptations of Soviet communism, the United States helped with the rebuilding of its national economies (and reinvigorating markets for the United States economy) with the Marshall Plan (1947–51). This was not the last international intervention by United States governments. The collapse of European colonialism in the 1940s and 1950s left a "third world" of former colonies under the influence of neither the Soviet "second world" nor the United States "first world." American leaders feared that the poverty of these countries would leave them vulnerable to the Soviet way and so in the 1950s and 1960s programs of aid were launched in order to develop third world countries. As with the Marshall Plan to Western Europe, these programs involved the export of American production techniques and values, an offshoot of which was the instigation of the American ethos of consumerism.

Given American dominance in its sphere of influence at the end of the Second World War it is little surprising that it should have had a major impact on the workings of the revived world economy. But the impact was not in the form of a mere recapitulation of the pre-war world economy, only now under American command. Rather, it was something new. Abandoning territorial imperialism, "Western [American] capitalism resolved the old problem of overproduction, thus removing what Lenin believed was the major incentive for imperialism and war" (Calleo 1987: 147). The motor of this sea change in the geography of the capitalist world economy was the emergence of high mass consumption across the industrial world. Following the broad outlines of the American model developed between the 1890s and 1930s, major industries increasingly traded across national boundaries, setting up subsidiaries, and investing on a world scale. All of this required the deepening of consumption across the industrial world rather than the creation of captive colonial markets. The United States had pioneered in paying high wages to factory workers to stimulate consumption. With the New Deal policies of the 1930s in which the United States federal government took a hand in encouraging economic growth through government spending programs and the spread of Keynesian economics, commitment to encouraging economic growth by stimulating demand through higher incomes and progressive income taxes became a global standard.

The famous American political theorist Louis Hartz (1955: 291–2) thought that "all this was basically alien to the national liberal spirit . . . Wasn't the whole meaning of 'Americanism' that America was a peculiar land of freedom, equality and opportunity?" Of course, Hartz claimed that America had always been a basically liberal society reliant on collective belief in individual liberty, equality, and capitalism in which the marketplace of goods and ideas was the basic testing ground of human achievement. Certainly, the founders of the United States, such as Thomas Jefferson, John Adams, and James Madison, drew on the essentially liberal, if also Puritan, ideas of the seventeenth-century English philosopher John Locke to justify their rebellion and the new institutions they created. If Hartz ignored the Puritan aspect of the founders (Dienstag 1996), he also largely missed the imperial element in American domestic politics. He particularly underplayed the racism upon which the American political economy had been constructed both with respect to the native Indians and the imported black slaves. The silence of the Declaration of Independence about the institution of slavery upon which the plantation economies of the South relied introduced an implicit double standard into American liberalism, privileging entrenched interests, such as slave holders and, later, corporations, and a European or white and male identity as that of the quintessential "American." The peculiarly American fusion of liberalism and imperialism in the world beyond national boundaries, therefore, was nothing new. It was not alien at all.

America's cold war

The Cold War was written in America largely as an inevitable clash between two systems: one (America) represented freedom, democracy, and individualism whereas the other (the Soviet Union) represented collectivism, communism, and totalitarianism. All parts of the world were implicated in this geopolitical order based on the geographical division of the world into two political-economic zones. Each state was either part of the First World led by the United States of America, the Second dominated by the USSR, or, in the space of conflict, the Third World, waiting to fall to communism unless bolstered by United States aid or military intervention. This geopolitical system allowed the narrative of the frontier to continue, this time unfolding against the barbarity of communism rather than that of European power politics or a harsh North American environment.

America's Cold War focused on geographically isolating and containing the Soviet Union. The two founding actions of this policy were the Truman Doctrine of 1947 and the formation of NATO in 1949. The first established the principle that the United States would "support free peoples who are resisting attempted subjugation by armed minorities or outside pressure." Initially directed at a radical insurgency in Greece, it was quickly seen as licensing opposition to any political change that could be construed as favorable to the Soviet Union. The second committed the United States to the military defense of Western Europe and led to a long-term American military presence in Europe that reversed the long-term American opposition to active involvement in power politics. If the Truman Doctrine favored a world-wide American opposition to Soviet-leaning political movements then NATO institutionalized the division of the world agreed to by President Franklin Roosevelt at Yalta in 1945.

In two different and potentially contradictory ways, therefore, the Soviet Union became the Other against which American identity was defined for the next forty years. This not only created a simplified totalistic opposition between the two sides with one of which each other country must choose to affiliate, it reinforced in the United States a strong sense of the American difference and suggested the need to adopt a "forward position" around the world in order to preserve it. Distant events, such as regime changes and civil wars, were connected to defense of the "national interest" by the idea of a "domino effect," such that a geographical chain was envisaged connecting threatening events back to the domestic condition of the United States (Agnew 1993).

This posture led to a vastly expanded military budget. As the list of political threats expanded so did military spending. Costs spiralled upwards to maintain United States pre-eminence in nuclear weapons but also to support troops stationed in Europe and, increasingly, to prop up pro-American regimes, particularly those in South Korea, Taiwan, and, in the 1960s, in South Vietnam. The fiscal difficulties brought on by excessive military spending and declining domestic investment plus opposition to an increasingly brutal war in Vietnam led to the collapse of the American "Cold War consensus" in the late 1960s and early 1970s. Although there were subsequent attempts at reinstalling this, most notably during the Reagan presidency in the 1980s, the Cold War's singular hold on the American political consciousness had been broken and was not to recover from the disaster of Vietnam.

The end of "victory culture"?

The expansion of the American world economy began to falter and decline with the economic crisis of 1969–72 brought about by a combination of domestic economic difficulties and military spending without raising taxes. At this point, American industry had started to stagnate in comparison to the more technologically innovative production championed by East Asian countries, most notably Japan, and the revived European economies. The success of the United States labour movement in raising wages and benefits had made labour costs high and so many American companies sought to increase competitiveness by moving production to other countries where labour was not so well organized and, as a result, cheaper. The organization of the world's major oil producers into OPEC in the early 1970s demonstrated America's dependence on petroleum products and its resultant vulnerability to global oil price rises. Finally, anxiety was created by the effects on American sovereignty of exposure to and penetration by foreign, particularly Japanese, investment. This "nippophobia" was not just about economic hegemony, although that was feared for a while in the 1980s, but perhaps a fear of the Japanese buying up things that were quintessentially "American" such as movie studios, record companies, and New York's Rockefeller Center (Morley and Robins 1995: 158). Given the geographical power of the idea of Orientalism, a distant, inscrutable, and collectivist East, it was unthinkable – and intensely frightening – to have to contemplate the need to learn from the Japanese, of the Orientalizing of America/the West.

One of President Richard Nixon's responses to economic crisis was to remove the dollar from the Bretton Woods system of semi-fixed exchange rates in 1971 and to replace this system with one of floating rates. This gave policy makers the ability to alter the dollar's value against other currencies: for example, to lower the price of exports. A corollary effect of this, however, was to remove one of the major instruments of government control over the United States and world economies and so create conditions for the further financial globalization of the world economy where there was now no controlling power over the direction of globalization. As Alan Henrikson (1980: 98) noted a few years later, Americans felt a loss of status but could not agree on whether this was

> due simply to the fact that other great powers have risen to challenge their primacy and centrality, and in so doing have "displaced" them, or whether it is due to an upheaval in the basis of the international system itself, in the underlying hierarchical-locational structure of international relations.

With the further rise of the global production line – the outcome of American projection of production and markets around the world – questions of protectionism versus free trade have become more complex. Now United States jobs are dependent upon decisions made

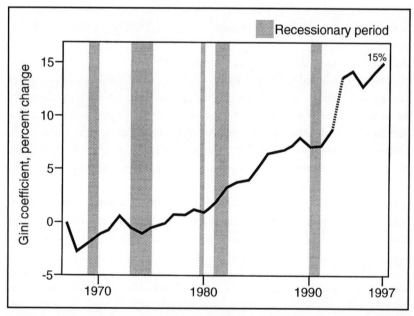

Figure 4.2 Household income inequality since the 1960s. The Gini coefficient measures the degree of concentration of households across the income distribution. The percent change shows the extent to which incomes are becoming more (if positive) or less (if negative) equally distributed across all households. Source: United States Bureau of the Census (1998).

in Europe, Japan, and Korea. Perhaps of more long-term significance to American culture is that the period since the mid-1970s has seen a widening of the income gap between rich and poor and a shrinking in the size of the middle class (Figure 4.2). To take one example, that of the "working poor," this segment of the population, employed overwhelmingly in the service and retail sectors, experienced rising incomes from 1966 to 1978 but since 1986 has experienced both a jump in numbers and a drop in incomes (*Business Week* July 10, 2000: 34). At the same time, wealth, or control over all assets, not just current income, has become even more concentrated than income as the United States bull market for stocks in the 1990s has benefited those who play the stock market and federal tax policies in the 1980s and 1990s have favored the wealthy at the expense of the poor and the middle class (*Business Week* June 19, 2000: 38). The American Dream of equal opportunity and progress for all faces significant challenge when the model can no longer function to generate increased incomes for more than a minority of the population.

Of course, the effects of the crisis beginning in the early 1970s were not only economic. This period has been named the "end of victory culture" by one commentator because of a crisis of confidence by many Americans in the seemingly inevitable – and necessary – expansion of American influence and the American way (Engelhardt 1995). American failure to win the war in Vietnam, for the global hegemon to have met its match in a seemingly insignificant third world country, has had a particularly profound effect on the national psyche. For some people, the right of America's Manifest Destiny to serve as global role model has been challenged by reports of the brutality of American soldiers towards Vietnamese soldiers and civilians alike. "We" were not supposed to behave like that. Winning somehow took place effortlessly and with a minimum of violence. Reports from Vietnam led to a re-examination of earlier wars, such as the Indian Wars of the 1800s and the United States occupation of the Philippines in 1900, suggesting a somewhat less noble application of force by United States troops to just about everyone, not just military combatants. This coincided with the growing power and effectiveness of the Civil Rights Movement in the 1960s and its forceful reminder of the ugly violence of American domestic history, from Indian massacres to lynchings of Blacks in the South in the aftermath of the Civil War. For others it is simply that the nation's might had been successfully challenged. Some interpretations have suggested that weak (and feminized) politicians were not sufficiently committed to the war (or to the American soldiers fighting it). The *Rambo* films illustrate this most clearly, with supine leaders refusing to back their men, instead looking to compromise and negotiation with the enemy (Jeffords 1989; Enloe 1993; Gibson 1994). The personal identities of many American men were particularly affected. The long-running American celebration of successful war (from Native Americans to the Nazis and Japanese) and returning warriors had come to an ignominious end in the jungles of Vietnam. Whatever the particular effect supposed, the depth of feeling is clear: the Vietnam War has been fought over and over again on American cinema and television screens, demonstrating an agonized contemplation of an American self-image that the war cast into doubt. The strange American fixation with gun ownership and the celebration of redemption, religious and political, through violence is an important indication of the continuing, if increasingly challenged, mythology of a nation nurtured on individuals taking the law into their own hands.

In addition to challenges to American moral leadership that arose from Vietnam, the post-Vietnam period also witnessed challenges to the territorial coherence of the United States structure of security. This was temporarily restored in the 1980s under President Reagan's rhetoric of America's moral battle with the "evil empire" of the Soviet Union. However, although the end of the Cold War with the political-economic collapse of the Soviet Union can be read as a victory for the American Way, it has led instead to an intensification of the end-of-victory culture. The unity and purpose of the Cold War appeared to collapse along with the Iron Curtain (e.g. Ruggie 1997). A singular American identity is now seen as under challenge from multiculturalists, feminists, and other pressure groups, or undermined by a hostile federal government. Despite America's apparent "winning" of the Cold War, the end of hostilities demonstrated the strain that the arms race (particularly under President Reagan) had put on the United States economy. Furthermore, the demise of America's Evil Twin (the Soviet Union) ended a powerful force for social cohesion within the United States. The Cold War offered a clearly inscribed battle ground on which American national citizens could triumph, as could the values seen as identifying the American national character. David Campbell (1992) has suggested that instead of being inherently threatening to American identity, the Soviet Union rendered such identity secure. The Soviet Union offered a mirroring space to that occupied by America; into this space were projected negative characteristics against which a positive image of the American character could be reflected. Rather, the problem emerged when the Cold War order broke down; now the geography which had contained both the Soviet Union and the possible contours of American citizenship ruptured, becoming fluid and uncontrollable. As a result, many commentators have noted that we are witnessing a period of renegotiation of national identity, a crisis of national purpose and an introspection: a critical turn inwards to find the root of problems whether this is presented as lying in too great a reliance upon intrusive government, a culture of victimism, the decline of the family as a result of working women, or the acceptance of homosexuality, the diluting effects of multiculturalism on "traditional" American culture, and so on. At least one prominent commentator has warned that Americans will miss the security and certainty of the Cold War world order (Mearsheimer 1990), whereas others have noted a lost romance now that the dangerous spaces that formed Cold War geopolitics have disappeared (McClure 1994).

Contemporary geographical impacts of the American world economy

The world the United States has created beyond its territorial bound-aries is no longer one in which all of America sees a positive reflection. Though the American economy has largely recovered from the worst negative trends of the 1970s and 1980s, the decline of the "victory culture" has created a crisis of confidence in the presumed identity of interests between American and world economies. There is good reason for this. Over the ten years 1989 to 1998 the best measure of economic performance, gross domestic product per capita, has aver-aged 1.6 percent, much the same as in Japan and much less than in Germany (see Figure 4.3). At the same time the main measure of what causes economic growth, change in level of productivity (efficiency of using capital, labor, and technology), has grown more slowly in the United States than in either Japan or Germany. In only one way does the United States now outperform either of these other industrial countries: job creation, with a 1998 unemployment rate below that of Japan's 4.6 percent. Over the entire decade, however, the United States did not outperform Japan (*Economist* 1999). Many of the new jobs also

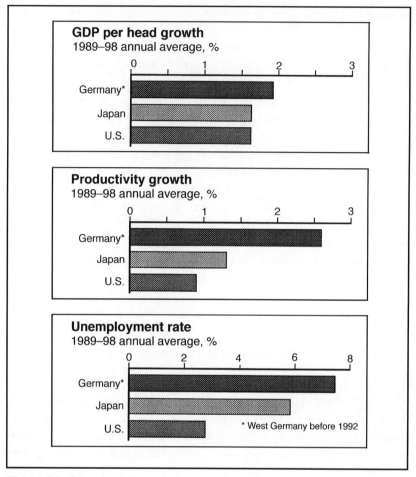

Figure 4.3 Gross domestic product per capita, change in productivity, and unemployment rate in the United States, Germany, and Japan, 1989–1998. Source: IMF (1999), *Annual Year Book.*

pay much less than the ones they have replaced. In Los Angeles, for example, state payroll records show that of the 300,000 new jobs created between 1993 and 1999 most pay less than the $25,000 average per year of the metropolitan area in 1993 and only one in 10 pays $60,000 or more per year; the number of jobs paying $15,000 or less has grown at an annual rate of 4 percent, more than twice the rate for all other income categories (Lee 1999).

Notwithstanding the hoopla over the long expansion of the United States economy from 1991 to 2000 and the explosion of the stock market, the American economic model, therefore, is no longer a global paragon (*Business Week* April 24, 2000: 32). It must now struggle alongside all of the others, producing higher growth than in the period 1970–89 but with wider income inequality than in most industrial countries. It is sometimes asserted that America has traded higher inequality for faster growth. Yet over the period 1989–98, average incomes have risen by similar amounts in Japan, Germany, and the United States, despite America's much bigger income differentials. In the United States the richest 20 percent earn nine times as much as the poorest 20 percent, compared with ratios of four times in Japan, and six times in Germany. Despite a higher average income in the United States, the poorest 20 percent in Japan are about 50 percent better off than America's poorest 20 percent (*Economist* 1999).

There is a marked regional aspect to the pattern of income stagnation and polarization in the United States (Figure 4.4). If in the period between 1945 and the early 1970s the major regions of the United States had converged in incomes, reflecting a nationwide process of growth in the middle class, the period since then has seen a trend towards the regional distinctiveness in development and incomes that had characterized earlier epochs in American history (Phillips 1991) (see this volume, Chapters 6 and 7). As a result of its economic domination by declining heavy manufacturing industries, the Midwest region has experienced the highest levels of job loss in middle-income categories, with only lower-income service sector jobs available as substitutes. At the other extreme, California and New England have benefited most from increased foreign trade and investment, particularly in high-tech industries and informational technology (see, for example, Table 4.1). The Northeast and West totally dominate with respect to new capital investment, reflecting concentrations of skilled workers, existing clusters of technological innovation, and the presence of capital locally in the hands of those who have profited from previous rounds of investment (*Business Week* February 7, 2000: 30). The new openness of the United States economy has had radically different political impacts in different regions depending on economic mix and vulnerability to foreign competition. Cultural differences between regions and localities have also never completely disappeared, even in the face of high levels of internal migration. In particular, the white South has maintained a high degree of particularity in its levels of religious enthusiasm, commitment to an aggressive Americanness (associated with an expansive

America more than with American constitutionalism), and hostility to the social changes in the status of women and minorities beginning in the 1960s.

Table 4.1 Leading and lagging states in the "new economy:" high-tech jobs, online population, and research and development investment, 1999. Source: Progressive Policy Institute News Release (1999). In the second quarter of 1999 some 80 percent of profits in the US came from high-tech companies even though they accounted for only 30 percent of revenue (Mandel 1999).

High-tech jobs Percentage of all jobs		Online population Percent of adult population with Net access		R&D investment As a percentage of total state economy	
		[Top 5]			
New Hampshire	7.8	Alaska	52	Michigan	4.9
Colorado	7.5	Colorado	47	Delaware	4.0
Massachusetts	7.5	Maryland	46	Massachusetts	3.8
California	6.2	Utah	46	New Mexico	3.6
Vermont	5.2	New Hampshire	41	Connecticut	3.3
		[Bottom 5]			
Mississippi	1.7	Kentucky	23	Louisiana	0.1
Hawaii	1.5	Louisiana	21	North Dakota	0.1
Louisiana	1.4	West Virginia	20	South Dakota	0.1
Montana	1.2	Arkansas	19	Montana	0.1
Wyoming	1.0	Mississippi	17	Hawaii	0

Data: Progressive Policy Institute

The twin phenomena of income stagnation and fading promise owe something to technological change as businesses substitute capital for labor. But this has actually declined in the United States since the early 1980s, suggesting that something else is also at work (Wolman and Colamosca 1997: 76–7). Part of the answer is that the growing service industries show much lower increases in productivity than do those in manufacturing (Rowthorn and Ramaswamy 1999). Globalizing capital and labor markets are also undoubtedly part of the answer. On the one hand, the increasing uniformity of regulations and accessibility across different national economies makes it easier for businesses to move investment from one to another. At the same time labor is now increasingly available on a global basis. In particular, skilled labor can be imported if a local economy provides an insufficient number of qualified workers. This also makes production more flexible as it also

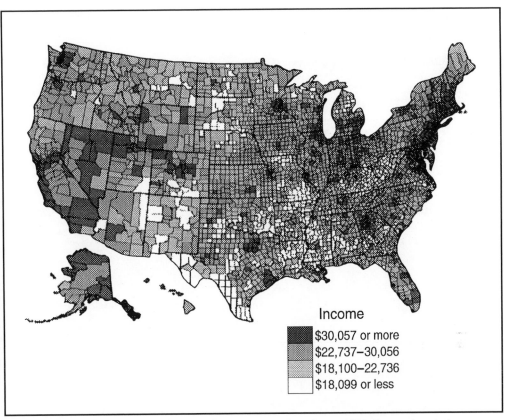

Figure 4.4 Median income by county in the United States, 1990 Census. America's median household income was $30,056 in 1990. But in top-ranked Fairfax County, VA (suburb of Washington, DC), median household income was more than six times greater than bottom-ranked Holmes County, MS. The median income is one in which half of all households in a county are above it and half are below it. The top twenty counties are all suburban areas close to the biggest cities with seventeen in the Northeast. The poorest twenty counties are all rural. Seven are in Kentucky and four are in Texas. The counties in Kentucky are overwhelmingly white, whereas those in Texas are Hispanic. In the South the poorest counties tend to have black majorities. Source: United States Bureau of the Census 1991.

makes it less dependent on relatively immobile local populations. As a result there is a potential global "levelling" of incomes. One political consequence of the increased openness of the American economy has been that the American states and various municipalities have embarked on programs to set up their own investment and trade policies without going through Washington DC, the national capital (see this volume, Chapter 5). For example, California, which has the seventh largest economy in the world, has its own health and pension policies and has tried to establish its own immigration policy.

Table 4.2 Major US capital flows, 1970–95 ($ billions, at current prices. Minus denotes outflows. G = goods, S = services, I = Investment). Source: United States Bureau of the Census (1988, 1992, 1998). The story told in this table is of a thinning of United States assets abroad relative to an increased dependence on capital and goods flowing in from outside. The low level of United States domestic saving is particularly important in generating the need for external financing of United States investment.

Year	1970	1980	1985	1990	1995
Balance on G + S + I	4	11	−101	−59	−123
Exports G + S + I	63	344	383	697	965
Imports G + S + I	−59	−334	−484	−757	−1088
Unilateral transfers	−3	−8	−23	−33	−30
US govt grants and					
pensions	−2	−7	−13	−20	−14
Private gifts	−1	−1	−10	−13	−16
US assets abroad	−8	−87	−40	−74	−280
Govt assets	−2	−13	−7	−4	−10
Direct investment	−4	−19	−14	−30	−97
Foreign securities	−1	−4	−8	−29	−94
US bank and other					
lending	−1	−51	−11	−11	−79
Foreign assets in the USA,					
net	6	58	141	122	426
Foreign official assets,					
net	—	15	−1	34	110
Foreign private assets,					
net	6	43	142	88	316
Direct investment	—	17	20	48	75
US Treasury securities	—	3	20	−3	99
Other US securities	4	5	51	35	95
US bank and other					
liabilities	2	18	51	8	47
Residual	1	27	23	44	7

Source: Bureau of the Census, US Department of Commerce
Statistical Abstract of the United States: 1988, 1992, 1998.

The sense of a more fragile and unstable economic future has given rise to a questioning of the "common sense" of the American ethos. Free trade and international economic competition are openly criticized in ways that would have been unthought of thirty years ago. Criticism draws on the sorry condition of the United States balance of payments in the 1980s and 1990s. The figures suggest an economy increasingly dependent on imports of goods and capital from elsewhere rather than a powerhouse economy dominating the rest of the world and invulnerable to foreign decision makers (Table 4.2). Yet trade and competition are vital corollaries of the extension of the frontier nation into the world at large. But the setting of wages at the lowest-cost location without attending to the collective consequences for Americans of expanding production overseas without commensurate increases in the earnings capacity for American consumption is seen as a violation of the American promise to its own population. Interestingly, criticism comes from both left and right ends of the political spectrum, as seen most dramatically in the protests against the World Trade Organization Meeting in Seattle in 1999. Both labor unions, environmental activists, and far-right militia groups take exception to the idea that the United States and its regions are just locations for investment and disinvestment rather than parts of the abstract space of economic promise bequeathed to them by the frontier nation. This attitude is manifested in the increase in isolationist positions on both economic and military issues. These question such core United States commitments as global diplomatic activism, leadership of liberal international organizations, such as the World Trade Organization, membership in the UN system, and various alliance structures, such as NATO. Though there is a range of "isolationisms," giving priority to different issues – from protecting existing jobs and environmental regulations to worrying about foreign cultural influences – all share a basic antipathy to the globalist status quo (Dumbrell 1999). Lurking within all of them is the imperative to squeeze the genie of globalization unleashed by the frontier nation back into the territorial bottle of the United States.

Yet, it would be mistaken to presume that the myth of American exceptionalism is simply fading away as a result of the excesses of globalization. Far from it. Even as doubt about the old ethos spreads, the rhetoric of techno-capitalism is now combining with that of American exceptionalism to suggest new frontiers that lie in cyberspace rather than in geographical space (see Chapter 10). At the same time, many Americans seem to accept, and even to relish, the social inequalities that the economic boom of the 1990s has entailed. Increasingly, as huge inequalities in wealth are taken as natural measures of market-based demonstration of success and worth, the federal government, journalism, academia, and Hollywood are excoriated by conservative politicians and pundits as populated by a motley "new class" systematically engaged in undermining faith in the "American way." Relationships to this "market populism," to use Thomas Frank's (2000) term, were at the center of the 2000 American presidential election with its amazing geographical polarization of the country between the largely skeptical coasts and the true believers in the American "heartland" in between. Neither the frontiers of cyberspace nor market idolatry, however, completely offsets the depredations of globalization and the image of an America on the receiving, rather than on the delivering, end of powerful forces from beyond its borders.

Conclusion

Americans, along with people around the world, now live with the consequences of the globalization that they promoted as they moved the frontier from a continental to a global scale. The world is now much more open to trade, investment, and cultural influences – especially, from an American perspective, due to the obvious global success of American culture – but also of increased economic competition and insecurity at home and abroad.

Moving from a peripheral to a central position within the world geopolitical order, the United States brought to that position its own unique ethos. American economic predominance at the end of the Second World War allowed the successful projection of the American ethos and its actual agents beyond American shores. Expansion seemed to produce economic and political benefits for Americans, particularly in the context of the Cold War. But the long-term benefits are now in greater doubt. Globalization of the world economy under American auspices has shifted control over parts of the United States economy to more distant seats of power without any sense of the "special" character of the space in which they are investing or disinvesting.

The political consequences of the turnaround are significant because the negative impacts of globalization have emerged into prominence at precisely the time when the dominant narrative about national origins and success has entered into crisis because of its projection into circumstances, above all the Vietnam War, that called it into doubt. In cinematic terms, Kevin Costner in *Dances with Wolves* replaces John Wayne in *Stagecoach*. The disintegration of the heroic story that bonded many Americans to its binary geography, to the dual claim to represent a unique "America" and yet offer that to the rest of the world in commodified form (i.e. in the form of things and images), the victory culture embodied in the myth of the frontier, leaves only America as a richly differentiated place, an ordinary country in which people struggle against powerful forces to win lives for themselves and their significant others. Less heroic, perhaps, but finally more realistic and more interesting.

References

Agnew, J. (1987), *The United States in the World Economy: A Regional Geography*, Cambridge: Cambridge University Press.

Agnew, J. (1993), "The United States and American Hegemony," in P. Taylor (ed.), *The Political Geography of the Twentieth Century*, London: Belhaven Press.

Agnew, J. (1999), "North America and the Wider World," in F. W. Boal and S. A. Royle (eds.), *North America: A Geographical Mosaic*, London: Arnold, pp. 303–16.

Anderson, B. (1983), *Imagined Communities*, London: Verso.

Business Week (7 February 2000), "Where venture capital ventures: to just a few states and industries," p. 30.

Business Week (24 April 2000), "Yes, the 90s were unusual. But not because of economic growth," p. 32.

Business Week (19 June 2000), "Surprise – the rich get richer. New data on wealth concentration," p. 38.

Business Week (10 July 2000), "A new economy, but no new deal. More full-time workers are poor," p. 34.

Calleo, D. P. (1987), *Beyond American Hegemony: The Future of the Western Alliance*, New York: Basic Books.

Campbell, D. (1992), *Writing Security: United States Foreign Policy and the Politics of Identity*, Minneapolis: University of Minnesota Press.

Cross, G. (2000), *An All-Consuming Century: Why Commercialism Won in Modern America*, New York: Columbia University Press.

Dienstag, J. F. (1996), "Serving God and Mammon: The Lockean Sympathy in Early American Political Thought," *American Political Science Review*, 90, pp. 497–511.

Dolan, F. (1994), *Allegories of America: Narratives–Metaphysics–Politics*, Ithaca, NY: Cornell University Press.

Dumbrell, J. (1999), "Varieties of Post-Cold War American Isolationism," *Government and Opposition*, 34, pp. 24–43.

Economist (1999), "Desperately Seeking a Perfect Model," April 10, p. 10.

Engelhardt, T. (1995), *The End of Victory Culture: Cold War America and the Disillusioning of a Generation*, New York: Basic Books.

Enloe, C. (1993), *The Morning After: Sexual Politics at the End of the Cold War*, Berkeley: University of California Press.

Forstall, R. (1994), *Population of States and Counties of the United States, 1790–1990*, Washington, DC: United States Bureau of the Census.

Frank, T. (2000), *One Market under God: Extreme Capitalism, Market Populism, and the End of Economic Democracy*, New York: Doubleday.

Gibson, J. W. (1994), *Warrior Dreams: Violence and Manhood in Post-Vietnam America*, New York: Hill and Wang.

Hartz, L. (1955), *The Liberal Tradition in America: An Interpretation of American Political Thought since the Revolution*, New York: Harcourt Brace World.

Henrikson, A. (1980), "America's Changing Place in the World: From 'Periphery' to 'Centre'?" in J. Gottmann (ed.), *Centre and Periphery: Spatial Variation in Politics*, London: Sage, pp. 73–100.

Jeffords, S. (1989), *The Remasculinization of America: Gender and the Vietnam War*, Bloomington: Indiana University Press.

Lee, D. (1999), "L.A. County Jobs Surge since '93, but Not Wages," *Los Angeles Times*, July 26, A1, A19.

Lynch, J. M. (1999), *Negotiating the Constitution: The Earliest Debates over Original Intent*, Ithaca, NY: Cornell University Press.

McClure, J. (1994), *Late Imperial Romance*, London: Verso.

Mandel, M. J. (1999), "The spoils of the new economy belong to high tech," *Business Week*, August 16, p. 37.

Mearsheimer, J. (1990), "Why We Will Soon Miss the Cold War," *The Atlantic*, 266(2), pp. 35–50.

Meinig, D. W. (1986), *The Shaping of America. Volume I: Atlantic America, 1492–1800*, New Haven: Yale University Press.

Morley, D., and K. Robins (1995), *Spaces of Identity: Global Media, Electronic Landscapes and Cultural Boundaries*, London: Routledge.

Phillips, K. (1991), *The Politics of Rich and Poor: Wealth and the American Electorate in the Reagan Aftermath*, New York: Harper and Row.

Richardson, J. (1905), *A Compilation of Messages and Papers of the Presidents, 1789–1902*, 12 vols., Washington, DC: Bureau of National Literature and Art.

Rosenberg, E. (1982), *Spreading the American Dream: American Economic and Cultural Expansion, 1890–1945*, New York: Hill and Wang.

Rowthorn, R., and R. Ramaswamy (1999), "Growth, Trade and Deindustrialization," *IMF Staff Working Papers*, 46, pp. 18–41.

Ruggie, J. R. (1997), "The Past as Prologue? Interests, Identity, and American Foreign Policy," *International Security*, 21, pp. 89–125.

Shapiro, M. J. (1997), *Violent Cartographies: Mapping Cultures of War*, Minneapolis: University of Minnesota Press.

Slotkin, R. (1973), *Regeneration through Violence: The Mythology of the American Frontier, 1600–1860*, Middletown, CT: Wesleyan University Press.

Slotkin, R. (1986), *The Fatal Environment: The Myth of the Frontier in the Age of Industrialization, 1800–1890*, Middletown, CT: Wesleyan University Press.

Slotkin, R. (1992), *Gunfighter Nation: The Myth of the Frontier in Twentieth-Century America*, New York: Atheneum.

Twitchell, J. B. (1999), *Lead Us into Temptation: The Triumph of American Materialism*, New York,: Columbia University Press.

Turner, F. J. (1896), "The Problem of the West," *The Atlantic Monthly*, 78, pp. 289–97.

Turner, F. J. (1920), *The Frontier in American History*, New York: Henry Holt).

United States Bureau of the Census (1988), *Statistical Abstract of the United States*, Washington, DC: United States Department of Commerce.

United States Bureau of the Census (1991), *1990 Census*, Washington, DC: United States Department of Commerce.

United States Bureau of the Census (1992), *Statistical Abstract of the United States*, Washington, DC: United States Department of Commerce.

United States Bureau of the Census (1996), *Statistical Abstract of the United States*, Washington, DC: United States Department of Commerce.

United States Bureau of the Census (1998), *Statistical Abstract of the United States*, Washington, DC: United States Department of Commerce.

Williams, W. A. (1969), *The Roots of Modern American Empire: A Study of the Growth and Shaping of Consciousness in a Marketplace Society*, New York: Random House.

Wills, G. (1997), *John Wayne's America*, New York: Simon & Schuster.

Wolman, W., and A. Colamosca (1997), *The Judas Economy: The Triumph of Capital and the Betrayal of Work*, Reading, MA: Addison-Wesley.

CHAPTER 5

Local territories of government: From ideals to politics of place and scale

Andrew E. G. Jonas

One of the most influential views about the nature of American politics has been that of Alexis de Tocqueville, the French aristocrat and liberal sympathizer who traveled widely in the United States in the early 1830s. Tocqueville's comments on the importance of local communities for American democracy and the power of the states relative to the federal government have become widely accepted in the United States as statements of "fact" about the essential political equality upon which the American "experiment" has been based, notwithstanding obvious problems with Tocqueville's account from a twenty-first-century perspective with the absence of women and African-Americans from the "calculus of consent." In particular, Tocqueville's claim that the importance of local territorial government set America apart from other countries has become widely accepted as a characterization of American democracy. For many years, of course, particularly from the 1930s to the 1960s as the federal government addressed perceived national social and economic problems at an increasing rate with increased impacts across the country, the role of local governments appeared in decline. In this chapter, the political geographer Andrew E. G. Jonas argues that local governments always kept important functions and powers that have been enhanced more recently both as a result of globalization eroding the regulatory role of the federal government and the increased attention given by interest groups to acting at the local and state levels. There is both an enhanced politics of place (associated with defending and pursuing locally-based interests) and a shift in the politics of scale (associated with the perceived greater efficacy of pursuing interests at the local rather than at the national level or creating new territorial units within which such interests can be pursued). After surveying the high degree of political fragmentation in the United States, the author explores some of the ideals that have influenced struggles around American local government, and then examines three case studies – public education in central Ohio, economic development in

Massachusetts, and conservation planning and property rights in southern California – to show the changing balance of both the politics of place and that of scale towards the local level. American management of the pressures of globalization – however imperfectly, inefficiently, and inequitably – takes place within the context of the ideals and practices of local territorial government which were broadly identified by Tocqueville.

. . . the Constitution of the United States . . . consists of two distinct social structures, connected, and, as it were encased one within the other; two governments, completely separate and almost independent, the one fulfilling the ordinary duties and responding to the daily and indefinite calls of a community, the other circumscribed within certain limits and only exercising an exceptional authority over the general interests of the country . . . The Federal government, as I have just observed, is the exception; the government of the states is the rule.

Alexis de Tocqueville

Placing American government: Tocqueville's "Rule"

Inspired by a "great democratic revolution" sweeping through Europe in the nineteenth century, the French aristocrat and liberal idealist, Alexis de Tocqueville, visited the youthful America in the 1830s in order to observe firsthand a system of government which, in his view, had given rise to "a condition of equality" that did not exist in class-divided Europe. In the event, he found and described two separate and distinctive systems of government in America, each fulfilling quite different functions. At one level, there was the federal government, charged with the responsibility of guaranteeing "liberty, justice, and freedom for all." Below this, and performing a different set of functions to do with "the daily calls of the community," was the system of local government comprising the states, the counties, and the townships. The discovery of this "dual social structure" led Tocqueville to the conclusion that to understand American democracy one first had to understand how the country's unique geographical and historical conditions had given rise to a political system founded on the principle of the sovereignty of the people. Accordingly, Tocqueville's influential treatise, *Democracy in America*, does not begin with an analysis of the federal government but rather with detailed discussions of the physical geography of America, its settlement history, and most of all the "small sovereign nations, whose agglomeration constitutes the body of the Union" (Tocqueville 1945/1963: 59). For Tocqueville, then, the basis of American political exceptionalism was the "rule" of local territorial government.

To this day, alongside such distinctive "American" values as the right to vote, freedom of expression, and respect for private property, the Tocquevillian principle of local democracy is deeply felt. This principle is thoroughly embedded in the country's territorial fabric. Materially, it takes the form of the fifty states and the thousands of counties, municipalities, and townships that are responsible for governing places as large as New York City and as small as Eastman, Georgia. Ideologically, it finds expression in arguments for local autonomy and home rule. Yet just as the definition of who is an "American" and what "rights" obtain to this status have been sources of struggle throughout the history of this country, so too has the local territorial form of American government. The aims of this chapter are to provide a geographical interpretation of struggles around local territories in the United States, and to examine whether contemporary processes of economic globalization and political devolution are placing new pressures on local government, which threaten to undermine the Tocquevillian "rule" about democracy in America.

Until relatively recently, political-geographic interpretations of territorial government in America were influenced by functionalist theories of the state. Such theories analyzed government policies and territorial outcomes in terms of their roles in facilitating economic growth, legitimating state intervention, or controlling social unrest (O'Connor 1973; Gutman 1988). Richard Hartshorne, for example, was able to show how the state, responding to the functional imperative, organized its territory in such a way as to facilitate economic development, minimize spatial disparity, and incorporate regional diversity (Hartshorne 1950). As far as the functions of local government are concerned, scholars have looked at the allocation of different functions between national and local government, seeing the allocation process as the outcome of class and political struggles (Clark and Dear 1984). A further set of studies (e.g. Dahl 1961) has examined community power structures in their own right but in these studies local politics are often separated from their functional-territorial context.

In recent years, scholarly treatments of the functional role and territoriality of national and local government in America have been all but eclipsed by studies of globalization and the alleged "demise" of the nation-state (Peck and Tickell 1994; Swyngedouw 1997). Many analysts believe that global communications and international trade and investment flows are breaking down national barriers, creating a "borderless world" in which the influence of the nation-state has been progressively undermined as the locus of political power has been displaced upwards (internationally), downwards (locally), and sideways (into civil society) (Jessop 1994; Ohmae 1995).

Political geographers have started to look above the national level to examine the ways in which geopolitical roles and relations are being reconstructed in the post-Cold War era. But globalization also appears to be enhancing the economic and political importance of "the local" (Cox 1997; Preteceille 1990). In the United States, this can be demonstrated in a variety of ways. In economic terms, global networks of production and consumption have been reorganized around highly innovative and competitive regional economies such as Silicon Valley, California. In the social and political realms, anti-capitalist protests, the property rights movement, and campaigns for social justice and the minimum wage offer evidence of the many ways in which civil society is reasserting itself. Together, these trends demonstrate the rising "power of the local" in the spheres of the economy, state, and civil society in America.

All of this assumes, of course, that somewhere along the way economic and political power in America had become too centralized at the federal level. There is certainly anecdotal evidence to suggest that many Americans have become distrustful of their national political leaders and no longer vote in federal elections. Presidential campaigns have degenerated into "beauty contests" featuring candidates whose political and ideological differences have become blurred. Confronting this "crisis" of national government, analysts on the political Right and Left point to recent devolutionary tendencies and the emergence of new forms of local political participation as evidence of the possibility for the revival of local democracy in America (Ferejohn and Weingast 1997; Staeheli, Kodras, and Flint 1997). Arguably, local territorial government has always been important in the United States political system. It has provided a focus for intense material and ideological conflicts over the years. Local political institutions have often struggled to incorporate the diversity of local interests, political ideals, and social values in America. Although globalization has given new momentum for these struggles, the territorial fabric of local democracy is firmly established. As the late Tip O'Neill (a Democrat and Speaker of the House of Representatives) allegedly once said, "all politics is local" (a reference to "pork barrel" politics in which representatives will vote on specific bills so long as federal spending occurs in their district). The question, therefore, is: how have local territories of American government adapted to the changing scope and scale of social, economic, and environmental interests and political pressures?

Bearing in mind the Tocquevillian "rule" about democracy in America, this chapter aims to provide a geographical interpretation of struggles around local territories of government. It is organized as follows. First, the chapter discusses the territorial organization of the American system of government, emphasizing the important role of local (sub-national) territories – the states, counties, municipalities, and so forth – in the system. As the number of local territories of government has proliferated, along with their functions and responsibilities, discussions of American government have inevitably focused on the matter of political fragmentation. In this chapter, political fragmentation refers not simply to the proliferation of local political units but also to the variety of powers, functions, and policies associated with these units. The chapter examines some of the political ideals that have influenced struggles around American local government, giving rise to more or less fragmented territorial forms.

We then turn to real-world examples of conflicts around local territories in the United States. In explaining the political processes at work in these examples, the chapter makes a distinction between the politics of place and the politics of scale. The politics of place refers to the mobilization of local groups around a collective interest, or set of interests, in a local territory. The politics of scale refers to the ways that in each of these cases local interest groups have engaged with different territories (levels of government) in order to articulate different views about the ideal territorial form of local government. The politics of place and scale are exemplified through discussions of recent struggles around public education in central Ohio, economic development in Massachusetts, and conservation planning and property rights in southern California. In the conclusion, we reflect upon the malleability of local territories of government in America in the face of local interest-group pressures. Some sort of territorial reorganization at the local level has often been seen as necessary in order that the political system may adapt to the changing scope and scale of social, economic, and environmental interests. In this respect, the Tocquevillian "rule" about American government continues to resonate despite the many new challenges facing local territories.

Local territorial government and American political exceptionalism

For Tocqueville, American government represented the culmination of a "great democratic revolution," yet he cautiously noted that

> no man [sic] can entirely shake off the influence of the past; and the settlers, intentionally or not, mingled habits and notions derived from their education and the traditions of their country with those habits and notions that were exclusively their own. (Tocqueville 1945/1963: 44)

In Tocqueville's geographical imagination, then, America represented a pluralistic democracy, comprised of independently governed communities, where citizens ("men") could participate in a new type of democracy, and where local political institutions were shaped by specifically local affairs and needs. From a twenty-first-century perspective, Tocqueville's treatise on American government is deeply problematic, not the least of which being its exclusion of women and African-Americans from the "great revolution" (for contemporary perspectives, see Staeheli 1994, and Gilbert 1999). Yet to this day it is often taken as a statement of "fact" about local democracy in America.

An important issue for the original founders of American government was how much power should be centralized since some centralization was seen as necessary to resist European domination, amongst other concerns. Centralization, however, had to be buttressed by the reality that the United States was for the most part an agrarian society constructed around relatively small trading communities, albeit increasingly inter-connected. The protection of private property, regulation of local commerce, and proper representation of local civic interests were central concerns for the framers of the Constitution. A system of government was to be designed that would be strong enough to resist external control and promote American national and international

economic interests, and yet at the same time flexible enough to encourage local enterprise, allow freedom of political expression, and secure
basic rights.

The United States Constitution served as a charter entered into by
the people of the United States with their government. United States
federalism was built upon the principle of the division of sovereignty
between the federal government, the states, and the people of the
states. The federal government acted as guarantor of individual rights
and civil liberties subject to constitutional checks and balances. State
ratification of the Constitution was required, leading to complicated
agreements between the states and the federal government about the
regulation of inter-state commerce and the assumption of public debt.
The states, in turn, were allocated key functions such as the police
power (which governs local land use planning) as well as procedures
for determining the formation of new local units of government. This
structure allowed each level of government to preside over the citizens
of its jurisdiction according to clearly defined "spheres of action"
(Skidmore and Wanke 1981: 21–2). Subsequent amendments to the
Constitution and the Bill of Rights attest to the extent to which this
system was to be treated as an ongoing "experiment." Crucially, maintaining the scope for the creation of new local territories (municipalities,
special districts, and other units of local government) has been crucial
to the success of this "experiment."

In the early years of the Republic, the United States operated as a
loose confederation of states rather than a unified federal system. The
Civil War proved the greatest test of national-territorial unity under
this system, with Southern states attempting to secede from the union.
After the Civil War, Washington, DC, effectively re-asserted control
and thus began a process of political centralization, which accelerated
in the twentieth century. Although to this day the states are key
players in the geographical matrix of power in the United States – the
first level of recourse for any test of the sovereignty of the people – this
reality has often been overlooked because of the dominance of political
centralization tendencies in recent American history.

The American states have retained at least six important functions,
both in relation to the federal government and their own territories.
First, the states have claims on sovereignty or "states' rights." However,
given that such claims have often served to mask deep social and racial
divisions across America, the federal Supreme Court has on frequent

occasions found it necessary to intervene in state and local affairs in its capacity as the ultimate guarantor of civil liberties. Second, state legislators can pass their own laws in order to regulate trade and economic activity, or effect fiscal redistribution, across their territories. Since state laws can either replicate or circumvent federal statutes, local public officials, citizens, business organizations, and community groups often lobby their state representatives before resorting to the Congressional "pork barrel." Third, states deliver and administer welfare programs, grants-in-aid, and many other services across their territories. Fourth, the states continue to serve as "laboratories of democracy," where experiments in new policies and regulatory reforms take place, thereby deflecting any blame for policy failures away from federal politicians, or claiming success for "model" local programs. Fifth, since the United States has no separate regional level of government, the states (or their boundaries) often serve as indicators of regional variation and cultural identity within America. Finally, and crucially, the creation of new territories of local government is contingent on state enabling legislation. Therefore, constitutionally local territorial government is subject in the first instance to state rather than federal oversight.

Political scientists and commentators are frequently divided on whether the level of political fragmentation (i.e. the extent and scope of local territorial government) is an asset or an obstacle to politics and government in America. In one widely used textbook on American government, Nigel Burrows suggests that "[d]iffusion and fragmentation, rather than concentration and coherence, characterise American government, and extraordinary vigour its society" (Burrows 1998: 16). Burrows implies that American government has somehow become detached from civil society; politics no longer reflects the will or desires of the people. The problem, it appears, is that political institutions have been colonized by special interest groups, such as corporations, industrial sectors and unions, and other interests, which possess the requisite resources, influence, and knowledge to manipulate public policy. The people and local communities, by contrast, have little opportunity to influence public policy and feel alienated from the political process and, in particular, the federal government.

While such criticisms apply with some justification to national government, the situation is more complicated at the state and local levels, although even there many people feel alienated from their political institutions. At the local level, the question of the extent and scope of political fragmentation sits uneasily with the issue of local autonomy. In practical terms, an absolute definition of local autonomy is not possible. This is true even in a federal system that allows for a high degree of decentralization of fiscal and administrative capacities such as exists in America (Brown 1994). Nevertheless, as an ideal local autonomy frequently informs local political practice and discourse in America, especially in sensitive areas like education (Reynolds and Shelley 1990). Perhaps more importantly, local interest groups have mobilized around their state and local governments precisely in order to counteract the centralization of political power in the hands of corporations, industry groups, unions, and federal bureaucracies. In this respect, political fragmentation has served to activate rather than obstruct local groups in civil society; geography – in the sense of local territorial government – has made a difference.

But there have been many times when the territorial malleability of American government has been severely tested. The bombing of the federal building in Oklahoma City in 1995 was one such occasion. The possibility that the perpetrators of the atrocity might have been from outside the United States evoked powerful senses of national unity and loss, calling for a strong federal response. The reality, however, pointed to the depth of anti-federal government feelings within the United States (Sparke 1998). Anti-federalism is a long-standing feature of domestic political struggle in America. But it is not always anti-nationalist by nature. Consider in this light the Sage Brush Rebellion, which was a move to assert commercial and states' rights over the use and control of public lands in Western states. Consider also the Southern states' backlash against the civil rights movement, which highlighted racial divisions across America. Whatever the issue, the system of local territorial government has frequently been at the centre of political struggle in America, a struggle often waged against "government" without necessarily posing a threat to the American territorial ideal.

Contemporary political struggles in America have revolved around such questions as: How much power should be returned to the states and the people of the states by the federal government? What responsibilities should states and localities have for economic development and social redistribution across and within their territories? Which level of government should be involved in policies to protect the environment? Let us first consider how the pressures of economic globalization and political devolution have impinged on these questions in recent years before we address the political fragmentation of local government in more detail.

Economic globalization, political devolution, and new pressures on local territorial government in America

During the twentieth century, political and economic power in America became far more centralized than ever before. But the latter part of that century saw concerted moves towards the reversal of that trend. Post-1930s federal intervention in local territorial government was the product of struggles and crises during the Great Depression, the scope and scale of which were well beyond the political, fiscal, and institutional capacities of states and municipal governments at that time. The Depression economic crisis called for a national political response, which took the form of the New Deal, a series of emergency measures as well as longer-term policies marking a new era of federal intervention in domestic economic and social affairs. From the 1940s to the late 1970s, national economic and social stability was constructed not simply around a "class accord" struck between large corporations and the industrial unions but also a new understanding about the relationship between the federal government and the cities (Salins 1993). The federal government became a major force of economic and urban development, using its borrowing capacity, regulatory authority, and urban policies to manage economic recovery and achieve social stability. Suburban development, the urbanization of the West and South, and the expansion of metropolitan areas throughout America were important territorial outcomes of this extended period of federal intervention (Florida and Jonas 1991).

The post-war class accord and the new relationship between the federal government and the cities began to unravel after the 1973 oil crisis, which symbolized the crisis of American Fordist production. This was a time when industry appeared to become very mobile as United States corporations relocated manufacturing activities on a global scale. In response to these economic trends, the 1980s saw a series of changes in national government policy, including cuts in federal urban policy programs, welfare reform, and other strategies to make the labor market more flexible to the changing needs of industry. Most crucially, the period marked the rise of the New Federalism, a political project that combined systematic reductions in federal spending on core social (or "urban") programs with the transfer of responsibility for these programs from Washington DC to the states. In the new "post-federal" era, states and localities have become key sites for domestic policy experimentation as politicians struggle to find "solutions" to the fiscal crisis of the state and the crisis of mass production. In certain areas of public policy, the solution might be seen in the devolution of government, albeit it could be argued that power has not so much devolved as been restored to its rightful location, namely, local territorial government; the Tocquevillian "rule" has simply been reasserted.

The neo-conservative view on devolution is founded upon the belief that the rightful place for government is the states and the localities. In this view, the federal government has become bureaucratic, wasteful, and untrustworthy; its role should be limited as far as possible to promoting national and global markets, protecting American interests abroad, and guaranteeing the rights of individuals at home. As far as social redistribution goes, the states are better placed than the federal government to respond to local voters and consumers; they should be given the opportunity to fulfil their idealized role as "laboratories of democracy." Echoing this view, Thomas H. Naylor (an economist) and William H. Willimon (a theologian) suggest that modern American institutions (principally United States government) have become too big, too intrusive, and too distant from people. Urging for "a post-modern political imagination which is specific, local, contextual and particular," their radical solution is to downsize government through a peaceful process of succession and community empowerment (Naylor and Willimon 1997: 246). Naylor and Willimon aver that devolution and local succession are political ideals for which American citizens should actively strive.

While neo-conservatives argue that political power should be returned to the states, neo-liberals are perhaps even more sanguine about the responsibilities of local territorial government. Given economic globalization, neo-liberals feel that states and localities should be more entrepreneurial, not simply administering social programs but also competing for high value-added economic activity. Emphasis is therefore given to forging "partnerships" between local government, business, community groups, and citizens around a range of issues including economic development, social policy, and environmental protection. This ideal sees the role of government as that of enabler, while giving greater political responsibility to local groups in civil society.

Some critics of devolution have doubts about the capacity of the states and localities to take on new responsibilities and sustain new partnerships. For example, John D. Donahue argues that the coupling of local entrepreneurialism with the devolution of responsibility for welfare and higher education would simply encourage a "race to the bottom" between the states with severe territorial-distributional consequences. In order to compete for mobile capital and labor, states would have had to cut the taxes needed to fund their new responsibilities (Donahue 1997). Donahue's conclusions are supported to some extent by a study of inter-state fiscal disparities conducted by Robert Tannenwald (Tannenwald 1999). Tannenwald developed an index of state "fiscal comfort" by dividing a state's tax capacity (revenue base)

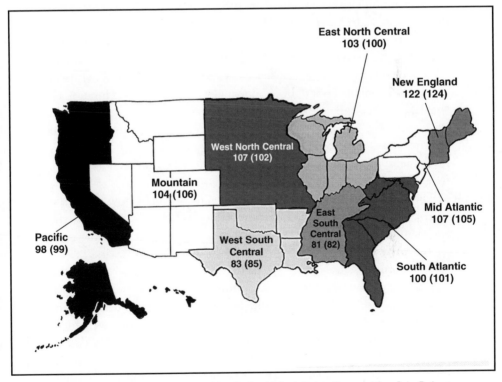

Figure 5.1 Regional fiscal disparities in the United States. Source: Map 3 in Robert Tannenwald (1999), "Fiscal Disparity among the States Revisited," *New England Economic Review*, July/August, 19, Copyright © 1999 Federal Reserve Bank of Boston. Used by permission of Federal Reserve Bank of Boston.

by its fiscal need (claims on expenditures). The "fiscal comfort" index was compared for Fiscal Years 1996 and (1994) (see Figure 5.1). Comfort levels decreased between 1994 and 1996 across most of the regions except West North Central, East North Central and Mid Atlantic. Moreover, there were significant disparities in fiscal comfort between regions, with the East South Central states showing the least comfort and the New England States the most. Tannenwald (1999: 19) suggested that the degree of fiscal disparity "pertains to the devolution debate, since devolution's detractors doubt the ability of fiscally stressed states to compete with their fiscally comfortable counterparts".

The fiscal pressures on states and localities in the United States were vividly illustrated by the predicament of Orange County, California, which was forced to declare bankruptcy in 1994 (Platte, Lait, and Petruno 1994). The Orange County crisis was significant because it affected a municipality in a wealthy suburban area with a conservative (Republican) administration. Mark Baldassare studied the Orange County fiscal crisis and concluded that three factors contributed to the crisis: (1) the extreme political fragmentation of local government in the county; (2) voter distrust of local (county) officials; and (3) fiscal austerity brought about by California's property tax limitations (Baldassare 1998). Baldassare proposed that the most practical solution to such a crisis would be greater regional cooperation among the local governments, and state control of local government spending and investment. Note, however, that this makes little or no mention of the federal government role.

The Orange County bankruptcy serves to highlight how much the recent devolution trend has already influenced the debate about the fragmentation of government in America. In addition, it illustrates the growing economic importance of local government in the face of globalization pressures. Local governments in America, such as Orange County, have invested considerable sums of public money in the stock market (e.g. employee pension funds, etc.). For their part, corporations and other investors have sunk billions of dollars into local government bonds. As a result, America and Americans have become very dependent upon the economic performance of local territories. With the system of local territorial government having to confront increasingly complex pressures and responsibilities, what scope is there for this system to incorporate the conflicts of local political ideals and material interests that inevitably result?

Political fragmentation and local territories of government in America

Few would disagree with Gregory Weiher's claim that the United States has one of the most fragmented political systems in the world (Weiher 1991: 1). Of course, the truth of this claim depends upon what is meant by "political fragmentation." Whilst it is possible to say that the number of local units of government has proliferated, particularly since Tocqueville's time, these units have a variety of powers and responsibilities, and often pursue very different policies (Baldassare 1998). Although local territories throughout the United States are under increasing economic pressures, the range of political responses can still vary from place to place, local government to local government. A geographical perspective is therefore essential for understanding the economic, social, and environmental effects of political fragmentation.

Local government fragmentation

Nancy Burns claims that at least fifty thousand new local government units have been formed across the United States since independence (Burns 1994). Hers seems to be a conservative estimate. A more likely total would be of the order of one hundred thousand local political units in America. Of these, the proliferation of special purpose districts has been an important feature of local political fragmentation in the United States. Unlike municipal governments, which perform a variety of functions, special districts provide a single function such as supplying water, treating sewerage, controlling pollution, or the like. A special district is normally not directly accountable to the public, being governed by appointed commissioners. Orange County, California, provides a good example of a local territory where there is a high level of political fragmentation (see Box and Figure 5.2).

> MANY LOCAL GOVERNMENTS
>
> County government is just one element of the fragmented political structure of local government in Orange County. There are also many cities, school districts, single-purpose regional agencies, and local special districts involved in local governance. Orange County has thirty-one municipal governments, each with its own mayor, city council members, and city budgets to provide local

public services (see Figure 5.2). This is a highly diverse group of
cities in terms of size and population composition. No city comes
close to representing a central city for this suburban region. The
largest places are Santa Ana and Anaheim, each with fewer than
300,000 residents. In 1990 seven cities had populations of over
100,000, ten cities had populations of more than 50,000 and less
than 100,000, nine cities had populations of fewer than 50,000 and
more than 25,000, and five cities had fewer than 25,000 residents.
Only about 6 percent of the population lived in the unincorpo-
rated areas served by the county government.

Figure 5.2 Local governments in Orange County. Source: Figure 2.2 in Mark
Baldassare (1998), *When Government Fails: The Orange County Bankruptcy*, Berkeley
and Los Angeles: University of California Press, p. 52. Copyright © 1998 The
Regents of the University of California. Used by permission of University of
California Press.

In addition to the thirty-one Orange County cities and county government, other key elements define the local government structure. The Orange County Transportation Authority is a massive single-function agency with its own budget, sales tax, and appointed board of directors. There are twenty-seven local school districts, which each have their own elected governing boards, bond financing, and budgets. There are 126 special districts that deliver water, sanitation, and other public services in certain areas, with their own budgets, financing, and elected officials. A full portrait of the politically fragmented government within this suburban region would thus include at least 186 local government entities.

Reproduced from Mark Baldassare (1998), *When Government Fails: The Orange County Bankruptcy*, Berkeley and Los Angeles: University of California Press, pp. 51–2. Copyright © 1998 The Regents of the University of California. Reproduced by permission of University of California Press. Figure 2.2 Local Governments in Orange County, p. 52.

The level of political fragmentation at the local level in the United States is related to urbanization and, in particular, suburbanization. Middle-class residents have traditionally voted for the incorporation of politically independent suburbs so as to avoid living under the jurisdiction of city government. Suburban residents tend to be anxious about crime, congestion, and high taxes, problems often associated with the failings of urban government. For the middle classes, the suburbs represent the American ideal, and are seen to reflect democratic principles such as local autonomy and home rule. Yet, perhaps ironically, another important development associated with suburbia is the creeping privatization of public space. Special districts and other examples of "shadow government" have become characteristic features in the political landscape of suburban America (Garreau 1991). Indeed, some of these "edge cities" are not even legally incorporated places.

Political fragmentation and public policy

Local government in America has a variety of powers and these powers are deployed for many different purposes. Land use planning is perhaps the most important local power specific to municipal and county government. Local jurisdictions use this power to influence the pattern and mix of land uses, including housing and industry, and hence also household characteristics, the nature of the local economy, and the tax base. Land use zoning can have important territorial-distributional effects. For instance, local governments in the suburbs are notorious for enforcing exclusionary zoning and restrictive ordinances (Teaford 1997). These land use policies serve to prevent "undesirable" local land use changes from occurring, such as the construction of noxious facilities or low-income housing. The exercise of local land use powers, therefore, tends to create inter-jurisdictional disparities in household characteristics, levels of economic activity, and fiscal capacity. In metropolitan areas, such disparities increase with the level of local political fragmentation (Weiher 1991).

Local political fragmentation is associated with another important distributional effect. Local governments are actively engaged in promoting economic development in their jurisdictions, using a variety of policy tools in addition to land use planning. Although this activity is sometimes seen as evidence of the local impact of economic globalization, there is in fact a well-documented history of place competition or local boosterism in the United States. For example, Sinclair Lewis evocatively portrayed early twentieth-century urban boosterism in the novel *Babbitt* (Lewis 1922). The reasons why place competition has arguably become more intense in recent years are twofold.

First, counties and municipalities are very dependent on local revenues, especially local property taxes but increasingly sales taxes, developer fees, hotel and motel taxes, and so forth. Local revenues are needed not only to fund public employee wages and basic services – libraries, schools, health facilities, parks, etc. – but also to pay the principal and interest on municipal bonds. These bonds are issued for infrastructure projects and capital spending. It is important for the issuing local public authority to maintain a good credit rating since bond investors use these ratings as indicators of the fiscal health and investment risk of the authority in question. Without a healthy local economy the local tax base is vulnerable, investors become nervous, and the local government could potentially face a fiscal crisis. The fiscal local dependence of local territories in the United States may have further intensified as a result of popular resistance to new taxes and other such political struggles (Cox and Mair 1988).

The second reason why local governments are interested in promoting themselves to potential investors has to do with the increasing geo-graphical mobility of capital. As has already been suggested, during the 1970s the American economy began to transform from mass pro-duction to more flexible forms of manufacturing and new forms of service provision. This "new economy" is far less dependent than mass production was on traditional "location factors" such as proximity to rail and river transportation, raw materials, water supplies, urban labor markets, and the like (Blair and Premus 1987). This is not to say that geography or "location" has become unimportant in the post-mass production economy; industries and investors still need to locate and invest somewhere. Evidently for some producers location outside the United States has become more desirable because of the availability of cheap labor and new markets (Bluestone and Harrison 1982). But for others, there is still a need for access to domestic skilled labor and regional markets. Rather the issue is the increasing locational flexibility of firms and the responsiveness of local territories in the US to this (Storper and Walker 1989).

The threat of capital mobility can be used in various ways to influ-ence the policies of local government. Mobile businesses may threaten to leave a particular jurisdiction unless the local authority undertakes to improve the local "business climate" by lowering taxes and utility charges, or changing local land use designations. Even immobile busi-nesses can be influential; they often use the threat of an investment boycott to put political pressure on local politicians to encourage inward investment or restrict union activity (Herod 1991). In this manner, almost every state, county, and city in the United States has at some point in its history operated like a "growth machine" seeking to attract jobs, increase its population, and enhance the local tax base (Molotch 1976; Logan and Molotch 1987).

Local governance

The proliferation of special purpose districts is a measure of the extent to which local public authority and power in America has not only become fragmented but also displaced away from local government. But political fragmentation also can refer to the policies of local gov-ernment itself, and how these vary from place to place. Given that public policies are often formulated beyond the electoral realm, and given that local government attracts a wide range of interest groups other than the main political parties, the term governance rather than government is often used to describe the relationship between civil society and public policy at the local level. The combination of actors and institutions shaping governance in any given locality is sometimes referred to as the local political regime (Elkin 1987; Stone 1993).

The character of the local political regime can vary from place to place, albeit certain regimes can achieve a degree of stability over time. For example, many local governments, already pro-growth in orientation, have found the transition to local entrepreneurialism relatively straightforward. Nevertheless, and depending on local politics, some local governments have supported growth management, social redistribution, or even a sustainable environment over and above economic development. In other localities – especially places where globalization has been seen as a threat – unions, workers, and community groups have put pressure on local government to protect local industries and the communities and businesses that depend upon these from external competition and control (Jonas 1995).

Despite these important spatial variations in local government policy, the overall tendency has been for state and local governments in America to become more entrepreneurial. And quite apart from the pressures of economic globalization, political devolution has been an important factor in this trend. Local policy makers have had to rely increasingly on their own local resources rather than those provided by federal authorities. In an attempt to measure the local impact of this trend, Susan Clarke and Gary Gaile conducted a comprehensive study of economic development strategies used by more than 170 cities across the United States since the 1970s (Clarke and Gaile 1998). They observed a shift from locational strategies, such as the use of tax breaks and zoning to attract manufacturing activities, to post-federal entrepreneurial policies, focusing upon high value-added activities. Post-federal entrepreneurial policies include the use of business incubators, greater metropolitan and regional cooperation, tax-increment financing, and other such local economic policy tools (Table 5.1). Although the variety and sophistication of policy instruments used by state and local governments have clearly expanded, most involve financial risk-taking on the part of local government officials. The Orange County fiscal crisis demonstrated just how far local officials are prepared to gamble with public revenues these days.

Table 5.1 Post-federal entrepreneurial local economic development strategies (ranked according to level of use)

Business incubators
More metro and regional cooperation
Tax increment financing
Special assessment districts
Foreign trade zones
Strategic planning
Land banks
Export and promotion
Equity participation
Taxable bonds
Streamlining
Tax abatements – targeted at new business
Equity pools: private-public consortia
Tax abatements – targeted at selected sectors
Enterprise zones
Enterprise funds for public services
Venture capital funds
Local development corporations
Linked deposits

Source: Adapted from Susan E. Clarke and Gary L. Gaile (1998), *The Work of Cities*, Minneapolis, MN: University of Minnesota Press, Table 3.5, pp. 81–2. Copyright © 1998 Regents of the University of Minnesota. Adapted by permission of University of Minnesota Press.

The aim of entrepreneurial local economic policy is to encourage investment in the local territory. The types of inward investment most sought after include high tech and so-called "knowledge-based" industries, flexible manufacturing, banking and finance, and cultural activities such as professional sports franchises (e.g. a major league football team) or the Olympic Games. Frequently it is important to attract these activities not because they generate jobs or increase the flow of revenue into the local area (in fact, cultural ventures can be a significant local tax burden), but because they help to raise the external profile and esteem of the locality in question. Place promoters in the United States are, it seems, concerned more about the ways in which their cities are represented to the wider world than about the needs of local residents (Short 1999). Of course, not every locality in the United States can be a Silicon Valley or an Olympic Games venue. Some localities settle for less glamorous ventures such as a new convention center, a resort facility, a casino, an extra runway at the airport, a county landfill, or even a state penitentiary. In these instances, local residents may be convinced by the argument that the new facility in question "creates jobs" and boosts revenues.

As far as its role in facilitating territorial economic competition is concerned, political fragmentation is often seen in a positive light. Paul Peterson, for example, believes territorial competition forces local governments, otherwise constrained by their fixed territorial limits, to be more responsive to mobile capital (Peterson 1981). However, we have seen evidence to the effect that local political fragmentation puts some localities at a fiscal disadvantage over others, and that there should be more cooperation between local government around important issues like economic development and public investment. Clearly, then, there are different views on the ideal form of local territorial government in the United States.

Ideal local territories of United States government

There are some well-established views about the most appropriate territorial form of local government in the United States. In this section, we examine four of the most important and influential views or "theories."

Public choice theory

This theory represents the conservative perspective on political fragmentation at the local level (Tiebout 1954; Ostrom, Bish, and Ostrom 1988). It suggests that ideally local public institutions should reflect the preferences of local voters and consumers. This ideal is not possible when people lack a choice of local government. Political fragmentation, however, is functional to this ideal because it serves as the mechanism by which preferences are revealed. Consumers who are not satisfied with a particular level of service provided by one local jurisdiction will "vote with their feet" and move to another, perhaps nearby, jurisdiction that can better satisfy their demands. By increasing the level of choice of local government, this mechanism not only forces local governments to be more responsive to consumer demands but also maximizes local fiscal effort.

Lyke Thompson's study of citizen attitudes to local service delivery mechanisms provides some empirical support to the public choice argument insofar as it confirms a preference for local provision (Table 5.2)

Table 5.2 Citizen attitudes to public service delivery in the United States

	Police		Street lighting		Garbage collection		Parks and recreation		Water and sewer		Libraries		Fire protection	
	A	B	A	B	A	B	A	B	A	B	A	B	A	B
Own city or township	88.6	70.4	62.6	70.7	54.2	54.6	78.9	68.2	66.3	65.1	79.9	72.5	90.7	83.0
Another city or township	2.1	1.5	1.7	1.9	1.2	1.4	1.9	1.6	14.7	10.5	2.8	2.4	1.9	1.9
County	5.2	4.6	3.0	3.9	1.2	1.7	5.6	8.1	3.0	3.9	4.3	6.1	1.0	1.9
Special district	0.6	1.3	0.1	0.7	0.6	0.6	0.3	1.5	0.6	2.0	1.2	2.3	0.3	0.7
Private firm	0.6	1.4	4.3	4.3	32.6	23.9	0.9	3.7	0.6	1.6	0.2	1.5	0.1	0.6
Other	1.1	1.4	1.2	1.1	0.6	0.5	2.0	3.5	2.9	2.3	1.7	1.9	1.8	1.0
No preference	NA	17.9	NA	15.5	NA	15.5	NA	11.4	NA	13.0	NA	11.9	NA	9.8
Don't know/NA	3.9	1.5	9.6	1.8	9.6	1.8	10.3	2.2	11.9	1.7	9.9	1.9	4.1	1.1

Explanation
A = Preferences for how services are offered
B = Preferences for how services should be offered
NA = No response
Numbers are the percentage of respondents surveyed in the 1994 Detroit Metropolitan Area Public Policy Survey, conducted by the Center for Urban Studies at Wayne State University. 1,200 telephone interviews were successfully completed for a response rate of 45.2 percent.

Source: Adapted from Table 1 in Lyke Thompson 1997 Citizen attitudes about service delivery modes *Journal of Urban Affairs* 19:13, 294–5.
Adapted by permission of Blackwell Publishers.

(Thompson 1997). After studying service delivery modes in metropolitan Detroit, Thompson concluded that when it comes to local services like police protection and fire fighting voters and consumers prefer things the way they are rather than delivered by alternative entities like counties or private contractors. In this respect, Thompson's findings suggest that Americans are generally conservative when it comes to their public service needs.

However, it is perhaps important to note that local providers and public employee unions have a vested interest in the status quo; they want to protect their revenue base and keep people employed. In other words, when it comes to understanding the pressures on local government, satisfying consumer preferences is not the end of the story.

The reform tradition

There is a political tradition in America dating back at least to the Progressive Era, which holds that the public interest transcends local political boundaries. Since local politicians are primarily interested in serving their districts and voters, they often lack an awareness of wider economic and social trends. Local government is thus often portrayed by reformers either as economically inefficient or incapable of promoting social equality. Reformers have proposed a number of alternatives: removing specialized services and planning functions from direct local electoral control; replacing district and ward elections with at-large elections and public ballot measures; creating more efficient public service management systems; spreading the tax burden and exploiting economies of scale; consolidating local governments into larger units; and so forth. Two developments of the reform tradition attest to its liberal ideals.

First, liberal reformers often associate fiscal and social disparities with the level of political fragmentation locally (Danielson 1976; Downs 1973; Weiher 1991). These types of disparity show little sign of disappearing; in metropolitan areas, in particular, they are deeply entrenched. The problem, then, is local political fragmentation, which acts as a mechanism of choice for some but exclusion for many others. Local jurisdictional boundaries serve to deny access on the part of needy social groups – the poor, the homeless, children from deprived households, particular "racial" groups, etc. – to services (housing, schools, etc.). The privileged, in contrast, can use local land use powers to exclude needy groups. In the liberal view, the solution is to circumvent the effects of local political boundaries by introducing more socially inclusive and equitable territorial arrangements.

Second, the proponents of metropolitan or regional government – corporate regionalism in America – have put forward the argument for economies of scale in public service provision (Bish 1971). In a mass-production economy, the efficient delivery of services and circulation of goods would be of prime importance, as is maintaining conditions conducive to mass consumption. Local government should enable housing and infrastructure to be produced in an affordable way but this is not possible when local government is fragmented. Fragmentation leads to irrational planning, over-regulation, fiscal inefficiency, and increased costs-of-doing business. The ideal solution is to consolidate multiple local land use planning and service delivery systems into single metropolitan or regional structures (Walker and Heiman 1981), which can then exploit economies of scale and deliver services more affordably and equitably.

Competitive regionalism

The idea of competitive regionalism has been promoted recently as a mechanism for encouraging metropolitan areas in the United States to compete more effectively in the global economy (Cisneros 1995). Neo-liberals believe that nurturing regional clusters of innovative firms is the key to success in the new economy. Although local governments have become more entrepreneurial, a problem is the lack of cooperation between local jurisdictions within city-regions. Political fragmentation tends to encourage local governments to compete with each other rather than to cooperate for the good of the region as a whole. City-regions with their fragmented jurisdictional arrangements are seen to lack the institutional capacity and political will to sustain regional clusters of innovative firms. Neo-liberal proponents of competitive regionalism suggest that incentives for regional governance provided by federal or state government could bring about greater cooperation among local governments.

The sustainable city-region

According to liberal ecologists, current growth trends across the United

States are environmentally unsustainable. Together, the depletion of non-renewable resources, pollution, and loss of biodiversity represents a major threat to the livelihoods of future generations. Internationally, there are pressures on local governments, including some places in the United States (Lake 2000), to seek ways of balancing their economic growth and environmental resource needs. The principle of sustainable urban development recognizes that actions need to be taken that over the long-term balance the growth and development of urban systems with their environmental resource base (Ravetz 2000: 8). If sustainable urban development necessitates analysis and actions at several spatial scales (Figure 5.3), particular emphasis is placed on the city-region as an integral economic and ecological unit requiring monitoring, long-term planning, and governance. In the United States the problem is that urban growth has occurred under a fragmented system of local government and governance; cities, people, and institutions have become disconnected from their immediate environment. From a planning and governance perspective, greater emphasis needs to be placed on the economic and ecological unity of the city-region. In this respect, the idea of the sustainable city-region offers the environmental alternative to competitive regionalism.

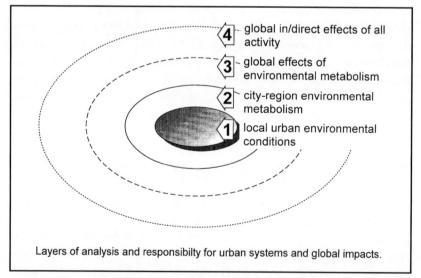

4 — global in/direct effects of all activity

3 ~ global effects of environmental metabolism

2 city-region environmental metabolism

1 local urban environmental conditions

Layers of analysis and responsibilty for urban systems and global impacts.

Figure 5.3 Ladder of local sustainability. Source: Figure 1.5 in Joe Ravetz (2000), *City Region 2020: Integrated Planning for a Sustainable Environment*, London: Earthscan Publications, p. 9. Copyright © 2000 Earthscan Publications. Used by permission of Earthscan Publications.

All of these theories capture different ideas about the role of government in American society. Should (local) government promote economic development? Or should it emphasize redistribution? How can the economic development and welfare functions of government be most efficiently and equitably reconciled at the local level? What is the role of local government in ecological management? But we should note that globalization has considerably changed the scale of reference for such questions, serving to exemplify Neil Smith's point that as the (American) space-economy has undergone crises and restructurings so also has its underlying territorial scales of organization (Smith 1984). Let us now consider some actual examples of the ways in which these political ideals have been, and continue to be, reflected in real struggles around local territories in the United States.

From ideals to reality: contested local territories in the United States

It is helpful to begin our discussion by making a distinction between the politics of place and that of scale. The politics of place refers to the mobilization of local interests upon the basis of a collective interest, or set of interests, in a given territory. Territorial interests can vary from place to place, as also do local territorial arrangements. The interests that preoccupy people in the United States are those to do with the places where they live and work – jobs, education, the quality of the local environment, and the like. Spatial restructuring in the economy, the reallocation of government resources, urban growth, and so forth, threaten these territorial interests. When this occurs, access to, or exclusion from, the powers and resources of local territories can become foci of conflict (Cox and Jonas 1993).

Conflicts around local territorial interests often lead to territorial projects and strategies, which might be pursued at the local or wider spatial scales. The politics of scale refers to the variety of ways in which interest groups engage with existing levels of government (federal, state, county, municipal, etc.) and/or pursue new territorial projects. A related concept here is that of "geographically-shifting political opportunity structures" (Miller 1994). This concept refers to the manner in which territorial interest groups mobilize around the spatial scale or level of government (local to national) at which they perceive they have the greatest opportunity to exercise political leverage and thereby gain access to available resources, regulatory arrangements, legal precedents, and the like. For instance, devolution implies that state government has become a "new" political opportunity structure and therefore a key arena of territorial conflict in the United States. Where groups in civil society are denied access to the powers and resources available at a given level of territorial government, or when such powers and resources are simply not available, they may press for some form of territorial reorganization. Thus they attempt to organize jurisdictional arrangements with attendant powers and resources that are more commensurate with their particular territorial scale-of-interest. As we will see these territorial projects are often informed by alternative ideas concerning the most efficient or equitable organization of local jurisdictions, perhaps from the standpoint of economic development, social redistribution, ecological benefits, or other such criteria.

Choice versus equity in local education provision in central Ohio

Struggles over elementary and high school provision in the United States frequently center upon a conflict between the ideals of choice and equity (Reynolds and Shelley 1990). On the one hand, many parents want to send their children to local school districts that are well resourced and whose educational policies and practices most closely reflect "middle-class" American values and aspirations. Increasingly for the upwardly mobile such schools are to be found in suburban districts. On the other hand, ever since the Supreme Court ruling in *Brown v Board of Education of Topeka* (1954), which found the attendance of children of different races at separate schools unconstitutional, the liberal reformist principle of equal provision has also applied to local education in America. Yet despite remedial measures such as bussing for racial balance disparities between central city and suburban districts have persisted and in some places widened.

The geography of education provision in Franklin County, Ohio, usefully demonstrates the conflict of territorial ideals in areas where inter-jurisdictional disparities in educational resources have persisted (see Cox and Jonas 1993; Jonas 1998). Franklin County, which includes the City of Columbus (population approximately one million), has sixteen school districts (Figure 5.4). The largest in size is the Columbus School District, but this comprises only 60 percent of the land area of

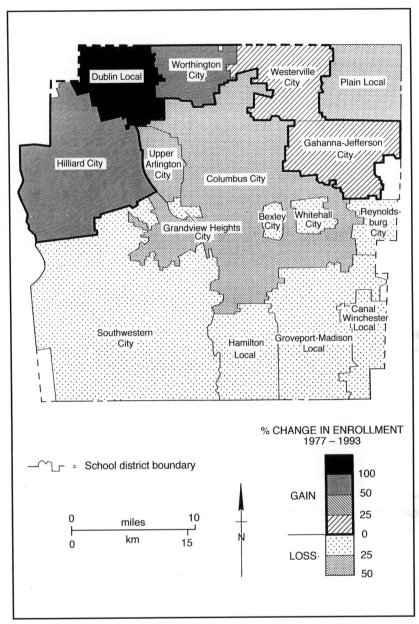

Figure 5.4 Inter-jurisdictional disparities in school district enrollment levels in Franklin County, Ohio. Source: Adapted from Figure 2 and Table 1 in Andrew E.G. Jonas (1998), "Busing, 'White flight' and the Role of Developers in the Continuous Suburbanization of Franklin County, Ohio," *Urban Affairs Review*, 34, pp. 340–58. Adapted by permission of author and Sage Publications, Inc.

the city. A large number of students living in Columbus attend suburban schools. Moreover, whereas about 25 percent of the population of the City of Columbus is African-American, the student population of the city's school district is 50 percent African-American. In this case, the persistence of inter-jurisdictional disparities – not untypical for a large metropolitan area, and highlighted by "racial" categories – is made even more vivid when one considers enrollment levels (Figure 5.4). In the period 1977–93, by far the greatest increases in enrollments were in suburban districts to the north and west of Columbus, such as Dublin, Westerville, Worthington, and Gahanna. By contrast, enrollments in the Columbus district declined over the same period.

An important point to make at this juncture is that these enrollment levels across metropolitan Columbus do not simply reveal a preference on the part of parents for suburban schools (some suburban districts in Franklin County have clearly not attracted new students); instead they are intricately related to the pattern of residential development in the county. In particular, there is a history of developers building outside the Columbus School District, in areas where they can obtain low-cost infrastructure (e.g. water and sewerage), and taking advantage of public perception about the quality of local schools. These areas have become even more attractive to homebuilders in the wake of the desegregation of Columbus schools (which began in the 1970s) and "white flight" out of the city school district.

Recent struggles around in education provision in Franklin County have, therefore, highlighted conflicting territorial ideals. On the one hand, there is the issue of equal provision. In attempts to meet the district's desegregation target and maximize educational resources, parents and school officials in Columbus have called for the matching of school district and city boundaries. There has also been some attempt at fiscal redistribution by the state so as to mitigate local dependence on the property tax, a perceived source of inequality. On the other hand, parents and school officials in the suburbs have fought to maintain the integrity of existing boundaries, often invoking the principles of choice and local control.

It should be noted, however, that suburbanization has also had a fiscal impact on the suburban school districts. New schools and facilities are needed in suburban areas and these have to be funded locally, but local residents have been reluctant to vote for the necessary bond issues and taxes. There is, therefore, a wider context to these struggles relating to the uneven growth of the metropolitan area and the external image of Columbus. Growth promoters in Columbus want to attract inward investment into the city-region but they feel the city's schools are not necessarily equipped to supply the students with skills and qualifications needed by local employers. Given this argument, there have been moves, often led by local growth interests, to abandon desegregation and develop new educational initiatives and encourage investment in the Columbus School District. These initiatives have not necessarily undermined the salience of ideals like public choice and equal provision; on the contrary these ideals continue to feature centrally in the political geography of education provision in central Ohio as well as other places in the United States. What has changed is the framing of these ideals by the politics of economic development and place competition.

Economic globalization and competitive regionalism in Massachusetts

As we have noted, all levels of United States government but particularly state and local levels are being called upon to respond to the pressures of globalization and political devolution. One approach to economic globalization that has been pursued locally within the United States is the idea of competitive regionalism. This idea encourages greater cooperation among local jurisdictions and stakeholders within city-regions where important economic activities are clustered. The idea of competitive regionalism is reflected in the recent economic policies of the Commonwealth of Massachusetts, a state that has actively sought to promote inward investment and economic development in its largest and most important economic region, Greater Boston (Horan and Jonas 1998).

Throughout Massachusetts, business organizations have a long tradition of lobbying city and state government to promote economic development. Since the 1920s, these policies were aimed at creating a business-friendly fiscal and regulatory environment so as to stop corporations and industry sectors relocating out-of-state. In recent years, however, the pressure of global competition has forced the state government to shift its policies from those that reduce the cost-of-doing business to those that facilitate entrepreneurialism in sectors such as high tech. In the 1980s, in particular, Massachusetts attracted the attention of national economic policy makers owing to its "economic miracle" built around high tech industry. One feature of this more entrepreneurial style of economic governance was the level of cooperation between state government, the education sector, and industry in the Greater Boston area. In short, Massachusetts became a model of competitive regionalism.

The Boston region remains an important territorial focus for economic development policy in Massachusetts. In addition to its cluster of educational and high tech institutions, the city-region has recently attracted some very large-scale infrastructure projects, which have been promoted and subsidized by state government. These include a $10 billion central artery linking downtown to the suburbs and a large new sports stadium (www.bigdig.com/thtml/mitigate.htm). To push these projects through complex local planning and land acquisition processes, the Commonwealth has found it necessary to broker conflict with and among the large number of well-organized civic groups in the region. Although the artery project in particular is seen as a key to the region's economic recovery, growth continues to engender conflict with local groups. In this respect, regional cooperation remains an ideal rather than a fact of life in the Boston city-region.

Conflicts around local economic development in Massachusetts have often been displaced to a wider scale. Increasingly, state government has been seen as a political opportunity structure for different interest groups, which have pursued different strategies and territorial projects across the state. For instance, business organizations representing high tech have wanted the state to become more open to inward investment, including foreign direct investment. These groups have supported tax cuts, welfare reform, the relaxing of environmental regulation, and changes to the Commonwealth's tax codes for corporations. However, these policies have conflicted with the interests of established manufacturers, industrial unions, public sector unions, and environmental groups. The debate about globalization has played an important role in the struggle between these factions, but in perhaps a surprising way. Between 1980 and 1990, the number of Massachusetts residents employed in United States affiliates of foreign companies more than doubled, yet the Commonwealth's manufacturing base declined dramatically, creating the perception that "globalization" (in the sense of foreign direct investment) was part of the problem rather than the solution. A coalition of manufacturing interests, public employee unions, and environmental groups was able to force through state legislation regulating foreign direct investment and promoting public investment in the state-wide infrastructure.

As a result, Massachusetts has in recent years created several new institutions for the purpose of regional economic development. For instance, it has set up MassDevelopment as a quasi-public agency providing financing for new business activities in the form of tax-exempt bonds and loans (Figure 5.5) (www.massdevelopment.com/). Its aim is to stimulate economic development in communities throughout the state. In the early 1990s, the Commonwealth also published its economic development strategy, *Choosing to Compete: A Statewide Strategy for Job Creation and Economic Growth* (www.magnet.state.ma.us/econ/toc.htm). This strategy highlights the importance of economic development not just in the Greater Boston area but in other localities as well. In Massachusetts, therefore, territorial struggles have focused attention not

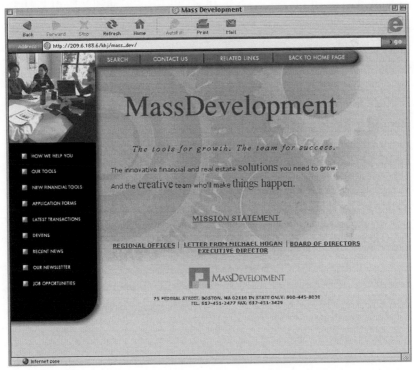

Figure 5.5 Home page for MassDevelopment: The new economic development bank of Massachusetts. Source: www.massdevelopment.com/. Used by permission of MassDevelopment, Boston, Commonwealth of Massachusetts.

only on the quality of inward investment and economic development but also on the uneven territorial impacts of globalization.

Sustainable urbanization? Conservation planning and property rights in southern California

A third example of the difference between ideal and actual local terri-tories in the United States concerns the development of sustainable approaches to urbanization in southern California (see Feldman and Jonas 2000). This is one of the fastest-growing city-regions in the United States, with growth occurring well beyond the urban cores of Los Angeles and San Diego in the neighboring counties of Orange, Riverside, and San Bernardino. In these areas, new suburban develop-ment poses a threat to the habitat of rare and endangered fauna and flora, and has raised concerns amongst local residents, environmental organizations, and conservationists about the sustainability of current growth trends. Specifically, rare and endangered species such as the California gnatcatcher (*Polioptila californica californica*) and the Stephens' Kangaroo Rat (*Dipodomys stephensi*) (Figure 5.6) have been federally listed, and hundreds more besides are threatened. Working under the framework of the 1973 Endangered Species Act (ESA), federal, state and local agencies are endeavoring to put in place habitat conservation plans (HCPs) to protect the region's biodiversity for future generations.

A key consideration is developing conservation plans that are suffi-ciently broad in temporal scope and geographical scale to ensure long-term habitat protection and species survival and recovery. Hitherto HCPs have tended to be rather limited in scope and scale: they have focused upon individual species only when they are federally listed, and fragments of habitat that fall within well-defined property and juris-dictional boundaries. This approach is neither ecologically sustainable nor fiscally efficient. It creates regulatory uncertainties for developers, utility companies, and local governments (these interests want to ensure that long-term development projects are not delayed by land use controls associated with HCPs). Moreover, it fails to cover sufficient acreage so as to ensure the survival of species, presenting legal problems for those local conservation agencies and governments attempting to comply with the ESA. More problematically, interim land use controls associated with HCPs have been opposed politically by local growth coalitions and have been legally challenged in the courts by property

Figure 5.6a and b In Southern California, conservation plans are being developed for federally listed threatened and endangered species, including (a) the California gnat-catcher (*Polioptila californica californica*) and (b) the Stephens' Kangaroo Rat (*Dipodomys stephensi*). Sources: Used by permission of (a) Photo © John Menge; (b) Photo © Karen Kirtland.

owners on the grounds that these plans amount to a "taking" of private property. In other words, local concerns about the ecological integrity of the city-region have come up against constitutional provisions for local property rights.

A desirable solution would be to develop a single conservation plan for a large area – possibly an entire ecosystem – so that as many species as possible are effectively "covered" by such a plan, including those species that are not yet officially listed as threatened. A single comprehensive plan covering a large area would also create a more predictable regulatory environment within which developers, utility companies, and local governments involved in land use projects that comply to ESA standards could operate. Finally, such an approach would seek to internalize property externalities by allowing for voluntary mitigation strategies developed on a regional basis. With these factors in mind, the State of California in 1991 introduced a procedure for implementing ecosystem-based conservation plans on private and public lands throughout the state. Natural Community Conservation Planning (NCCP) aims to replace species-by-species approaches typical of plans developed under the ESA with voluntary ecosystem plans undertaken under procedures delegated from the federal to the state level. In terms of scope and scale, the NCCP process encompasses entire ecosystems rather than single species and defines a process for saving critical habitat in areas undergoing urban development before a listing of a species as threatened or endangered becomes necessary. The NCCP approach has generally been welcomed by conservationists, large-scale developers, utility companies, and other stakeholders in Southern California, where a pilot program has been introduced for the coastal sage scrub ecosystem, which covers all or parts of five counties (Figure 5.7).

Although there is a great deal of state support for ecosystem conservation planning under the NCCP program, the pilot program has confronted three major obstacles. First, and most significantly, constitutional protection for private property rights remains a sticking point. Conservation agencies often face bitter opposition to their plans from local landowners who feel they have suffered a taking of their property. Second, there is a question of defining appropriate territorial limits for the ecosystem in question: in short, what is the ecosystem boundary and how does this match the boundary of the city-region? It has proven especially difficult to establish reserve boundaries that meet ESA standards for species survival and recovery and yet also match

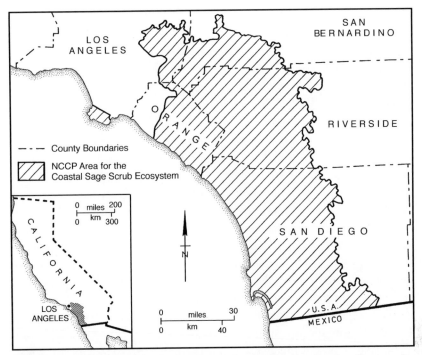

Figure 5.7 Planning region for the Natural Community Conservation Program for coastal sage scrub in Southern California. Source: Adapted from Figure 1 in Thomas D. Feldman and Andrew E. G. Jonas (2000), "Sage Scrub Revolution? Property Rights, Political Fragmentation and Conservation Planning in Southern California under the Federal Endangered Species Act," *Annals of the Association of American Geographers*, 90:2, p. 258. Adapted by permission of author and Blackwell Publishers.

local property and jurisdictional boundaries. Third, cities and counties continue to claim "sovereignty" over local land use planning and consequently have been reluctant to surrender land use control to a larger authority such as a state or federal conservation agency. As a result of these obstacles, the NCCP pilot program for Southern California appears to have politically fragmented into its constituent sub-regions. On a more positive note, however, some county governments in the region have been able to integrate habitat conservation planning into their local and regional land use and transportation plans, holding some promise for more sustainable approaches to urbanization and development at least within those local jurisdictions (see http://ecoregion.ucr.edu/mshcp/).

Conclusion

In reflecting upon the relationship between equality, democracy, and political institutions in America, Alexis de Tocqueville concluded that the federal government was the exception, local government the rule. In other words, Tocqueville believed that in order to understand the workings of American democracy one had to look in the first instance to the principle of the sovereignty of the people and how this was realized in the system of local territorial government. From today's perspective, Tocqueville's conclusion seems naïve, especially when one thinks of the hugely important role the federal government played in the post-Depression American economy and society, and also in view of more recent ideas that economic globalization and place-transcending networks and flows of information and materials have undermined the power and efficacy of territorial government. Nevertheless, the maintenance of a dual political system constructed around local territories within a larger federation remains the foundation of a "democratic revolution" that, in the eyes of Tocqueville and his many followers, has found its ultimate expression in America.

In this chapter, we have seen how the pressures of globalization and devolution are testing this system quite literally to its territorial limits. As new responsibilities have been foisted onto local territories, the political ideals that traditionally have shaped the organization of local government in the United States have been found wanting. Across the United States, new pressures on local government are calling for new territorial strategies and projects. In central Ohio, parents, children, and school district officials have struggled with the redistributional consequences of liberal policies such as schools desegregation. In Massachusetts, global competition and pressures to promote economic development have led to calls for regional approaches to economic governance. In southern California, urban growth has threatened the habitat of endangered species, prompting state and local government to develop alternative, sustainable approaches to urbanization including ecosystem and multiple-species habitat conservation plans. Examining these struggles more closely, one is impressed by the diversity, scope, and scale of territorial interests and projects at the local level of government in America.

In these examples, moreover, local territorial outcomes have had little to do with liberal or conservative ideals such as equality, choice, and freedom, let alone the Tocquevillian "rule" about American democracy. That said, none of these examples actually violates the "rule;" much can still be learnt about the workings of American government by looking closely at its local territories, at the local groups and their political values that shape and reshape local institutions of government and governance. If anything, one is struck by the great high degree of malleability of local territories in the United States. Quite apart from what happens at the federal level, there is still a great deal of scope for local interest groups in America to shape their local territorial institutions of government. But at the same time we should be careful not to imply that local territorial government is somehow functional to wider economic, social, or political imperatives. As Kevin Cox and Andrew Jonas argue, to understand struggles around local territories one has to look not at abstract principles or functional needs but at concrete, local interests:

> there is a good deal of plasticity to the jurisdictional arrangements through which local interests can be realized. Judged at a high level of abstraction there is no necessary relation between local interests and local jurisdictional arrangements. At a more concrete level, however, the relation between the two loses its contingent character and serves to give a concrete form to local interest. (Cox and Jonas 1993: 14)

Local territorial outcomes reflect the variety of ways in which place-based interests have mobilized around existing (local) levels of government or sought to create new jurisdictional arrangements that are commensurate with the changing scope and scale of their interests. In this respect, local territories and institutions in the United States embody collective societal values as rooted in particular places, or, as Nancy Burns puts it, "those who engage successfully in collective action embed their own private values in these public institutions of local government" (Burns 1994: 20). Local territories of government do not reflect some sort of abstract "rule" about the relationship between democracy, equality, and government in America; rather they are the concrete expression of collective interests and struggles based in particular places.

Of course, the political system has had to adapt to the changing geographical scope and organizational scale of the American economy and society. The system Tocqueville observed was for the most part based around small-scale agrarian communities that were only partially integrated in a world economy focused around manufacture, international trade, and a few urban centers. America today is thoroughly urbanized, a centre of flexible manufacturing, and fully integrated into the global economy. It is not surprising that the American system of local territorial government, which was founded upon social relations and democratic principles specific to one time period, has struggled to adapt to changes in these social relations and principles. But if American government is being stretched to its limits, these limits are as much about the organization of the country's internal territories as about its changing external relations.

In America, the form of nation-state "hollowing out" has been different to that which has been observed in the European context. In unitary European states, political devolution has changed the territorial form of government without necessarily undermining the power of central government (Jessop 1994). In the United States, by comparison, it has not so much been the case that the federal government has devolved powers and responsibilities to the states and the people as a situation where changes in policy at the national level have activated powers and responsibilities already residing in local territories. Place-based struggles over local territorial outcomes in the United States remain absolutely central to the process and politics of globalization – how economic development, social inequality, and environmental decay in the global era should be managed – and political devolution – what sorts of local "policy experiments" are occurring, which of these work or are resisted, and which are diffused to a wider political arena. In that respect, the Tocquevillian "rule" continues to offer a basis from which to observe and reflect upon the ideals and practices, the strengths and weaknesses, of democracy and government in America.

References

Baldassare, Mark (1998), *When Government Fails: The Orange County Bankruptcy*, Berkeley and Los Angeles: University of California Press.

Bish, Robert L. (1971), *The Public Economy of Metropolitan Areas*, Chicago: Markham Publishing Company.

Blair, John P., and Robert Premus (1987), "Major Factors in Industrial Location: A Review," *Economic Development Quarterly*, 1, pp. 72–85.

Bluestone, Barry, and Bennett Harrison (1982), *The Deindustrialization of America*, New York: Basic Books.

Brown, Michael P. (1994), "The Possibility of Local Autonomy," *Urban Geography*, 13:3, pp. 257–79.

Burns, Nancy (1994), *The Formation of American Local Governments: Private Values in Public Institutions*, New York: Oxford University Press.

Burrows, Nigel (1998), *Government and Politics of the United States*, 2nd edn., Basingstoke and London: MacMillan Press.

Cisneros, Henry G. (1995), *Regionalism: The New Geography of Opportunity*, Washington, DC: United States Department of Housing and Urban Development.

Clark, G. L., and M. Dear (1984), *State Apparatus*, Boston: Allen and Unwin.

Clarke, Susan E., and Gary L. Gaile (1998), *The Work of Cities*, Minneapolis, MN: University of Minnesota Press.

Cox, Kevin R. (ed.) (1997), *Spaces of Globalization: Reasserting the Power of the Local*, New York: Guilford Press.

Cox, Kevin, and Andrew Mair (1988), "Locality and Community in the Politics of Local Economic Development," *Annals of the Association of American Geographers*, 78, pp. 307–25.

Cox, Kevin R., and Andrew E. G. Jonas (1993), "Urban Development, Collective Consumption and the Politics of Metropolitan Fragmentation," *Political Geography*, 12:1, pp. 12–32.

Dahl, Robert A. (1961), *Who Governs?* New Haven, CN: Yale University Press.

Danielson, Michael N. (1976), *The Politics of Exclusion*, New York: Columbia University Press.

Donahue, John D. (1997), *Disunited States*, New York: Basic Books.

Downs, Anthony (1973), *Opening Up the Suburbs*, New Haven: Yale University Press.

Elkin, Stephen (1987), *City and Regime in the American Republic*, Chicago: University of Chicago Press.

Feldman, Thomas D., and Andrew E. G. Jonas (2000), "Sage Scrub Revolution? Property Rights, Political Fragmentation and Conservation Planning in Southern California under the Federal Endangered Species Act," *Annals of the Association of American Geographers*, 90:2, pp. 256–92.

Ferejohn, John, and Barry R. Weingast (eds.) (1997), *The New Federalism: Can the States Be Trusted?* Stanford, CA: Hoover Institution Press.

Florida, Richard L., and Andrew Jonas (1991), "US Urban Policy: The Postwar State and Capitalist Regulation," *Antipode*, 23:4, pp. 349–84.

Garreau, Joel (1991), *Edge City: Life on the New Frontier*, New York: Doubleday.

Gilbert, Melissa (1999), "Place, politics, and the Production of Urban Space: A Feminist Critique of the Growth Machine Thesis," in Andrew E. G. Jonas and David Wilson (eds.), *The Urban Growth Machine: Critical Perspectives Two Decades Later*, Albany, NY: State University of New York Press, pp. 95–108.

Gutman, Amy (ed.) (1988), *Democracy and the Welfare State*, Princeton, NJ: Princeton University Press.

Hartshorne, Richard (1950), "The Functional Approach in Political Geography," *Annals of the Association of American Geographers*, 40, 95–130.

Herod, Andrew J. (1991), "Local Political Practice in Response to a Manufacturing Plant Closure: How Geography Complicates Class Analysis," *Antipode* 23, pp. 385–402.

Horan, Cynthia, and Andrew E. G. Jonas (1998), "Governing Massachusetts: Uneven Development and Politics in Metropolitan Boston," *Economic Geography*, Special Issue for the 1998 Annual Meeting of the Association of American Geographers, Boston, MA, March 25–9, pp. 83–95.

Jessop, Bob (1994), "Post-Fordism and the State," in Ash Amin (ed.), *Post-Fordism: A Reader*, Oxford: Blackwell, pp. 251–79.

Jonas, Andrew E. G. (1995), "Labor and Community in the Deindustrialization of Urban America," *Journal of Urban Affairs*, 17, pp. 183–99.

Jonas, Andrew E. G. (1998), "Busing, 'White Flight' and the Role of Developers in the Continuous Suburbanization of Franklin County, Ohio," *Urban Affairs Review*, 34, pp. 340–58.

Lake, Robert L. (2000), "Contradictions at the Local Scale: Local Implementation of Agenda 21 in the USA," in Nicholas Low, Brendan Gleeson, Ingemar Elander, and Rolf Lidskog (eds.), *Consuming Cities: The Urban Environment in the Global Economy after the Rio Declaration*, London: Routledge, pp. 70–90.

Lewis, Sinclair (1922), *Babbitt*, New York: Collier.

Logan, John R., and Harvey L. Molotch (1987), *Urban Fortunes: The Political Economy of Place*, Berkeley and Los Angeles: University of California Press.

Miller, Byron (1994), "Political Empowerment, Local-Central State Relations, and Geographically Shifting Political Opportunity Structures: Strategies of the Cambridge, Massachusetts, Peace Movement," *Political Geography*, 13, 393–406.

Molotch, Harvey L. (1976), "The City as a Growth Machine: Toward a Political Economy of Place," *American Journal of Sociology*, 82, pp. 309–30.

Naylor, Thomas H., and William H. Willimon (1997), *Downsizing the U.S.A.*, Grand Rapids, MI: Eerdmans.

O'Connor, James (1973), *The Fiscal Crisis of the State*, London: St. Martin's Press.

Ohmae, Kenichi (1995), *The Borderless World: Power and Strategy in the Interlinked Economy*, New York: Harper Business.

Ostrom, Vincent, Robert Bish, and Elinor Ostrom (1988), *Local Government in the United States*, San Francisco: Institute for Contemporary Studies.

Peck, Jamie, and Adam Tickell (1994), "Searching for a New Institutional Fix: The After-Fordist Crisis and the Global-Local Disorder," in Ash Amin (ed.), *Post-Fordism: A Reader*, Oxford: Blackwell, pp. 280–315.

Peterson, Paul (1981), *City Limits*, Chicago: University of Chicago Press.

Platte, Mark, Matt Lait, and Tom Petruno (1994), "Orange County Officials Urge Calm as Crisis Fallout Spreads," *Los Angeles Times*, December 8, A1 and A28.

Preteceille, Edmund (1990), "Political Paradoxes of Urban Restructuring: Globalization of Economy and Localization of Politics," in John R. Logan and Todd Swanstrom (eds.), *Beyond the City Limits*, Philadelphia: Temple University Press, pp. 27–59.

Ravetz, Joe (2000), *City Region 2020: Integrated Planning for a Sustainable Environment*, London: Earthscan Publications.

Reynolds, David R., and Fred M. Shelley (1990), "Local Control in American Public Education," in Janet E. Kodras and John Paul Jones (eds.), *Geographic Dimensions of United States Social Policy*, London: Edward Arnold, pp. 107–33.

Salins, Peter D. (1993), "Cities, Suburbs, and the Urban Crisis,' *The Public Interest*, Fall, pp. 91–104.

Short, John R. (1999), "Urban Imagineers: Boosterism and the Representation of Cities," in Andrew E. G. Jonas and David Wilson (eds.), *The Urban Growth Machine: Critical Perspectives Two Decades Later*, Albany, NY: State University of New York Press, pp. 37–54.

Skidmore, Max J., and Marshall Carter Wanke (1981), *American Government: A Brief Introduction*, 3rd edn., New York: St. Martin's Press.

Smith, Neil (1984), *Uneven Development*, Oxford: Basil Blackwell.

Sparke, Matthew (1998), "Outsides Inside Patriotism: The Oklahoma Bombing and the Displacement of Heartland Geopolitics," in Gearoid O. Tuathail and Simon Dalby (eds.), *Rethinking Geopolitics*, London: Routledge, pp. 198–223.

Staeheli, Lynne A. (1994), "Gender Relations in Urban Growth Politics," in David Wilson and Jim O. Huff (eds.), *Marginalized Places and Populations: A Structurationist Agenda*, Westport, CN: Praeger, pp. 129–48.

Staeheli, Lynn A., Janet E. Kodras, and Colin Flint (eds.) (1997), *State Devolution in America*, Urban Affairs Annual Reviews, 48, Thousand Oaks, CA: Sage Publications.

Stone, Clarence N. (1993), "Urban Regimes and the Capacity to Govern: A Political Economy Approach," *Journal of Urban Affairs*, 15, pp. 1–28.

Storper, Michael, and Richard Walker (1989), *The Capitalist Imperative: Territory, Technology and Industrial Growth*, Oxford: Basil Blackwell.

Swyngedouw, Eric (1997), "Neither Global Nor Local: 'Glocalization' and the Politics of Scale," in Kevin R. Cox (ed.), *Spaces of Globalization: Reasserting the Power of the Local*, New York: Guilford Press, pp. 137–66.

Tannenwald, Robert (1999), "Fiscal Disparity among the States Revisited," *New England Economic Review*, July/August, pp. 3–25.

Teaford, Jon C. (1997), *Post-Suburbia: Government and Politics in the Edge Cities*, Baltimore, MD: Johns Hopkins University Press.

Thompson, Lyke (1997), "Citizen Attitudes about Service Delivery Modes," *Journal of Urban Affairs*, 19:13, pp. 291–302.

Tiebout, Charles M. (1954), "A Pure Theory of Local Expenditures," *Journal of Political Economy*, 64, pp. 416–24.

Tocqueville, Alexis de (1945, 1963), *Democracy in America*, New York: Alfred A. Knopf.

Walker, Richard A., and Michael K. Heiman (1981), "Quiet Revolution for Whom?," *Annals of the Association of American Geographers*, 71, pp. 67–83.

Weiher, Gregory R. (1991), *The Fractured Metropolis: Political Fragmentation and Metropolitan Segregation*, Albany, NY: State University Press of New York.

CHAPTER 6

Urban and regional restructuring in the second half of the twentieth century

David L. Rigby

A set of economic complaints was of importance in motivating the American Revolution. There were resentments about restrictions on American settlement beyond the Appalachian Mountains and concerns about the duties placed on American imports. Above all, many among the American colonists thought that they were not masters in what they increasingly saw as their own economic house. The founders of the United States, however, had different ideas about how a national economy should be organized. For example, Alexander Hamilton wanted a powerful central government to create an integrated national economy that could hold up to European (British) competition. Thomas Jefferson was more concerned to defend the identity and interests of small producers in frontier areas rather than the traders of the Northeast and the big planters of the coastal South (even though he was one of the latter). The economy of the newly-independent United States was really a set of distinctive local and regional economies tied together only weakly. Though federal-government legislation from 1817 onwards was geared towards protecting infant manufacturing industries and encouraging the creation of a national economy, the various parts, the cotton-growing South in particular, remained tied in distinctive ways into circuits of trade and commerce within a wider Atlantic economy. Only after the Civil War had definitively destroyed the slave-based plantation economy of the South, Northern businesses had embarked on making national markets for consumer goods, and federal initiatives had led to the construction of transcontinental railroads did an American national economy begin to take shape. The American gospel of business-led growth based on mass production trickling down to stimulate mass consumption by the broad masses of the population emerged at much the same time. Initially based on a Northeastern manufacturing belt and resource peripheries in the South and the West, the last fifty years of the twentieth century have seen a profound transformation in both the structure and the geography of the American economy. Economic geographer David L. Rigby (1) shows how the recent changes in the American economy have been explained by economists and others, (2) ties these changes definitively to the increased openness of the United States economy to external influences (trade, investment, etc.), and (3) details the trends in the United States economy at the national, the regional, and the metropol-itan geographical scales of analysis. If the most important national-level trends have been the overall decline in manufacturing in the United States economy and the shift in employment growth from the Northeast to the South and West, the most important metropolitan-level trend has been the abandonment of central cities (and their poorer, minority populations) by manufacturing industries. In tracing the impact of globalization on the recent past of the American economy, the chapter suggests that the United States is now returning to the position of dependency on the larger world economy that it once had and the American Revolution was at least in part designed to restrict.

Introduction

At the close of the twentieth century the United States economy produced approximately five times more output than in 1950. The pace of growth over this period was uneven. Whereas real output expanded at an annual average rate of 3.9 percent between 1950 and 1973, annual growth rates declined to around 1.8 percent from 1973 until the deep recession of the early 1980s (United States Department of Commerce, *Annual Survey of Manufactures*, various years). Through the 1980s the economy recovered slowly, and following the Cold-War slowdown of 1989–91, United States economic output accelerated sharply at rates close to those of the postwar "golden age." Economic growth has also been uneven from place to place. At the end of the Second World War, almost 60 percent of the nation's employment was concentrated in the old industrial core comprising the New England, Mid-Atlantic and East North Central census regions. Today these regions contain only 37 percent of United States jobs, testimony to the development of new industrial places in the south and west of the country. At a more disaggregate scale, employment across the country generally has shifted from older to newer metropolitan centers and from inner cities to exurban regions.

The expansion and the geographical realignment of the United States economy over the last fifty years of the twentieth century have been paced by a series of other significant changes. Following patterns observed across most advanced industrialized nations, over the second half of the twentieth-century workers in the United States economy were increasingly likely to be employed in service industries and less likely to be employed in manufacturing. Indeed, between 1950 and 1996, the share of workers found in the manufacturing sector declined from 29 percent to 14.6 percent, while the service sector employment share grew from 13.7 percent to 28.7 percent (United States Department of Commerce, *County Business Patterns*, various years). And as the mix of industries in the United States economy has changed, so has the nature of employment, with part-time, contractual, and other non-standard types of employment increasingly replacing the full-time worker. These changes, coupled with a drop in rates of unionization and an acceleration in the pace of skills obsolescence have translated into less and less employment security for the average United States worker and virtually no gains in real income since the mid-1970s.

This chapter details the process of industrial and regional economic restructuring in the United States economy over the last half of the twentieth century. The chapter is organized as follows. The first section provides a brief overview of competing theories of restructuring. The second section highlights the postwar emergence of a global economy and the position of the United States in that economy. Postwar economic growth and subsequent decline at the national level are examined in the third section, alongside discussions of the changing character of the United States economy and consequences for the distribution of income. In the fourth section attention turns to geographical issues, in particular the snowbelt to sunbelt migration of jobs and the population, to the growth of new urban and ex-urban places, and to regional variations in economic performance and incomes. The fifth section concludes the chapter.

Different models of industrial restructuring

Between 1950 and 1973, the output of OECD nations grew at an annual average rate of 4.9 percent. From 1973 to 1996, the annual growth rate of OCED output slowed to about 2.8 percent. This slow-down in economic growth was widespread across the advanced industrialized nations, though national differences in growth rates and the timing of the slowdown were significant (Webber and Rigby 1996).

The extent of the slowdown and the attendant job loss, particularly in the manufacturing sector, spawned a number of theories to explain the crisis and characterize the subsequent phase of renewed accumulation. Four of the most popular frameworks are very briefly sketched below. Webber (1991) and Amin (1994) offer more detailed reviews and criticisms of some of these frameworks.

Freeman and Perez (1988) develop a neo-Schumpeterian account of long waves (Kondratieff cycles) of growth and decline that supposedly exhibit a periodicity of about fifty years. The long waves are viewed as phases of accordance and discordance between new technology systems and socio-institutional frameworks. Thus, periods of rapid growth are claimed to rest upon radical innovations and new modes of social management that complement the essential character of the new technologies. Periods of slowdown are characterized by diminishing returns to a particular "techno-economic paradigm," by the search for new technologies and development of new regulatory approaches. So Freeman and Perez (1988) view the slowdown of the 1970s as the end of the fourth Kondratieff cycle, the exhaustion of the potential of Fordist mass production technologies in the automobile and other consumer durables sectors.

Mandel (1978) also develops an account of postwar decline that is linked to long waves. Rather than linking long waves directly to new technology systems, Mandel offers a Marxian explanation of the lower and upper turning points of these cycles of accumulation. For Mandel, the boom resulted from the last crisis, the devaluation of capital and labor power and the attendant rise in the rate of profit. The 1950s and 1960s were seen as years of rapid accumulation, with a high rate of profit resting upon the super-exploitation of labor. The rapid pace of accumulation itself generated the crisis of the 1970s: as economic growth increased the demand for labor, wages were bid-up. Capitalists responded with mechanization, raising problems of underconsumption. Squeezed by higher wages, a rising organic composition of capital and flooded markets, the rate of profit was forced lower and growth faltered.

Piore and Sabel (1984) view the slowdown of the 1970s as an industrial divide. According to them, capitalist production tends toward one of two essential types: mass production or flexible specialization. Mass production is an arrangement where dedicated (single purpose) capital equipment and semi-skilled workers, who perform specific, routine tasks, are employed to manufacture standardized goods, typically within a single, large factory. Flexible specialization is a quite different production arrangement where skilled, polyvalent workers use general-purpose equipment and machinery to produce a variety of customized goods. Flexibility is also assisted by the social division of labor, by the fragmentation of production among many firms that constitute an industrial network. Piore and Sabel (1984) maintain that these two types of production system have co-existed since the nineteenth century, but that for social and political reasons one system typically dominates the other, with the phase of transition between systems known as an industrial divide. Piore and Sabel contend that the Fordist system of mass production dominated from the 1920s–1930s until the 1970s. In the early 1970s, overproduction crises and falling levels of productivity generated considerable economic instability and raised doubts about the viability of Fordist, mass production, ushering in a period during which the two production arrangements competed for hegemony. The character of the new post-Fordist regime is still hotly debated (Schoenberger 1988; Gertler 1988).

Regulation theorists view the history of capitalist accumulation slightly differently (Aglietta 1979; Lipietz 1986). They too characterize that history as a series of phases of relative stability and rapid accumulation interrupted by periods of crisis. For the regulationists, each regime of accumulation hinges both on a particular way of organizing production and on an attendant mode of regulation, a set of institutions that manage the reproduction of the social, political, and economic relations of capitalism. Thus, the so-called "golden age" of the 1950s and 1960s was characterized by a Fordist system of mass production, and the stability of this regime was underpinned by institutions such as collective bargaining that linked productivity gains with increases in the real wage to ensure market-clearing. The end of this regime is usually explained by the downturn in productivity, by the globalization of production, and the consequent inability of national policies to manage production and consumption, and thus by the collapse of the regulatory institutions that maintained stability.

Unquestionably, aspects of all these accounts offer some theoretical purchase in terms of trying to understand the broad swings in economic growth that characterize the capitalist economy. Mandel's (1978) Marxian framework does the best job of outlining the essential dynamics of capitalist production, although at a cost of some specificity. Freeman and Perez (1988) flesh out Mandel's arguments, providing a richer theoretical model of the relationship between technology and growth. Piore and Sabel (1984) provide yet more depth in terms of the links between technology and industrial organization over the course of the last 150 or so years, and the regulationists complement these claims by providing institutional detail.

The United States in the emerging global economy

Over the second half of the twentieth century the pace of global economic integration accelerated markedly. By the mid-1990s global annual marketed output approached $25 trillion. In real terms this was six times the level of 1950. International commodity trade grew even faster: between 1950 and the 1993 world trade expanded tenfold (UNCTAD 1996). The growth of trade is closely related to the increasing fragmentation of production and to the separation of production processes across nations and regions. One consequence of this is that we no longer live in places where social, political, and economic values are locally produced and controlled. Of course the extent of control varies from one country and region to the next. Not surprisingly, the first world, industrialized nations enjoy most influence, though even they are not immune from economic crisis.

The origins of the global economy are traced by Dicken (1998), and others such as Braudel (1984) and Wallerstein (1979), to imperial expansion, especially that of European nations during the late fifteenth and early sixteenth centuries, and to the emergence and dominance of the capitalist mode of production. International trade accelerated rapidly through the nineteenth century, fuelled by industrialization and a geographically extensive search for sources of cheap inputs and markets for manufactured goods around the world. A product-based division of labor developed comprising a core group of industrialized economies that exchanged manufactured goods in return for resources from a non-industrialized and heavily dependent periphery. The rapid pace of technological change in transportation systems and in communications shortly after the Second World War, the integration of global financial markets, the reorganization of production, and growth of multi-national corporations hastened the development of a new post-war international division of labor. This new spatial division of labor is largely based upon the disintegration of commodity production, upon region-specific process specialization and upon the functional integration of spaces of production across the world (Dicken 1998).

While Britain dominated the production of manufactured goods through the nineteenth century, the United States had assumed the lead role by 1913 (Dicken 1998). With European and Japanese economies in turmoil at the close of the Second World War, and with economic recession looming, the United States was saddled with the problem of European economic reconstruction made ever more urgent by the threat of Soviet socialist expansion (see Chapter 4, this volume). Not wanting to repeat the protectionism and economic insularity that deepened the global depression of the 1930s, the United States championed a new financial order and a system to encourage international trade. The 1944 Bretton Woods agreement sought to stabilize international currencies by linking them, in a less rigid fashion than previously, to a new gold standard and by promising short-term support for countries with significant balance of payments deficits through the International Monetary Fund and the International Bank For Reconstruction and Development (later the World Bank). Since the dollar was really the only convertible currency at the end of the war, Bretton Woods effectively made the dollar equal to gold. Linking the dollar and gold was a boon to trade and the emerging postwar international financial system. Dollars could be produced more easily than gold, and thus international liquidity accelerated more rapidly than would have been possible under a pure gold standard (Moffitt 1983; Walter 1991). With dollars as lubricant, another institution, the General Agreement on Tariffs and Trade, was established in 1947 with the aim of stimulating growth through the reduction of tariff and non-tariff barriers to trade.

European economic reconstruction faltered until 1948 and the introduction of the Marshall Plan, a series of loans from the United States totaling $12 billion. The Marshall Plan eased the shortage of capital and provided the necessary spur to European redevelopment. These same funds accelerated economic growth in the United States as European, and other, economies imported manufactured goods from American firms. With virtually no foreign competition in the immediate postwar period the United States economy enjoyed substantial trade surpluses year after year. Apart from the Marshall Plan, the United States flooded the world with dollars through running regular balance of payments deficits after the Second World War. These deficits resulted from massive increases in military spending outside the United States and from overseas investments by United States corporations and other types of international capital flows. It is estimated that of an $8.5 billion increase in international money during the 1950s, United States balance of payments deficits provided close to $7 billion (Solomon 1977). On the one hand these deficits contributed to the success of the Bretton Woods system by increasing international liquidity. On the other hand, however, they also undermined that system, raising doubts about the ability of the United States Treasury to convert dollars to gold (Triffin 1969).

By the mid-1960s, it was clear that the dollar and the United States economy were in trouble: United States balance of payments deficits that had been averaging about $1 billion jumped to over $3 billion annually after 1965. The surge in the deficit was driven by international economic competition from Europe and Japan, that steadily intensified through the 1960s such that the United States trade surplus was steadily reduced (see Figure 6.1), and by the cost of the Vietnam War. The pressure on the dollar triggered a significant jump in United States inflation and this compounded the problem making it more and more difficult for United States firms to compete in international markets with an overvalued dollar. Indeed, in 1971 the United States economy posted its first trade deficit of the postwar period. Spending his way out of recession, President Nixon only worsened the dollar problem and hastened the flight of capital from the United States economy as interest rates slumped and investors awaited the inevitable devaluation of the dollar. Moffitt (1983) reports that between 1970 and 1971 the dollar holdings of foreign governments increased from $24 billion to over $50 billion. Private currency market speculators stepped up their attacks on the dollar and European central banks closed their currency markets, no longer willing to maintain the dollar and ultimately the fixed exchange rates of Bretton Woods. The official end of the fixed exchange system came on August 15, 1971, when Nixon closed the "gold window" suspending the convertibility of the dollar for gold.

Attempts by the United States government to reduce the balance of payments deficit and to prevent the massive outflow of private capital in the late 1950s also backfired. United States banks quickly established foreign branches around the world to sidestep regulations on capital flows. Park and Zwick (1985) note that in 1960 13 United States banks controlled 211 foreign branches and by 1970 79 banks controlled

Figure 6.1   United States trade. Source: United States Department of Commerce, Bureau of Economic Analysis, *Survey of Current Business,* various years.

532 foreign branches. In 1965 United States banks held $377 billion in domestic loans and $9 billion in foreign branch loans. By 1976 assets in foreign branches had risen more than twenty times while domestic assets merely tripled. Most of these assets supported the growth of the Eurodollar market, a single global money market largely unregulated by government, created in the late 1950s as European and United States banks sought to replace the increasingly regulated United States bond market with a European alternative. In the 1960s and 1970s international bank lending was growing three times faster than world trade and nearly five times as fast as global production (Moffitt 1983). International bank holdings rose steeply after the OPEC oil price increase of 1973, that was itself, in large part, driven by the

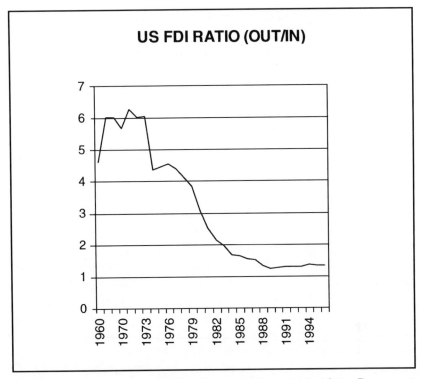

Figure 6.2 United States foreign direct investment. Source: United States Department of Commerce, Bureau of Economic Analysis, *Survey of Current Business*, various years.

devaluation of the dollar. OPEC nations did not have the infrastructure to absorb their expanding trade surpluses and thus channeled large sums into international banks. Once more, the result was a significant increase in international liquidity, now in the form of low interest loans from sources such as the Eurodollar market. Quick to take advantage of these loans, a number of newly industrializing economies such as Hong Kong, Singapore, Taiwan, and South Korea, rapidly expanded their manufacturing base, flooding international markets and dramatically raising the level of competition for countries such as the United States (Webber and Rigby 1996).

The initial flow of capital out of the United States was largely driven by portfolio investment. By the mid-1960s, however, a faltering economy spurred significant increases in the volume of foreign direct investment (FDI) as United States firms extended their domestic operations into the international arena (Figure 6.2). By the end of the 1960s approximately six times more foreign direct investment was flowing out of the United States than was flowing into the country. Figures 6.3a–d show the industrial and geographical patterns of foreign direct investment flows in and out of the United States in 1973 and in 1996. There has been considerable stability in the geography of FDI: correlation coefficients of the proportions of inward and outward FDI in 1973 and 1996 for the places listed in Figures 6.3a and 6.3b are 0.57 and 0.76, respectively. About 85 percent of capital inflows to the United States originated in Canada and Europe in 1973, and these regions sourced more than 75 percent of FDI entering the United States in 1996. Of the flows of FDI from the United States, Canada and Europe received a little more than 60 percent each year since 1973. The most notable changes in the geography of FDI between 1973 and 1996 has been the growth of Japan, especially as a source of FDI into the United States, and the relative decline in the importance of Canada as both a source and destination for United States FDI. In terms of the industrial composition of FDI flows, the trade sector has changed little in significance, manufactures have declined slightly, more so in terms of foreign investment in the United States, FDI focused on petroleum has dropped sharply, and most FDI growth has taken place around the services sector, especially banking and finance (see Figures 6.3c and 6.3d).

As capital flowed out of the United States economy, the annual pace of investment in the domestic manufacturing sector slowed from over 4 percent on average in the 1960s to around 3 percent on average through the 1970s. Investment is one of the key mediums through which new technologies are introduced into the economy. The slowdown in the pace of investment in the 1970s had a rapid and severe impact upon much of the manufacturing sector. Between 1963 and 1973 manufacturing productivity (real value added per worker) increased by 1.8 percent on average each year. After 1973 the growth of manufacturing productivity essentially halted for a decade. Indeed, productivity levels were lower in 1982 than they were 10 years earlier. The decline in United States productivity growth intensified competitive pressures from foreign producers. Baumol, Nelson, and Wolff (1994), Fagerberg (1994), and others have demonstrated that productivity in a number of industrialized and newly industrialized economies converged rapidly on United States levels through the 1970s and 1980s.

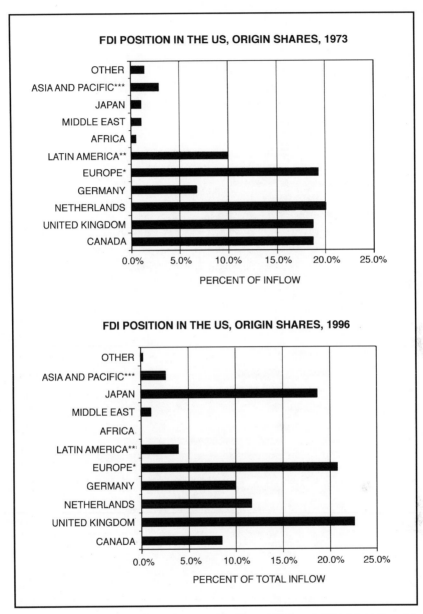

Figure 6.3a FDI in the United States, origin Shares, 1973 and 1996. Note: Europe* excludes the UK, Germany and the Netherlands; Latin America** includes western hemisphere countries; Asia and Pacific*** excludes Japan. The Foreign Investment position in the US was $20.6 Billion in 1973 and $631.0 Billion in 1996 (historical cost basis). Source: US Department of Commerce, Bureau of Economic Analysis, Survey of Current Business, various years

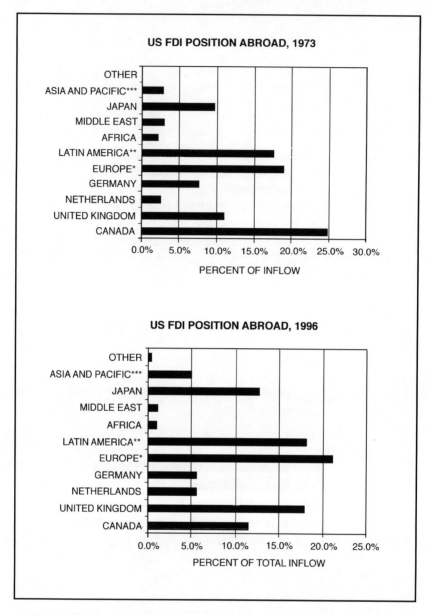

Figure 6.3b United States FDI position abroad, 1973 and 1996. Note: Europe* excludes the UK, Germany and the Netherlands; Latin America** includes western hemisphere countries; Asia and Pacific*** excludes Japan. The Foreign Investment position in the US was $101.3 Billion in 1973 and $796.5 Billion in 1996 (historical cost basis). Source: US Department of Commerce, Bureau of Economic Analysis, Survey of Current Business, various years.

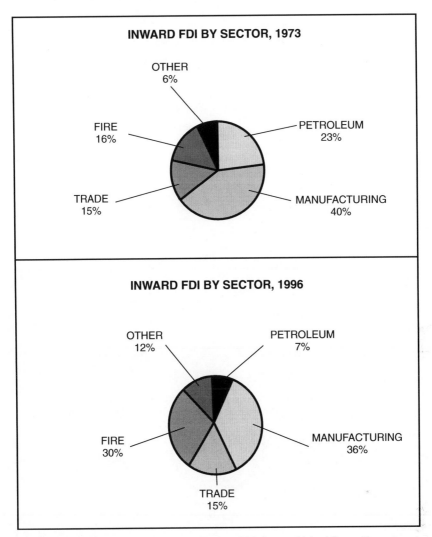

INWARD FDI BY SECTOR, 1973

OTHER
6%

FIRE
16%

PETROLEUM
23%

TRADE
15%

MANUFACTURING
40%

INWARD FDI BY SECTOR, 1996

OTHER
12%

PETROLEUM
7%

FIRE
30%

MANUFACTURING
36%

TRADE
15%

Figure 6.3c Inward FDI by sector, 1973 and 1996. Source: United States Department of Commerce, Bureau of Economic Analysis, *Survey of Current Business*, various years.

Manufacturing decline and national economic change

The United States emerged from the Second World War with an economy that dominated global production. In 1950 United States manufacturing output totaled $90 billion, more than four times greater than that of the second largest manufacturing nation. Total manufacturing employment then numbered close to 15 million, almost twice the size

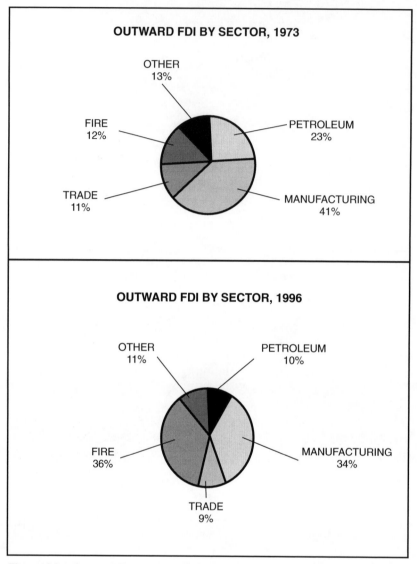

Figure 6.3d Outward FDI by sector, 1973 and 1996. Source: United States Department of Commerce, Bureau of Economic Analysis, *Survey of Current Business*, various years.

of the workforce of the United Kingdom and several times greater than in Japan. In the early postwar years manufacturing investment in the United States was higher than elsewhere in the world and American technology and management were second to none (Dertouzos, Lester, and Solow 1989). With its manufacturing capacity intact, with its scale advantages, and its abundant capital, the United States seemed poised to tighten its grip on the global economy.

Postwar expansion was relatively short-lived, however, as the United States economy was unable to escape the global recession that took root at the end of the 1960s. Indeed, after growing relatively rapidly throughout the mid-1950s and early 1960s, direct production employment in United States manufacturing declined from 14.4 million workers in 1969 to about 11.8 million in 1986, less than the number employed in 1950. Over the same period, the real rate of growth of United States manufactured output, measured between peaks of the business cycle, declined from 5.05 percent per annum between 1955 and 1965 to 2.49 percent per annum between 1965 and 1973, to 2.74 percent per annum between 1973 and 1979, and between 1979 and 1990 manufacturing output actually contracted at a little over 1 percent each year on average. After producing 40 percent of world manufactured output in 1963, the United States share of global production fell to less than 30 percent by 1980 (Dicken 1998). The share of world exports of manufactured goods originating in the United States also declined by 20 percent between 1963 and 1976 (Watts 1987).

A general barometer of the performance of the economy, the United States manufacturing profit rate declined sharply after 1965, falling by almost 40 percent to its postwar low in 1982. After fluctuating around a generally rising trend between the early 1980s and the recession of the early 1990s, the rate of profit has rebounded more steadily through the 1990s (Figure 6.4). Increasing competitive pressure from Europe and Japan undoubtedly contributed to the decline in the United States rate of profit. That decline predates the growth of a number of the newly industrializing economies, as well as the oil price shock of 1973, however, and thus reasons for the deteriorating performance of the United States manufacturing sector must be located elsewhere. Indeed, as outlined above, the growth of the NICs in part was fueled by falling profits in the United States and the export of capital in search of higher returns. Webber and Rigby (1996) examine the different forces acting on the United States manufacturing rate of profit after 1960. They show that the downturn in profitability resulted from increases in the amount of capital inputs used per worker which were not offset by corresponding increases in output. Thus, overall manufacturing productivity declined.

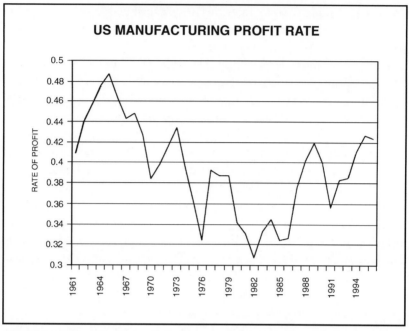

Figure 6.4 United States manufacturing profit rate. Source: United States Department of Commerce, Bureau of Economic Analysis, *Annual Survey of Manufactures*, various years.

As profitability declined in manufacturing so did the rate of investment. The result was a steady reduction in the relative size of the manufacturing component of the United States economy that was paced by growth in the service sector. Figure 6.5 reveals how the industrial composition of the United States economy changed between 1950 and 1996. The decline in the relative size of the manufacturing sector began as the Second World War ended and continued throughout the latter half of the twentieth century. Between 1950 and 1973, manufacturing employment fell from 29.03 percent of the overall United States workforce to 23.6 percent. The pace of manufacturing decline accelerated with the onset of economic crisis in the late 1960s and early 1970s: by 1996 manufacturing's share of United States employment stood at 14.6 percent. As manufacturing activity became a smaller component of the United States economy, the service sector expanded its influence from 13.7 percent of total United States employment in 1950 to 28.9 percent by 1996. The finance, insurance, and real estate sector doubled in relative size over this same period and the retail sector also enjoyed robust growth. Even more dramatic changes were recorded in the agriculture, forestry, and fishing sectors where the relative employment share fell from just under 5 percent in 1950 to less than 2 percent only twenty years later. Unfortunately, a richer story of economic change in the non-manufacturing sector of the United States economy is difficult to provide because of the paucity of data. However, economic change in the services sector has been extensively examined in the United States by Beyers (1989) and more generally by Daniels (1993).

These relatively broad shifts in the industrial composition of the United States economy have been paralleled by a series of more subtle changes. Within the manufacturing sector, for example, capital- and technology-intensive industries such as electronics, rubber, plastics, and chemicals have grown rapidly, while low-technology, labor-intensive

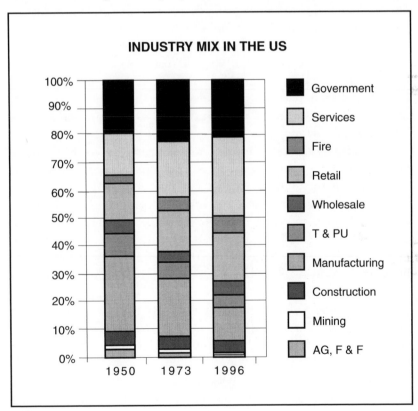

Figure 6.5 Industrial mix of the United States, 1950, 1973, and 1997. Source: United States Department of Commerce, *County Business Patterns*, various years.

sectors such as apparel have declined just as quickly. In part, these changes are associated with the process of globalization, with increased international trade and economic specialization (Dicken 1998). Super-imposed on these shifts in the economic base, the nature of industry organization has also altered as many firms have abandoned Fordist mass-production strategies in favor of post-Fordist alternatives such as flexible manufacturing.

The trends noted above have significantly impacted the character of work in the United States, the demand for specific skills, and the incomes of different groups in the population. Gittelman and Howell (1995) examine changes in the structure and quality of jobs in the United States from 1973 to 1990. They identify six "job contours," based on earnings and benefits, skill requirements, working conditions, employment status, and institutional setting, and they show that the distribution of employment shifted after 1973 to favor jobs in the highest job contour, largely at the expense of jobs in medium contours, typi-cally blue-collar jobs. Levine (1996) also summarizes evidence of an increase in skill levels within the United States workforce. This is typically attributed to changes in the mix of industries and the growth of more skills-intensive sectors, to changes in the occupational distrib-ution within sectors, and to the upgrading of skill requirements within individual jobs (Howell and Wolff 1991).

Increasing specialization in the United States economy favors those with the right skills and passes the costs of adjustment to those at the lower end of the skills hierarchy. This too represents a significant shift. Levy (1998) notes that in the 1950s mechanization of agriculture displaced large numbers of relatively low-skilled farm laborers in the United States South. Many of these workers were able to find higher-paying factory jobs. At the close of the second half of the twentieth century, less-skilled unemployed workers faced a much more difficult time finding jobs, especially those paying a "living wage". Gittelman and Howell (1995) also examine the impact of the changing character of work on different groups. They show how the costs of adjustment were borne more heavily by black and Hispanic men and women (see also Wilson 1987).

Closely related to these changes in the nature of employment, the distribution of incomes and the trajectories of blue- and white-collar wages have altered markedly over the postwar period. From the end of the Great Depression through the early 1970s income inequality in the

United States declined significantly. Since the mid-1970s, however, income inequality has grown, with the wealthiest 5 percent of families enjoying over 20 percent of all wage income (excluding capital gains) in the country in 1996 (Levy 1998). Bound and Johnson (1992) review competing explanations of growing wage inequality over the 1980s and find that skilled-labor-biased technological change was the most important determinant.

As income inequality has grown, average wage levels have remained largely unchanged for an extraordinarily long time. Between 1950 and 1973, private non-agricultural real hourly earnings increased at an annual average compound rate of 2.05 percent. However, since 1973, the trajectory of real hourly earnings has been downward. Indeed, in 1997 real hourly wages for private non-agricultural workers in the United States were lower than in 1966 (Bureau of Labor Statistics, various years). The decline in average real wages since the late 1960s/early 1970s is linked to the slowdown of productivity growth in the 1970s, to the rapid decline in demand for semi-skilled manufacturing workers in the 1970s and 1980s, and to a decline in rates of unionization, from around 25 percent in the mid-1970s to about 14 percent by 1997 (Levy 1998; and see Chapter 7, this volume).

Regional restructuring

Between 1951 and 1997 approximately 67 million workers were added to the United States economy in private sector (non-government) jobs: an expansion of 179 percent. These new jobs were disproportionately located in the south and west of the country so that the geography of United States employment at the end of the twentieth century looked quite different from that of only fifty years earlier. Figure 6.6 shows total private sector employment in the nine census regions of the United States in 1951 and 1997. What is quite striking from this figure is the relative decline of the old industrial core, comprising the New England, Mid-Atlantic and East North Central census regions. This decline is often described as the snowbelt–sunbelt shift. The South Atlantic and Pacific census regions experienced the largest absolute increases in their share of United States employment in the second half of the twentieth century, and the Mountain region recorded the greatest relative growth, starting as it did from a relatively small employment base.

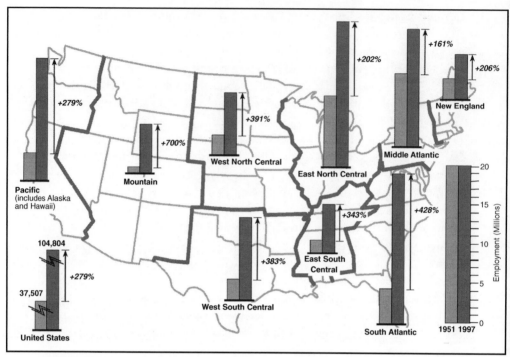

Figure 6.6 Regional Distribution of Employment, 1951 and 1997. Source: United States Department of Commerce, *County Business Patterns*, various years.

It is surprising that we know relatively little about the determinants of the changing geography of United States employment. We can begin to account for these changes by separating the impacts of the changing mix of industries found in the United States economy (see above) from region-specific influences on employment growth and decline. This is conventionally done using the technique of shift-share analysis (Fothergill and Gudgin 1979; Barff and Knight 1988; Rigby 1992). Shift-share analysis is a descriptive technique that allows net changes in a region's employment (or some other variable) to be decomposed into three elements: that due to the national rate of employment growth; that due to the industrial structure of a region; and a residual element that may be interpreted as indicating the locational advantages or disadvantages of a regional economy. The results of a shift-share analysis of employment change across the nine United States census regions are shown in Table 6.1. The analysis used industry data defined at the one-digit level of the Standard Industrial Classification.

Table 6.1 Shift share analysis of United States employment change, 1951–97

Census regions	Total shift	Proportional shift	Differential shift
ENC	−6947.2 (−76.6)	−2406.3 (−26.5)	−4540.8 (−50.1)
ESC	1149.5 (64.0)	−94.2 (−5.2)	1243.7 (69.2)
MA	−11071.0 (−118.4)	−528.6 (−5.7)	−10542.0 (−112.7)
MTN	3810.0 (420.7)	531.7 (58.7)	3278.3 (362.0)
NE	−2043.2 (−72.9)	−894.6 (−31.9)	−1148.6 (−41.0)
PAC	5295.0 (144.9)	1642.2 (44.9)	3652.8 (100.0)
SA	6657.1 (149.3)	256.7 (5.8)	6400.3 (143.5)
WNC	314.3 (11.5)	675.1 (24.8)	−360.8 (−13.2)
WSC	2835.0 (103.6)	817.7 (29.9)	2017.3 (73.7)

Notes: Absolute shift-share values are presented in thousands of workers. Figures in parentheses are percentages. The one-digit industries employed in the analysis were: agriculture, forestry, and fishing; mining; construction; manufacturing; transportation and public utilities; wholesale trade; retail trade; finance, insurance, and real estate; services. ENC is East North Central; ESC is East South Central; MA is Mid Atlantic; MTN is Mountain; NE is New England; PAC is Pacific; SA is South Atlantic; WNC is West North Central; WSC is West South Central. Source: United States Bureau of the Census: *County Business Patterns*, various years.

Table 6.1 shows absolute and relative shift-share components (in parentheses) for the nine census regions of the United States. The total shift represents the employment gain/loss in a region relative to that expected on the basis of national employment growth. Thus, a positive(negative) total shift indicates that the region grew faster(slower) than the nation over the period in question. As an example, the total shift value for New England means that this region had 2.043 million fewer jobs in 1997 than would have been the case had the region grown at the same rate as the nation between 1951 and 1997. In relative terms, New England gained 72.9 percent fewer jobs between 1951 and 1997 than would have been predicted on the basis of national growth. The total shift values are the sum of the proportional and differential shift values. The proportional shift measures the impact of changes in the region's industry mix on employment growth/decline. A positive(negative) proportional shift indicates that a region's employment is concentrated in industries that are growing faster(slower) than average. The differential shift measures the performance of industries in a region relative to their performance in the nation and thus is thought to index regional competitiveness. A positive(negative) differential shift means that the region is performing better(worse) than the nation on an industry-by-industry basis.

The shift-share results indicate the poor performance of the snowbelt after 1951. They also show that while employment in the snowbelt was concentrated in industries that have declined over the postwar period, the main reason for the decline of the old industrial core appears to be inefficiencies in production at the industry level. In contrast, sunbelt census regions have all performed better than the nation since 1951 in terms of employment. The strong performance of the sunbelt was buoyed by an advantageous industry mix, except in the East South Central census region. The large, positive differential shift values across most of the sunbelt indicates that region-specific advantages were the driving force behind the relative employment gains of this region.

These results are consistent with those providing a more disaggregate analysis of individual manufacturing sectors. For example, Rigby (1992) details the manufacturing employment gains of the sunbelt and shows that these were associated with rapid improvements in productivity. A similar story of relative decline in the snowbelt and growth in the sunbelt is also evident in the manufacturing capital stock data of Table 6.2. These data suggest that the relative demise of the old manufacturing core was a gradual process that began at the end of the Second World War. While the analysis of employment shifts shows some acceleration in the flight of jobs from the sunbelt in the 1970s, there is little such evidence in the capital stock data. The capital stocks of the Mid Atlantic, East North Central and West South Central census regions were also found to be older than average in 1989 (the average age of capital is reported in parentheses), further evidence of an older pattern of investment and older technologies (see also Varaiya and Wiseman 1981).

Table 6.2 The regional distribution of manufacturing net capital stocks

Census regions	1955^P	1961^T	1965^P	1970^T	1973^P	1976^T	1979^P	1982^T	1989^P
ENC	32.20	31.88	31.02	30.19	29.41	28.44	27.27	26.32	24.56 (8.38)
ESC	4.60	5.00	5.45	6.10	6.25	6.58	6.84	6.97	6.84 (7.76)
MA	20.93	20.33	19.66	18.53	18.09	17.24	16.10	15.16	14.18 (8.50)
MTN	1.97	2.12	2.13	2.02	2.21	2.42	2.49	2.67	3.10 (7.47)
NE	6.22	5.86	5.69	5.54	5.36	5.42	5.32	5.33	5.69 (7.59)
PAC	9.26	9.80	10.15	10.20	10.03	10.03	10.19	10.89	12.26 (7.47)
SA	11.34	11.42	12.02	12.70	13.54	13.78	13.48	13.41	14.34 (7.50)
WNC	5.21	5.19	5.34	5.10	5.23	5.26	5.65	5.76	6.22 (7.66)
WSC	8.17	8.39	8.54	9.62	9.87	10.83	12.67	13.48	12.81 (8.34)

Notes: Superscripts P and T denote business cycle peaks and troughs, respectively. All figures are proportions of the national total in the given year. The average age of capital is measured in years. Source: Rigby (1995).

Another way of illustrating the regional shifts in manufacturing activity within the United States economy is to examine spatial patterns of plant entry and exit. Figures 6.7a–d show state variations in the proportion of manufacturing plants that are classified as incumbents, entrants, and exits. These data are averaged over the quinquennial census periods between 1963 and 1992. Entrants are defined as plants that are less than five years old. Exiting plants are defined as those that go out of business between a pair of census years, and incumbents are plants that remain in business at the start and at the end of each inter-census period. The figures allocate states to one of five quintiles, in each case darker shading represents an increasing share of plants in the respective category.

The geographical distribution of the share of incumbent plants is striking, as Figure 6.7a illustrates. State shares of incumbent plants range from 31 percent to 53 percent. The traditional manufacturing core of the United States has an above-average share of incumbent plants. Nine states have shares of incumbent plants that are more than one standard deviation greater than the United States average of 44.531 percent for the period 1963 to 1992; all are located in the snow-belt. Across the south and west of the country, the share of incumbent

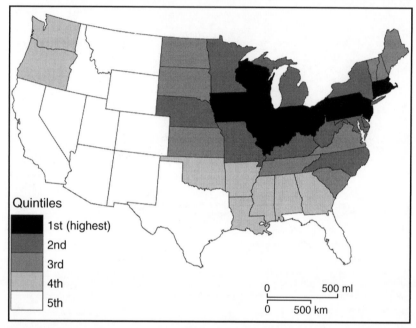

Figure 6.7a The share of incumbent plants in manufacturing, 1963–92. Source: United States Department of Commerce, United States Bureau of the Census, Longitudinal Research Database.

plants is below average. Nine states have shares of incumbent plants that are one or two standard deviations below the mean and all these states are found outside the old manufacturing core.

Figures 6.7b and 6.7c show the average shares of entering and exiting plants by state between 1963 and 1992. As might be expected, these figures show broadly similar variations to the map of incumbents. The proportion of entering and exiting plants is typically higher than average in the sunbelt and lower than average in the snowbelt, though there are some notable exceptions. State shares of entering plants range from 23 percent to 42 percent, and shares of exiting plants range from 22 percent to 30 percent. The pattern of entry is

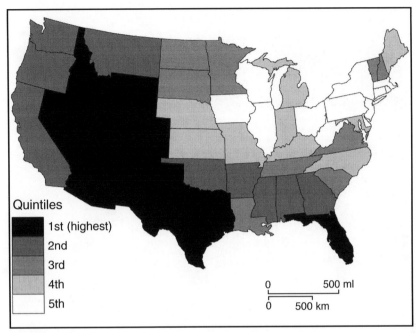

Figure 6.7b The rate of manufacturing plant entry, 1963–92. Source: United States Department of Commerce, United States Bureau of the Census, Longitudinal Research Database.

clearer than the pattern of exit. Seven states have shares of entering plants more than one standard deviation above the United States average of 29.808 percent, and all these states are located in the south and west. Nine states have entry shares more than one standard deviation below the United States average. These nine states are all found in the old manufacturing core. In the traditional manufacturing belt, the share of exiting plants in different states is quite variable. Rates of plant exit tend to be highly correlated with entry rates and, to a lesser extent, the overall vitality of the manufacturing sector. Thus, relatively low shares of exiting plants in Wisconsin, Illinois, Ohio, and Connecticut reflect low entry rates rather than manufacturing buoyancy. At the same time, relatively high rates of exit, coupled with average rates of entry in New York and Maine, signify substantial declines in the population of manufacturing plants. Across much of the south and west, relatively high exit rates are related to above average rates of entry (Figure 6.7d). Overall, these results show that manufacturing plant turnover is significantly lower in the snowbelt than in the sunbelt

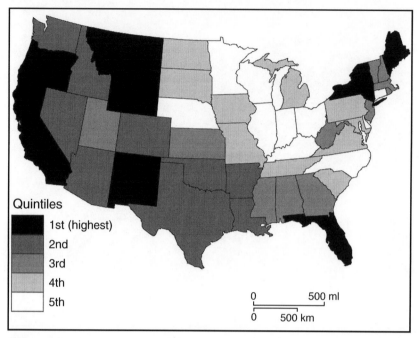

Figure 6.7c The rate of manufacturing plant exit, 1963–92. Source: United States Department of Commerce, United States Bureau of the Census, Longitudinal Research Database.

states of the United States. Consequently, the average age of manufacturing establishments should be somewhat greater than average in the traditional manufacturing core.

Table 6.3 Regional and temporal variations in the manufacturing rate of profit

Year	ENC	ESC	MA	MTN	NE	PAC	SA	WNC	WSC	US
1963	46.5	48.6	44.5	38.5	40.9	48.9	44.5	52.8	34.8	45.7
1982	34.5	26.9	29.8	29.2	22.3	35.8	30.5	38.7	22.9	30.7
1996	36.2	44.7	36.8	68.7	37.1	47.2	48.5	53.4	37.3	42.4

Notes: The figures shown are all percentages. The profit rate is defined as (value added − total wages)/(net capital stock + owned inventory).
Source: United States Bureau of the Census: *Annual Survey of Manufactures and Census of Manufactures*, various years.

These broad regional shifts of United States manufacturing activity are, in part, a response to regional variations in economic performance,

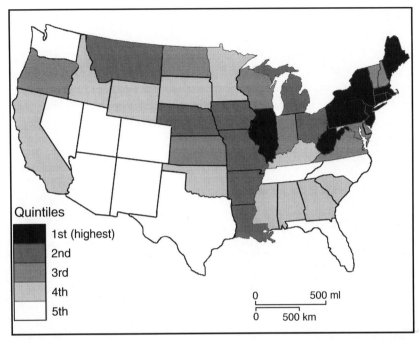

Figure 6.7d The ratio of manufacturing plant exit to plant entry, 1963–92. Source: United States Department of Commerce, United States Bureau of the Census, Longitudinal Research Database.

particularly the rate of profit. Table 6.3 shows manufacturing profit rates in the nine census regions of the United States in 1963, 1982, and 1996. It is clear from the table that there are significant spatial and temporal variations in manufacturing profitability. On average, manufacturing performance has been worse in snowbelt states (those of the NE, MA, and ENC census regions) than in sunbelt states, and the difference between snowbelt and sunbelt performance widened after 1963.

One of the key components of the rate of profit is wages. Table 6.4 reveals regional differences in average (mean) real hourly wage rates for manufacturing production workers. Significant differences between the census regions are apparent. In 1963, the average wage rate for production workers in South Atlantic manufacturing was only 71 percent of that in the Pacific region. In 1996, the average wage rate for production workers in South Atlantic manufacturing was only 78 percent of that in the East North Central region. Wage differences at the state level are even more pronounced: in 1963, the average hourly manufacturing wage in North Carolina was only 52 percent of that in Alaska; in 1996, the average hourly manufacturing wage in South Dakota was only 60 percent of that in Michigan. While income differences at the state level appear to be converging for all economic activity (Carlino and Mills 1996; Rey and Montouri 1999), within manufacturing they are not: between 1963 and 1996, the coefficient of variation for average hourly manufacturing wages across the fifty states increased from 0.061 to 0.144.

Table 6.4 Regional and temporal variations in real hourly manufacturing wages

Year	ENC	ESC	MA	MTN	NE	PAC	SA	WNC	WSC	US
1963	10.78	8.89	9.68	10.21	8.86	10.88	7.55	9.64	8.55	9.57
1982	11.81	8.66	9.82	9.90	9.00	10.54	8.30	10.40	9.81	9.98
1996	12.02	9.52	10.69	9.95	11.09	10.37	9.43	10.42	9.89	10.74

Notes: Real hourly wages are wages/production hours worked in manufacturing (in 1987 dollars).
Source: United States Bureau of the Census: *Annual Survey of Manufactures and Census of Manufactures*, various years.

As overall income levels converged across United States states, intraregional income levels diverged, largely as a result of growing inequalities between central cities and suburban areas after the Second World War. In 1950 a large proportion of manufacturing and service sector jobs was tied to central city locations by accessibility and the high cost of transport. Middle-income as well as low-income families still resided close to the city center and their places of employment and, consequently, median incomes of central-city families were only slightly lower than those of suburban families (Long and Dahmann 1980). However, by the early 1990s the median household income of inner-city residents was about 25 percent lower than that of suburban residents (United States Bureau of the Census, *County and City Data Book*, 1995).

The relative decline of the inner city and the well-being of its residents reflects a complex mix of factors (see Wilson 1987; Waldinger 1996). Probably most important, from the 1950s on, the suburban relocation of people and jobs accelerated dramatically, fuelled by new home construction, highway development, and rising automobile use (Table 6.5). Between 1950 and 1990, while the United States population expanded by 64.4 percent, the population of the fifty largest cities in

1950 increased by only 1.8 percent. Over the same period, the suburban (non-central city) population of these cities grew by 143 percent. A similar picture of inner-city de-industrialization emerges from a survey of manufacturing data (Bluestone and Harrison 1982). Initially a slow trickle, the exodus of manufacturing jobs from the inner city became a torrent after the economic slowdown of the mid-1970s, particularly in the older cities of the manufacturing heartland. While the United States manufacturing sector added about 1.7 million jobs between 1950 and 1990 (about 10.6 percent of the 1950 total), the largest fifty cities of 1950 lost close to one-third of their manufacturing employment, at the same time as suburban areas around these fifty cities experienced manufacturing job growth of about 160 percent.

Table 6.5 Inner-city versus suburban change, 1950–90

Region	1950–90		
	Population change	Manufacturing employment change	Total employment change
Largest 50 cities in 1950	1.77	–30.31	10.10
Suburban areas of the largest 50 cities	143.00	164.84	201.31
US total	64.38	10.53	156.56

Notes: Suburban data equal the county minus the city figures for the counties in which the largest cities are located. The figures are in percentages.
Source: United States Bureau of the Census: *County and City Data Book*, various years.

In terms of overall employment the fifty largest cities in 1950 performed somewhat better, adding 10 percent to their employment levels by 1990. However, the new jobs created were typically white collar and divided into two sorts: relatively high-skilled, high-wage jobs demanding higher education, and low-skilled jobs that demanded very little and paid the same in return. Because large numbers of skilled workers had left the inner city to chase employment in the suburbs, the disadvantaged low-skilled, non-white, and increasingly immigrant populations that remained were ill-suited to perform the more highly-skilled jobs, giving rise to the so-called spatial mismatch problem (Holzer 1991).

Postwar prosperity was not enjoyed by the majority of inner-city residents. Indeed, poverty in the United States has increasingly become an urban problem: whereas in the 1970s most of the "poor" lived in rural or non-metropolitan areas, by the 1990s almost 80 percent of the "poor" lived in metropolitan areas (Levy 1998). In 1990, the largest cities of the United States had poverty rates on average over 50 percent greater than the United States as a whole, they experience significantly higher than average rates of unemployment, and inner-city residents especially were plagued by a host of social ills that threatened to undermine much hope of any future at all (United States Census Bureau, *County and City Data Book*, various years).

Conclusion

Over the second half of the twentieth century, the United States economy underwent significant change. At the end of the Second World War United States producers dominated the world economy in terms of manufactured output, merchandise trade, and foreign investment. By the close of the twentieth century the relative share of the United States in world manufacturing production had declined close to 50 percent from its postwar peak, its trade dominance was severely weakened, particularly on the export side, and from sourcing almost half the world's FDI in 1960 the United States was now sourcing under 25 percent. In part these changes have resulted from the globalization of the world economy, by the increasing fragmentation of production, and the geographic separation of different stages of work. These changes make it much more difficult to measure accurately the size of a national economy as the production chains of multinational corporations extend across many countries, the value of trade data is inflated or deflated by the cross-hauling of commodities at different stages of manufacture, and as capital flows increasingly rapidly, and in increasing volume, from one financial center to another.

Alongside the changing international position of the United States, the domestic economy has witnessed profound shifts, from the relative decline of the manufacturing sector and the rise of the services industry, to the geographic realignment of population and jobs in new economic spaces, particularly across the south and west of the country. Inner cities across the country also suffered as economic activity increasingly moved to exurban locations. Of course, these shifts in the structure and geography of the United States economy have not impacted the population evenly. In general, the new economy favors skilled workers, in white-collar sectors outside the old manufacturing centers of the country. The relatively disadvantaged population expanded rapidly through the late 1970s and early 1980s as the structural adjustments described above accelerated. The rapid economic growth of the last decade of the twentieth century ameliorated the disparities to some extent, spreading growth more broadly across the nation. How the profits of the 1990s were reinvested in the United States economy would determine the character and the beneficiaries of economic development at the beginning of the twenty-first century.

References

Aglietta, M. (1979), *A Theory of Capitalist Regulation*, London: New Left Books.

Amin, A. (1994), "Post-Fordism: Models, Fantasies and Phantoms of Transition," in A. Amin (ed.), *Post-Fordism: A Reader*, Oxford: Blackwell, pp. 1–39.

Barff, R., and P. Knight (1988), "Dynamic Shift-Share Analysis," *Growth and Change*, 19, pp. 1–10.

Baumol, W., R. Nelson, and E. Wolff (eds.) (1994), *Convergence of Productivity: Cross National Studies and Historical Evidence*, New York: Oxford University Press.

Beyers, W. (1989), *The Producer Services and Economic Development in the United States: The Last Decade*, Washington, DC: Economic Development Administration.

Bluestone, B., and B. Harrison (1982), *The Deindustrialization of America*, New York: Basic Books.

Bound, J., and G. Johnson (1992), "Changes in the Structure of Wages in the 1980s: An Evaluation of Alternative Explanations," *American Economic Review*, 82, pp. 371–92.

Braudel, F. (1984), *Civilization and Capitalism*, 3 vols., New York: Harper and Row.

Carlino, G., and L. Mills (1996), "Convergence and the United States States: A Time-Series Analysis," *Journal of Regional Science*, 36, pp. 597–616.

Daniels, P. (1993), *Service Industries in the World Economy*, Oxford: Blackwell.

Dertouzos, M., R. Lester, and R. Solow (1989), *Made in America: Regaining the Productive Edge*, Cambridge, MA: MIT Press.

Dicken, P. (1998), *Global Shift*, 3rd ed., London: Chapman.

Fagerberg, J. (1994), "Technology and International Differences in Growth Rates," *Journal of Economic Literature*, 32, pp. 1147–75.

Fothergill, S., and G. Gudgin (1979), "In Defence of Shift-Share," *Urban Studies*, 16, pp. 309–19.

Freeman, C., and C. Perez (1988), "Structural Crises of Adjustment: Business Cycles and Investment Behavior," in G. Dosi, C. Freeman, R. Nelson, G. Silverberg, G. and L. Soete (eds.), *Technical Change and Economic Theory*, London: Pinter, pp. 38–66.

Gertler, M. (1988), "The Limits to Flexibility: Comments on the Post-Fordist Vision of Production and Its Geography," *Transactions, Institute of British Geographers*, 13, pp. 419–32.

Gittelman, M., and D. Howell (1995), "Changes in the Structure and Quality of

Jobs in the United States," *Industrial and Labor Relations Review*, 48, pp. 420–40.

Holzer, H. (1991), "The Spatial Mismatch: What Has the Evidence Shown," *Urban Studies*, 28, pp. 105–22.

Howell, D., and E. Wolff (1991), "Trends in the Growth and Distribution of Skills in the United States Workplace, 1960–1985," *Industrial and Labor Relations Review*, 44, pp. 4–21.

Levine, L. (1996), "The Changing Skill Requirements of Manufacturing Jobs," in I. Garvardina (ed.), *Jobs in America*, Commack, NY: Nova Science Publishers Inc., pp. 11–24.

Levy, F. (1998), *The New Dollars and Dreams*, New York: The Russell Sage Foundation.

Lipietz, A. (1986), "Behind the Crisis: The Exhaustion of a Regime of Accumulation. A 'Regulation School' Perspective on Some French Empirical Work," *Review of Radical Political Economics*, 18, pp. 13–32.

Long, L., and D. Dahmann (1980), "The City-Suburb Income Gap: Is It Being Narrowed by a Back-to-the-City Movement?" United States Bureau of the Census, Special Demographic Analyses, CDS-80-1, Washington, DC: United States Government Printing Office.

Mandel, E. (1978), *Late Capitalism*, London: Verso.

Moffitt, M. (1983), *The World's Money: International Banking from Bretton Woods to the Brink of Insolvency*, New York: Simon & Schuster.

Park, Y., and J. Zwick (1985), *International Banking in Theory and Practice*, Reading, MA: Addison-Wesley.

Piore, M., and C. Sabel (1984), *The Second Industrial Divide*, New York: Basic Books.

Rey, S., and B. Montouri (1999), "United States Regional Income Convergence: A Spatial Econometric Perspective," *Regional Studies*, 33, pp. 143–56.

Rigby, D. (1992), "The Impact of Output and Productivity Changes on Employment," *Growth and Change*, 23, Fall, pp. 403–25.

Rigby, D. (1995), "Investment, Capital Stocks and the Age of Capital in U.S. regions," *Growth and Change*, 26, Fall, pp. 387–414.

Schoenberger, E. (1988), "From Fordism to Flexible Accumulation: Technology, Competitive Strategies and International location," *Environment and Planning D: Society and Space*, 6, pp. 245–62.

Solomon, R. (1977), *The International Monetary System, 1945–1976*, New York: Harper and Row.

Triffin, R. (1969), *Gold and the Dollar Crisis*, New Haven: Yale University Press.

UNCTAD (1996), *Trade and Development Report 1996*, New York: United Nations.

United States Department of Commerce, *Bureau of Labor Statistics*, various years, Washington, DC: United States Government Printing Office.

United States Department of Commerce: *County and City Data Book*, various years, Washington, DC: United States Government Printing Office.

United States Department of Commerce: *County Business Patterns*, various years, Washington, DC: United States Government Printing Office.

United States Department of Commerce, Bureau of Economic Analysis, *Survey of Current Business*, various years, Washington, DC: United States Government Printing Office.

United States Department of Commerce, Bureau of the Census, *Annual Survey of*

Manufactures, various years, Washington, DC: United States Government Printing Office.

Varaiya, P., and M. Wiseman (1981), "Investment and Employment in Manufacturing in United States Metropolitan Areas, 1960–1976," *Regional Science and Urban Economics*, 11, pp. 431–69.

Waldinger, R. (1996), *Still the Promised City?* Cambridge, MA: Harvard University Press.

Wallerstein, I. (1979), *The Capitalist World Economy: Essays*, New York: Cambridge University Press.

Walter, A. (1991), *World Power and World Money: The Role of Hegemony and International Monetary Order*, New York: St. Martin's Press.

Watts, H. (1987), *Industrial Geography*, Harlow, Essex: Longman.

Webber, M. (1991), "The Contemporary Transition," *Environment and Planning D: Society and Space*, 9, pp. 165–82.

Webber, M., and D. Rigby (1996), *The Golden Age Illusion*, New York: Guilford.

Wilson, W. (1987), *The Truly Disadvantaged*, Chicago: Chicago University Press.

PART III

Social and cultural dimensions of Americanness

CHAPTER 7

"With liberty and justice for all": Negotiating freedom and fairness in the American income distribution

Janet E. Kodras*

The American Revolution was certainly no call to economic equality in the sense that the French and Russian Revolutions were. Indeed, it was in many respects a revolution undertaken by some of the most favored and powerful interests in their own behalf. Independence was about increasing their opportunities not about equalizing material conditions for all. Nevertheless there was an egalitarian impulse within the ranks of the revolutionaries and this ideological current has episodically reappeared within American political life in the years since, from the Jackson administration in the late 1820s to the Roosevelt New Deal years of the 1930s and the Johnson Great Society programs of the mid-1960s. This approach has emphasized that extreme inequalities in incomes and wealth undermine the promise of political equality by limiting political access and participation and potentially threaten the political order by deepening class resentments and producing regional and local differences in political power that can erupt in riot and rebellion. Of course, what is meant by poverty, justice, and inequality have varied over time and place as expectations and opportunities have changed. Persisting social and geographical patterns of poverty and income inequality, however, challenge the basic claim to the possibility of upward social mobility for all upon which the American story of individual advancement and prosperity rests. In this chapter, social geographer Janet E. Kodras contrasts the ways in which American conceptions of social justice and inequality have been framed with the actual ways in which incomes are distributed across the United States. She draws on David Harvey's relational concept of justice, that various arguments about what is and is not just must be related to the material conditions in which they are used, to address how the polarization of incomes and wealth in the United States takes place and is justified as just and proper. Kodras shows

*I wish to acknowledge the contributions of Mr. Christopher Cook for his assistance in data and literature searches for this study. Any errors remain my own.

how local social order, markets, government policies, and discourses about justice combine to produce patterns of poverty and inequality, using James Agee's book, *Let Us now Praise Famous Men* (1939), as her illustrative starting point. She maps income and poverty differentials across the United States and in comparison with some other countries, noting that rather than equalizing, incomes across the United States are increasingly polarized by class, race, sex, and place. But she also points to areas of persisting poverty – such as the Mississippi Delta region – and affluence – such as Northeastern suburban areas – strongly suggestive that place-based variation is neither temporary nor residual but can become "locked in" for considerable periods of time.

Wherever there is excessive wealth, there is also in the train of it excessive poverty, as when the sun is brightest, the shade is deepest.
Walter Savage Lander, 1850

The landscapes of American poverty are diverse, ranging from Chicago's infamous Henry Horner projects to the desolate hinterlands of American Indian reservations; from the wood shacks of the Mississippi Delta to the gutted factory zones of the industrial heartland; from the burnt-out barrios of south-central Los Angeles to the remote farms of Maine; and, to an increasing extent, hidden behind the facade of suburban tract houses, with paint peeling and the mortgage overdue. The landscapes of American wealth are equally varied, ranging from the patrician homes of Philadelphia's Main Line to Texas ranches stretching across counties, from the sun-bleached palaces of Palm Beach to the million-dollar log cabins on the slopes of the Colorado Rockies. There are many ways to be poor and many ways to be rich in America.

Yet for all the visible evidence of disparity and indeed divergence in affluence levels, there is surprisingly little acknowledgment of the sharp contrast between the country's founding principles of justice and equality versus the realities of life sketched across the American landscape. There is even less recognition that the landscapes of wealth and poverty are mutually constituted, each materially produced in opposition to the other, creating a distinctly American form of spatial injustice (Figure 7.1; see also, Mitchell 1996; and Chapter 9, this volume). It is to be expected that a capitalist economy, where individuals are granted the liberty to compete for profit and advantage, would generate variable outcomes of affluence and reward. Inequality is inherent in

ARTIST AT LARGE BY RONALD SEARLE

THE BIG APPLE

Figure 7.1 Juxtapositions of wealth and poverty in the United States. Ronald Searle Cartoon originally appearing in *The New Yorker*, April 12, 1993. Reproduced by permission.

such a system, but the fact that the net worth of a single individual (Bill Gates, CEO of Microsoft, Inc.) currently exceeds the combined net worth of 40 percent of all Americans (106 million people) does raise questions about the degree of inequality deemed acceptable. How best to negotiate the freedom and fairness of competition in a capitalist political economy?

The purpose of this chapter is to examine reasons for the substantial and increasing economic disparities in American society, cast within changing notions of social justice. I begin with a discussion of the major forces shaping the American income distribution. I develop a conceptual framework to illustrate how material and discursive practices in the market, state, and civil society combine to generate a dynamic national map of affluence and poverty, whose contours are shaped by geographic variations in class, race, gender, and other social relations. I incorporate into the framework the perceptive work of David Harvey (1996) who defines social justice as a negotiated process, embedded in the material conditions of life. To illustrate how the conceptual frame helps to explain real-world situations, I present a brief case study of the changing global-to-local forces generating race and class injustice in a rural area of Alabama over the course of the twentieth century, drawing upon James Agee's extraordinary ethnographic work, *Let Us now Praise Famous Men* (1939) and other historical and contemporary documents.

I then broaden my illustration, applying the conceptual framework to examine recent trends and patterns in American income disparities that reflect changes in the nation's political economy and dominant notions of social justice over the last twenty-five years of the twentieth century. Here I link recent restructurings in the market and state to changing notions of acceptable disparities in the income distribution. I document the recent ascendance of "market justice" attending economic globalization and political neo-liberalism that attempts to justify growing differentials in affluence. I conclude by returning to the notion of social justice as a negotiable principle, raising questions about the particular forms of justice we will create in the future.

Understanding the forces affecting income disparities

In post-industrial capitalist countries such as the United States, affluence is gauged according to a household's control over economic resources, including both income (the flow of resources over time) and wealth (the stock of resources held at any one point in time). The extent to which society exhibits disparities in affluence is thus expressed as the distribution of incomes and the dispersion of assets across households.[1] In recent years, both income and assets have become increasingly polarized, as changes in the economy, political system, and society have reconfigured the distribution of resources, leaving an increasing number to struggle in destitution, the majority to stagnate despite a growing economy, and a select few to amass fortunes. To explain why this is happening, I begin with a general outline that identifies how these forces affect affluence levels.

Conceptual framework

The distribution of wealth and incomes across the American population is fundamentally influenced by material and discursive practices in the market, the state, and civil society that vary through time and across places.[2] First, the market has the greatest structural effect on affluence levels, as it contains the mechanisms (e.g. labor markets, capital markets, property markets) that distribute economic resources (e.g. wages, profits, dividends, capital gains). Although the market consists of many different entities (big business v small enterprises, transnational corporations v locally dependent firms) and sectors (agriculture, manufacturing, services), the motive of each is to secure profit and accumulate capital.

Second, the state affects affluence levels. The state consists of different institutions and agencies working at different levels of the federal hierarchy (e.g. national, state, local). In contrast to the single motive pursued in the market, the state plays a dual role in a liberal democracy: accumulation and legitimation. On the one hand, the state assists the market, by providing the conditions (e.g. stable monetary, legal, infrastructure, and defense systems) necessary for capital accumulation and economic growth. On the other hand, the state assists civil society, by providing the conditions (e.g. education, health and safety regulations, individual rights legislation) necessary to gain legitimacy from citizens and thus ensure a stable society. The state is under constant pressure to balance these two, often contradictory, roles in ways that simultaneously bolster the power of capital and yet protect the interests of citizens. Whereas a capitalist market system tends to concentrate income and wealth unevenly across society, the state either reinforces or counters this tendency, depending on the primacy of its accumulation or legitimation roles.

Third, the market and the state are not abstract forces; they are populated by actors who affect affluence levels through their decisions and practices. Specifically, each individual living in civil society is situated within complex social networks, finding personal affiliation within the coarse webbing of relations that broadly define the social order (e.g. class, race, gender, sexuality, religion, age relations) and the fine netting of relations experienced in everyday life (e.g. relations in the family, on the job, in the shopping mall, on the street).

These social relations are by definition unequal, granting privilege of position to some, disadvantage to others. In some cases, the inequality takes extreme forms of oppression, while in others the distinction is inconsequential. Power is vested in those who hold privilege of position in class, race, gender, and other social relations. Such power translates into a relative ability to control situations to one's advantage. In particular, corporate and government leaders have the greatest command and authority over American affluence levels and disparities, because their decision-making power in the market and state positions them to set wage levels, secure profits, and create legal rules over property rights, capital gains, minimum wage levels, interest rates, and the like. Individuals who are not in such positions of power may have an effect also, if they actively negotiate with corporate and political leaders through trade unions, voting, social movement activism, and so forth.

The aggregation of these individual decisions and negotiations imprints class differentials in power into the practices and institutions of the market and state that shape the American income distribution. Furthermore, power over the dispersion of incomes and wealth involves complex interactions of class with race, gender, and other social relations. Although these multifaceted differentials in control over affluence levels operate primarily through the market and the state, they saturate all arenas of American life, extending into the community and the home.

This ongoing negotiation between actors in civil society, using the market, state, and other arenas in a complex power play for advantage and reward, is called politics, in the broadest sense of the word. And one outcome of this negotiation at any given point in time is reflected in the distribution of wealth and incomes across American society. Further, the position of each individual within the national distribution is influenced, although by no means determined, by the relative advantage one holds in this intricate play of power defined by class, race, gender, and other social relations.

Fourth, the power to affect affluence levels is exerted through both material and discursive practices. The discussion to this point has focused on readily-identifiable material actions, whereby relatively powerful actors ultimately decide how economic resources (e.g. wages, profits, dividends, capital gains, private property, taxes, credits) are to be distributed. But those with the greatest control over these material processes also seek to justify their positions of power by deploying discursive practices. For example, private firms use advertising to create consumer demand for their products as an important discursive strategy to secure profit. Also, government agencies use the extensive public information systems at their disposal to persuade civil society that the state is working on its behalf. As these examples show, powerful actors in both private firms and public institutions seek to assure other individuals that the best interests of the market and the state are also and always the best interests of consumers and citizens. The powerful have disproportionate control over this societal discourse, imposing visions of the world that serve their own best interests, thus structuring perceptions of reality for others and framing the sense of what is possible. As a result, material and discursive forms of power are entwined, each influencing the other. Those with material power hold a discursive advantage, which then solidifies their power, making it difficult, although by no means impossible, for others to confront them by challenging the dominant discourse with effective counter-discourses.

The principle of justice is a key point of conflict within these discursive negotiations over the distribution of American wealth and incomes (Harvey 1973, 1996; White 1991). This point requires some explanation, as it is essential to understanding how inequalities in affluence levels are justified and naturalized. While most people can readily and cleanly define justice to mean equity, fairness, impartiality, righteousness, and the like, complexities arise upon deeper reflection. The history of Western thought has produced many different theories of justice (e.g. egalitarian, utilitarian, positivist, intuitionalist, social contract, natural rights, relative deprivation, etc.) but, precisely because these are theories of justice, they collectively contain within them the societal rules for ascertaining what is "right." The problem is that there exists no overarching and universally accepted means for judging the relative "rightness" of these various theories. One recent response to this dilemma is the postmodern critique of all such universal theories of justice, which argues against the imposition of any one principle of justice in a world of great diversity. Postmodernists further argue that "we are far too ready to attach the word 'just' to cognitive, ethical and political arrangements that are better understood as phenomena of power and that oppress, neglect, marginalize, and discipline others" (as summarized in White 1991: 115). While contributing the important point that all theories of justice embed power relations within them, the postmodern position easily devolves into a situation where any charge of "injustice" is just a "localized and contingent complaint," as its distrust of universal principles leaves no means for distinguishing the depth and degree of oppression (Harvey 1996: 342; also, White 1991).

David Harvey (1996) articulates this tension between universal and particularist notions of justice and then provides the key to their resolution. He agrees that the universal application of any concept of justice creates injustice, as it is a discursive strategy of the powerful over others:

> too many colonial peoples have suffered at the hands of western imperialism's particular justice, too many African-Americans have suffered at the hand of the white man's justice, too many women from the justice imposed by a patriarchal order and too many workers from the justice imposed by capitalists, to make the concept anything other than problematic. (Harvey 1996: 342)

On the other hand, he argues against the postmodern obliteration of societal principles:

> at the end of a road of infinite regret for any founding act of violence, of questioning the superimposition of singular rules in a situation of infinite heterogeneity, and insisting upon open-endedness about what justice might mean, there lies at best a void or at worst a rather ugly world in which the needs of the exploiters or oppressors . . . can be regarded as "just" on equivalent terms with those of their victims. (Harvey 1996: 347)

To resolve this tension between the universal and the particular, Harvey advances a relational concept of justice, which holds that discursive representations of justice must be critically examined in relation to the larger material conditions in which they are deployed. He argues that concepts of justice are developed and debated through a process of negotiation between actors with varying levels of power in the larger political economy, each seeking to impose the concept serving its own material best interests as the dominant societal notion of justice. Applied to the contemporary capitalist political economy, Harvey sees this negotiation as a class struggle, although it is rarely perceived as such in the larger society. In particular, capitalists have a vested interest in promoting a notion of justice that favors profit making in the market:

> Just desserts, it has long been argued by the ideologues of free-market capitalism (from Adam Smith onwards), are best arrived at through competitively organized, price-fixing markets in which entrepreneurs are entitled to hang on to the profit engendered by their efforts. There is then no need for explicit theoretical, political, or social argument over what is or is not socially just because social justice is whatever is delivered by the market. Each "factor of production" (land, labor, and capital), for example, will receive its marginal rate of return, its just reward, according to its contribution to production. The role of government should be confined to making sure that markets function freely. (Harvey 1996: 343)

There is an alarming and intimidating beauty to this argument. It is discourse presented as being above discourse – advancing a particular form of justice that appears to be the natural result of abstract forces in the market rather than the self-interested result of concrete practices by the powerful. Further, it is discourse holding that there is no need for discourse, thus attempting to silence any counter-argument that might challenge it. No wonder it is difficult to detect and comprehend discursive strategies influencing the distribution of incomes and wealth in American society.

Harvey goes on to argue that the most effective rebuttal to the "rough justice of the market" is to confront the discourse favoring capitalists' interests in profit making with a counter-discourse emphasizing civilian rights to adequate compensation, health, safety, and dignity. He emphasizes that this discursive confrontation "is not the arbitration between competing claims according to some universal principle of justice, but class struggle over the particular conception of justice and rights which shall be applied to a given situation" (1996: 345).

With some modification, Harvey's relational concept of justice makes a key contribution to the conceptual framework I present here regarding disparities in American affluence. As we have seen, ongoing material and discursive negotiations between actors in civil society – using the market, state, and other arenas in a complex power play for advantage and reward – are reflected in the distribution of wealth and incomes across American society. Ascertaining the justice of these practices and their outcomes is a crucial aspect of the discursive negotiations. And in these, powerful decision makers in the market tend to hold advantage over other civilians trying to counter the dominant market–justice paradigm.

The state, given its dual role in assisting the power of capital even as it protects the interests of civil society, plays an important part in this discursive conflict over what justice means. Due to the intertwining of economic and political power in American society, capital has an advantage in aligning the state with its interests. Part of this advantage is gained by discursively deploying the notion inherent in the market–justice paradigm that the government's role should be limited to assisting the market. And yet, other forces in civil society can exploit the state's dual function to ensure that the state protects against market excesses in a broader support of human rights. It is important to recognize that this discursive confrontation over justice is not a simple transaction between equal and competing claims, bartering for the support of a neutral and arbitrary state. The state is itself a powerful force in American life, so much so in fact that its support can be decisive in confrontations over the principle of justice. For example, it is particularly difficult for civilian groups to challenge the combined force created when the state aligns with capital in a dual projection of the market paradigm of justice, given the state's self-perpetuated image of neutrality. Although discursive practices (such as the strategic representation of justice) are more difficult to detect than material practices (such as minimum wage laws), both play an important role in affecting the distribution of wealth and incomes in American society.

Fifth and finally, to understand how material and discursive practices in the market, state, and other arenas intersect with power hierarchies in civil society to affect affluence levels, it is necessary to consider these interactions in particular places and times. Aside from the indisputable point that inequality is inherent in a capitalist political economy, the role of the market and state in generating disparities in affluence cannot be studied in the abstract, as these take concrete forms and perform specific functions according to the particular place and time in which they are embedded. Specifically, each place at a given time consists of a distinct local social order, a particular pattern of inequality defined by overlapping power differentials in class, race, gender, and other social relations. The local social order is created through the interaction of material processes and discursive practices. Material conditions in the local political economy structure the types of jobs and other opportunities available to people with certain attributes and skills, creating local patterns of affluence and reward. The particular power relations thus embedded in this local social order then affect the nature of discursive practices. The principle of justice is a critical, although often submerged, issue in these discursive negotiations, as groups with differing interests and power within the local political economy each seek to impose notions of justice that serve their own purposes.

The relatively powerful have an advantage in articulating what is an acceptable and just distribution of incomes and wealth in the locale, although the particular forms and degree of power generated in the local political economy greatly affect the outcome. Sometimes, power is extreme and unquestioned; other times, subordinate groups successfully project an alternate sense of fairness. Sometimes this discursive confrontation over justice is drawn along class lines; other times the struggle is defined by race or gender, or by religion, language, or other social divisions. Sometimes, multiple forms of oppression coalesce into a forceful attack on an intolerable oppressor; other times, a difference of opinion is difficult to discern.

Whoever prevails, the outcome of this discursive negotiation then feeds back into material conditions, as locally accepted notions of justice help to produce and reproduce patterns of inequality and differentials in power. For example, the market–justice paradigm driving income disparities, when combined with exclusionary practices such as racial discrimination and sexism, fracture affluence levels along fine lines, creating multiple and overlapping forms of inequality. The particular mix of these discursive justifications of inequality vary substantially from place to place across the United States, shaping mechanisms in the market, state, and other arenas that influence whether the distribution of affluence is broadly egalitarian or is sharply divided by class, race, and gender.

Material patterns of inequality and discursive notions of justice become embedded in place and over time, naturalizing the local sense of the appropriate distribution of wealth and incomes in an ongoing "justice-ification" of power differentials. In fact, inequalities in the local social order get formed through specific exclusionary practices that emerge within the particular structures of the local political economy and then take on a life of their own, as they become generally accepted "without misunderstanding" (Harvey 1996: 332). When these power differentials become naturalized, it is difficult for people living their everyday lives to discern that the local social order is socially constructed to serve particular sets of interests and that the present circumstances can be changed. Yet the potential for change is always there.

One key strategy used by subordinate groups to confront the locally dominant representation of justice is to look to other local places and to the regional, national, and global scales, searching for relevant models of justice that hold elsewhere. Indeed, although the material and discursive practices affecting affluence levels are specific to place, they are by no means generated solely within a given place, but are instead developed through an evolving relationship of that particular place to the larger world. For example, patterns of inequality in a given place are formed by the material position of the locality within the regional, national, and global political economy, as its specialization in particular industries and occupations affects affluence levels and disparities. By the same token, local discourse over the justice of these disparities does not develop in isolation, but is instead informed by multiple concepts of justice filtering in from other local places and from the regional, national, and global levels. Drawing upon these alternative models of justice is one means for changing local acceptance of inequality.

In summary, the conceptual framework outlined here holds that the distribution of wealth and incomes in American society is fundamentally affected by material and discursive practices in the market, the state, and civil society that vary through time and across places. I have highlighted the importance of discursive representations of justice in this ongoing power play, working from the position that "justice" is a socially constituted set of beliefs, discourses, and institutionalizations expressive of social relations and contested configurations of power that have everything to do with regulating and ordering material social practices within places for a time. Once constituted, the trace of a particular discursive conception of justice across all moments of the social process becomes an objective fact that embraces everyone within its compass. Once institutionalized, a system of justice becomes a "permanence" with which all facets of the social process have to contend (Harvey 1996: 330).

Thus, principles of justice must be critically examined in relation to the larger material conditions in which they are deployed, because the particular articulations of power generated in the local political economy and embedded in the local social order help to shape, and are shaped by, locally dominant notions of justice. In studying any particular situation, it is important to ask who controls the discursive representation of justice? To illustrate the significance of this question, the next section brings the conceptual framework to life with a particular local example.

A local case study

In the summer of 1936, writer James Agee and photographer Walker Evans traveled to Alabama to write a piece for *Fortune* magazine on tenant farming. Agee's book, the odd and brilliant *Let Us now Praise Famous Men*, was the eventual result (1939). Born and bred in the South, Agee was acutely sensitive to the irony of documenting rural agonies of the Great Depression for such a bastion of high capitalism as *Fortune*, and he opened the book with this passage:

> It seems to me curious, not to say obscene and thoroughly terrifying, that it could occur to an association of human beings drawn together through need and chance and for profit into a company, an organ of journalism, to pry intimately into the lives of an undefended and appallingly damaged group of human beings. (1939: xxvi)

Read in retrospect, this intrusion of which Agee was so conscious provides an extraordinary example of social injustice cast within the material conditions of a particular place/time context. The local social order – developed through a long agrarian history, a tradition of economic and political control by local elites, and a heritage of exploitative class, race, and gender relations – shaped practices and institutions in the market, state, and other arenas in such a way as to ensure a strict hierarchy of wealth and power.

Specifically, the sharply defined power hierarchies existing in rural Alabama in the 1930s were grounded in the particular market system that had developed in the region – originating in the plantation economy (an agricultural production system in which white landowners purchased and used large numbers of black African slaves to produce cotton on their vast estates) and continued after the Civil War in tenant farming (a system in which landowners rented land to freed slaves as tenants). Due to the lack of mechanized alternatives at the time, white landowners used legions of black workers to do the arduous, labor-intensive work in the cotton fields. The particular forms of work organization embedded in the plantation and tenant systems were efficient and profitable, but the production of agricultural commodities based on cheap labor-intensive work patterns skewed labor, capital, and property markets, and thus created strong inequalities in affluence, power, and freedom.

The local state helped to generate and perpetuate these disparities created through the local market system. Government in the rural South of the 1930s was under the firm, and rarely contested, control of local landowning elites. This disproportionate political power was discursively justified as being characteristic of a traditionalist political culture, which held that formal politics should be consigned to particular "political" families in the area, with little participation by the rest of the population (Elazar 1973). As a result, power in the local market and local state accumulated into the hands of a small elite landowning group, and, not surprisingly, the state favored accumulation over legitimation. Indeed, there was little need for the local state to serve its legitimation role when African-Americans, often a large majority of the population in local Southern jurisdictions, were forbidden to vote or otherwise participate in the political process. It was within these circumstances that systematic injustice was legalized through Jim Crow laws and the like. Clearly, such obvious differentials in power and wealth required strong discursive "justice-ification" if they were to be maintained. The elitism, racism, and sexism embedded in the work patterns and political systems prevailing in the rural South during the 1930s coalesced into paternalism, an intricate system of reciprocal obligations and unspoken protocol which bound agricultural landowners and workers into an ongoing relationship that solidified the local political economy (Alston and Ferrie 1999). The landowner essentially treated the workers as children, providing them with minimal food, rudimentary housing, and basic health care, so as to reproduce his lifetime labor force for the following cotton seasons. The workers generally accepted this system because they lacked the civil rights to alter the situation.

Thus, sharp power differentials were naturalized within the paternalistic system, and generally came to be accepted "without misunderstanding," although the potential for revolt always lay just beneath the surface. One of the reasons why active discursive negotiations over the justice of these practices were so rare was that elites, through their control of the local state and political process, restricted workers' educational opportunities and knowledge of alternative models of justice available in the outside world. In such circumstances, it is remarkable that resistance was raised at all, yet the history of the rural South is peppered with sporadic, most often failed, insurrections. We see here how the discursive representation of justice evolves within the material conditions of life and then feeds back upon and supports the local social order. The following passage from Agee's book demonstrates how uneven social relations combined within the local political economy of 1930s rural Alabama to create temporally- and spatially-specific norms of justice, even as it contained the seeds of change. In this passage, Agee accompanies a white, male landowner on a visit to a cluster of shacks housing the black tenant workers on his lands. It is a remarkable study in power, manifested through subtleties in facial expression, body positioning, and discursive conventions:

Here at the foreman's home we had caused an interruption that filled me with regret: relatives were here from a distance, middle-aged and sober people in their sunday clothes, and three or four visiting children, and I realized that they had been quietly enjoying themselves, the men out at the far side of the house, the women getting dinner, as now, by our arrival, they no longer could. The foreman was very courteous, the other men were non-committal, the eyes of the women were quietly and openly hostile; the landlord and the foreman were talking. The foreman's male guests hovered quietly and respectfully in silence on the outskirts of the talk until they were sure what they may properly do, then withdrew to the far side of the house, watching carefully to catch the landowner's eyes, should they be glanced after, so that they might nod, smile, and touch their foreheads, as in fact they did, before they disappeared. The two men from the third house came up; soon three more came, a man of forty and a narrow-skulled pair of sapling boys. They all approached softly and strangely until they stood within the shade of the grove, then stayed their ground as if floated, their eyes shifting upon us sidelong and to the ground and to the distance, speaking together very little, in quieted voices: it was as if they had been under some sort of magnetic obligation to approach just this closely and to show themselves. The landlord began to ask of them through the foreman, How's So-and-So doing, all laid by? Did he do that extra sweeping I told you? – And the foreman would answer, Yes sir, yes sir, he do what you say to do, he doin all right; and So-and-So shifted on his feet and smiled uneasily while, uneasily, one of his companions laughed and the others held their faces in the blank safety of deafness. And you, you been doin much coltin lately, you horny old bastard? and the crinkled, old, almost gray-mustached negro who came up tucked his head to one side looking cute, and showed what was left of his teeth, and whined, tittering, Now Mist So-and-So, you know I'm settled down, married-man, you wouldn't – and the brutal negro of forty split his face in a villainous grin and said, He too ole, Mist So-and-So, he dont got no sap lef in him; and everybody laughed, and the landowner said, These two yere, colts yourn ain't they? – and the old man said that they were, and the landowner said, Musta found them in the woods, strappin young niggers as that; and the old man said, No sir, he got both of them lawful married, Mist So-and-So; and the landowner said that eldest on em looks to be ready for a piece himself, and the negroes laughed, and the two boys twisted their beautiful bald gourdlike skulls in a unison of shyness and their faces were illumined with maidenly smiles of shame, delight and fear . . . (Agee 1939: 27–8)

We see in this Sunday morning conversation a synthesis of power relations defined by the prevailing class, race, age, and sexuality norms of rural Alabama in the midst of the Depression. Class and race hierarchies are most clearly evident in the passage above, as throughout the discussion, the white landowner commands the attention of all the black males, who "approached softly and strangely until they stood within the shade of the grove, then stayed their ground as if floated," as if they had been "under some sort of magnetic obligation." Fine divisions of social rank are demonstrated when the landowner speaks to the foreman about work performed by a tenant worker, who is standing in his presence. And the hierarchy extends beyond a formal work relation, as the workers' guests

> hovered quietly and respectfully in the silence on the outskirts of the talk until they were sure what they may properly do, then withdrew to the far side of the house, watching carefully to catch the landowner's eyes, should they be glanced after, so that they might nod, smile, and touch their foreheads, as in fact they did, before they disappeared.

The tensions underlying this sharp power division are revealed in the repeated use of the term "uneasily" – one individual responding to the situation in nervous laughter, the others receding into "the blank safety of deafness."

These class and race differentials in power are also expressed through age and sexuality. Showing a lack of deference to one older than himself, the landowner inquires as to the sexual behavior of a graying tenant worker, who responds by assuring the landowner that his conduct falls within the prescribed norms of lawfully married relations. In a further demonstration of his right to discuss the behavior of others, the landowner jokes that two young boys are old enough for sexual relations, and their response is one of subservience, "twisting their beautiful bald gourdlike skulls in a unison of shyness," their faces "illumined with maidenly smiles of shame, delight, and fear" but not, you will note, with anger at the imposition.

In this particular case, all power resides in the white, male landowner whose position in this social order allows him to interrupt the religious and leisure activities of others, to remind others of their economic subservience and obligation to him, and to presume to speak of others' intimate lives. No one in this gathering would intrude on his leisure, question his productivity, or inquire of his personal life – such questions lie outside the purview of conversation in this social order. The only challenge to the multiple hierarchies that combine to place him in control is the "quietly and openly hostile" eyes of the women, symbolic of an underlying resistance to the social order.

And indeed, conditions in rural Alabama have changed since the

1930s, as restructuring of the local political economy and changing notions of social justice have fed upon each other. The local area Agee visited has diversified its economic base beyond cotton and now specializes in the raising and processing of catfish, dairy farming, and timber production. Tenant farming no longer exists and work patterns enable some greater opportunities for personal advancement. The political system now allows blacks to vote and participate in ways that were impossible during the 1930s. Some of these changes came from the outside. Local resistance to the sharp material inequities in affluence and the skewed discursive representations of justice were emboldened by the national civil rights movement in the 1960s. Also at that time, the national government took a more activist role in guaranteeing human rights in the South, often conducting an end-run around state and local governments by providing food, housing, and health assistance directly to individuals through nationwide entitlement programs. Local elites in many areas of the rural South bitterly contested this intrusion of alternative forms of justice. Although the strength of Southern politicians in the United States Congress had defeated such programs throughout the first half of the century, by the 1960s, the diminishing global competitiveness of Southern cotton, and thus the ebbing of the paternalist relation, enabled passage of such legislation. Transformations in the local market and state following the end of the cotton era created new patterns of work organization and some political freedoms.

The past does inform the present, however. The structural disadvantages embedded in rural labor markets still leave low-wage workers with relatively few opportunities, as evidenced by the work conditions existing in local catfish processing plants (Bates 1993). And the elitism, racism, sexism, and paternalism engendered by the plantation and tenant-farming systems have left a distinctive legacy of discrimination in areas where they predominated. In Hale County, Alabama, the site of Agee's study, fully one-third of the population live below the poverty line (U.S. Bureau of the Census 1990). Racial disparities in poverty are still clearly evident, varying from 8 percent for white married-couple families to 31 percent for black married-couple families. The rates are substantially higher among female-headed families with children, and here the racial differential is even greater, varying from 21 percent for whites to a shocking 73 percent for black women heading families. The legacy of racial discrimination in educational systems is also evident.

While only 11 percent of white adults have less than a ninth grade education, the rate among black adults is fully 31 percent. The persistence of racial problems is also indicated in the rash of black Baptist church burnings in the area. During 1996 alone, 6 such churches were torched within a fifty-mile radius of Hale's county seat. Nationwide, 155 black churches were burned that year, and although the national commission charged with studying the outbreak found a range of motives, from "blatant racism and religious hatred to financial profit, to personal revenge, burglary or vandalism," the cause of several in western Alabama was determined to be explicitly racial (Federal News Service October 22, 1998; *Washington Times* March 20, 1997; CBS Evening News June 4, 1996; CNN News June 3, 1996). For example, the instigator of one fire in rural Alabama, interviewed from her prison cell in Tallahassee, Florida, testified to using racial slurs in encouraging four friends to set the fire (Associated Press, January 4, 1999). The heritage of racial discrimination structurally generated within the local political economy and social order of the plantation system is currently manifested in the charred remains of small rural churches in Hale County, Alabama.

Power hierarchies articulating the local political economy in most places across the United States are more complex, more nuanced, than existed in rural Alabama in the 1930s and principles of social justice have also changed substantially. Social justice is a negotiated principle, woven into material conditions and power hierarchies prevailing in a given place and time context.

To develop a broader understanding of the processes affecting affluence and justice, as outlined in the conceptual framework and illustrated in the Agee case study, I now review recent trends in the market, state, and civil society that have altered income disparities across the American population over time.

Restructuring the American political economy*

The United States was created in the name of social justice and equality, with such terms liberally sprinkled throughout the founding documents. Yet it is important to recognize that sharp class differentials have existed throughout American history. The best estimates hold

---

*Parts of this section are drawn from Kodras 1997a, 1997b, 1997c.

that, at the time of the American Revolution, the most affluent 10 percent of the population possessed approximately 50 percent of the
wealth (Jones 1980). By the Civil War, the top decile had captured
about 70 percent of the wealth and at the height of the Progressive Era
in the early 1900s the figure had risen to 90 percent (Huston 1998).
Following the New Deal of the 1930s, inequalities substantially
moderated, until 1980, when they approximated levels at the time of
the Revolution. Over the past two decades, disparities have begun to
rise again.

The individuals defining the American ethos at the time of Independence were primarily landowning elites, including Madison, Adams,
and Hamilton, who wrote explicitly about the primacy of class controversy in the country's founding (Galloway 1991: 4–8; Kairys 1993).
How to reconcile the importance of principles such as justice and
equality within such a sharply divided society? The key is to understand
that the American ethos was created within the context of, and in
contrast to, stricter European hierarchies of wealth and inheritance.
The United States was founded on the prospects for social mobility
afforded by a fresh start in a new and expanding territory. This tension
between the principles of justice and equality versus the realities of
class division has come down through American history, with regions
and groups variously advantaged or disadvantaged in an American
economy fit within larger international dynamics (Agnew 1987; Meinig
1986).

Since World War II, the United States has served as the hegemonic
power of the global political economy, although both the world system
and the United States' role within it have undergone tremendous
transformation over this time period (Agnew 1987; Bluestone and
Harrison 1982). Between World War II and the mid-1960s, the United
States economy experienced a twenty-year expansion, with annual
growth rates in the gross national product averaging 4 percent. Based
largely on the Fordist model of industrial production, American firms
prospered, enjoying annual returns on investment of more than 15
percent.

This strong economic growth involved deliberate state orchestration
working in concert with expansive market forces (Kolko 1988). The
United States government drew upon the tenets of free trade, a stable
financial system, and containment of communism to establish the
institutional framework for the postwar era. At the international level,

the government used investment, loans, negotiation, coercion, and out-right intervention to induce the allegiance of other countries into a postwar world order that generally advanced the interests of the United States. In addition, the United States government underwrote postwar expansion by facilitating the growth and profitability of major domestic corporations, especially in the penetration of overseas markets. Thus, in a strong assertion of its role in assisting capital accumulation, the state helped to position the United States as the hegemonic power of the global political economy.

An increasing majority of Americans prospered during this period, although rising affluence levels were more of a struggle than might first appear. Due to high corporate profits and low unemployment rates, workers were able to bargain for wage and security benefits from capital and the state. Specifically, a number of large corporations and labor unions negotiated a "social contract" that tied wage increases to rising productivity in exchange for guarantees against strikes. This agreement provided management with the stability needed to increase profits and gave workers sufficient purchasing power to consume the commodities thus produced. The social contract, whose direct effect was limited to those working in large unionized firms, had a ripple effect on working conditions throughout much of the economy as workers gained further concessions from the state regulatory system: obtaining minimum wage levels, occupational health and safety standards, fair labor regulations, and improved workers' compensation. These, combined with the general postwar Keynesian policy of encouraging economic growth through the stimulation of consumer demand for America's industrial production, were instrumental in creating the broad-based affluence that typified the 1950s and 1960s.

Many Americans were left out of the growing prosperity, however (Harrington 1962). Fully one-quarter of the United States population earned incomes below the poverty level during the early postwar period. The dominant discourse of the times held that poverty was a remnant of former times, soon to be eliminated by technological progress in the world's strongest country. By the early 1960s, however, it became clear that the poor were often the victims of technological innovations, such as the mechanization of agriculture that released large numbers of poorly educated workers. With the increasing recognition that the hardship experienced by many low-income Americans could not be directly addressed by general economic growth, the United States government expanded its role in social provision with a set of initiatives known as the War on Poverty.

Combining its accumulation and legitimation roles, the United States government established the War on Poverty to make low-income individuals more effective participants in the labor force through a variety of policy mechanisms addressing education, job training, citizen participation, and community development. The federal government's increased commitment resulted from a combination of several factors, including pressure from the civil rights movement to put poverty on the national political agenda and the prevailing optimism that social problems could be easily accommodated within a prosperous and growing American economy. President Lyndon Johnson oversold the initiative, declaring that his "unconditional war on poverty" could eliminate hardship, then underfinanced it as costs of his other war, in Vietnam, accelerated (Harrington 1985). Declining poverty rates were modest but steady through the 1960s, but when the programs failed to register spectacular results unmet expectations erupted into rage and violence across American cities. In addition, the failure to fund programs adequately promoted as the liberal solution to social problems would give conservatives in the 1980s the ammunition to shoot down the liberal approach (e.g. Murray 1984).

By the early 1970s, the United States began to falter in the global economy as foreign corporations primarily based in Europe and Asia challenged United States' control of international markets and began to cut into its domestic market as well (Knox and Agnew 1989). United States' economic growth decelerated from more than 4 percent per annum during the 1960s to 2 percent in the 1970s. To reassert the United States' competitive position, American corporations could have chosen to focus on technological innovations and improved product quality. Instead, they chose to restructure by cutting capital investment, closing plants, shifting jobs overseas, transferring resources from manufacturing to services and speculative ventures, demanding wage and benefit concessions from labor, and replacing full-time workers with contingent labor, mechanisms whose combined effect substituted capital for labor, seriously reducing employment (Harrison and Bluestone 1988). Corporate acquisitions, mergers, and takeovers reshuffled assets rather than productively investing in new plants, equipment, and technologies.

Furthermore, the state began actively to strengthen these corporate restructurings by deregulating business, attacking labor unions, slashing social programs, and the like. The recessions of the early 1980s were politically orchestrated to bring down inflation by reducing interest rates, at the cost of increased unemployment. Because the negative effects of inflation focus on the relatively affluent while the adverse effects of unemployment concentrate on low-income groups, the recessions created by the government in the early 1980s had disproportionate impact on the poor (Galbraith 1992).

The affluence generated during the postwar era had been sufficient to provide some degree of state assistance to the low-income population, but as the economic system began to weaken a fiscal crisis developed and the welfare state lost the ability to address needs. Rather than viewing failures in the welfare system as a consequence of problems in the larger economy, however, the argument was reversed. Ronald Reagan won the 1980 presidential election, charging that rises in government spending, particularly in welfare, was the source, rather than the result, of national economic problems. He argued that the country's prosperity had been squandered on social programs for the indolent and that only the elimination of such programs would restore the United States to its previous position of global dominance. As increasing numbers of Americans faced economic insecurity through rising unemployment, falling real wages, declining benefits, and dwindling savings, many accepted the rationale that the government lavished their hard-earned tax dollars on the undeserving, despite the fact that less than 4 percent of the federal budget was allocated to means-tested public assistance (Ellwood 1988). Thus, there was little public upheaval when more than half of the budget cuts in 1981 were levied on programs serving the poor (Harrington 1985).

In the midst of the economic crisis, the dominant discourse on justice held that sufficient opportunities existed for anyone who bypassed the enticements of welfare and went to work. In the United States, welfare assistance is generally a function of the bargaining position between capital and labor, which is in turn dependent on rapid economic growth and labor shortage. In the 1970s labor shortages disappeared as the economy stagnated and competition for remaining jobs was heightened by the entry of the baby boom generation and unprecedented numbers of women into the labor force. As labor lost its former bargaining position, the state reversed its postwar role of countering inequalities generated by the market, reinforcing disparities in the

1980s (Kodras 1997a). The changes of the decade had far-reaching effects on the American standard of living, reshaping the occupational structure and expanding income disparities. The size of the middle class declined, poverty levels rose and efforts to address racial and gender discrimination in the labor market were attacked (Goldsmith and Blakley 1992; Newman 1992; Schwartz and Volgy 1992).

Thus, fundamental changes in the market and the state, beginning in the 1970s, have greatly altered affluence levels and disparities in American society. The change in market practices is often referred to as a transition from "Fordism" to "economic globalization," while the change in state practices is typically described as a shift from "Keynesian welfarism" to "political neo-liberalism." Globalization is arguably the central defining concept of the contemporary era, yet there is little understanding of the actual processes involved, much less their conse-quences in a rapidly changing world (Watkins 1997). The geographic processes of globalization – notably, the increasing international mobility of capital and technology, the deepening global integration of markets, and the expanding spatial segmentation of production – have been ongoing for decades and in some cases centuries, but the com-plexity and rapidity of changes, and the breadth and depth of their effects, distinguish the present era from the past.

Specifically, the effect of market practices on local social orders has changed under the processes of globalization. In the accelerating inter-national competition, mobile capital scans the global stage for the most favorable locations. Its very mobility highlights minute differences between places, throwing into sharp relief local advantages in labor supply, political interests, resources, and infrastructure (Harvey 1990). Caught in this larger competition, each place presents a distinct local mix of material and discursive conditions that influence its ability to accommodate the shifting needs of the market and thus thrive within a globalizing economy. This depends not only on the match of local productive specializations to changing demands of the larger economy, but also on the fit of the local social order to the changing needs of global capital. In their search for the least-cost and therefore highest-profit locations, mobile firms take advantage of distinct geographic variations in workforce attributes, a spatial division of labor defined by the social composition of the population, given prevailing hiring practices that typecast minorities as working for less than whites, women for less than men, foreigners for less than the native-born, etc. Firms are also sensitive to the legacy of social relations defined by class, race, gender, nationality, and the like, as these set the discursive context in which the firm would operate. Included here would be local traditions of unionization and worker rights that set the relations between labor and capital or local traditions of racism, patriarchy, and nativism that discursively justify different types and degrees of exploitation. The relations between the various local groups are socially constructed in place and unique to it, but do reflect traditions of discrimination and bias in the larger society that are refracted into a particular place context, local variations on an American theme (Massey 1984, 1994). As globalization rewrites production landscapes based on this finely-calibrated and historically-derived spatial division of labor, complex geographies of vulnerability and exclusion, power and privilege, materialize (Sibley 1995; Wolch and Dear 1993; Zukin 1991).

The intensifying competition of social groups jockeying for position within the globalizing United States economy plays out in the political arena, from the local to the national levels. The ability of different groups to secure position is affected by their participation in both formal politics (who votes; whose interests are represented by the state) and extra-governmental activism (social movements; political violence). In recent years, a great variety of social interest groups, each in their own way threatened by the fluctuations and insecurities of a globalizing American economy, have increasingly vocalized their political discontent, and the ascendance of "identity politics" to a major role in national political discourse has altered the strategies and priorities of these interest coalitions, including a reconsideration of the appropriate role of government in a changing American society. Many of these individual threads of discontent have been woven into a pervasive challenge of the national government, under charges ranging from sinister domination to blustering ineffectiveness, from over-regulation to neglect of responsibilities, from profligate spending to abandoning priorities.

The increasing rancor and divisiveness that characterize American politics (at the time of writing) largely reflect the economic polarization and social fragmentation engendered by changing market practices under globalization, yet political leaders, lacking a great deal of leverage to change conditions in the global market, increasingly charge that the state is responsible for stagnating affluence and diminishing prospects.

The result has been a notable shift in the role of the state within American society, from an uneasy balance between its accumulation and legitimation roles that typified the Keynesian welfarism era to a heightened focus upon accumulation characterized as neo-liberalism. Specifically, globalization of production and finance is subverting the power of even the world's most powerful state, as the volume and speed of transnational capital mobility limits the government's policy options. In response, the state has increasingly come to align itself with the values of global capitalism, deregulating capital markets and retracting the system of welfare and protection of citizen rights and livelihoods in a spirit of neo-liberalism (Peck 1996).

The increasing disparities in American affluence levels accompanying economic globalization and political neo-liberalization are discursively justified through the ascendance of the market paradigm of justice (Harvey 1996). In recent years, a confluence of powerful interests in the market and the state have quite successfully implanted the notion that justice is precisely what is delivered by the market, even as the globalizing market system increases inequalities in American living standards. In the process, income disparities manifested in the current American political economy have been materially produced and discursively represented as the natural order of things. In the next section, I illustrate how transformations in the material practices of the market and state in an era of economic globalization and political neo-liberalism, as well as shifts in the discursive representation of justice, have affected American affluence levels.

Patterns and trends in United States' income disparities*

I now present a series of maps and graphs that portray income disparities from the global and national scales to the regional and local levels, linking these to recent transformations in the American political economy.

---

*Given the paucity of data measuring disparities in wealth for different social groups and scales of analysis, this section addresses variations in income only. Unless otherwise noted, income data are drawn from the United States Bureau of the Census 1970, 1980, and 1990. Trends in income disparities are calculated in constant dollars for the period 1970–90 to ensure compatibility through time and across variables.

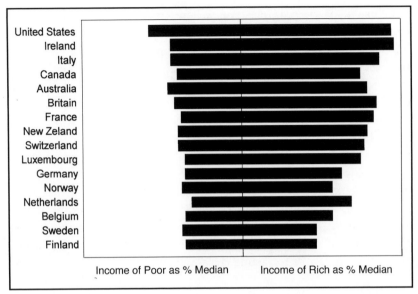

Figure 7.2 Income disparities in OECD countries. For each country, bars extending to the right measure the percent by which income of the top decile exceeds the national median income. Bars extending to the left measure the percent by which the bottom decile falls below the national median. See footnote below.

The global level*

First, to put the United States' situation in larger perspective, I show income disparities for sixteen comparable countries (Figure 7.2). The income gap between the wealthy and the poor is wider in the United States than in any of the others. In the United States, the wealthiest decile earns more than double the median income, while the poorest decile earns only one-third of the median. Although the United States contains the world's largest economy and has reigned as the hegemone of the world system since World War II, the particular practices and institutions of the market, state, and civil society, as described above, concentrate wealth to a greater extent than do those in comparable countries.

* Data are drawn from the Luxembourg Income Study, commissioned by the Organization for Economic Cooperation and Development (Atkinson, Rainwater, and Smeeding 1995). For each country, median income was calculated after taxes and adjusted for differences in family size. Personal incomes were ranked around the median and then the income level of the wealthiest decile (the top 10 percent of the population) was compared with the income of the poorest decile (the bottom 10 percent of the population).

Of particular importance, the welfare state is relatively less developed in the United States. The welfare state refers to the entire set of government policies and services that support the standard of living through full employment, minimum wages, and safe working conditions, as well as assistance in health, housing, education, and nutrition (Pinch 1997). At the height of the welfare state era in the mid-1970s, European states averaged one-quarter to one-third of GNP in social expenditures, while the United States committed less than 20 percent (Pierson 1991). The relatively limited welfare state in the United States is generally attributed to the discursive dominance of individualism and the market justice paradigm, the decentralized federal structure of governance, and the combined effects of racism and sexism (Pinch 1997). The ascendance of the market paradigm of justice in the United States has now spread widely among this set of countries, all of which are in the process of retracting their welfare states.

The national level

At the national level, the distribution of United States household incomes is notably skewed, exhibiting a strong clustering of households at low to middle income levels (Figure 7.3).[3]

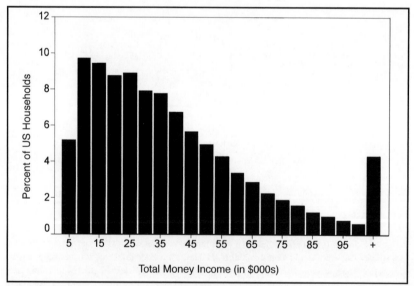

Figure 7.3 United States income distribution, 1990. Source: United States Bureau of the Census.

This lopsided distribution differs considerably from an idealized bell-shaped curve, countering the popular notion that American incomes center on a true middle-income level. In fact, one-fourth of all United States households acquired less than $15,000 in total money income, and fewer than 5 percent made more than $100,000 in 1990. The relatively large proportion of households with lower-middle incomes helps to explain why many Americans feel economically vulnerable in the current economic climate, despite strong aggregate growth. At the national level, disparities in affluence declined throughout the 1960s and early 1970s, as the state helped to distribute the proceeds of strong market growth. Since the early 1980s, disparities in income and wealth have increased, as the state has reversed its postwar role of countering inequalities generated by the market and began to reinforce those disparities. In fact, an overwhelming 98 percent of the national gain in household income over the last two decades went to the wealthiest 20 percent of United States households. The poorest 20 percent of United States households experienced a 7.5 percent decline in real income over the period. Racial and ethnic divisions are evident in the simple but appalling fact that 40 percent of African-American and Latino children live in poverty.

The regional level

Regional trends in income distribution reflect the spatial dynamics of the United States economy during this period. Throughout the 1970s and 1980s, the South exhibited distinctly lower average incomes than elsewhere. All regions experienced sharp declines in median household income during the recessions of 1973–5, 1980, and 1981–2, although the time at which each entered or emerged from recession varied among them. The Midwest was particularly unfortunate, as the median income declined more than 10 percent in just five years ($28,437 in 1978 to $25,230 in 1983), forceful evidence of the disproportionate effect of industrial restructuring on the Midwest. In contrast, the Northeast registered the strongest recovery after 1982, ending the period with a median household income of more than $30,000, the highest of all regions and a legacy of the accelerating concentration of financial power in the large metropolitan areas of this region that has accompanied globalization and neo-liberalization.

The Northeast and West outpaced the interior during the 1980s,

generating the so-called "bicoastal economy," which had also characterized the pro-business periods of Gilded Age in the late nineteenth
century and the Roaring Twenties (Phillips 1990). During much of the
1980s, the Eastern seaboard and Pacific coast held advantage, as they
possessed the major agglomerations of flourishing high-level services
(particularly finance, insurance, and producer services); received a
disproportionate share of defense and other federal spending; and
served as transfer points for the surge of imports drawn in by a strong
dollar (Markusen, Hall, Campbell, and Deitrick 1990). Meanwhile, the
interior of the country, heavily dependent on agricultural, mineral,
and industrial exports, suffered from the strong dollar.

Figures 7.4a and 7.4b show two-decade trends in income disparities
for the two largest racial groups across four census regions.[4] Both
blacks and whites experienced increasing income disparities during the
1970s and 1980s, as the ongoing processes of deindustrialization and
service expansion generated a widening gulf between rich and poor.
Racial differences in income levels have not changed noticeably over
the past two decades.

Among whites, income disparities increased fairly consistently across
all four regions. The single greatest change was a surge in the proportion of the white population earning high relative incomes in the
Northeast during the 1980s. The deepening concentration of corporate
headquarters and high finance in the major cities of the Northeast
during this time played a major role. We see here evidence of disproportionate advantage accruing to the core social group in the core
region during the 1980s.

In contrast, many whites in the Northeast suffered substantially
from economic restructuring during the 1970s and 1980s. In fact,
white poverty rates were highest in the central cities of the Northeast,
compared to all region–residence categories. The majority of these
were Hispanic. For example, Puerto Ricans endured a dramatic decline
in economic well-being during this period, the result of their concentration in Northeastern central cities experiencing intense economic
dislocation, their overrepresentation in job sectors most adversely
affected by such restructurings, and their vulnerable position at the
bottom of ethnic hiring queues.

Regional dynamics in black incomes are more complex, particularly
in the Midwest and the South. Blacks living in the Midwest bore the
full brunt of economic restructuring during the late 1970s and 1980s,

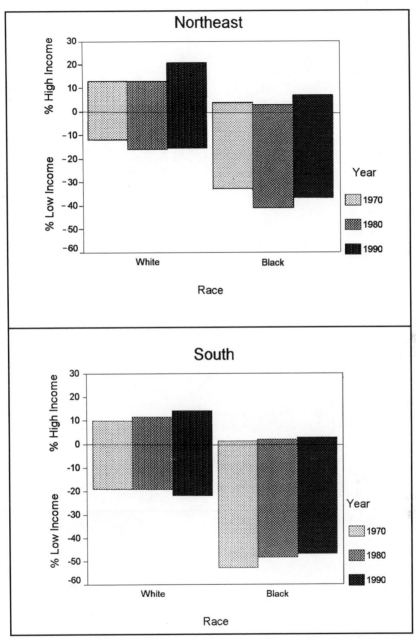

Figure 7.4a Trends in regional income disparities by race, 1970–90: northeast and south. Bars extending up from the central axis measure the percent with incomes greater than twice the United States median. Bars extending below the central axis measure the percent with incomes less than half the United States median. See endnote 4.

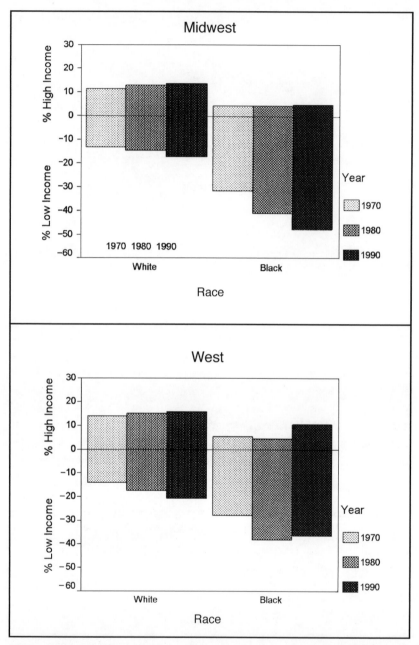

Figure 7.4b Trends in regional income disparities by race, 1970–90: midwest and west. Bars extending up from the central axis measure the percent with incomes greater than twice the United States median. Bars extending below the central axis measure the percent with incomes less than half the United States median. See endnote 4.

experiencing the sharpest declines in relative incomes over the period. The fraction of the Midwestern black population with high relative incomes remained stagnant throughout the period, but the fraction with low incomes grew dramatically. By 1989, almost half of the black population living in the Midwest had low relative incomes, for the first time surpassing the situation for blacks in the South. This worsening income situation for Midwestern blacks was due to their concentration in the lower echelons of heavy manufacturing, the sector hardest hit during deindustrialization. During the heyday of Fordism, large numbers of blacks migrated from the rural South to work in Midwestern factories, for the first time bringing a discernible proportion into the working class, although they tended to be employed as routine manufacturing operatives and in small input firms, rather than in the leading corporations offering the best pay and benefits. These small feeder firms were the most directly hit during the downfall of the Fordist system.

In the South, blacks registered some improvement over the two-decade period, although incomes remained low and disparities great. The improvement is seen primarily at the bottom of the income ladder. In 1969, more than half of all Southern blacks had low relative incomes; by 1989, this figure had improved slightly to 46 percent. This remains a strikingly high proportion with low incomes, demonstrating the continued deprivation of many blacks residing in the Southern United States. As has traditionally been the case given the South's long agrarian history and heritage of racial discrimination, the poverty rate among blacks living in the non-metropolitan South is exceptionally high, at more than 40 percent (Falk and Rankin 1992). The long historical legacy of racial discrimination in Hale County, Alabama, is but one element informing this graph of black income disparities in the South.

The local level

Finally, to examine variations in affluence at the local level, I present county-level maps portraying the percentages of the United States population with especially high and low incomes (Figures 7.5 and 7.6). The map showing the percent with annual earned incomes over $150,000 highlights urban-rural disparities in affluence, with the largest concentrations of high income earners largely reflecting the layout of

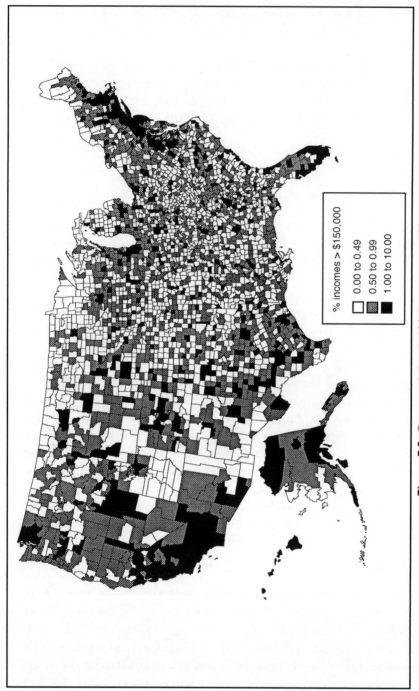

Figure 7.5 County variations in high-income rates, 1990.

metropolitan areas across the country (Figure 7.5). Continuous stretches of high income line the Eastern seaboard, the south Florida peninsula, and the California coast, while metropolitan centers scattered across the country register higher incomes than the hinterlands they dominate. The few non-metropolitan counties with unusually high incomes typically specialize in large-scale export-oriented agriculture or petroleum extraction or are supported by recreation and retirement economies.

In contrast to the urban-rural differentials at the high income end, the map showing the proportion of county populations earning below the poverty level is more regionally extensive (Figure 7.6). The highest poverty rates are concentrated in the Mississippi Delta, where in many counties a majority of the population lives below the poverty line. There are four extensions outward from this poverty core – to the east through the small towns and rural areas of the Southeast; to the southwest through the Oil Patch and extending along the Texas border with Mexico; to the west into the Ozarks and Ouachita; and to the northeast into Appalachia. Areas of severe poverty are also scattered throughout the interior West, particularly the American Indian reservations in the Dakotas and the Four Corners area.

These two maps are one-point-in-time snapshots of American income disparities that reflect the geographically- and historically-accumulated practices and institutions in the market, state, and civil society that distribute material resources. As we have seen, the economic effects of globalization on the United States population over the past several decades include stagnation in median household incomes, redistribution of earnings and wealth from low- and middle-income households to the most affluent, and deepening income disparities across local labor markets (O'Loughlin 1997). In the United States as elsewhere, the playing field was uneven, so that the positive effects have accrued primarily to wealthier peoples and places, while the negative effects have been greatest among marginalized peoples and places, unable to secure favorable position within the internationalizing competition:

a new world order is emerging which is surprisingly stable in its expanding core areas, and which has ridden out the very real threats presented by inflation, debts, balance of payments deficits and economic nationalism, but which is "orderly" in part because of *a new capacity to write off regions, countries and communities that are marginal to the development of this geopolitical economy* . . . the real costs

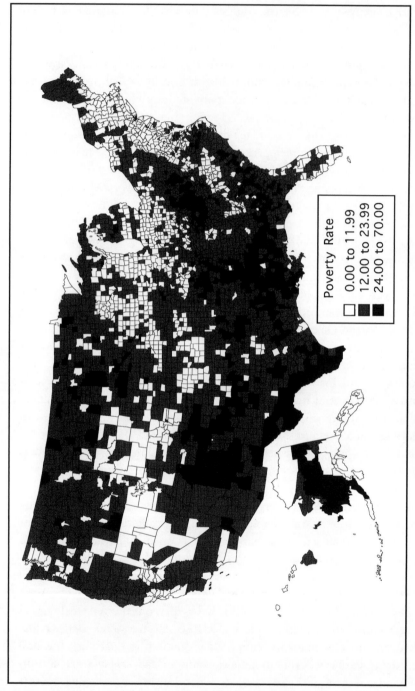

Figure 7.6 County variations in poverty rates, 1990.

of the crises of the past twenty years have fallen most heavily on certain countries, regions, and classes in the poorer regions of the "Third World" . . . and on those classes and communities in the First and Second Worlds that have to live in the deadlands created by economic restructuring. (Agnew and Corbridge 1995: 192–3, emphasis mine)

This last point brings us full circle, from the local level back to the global. Although income disparities in the United States are large relative to those in comparably industrialized countries, they pale in comparison to the vagaries of life in poorer countries. But given the interdependencies and international divisions of labor that comprise the global economy, American prosperity in the new world order must be recognized as coming at the expense of peoples living in many other places. The true income disparities generated through practices of the American market and state are global in scope. For example, one measure of the impact of transformations in the global political economy during the hegemonic period of the United States is that, in 1960, the top fifth of the world's population earned thirty times as much as the poorest fifth, whereas currently the top fifth earns seventy-five times more. This concentration of global wealth is greatest at the extreme high end. In just four years ending in 1998, the richest 200 individuals in the world more than doubled their net worth to $1 trillion, which is greater than the GNP of countries such as Canada, Russia, Brazil, or South Korea (UNDP 1999).

Conclusion

I have examined here the primary reasons for substantial and increasing economic disparities in American society, cast within changing notions of social justice. I began with a conceptual framework of the forces shaping the American income distribution, which described how material and discursive practices in the market, state, and civil society combine to generate a dynamic national map of affluence and poverty, whose contours are shaped by class, race, gender, and other social relations. I then applied the framework to a particular local case study and to a review of recent transformations in the American political economy that have altered income disparities. Fundamental transitions in the market and the state, most recently through the material processes and discursive practices involved in economic globalization and political neo-liberalization, have differentially affected specific regions and populations, as the shift in economic base from manufacturing to services, the acceleration of labor-saving technological innovations, the replacement of secure full-time employment for contingent labor, as well as rising unemployment, stagnating wages, and a host of related changes have altered well-being and the prospects of life.

These recent restructurings in the American political economy have been accompanied by changing notions of acceptable disparities in the income distribution. This has been accomplished primarily through a shift in poverty discourse, from the focus on individual rights and entitlements that dominated in the 1960s to the targeting and scapegoating of the poor that has dominated since the 1980s. The market–justice paradigm currently dominates, asserting a particular form of justice that appears to be the natural result of abstract forces in the market rather than the self-interested result of concrete practices by the powerful. The notion inherent in the market paradigm of justice that the state's function should be limited to assisting the market has helped to shift the state away from its legitimation role and toward accumulation. In consequence, the function of the state in American society has been thrown out of balance, as the government has diminished its role in protecting the interests of civil society and expanded its role in assisting the interests of capital, caught in the accelerating international competition of globalization.

Given the combined power of global capital and the national state in projecting the market paradigm of justice, it is difficult for people busy in their everyday lives to perceive, much less confront, this concept of justice, which has by now become so discursively "justice-ified" that it appears to be the natural order of things. Although this specific notion of social justice is well suited to the interests of powerful actors in the market who benefit from the concentrated wealth and power generated through globalization, it excuses and seeks to justify considerable and rising inequities in life chances from the local to the global levels. It is not the only choice available. The key is to recognize that social justice is a negotiated principle embedded in the material conditions of life. Concepts of justice are historically and geographically constituted in an ongoing process of societal valuation, and the widespread loss of individual security in a globalizing world is leading increasing numbers of people to search for an alternative concept of justice that protects their interests. Accordingly, the most effective challenges to market idolatry currently emerging tend to involve efforts by individuals in civil society to exploit the traditional dual role of the state, drawing the state back into a better balance between its legitimation and accumulation roles, such that it protects the rights and livelihoods of citizens even as it assists the power of capital. Although the state's authority has diminished under the pressures of globalization, it remains the strongest potential counter-force to the power of global capital, if pushed by civic action to do so.

The evidence provided in this study of substantial transformations in material affluence, as well as changes in the discursive justification of the increasing disparities, over the course of the last half-century raises questions as to the kind of future we will create over the next half-century. Active engagement in the struggle to define social justice is a key component of the answer.

Endnotes

1. This study focuses on variations in affluence levels, as measured by income and wealth, but it is important to recognize that a fuller understanding of variations in human well-being is achieved by examining people's freedoms of economic opportunity, or capabilities, to choose among options that achieve a high quality of life (see the accumulated works of Nobel Laureate Amartya Sen, especially 1999, Chapter 3). See also the deeply informative work of Lakshman Yapa, whose postmodernist perspective on poverty demonstrates how scarcity is socially constructed within a nexus of production relations – technical, social, cultural, political, ecological, and academic (Yapa 1996; http://www.geog.psu.edu/~yapa/ Discourse.html [1996]).

2. Although capital, the state, and civil society are necessarily presented as separate spheres in this study, it is important to recognize throughout that these are complex and overlapping entities. For example, private firms (capital) or charities (civil society) increasingly subcontract to provide government services (the state). Furthermore, the agents controlling the market and state are also individuals living in civil society. The same economic agents who support a state action favoring accumulation may question the legitimacy of its social effects.

3. The wide and skewed distribution of United States incomes demonstrates why income averages are inappropriate indicators of American well-being. Specifically, average income can be measured by either the mean or the median, but the choice has political implications. The mean household income for 1990 was $37,403. This value artificially inflates the average income because the mean of a skewed distribution is drawn toward the extreme values in the tail. The median household income that same year was $29,943 – half the households in the country obtained a higher income than this value and half received less. The

median is a less distorted measure of average income, as it is insensitive to the outermost values in the tail of the distribution. The consequences of selecting one over the other should be clear, as the median was only 80 percent of the mean in 1990.

4. Bars extending upward from the central axis measure the proportion of a group whose income is greater than twice the United States median, in other words, the fraction with high relative incomes. Bars extending downward from the central axis measure the proportion of a group whose income is less than half the United States median, that is, the fraction with low relative incomes. Taken together, the total length of a bar measures the proportion of a population in the highest and lowest income categories, or the obverse, the proportion of the population outside the middle-income category. Increasing bar lengths from decade to decade give evidence of rising income inequality over time.

There are several measures of income inequality from which to choose, and once again the choice affects interpretation. The Gini index of income concentration condenses the degree of inequality into a single, intuitive value, ranging from 0.0 (perfect income equality across a population) to 1.0 (perfect inequality, i.e., income is confined to one individual). By all accounts, the degree of income concentration in the United States rose during the 1980s, as the Gini increased from 0.403 in 1980 to 0.429 in 1990. United States maps of county-level Gini values show both regions of stability and areas of change between 1970 and 1990 (Lobao, Rulli, and Brown 1999). The Gini must be used with caution, however, because the single value gives no indication of the shape of an income distribution. As a result, two distinctly different income distributions, one centered on high incomes and the other centered on low incomes, can yield the same Gini value. For this reason, the Gini is of limited utility here; it measures the degree of income concentration but not the nature of that disparity, as is the concern in this chapter.

The income quintile method, by contrast, does suggest the shape of an income distribution, in that it compares the tails of the distribution, the 20 percent of the population with the highest incomes against the 20 percent of the population with the lowest incomes. Disparities are also evident with this measure, as the top 20 percent of households captured almost half of total United States income in 1990, while the bottom quintile earned only 4 percent of all income (United States Bureau of the Census, 1991a). In comparison with the Gini index, the income quintile measure gives a stronger sense of "who gets what" in that it identifies where national income is clustered along the spectrum. One serious shortcoming, however, is that the income quintile method is sensitive to changes in average household size, making it unreliable as a means for detecting shifts in income disparities over spans of time.

A third indicator of income inequality, not subject to the problems identified above, is the relative income measure (United States Bureau of the Census, 1991b). It indicates the extent to which a person's income differs from the median income of the total group. For example, a person with a relative income of 0.50 earns only one-half the income of an individual in the middle of the distribution, while a person with a relative income of 2.00 earns twice that of an individual in the middle. The income of each individual is compared to the median for all individuals of the same household size, effectively controlling for changes in household structure over time. Consequently, the measure can be used to track temporal shifts in income disparities, an important feature for our purposes here, as we examine changing American inequalities in the light of economic transformations during the 1970s and 1980s. I use this third measure of income inequality.

References

Agee, J. (1939), *Let Us now Praise Famous Men*, Boston: Houghton Mifflin.

Agnew, J. (1987), *The United States in the World Economy: A Regional Geography*, Cambridge: Cambridge University Press.

Agnew, J., and S. Corbridge (1995), *Mastering Space: Hegemony, Territory, and International Political Economy*, London: Routledge.

Alston, L., and J. Ferrie (1999), *Southern Paternalism and the American Welfare State*, Cambridge: Cambridge University Press.

Associated Press (January 4, 1999), "Convicted Church Arsonists Speak to Teens through Prison Video."

Atkinson, A., L. Rainwater, and T. Smeeding (1995), "Income Distribution in OECD Countries: Evidence from the Luxembourg Income Study," *OECD Social Policy Studies*, 18, Paris: Organization for Economic Cooperation and Development.

Bates, E. (1993), "The Kill Line," *Southern Exposure*, 21, pp. 122–3.

Bluestone, B., and B. Harrison (1982), *The Deindustrialization of America: Plant Closings, Community Abandonment, and the Dismantling of Basic Industry*, New York: Basic Books.

Brown, D. L., and T. A. Hirschl (1995), "Household Poverty in Rural and Metro-politan-Core Areas of the United States," *Rural Sociology*, 60, pp. 44–66.

Cammisa, A. M. (1998), *From Rhetoric to Reform? Welfare Policy in American Politics*, Boulder, CO: Westview.

CBS Evening News (June 4, 1996), "Black Church Torched in Greensboro, Alabama."

CNN News (June 3, 1996), "Fire at Black Church Becomes Latest in Arson String."

Cope, M. (1997), "Responsibility, Regulation and Retrenchment: The End of Welfare?" in L. Staeheli, J. Kodras, and C. Flint (eds.), *State Devolution in America: Implications for a Diverse Society*, Thousand Oaks, CA: Sage, pp. 79–96.

Cox, R., and D. Skidmore-Hess (1999), *U.S. Politics and the Global Economy: Corporate Power, Conservative Shift*, London: Lynne.

Elazar, D. (1973), *American Federalism: A View from the States*, New York: Harper & Row.

Ellwood, D. (1988), *Poor Support: Poverty in the American Family*, New York: Basic Books.

Falk, W., and B. Rankin (1992), "The Cost of Being Black in the Black Belt," *Social Problems*, 39, pp. 299–313.

Federal News Service October 22, 1998, *In the News*.

Galbraith, J. K. (1992), *The Culture of Contentment*, Boston: Houghton Mifflin.

Galloway, R. (1991), *Justice for All? The Rich and Poor in Supreme Court History, 1790–1990*, Durham, NC: Carolina Academic Press.

Gans, H. (1995), *The War against the Poor: The Underclass and Anti-Poverty Policy*, New York: Harper Collins.

Goldsmith, W., and E. Blakely (1992), *Separate Societies: Poverty and Inequality in U.S. Cities*, Philadelphia: Temple University Press.

Harrington, M. (1962), *The Other America: Poverty in the United States*, Baltimore: Penguin.

Harrington, M. (1985), *The New American Poverty*, New York: Penguin.

Harrison, B., and B. Bluestone (1988), *The Great U-Turn: Corporate Restructuring and the Polarizing of America*, New York: Basic Books.

Harvey, D. (1973), *Social Justice and the City*, London: Edward Arnold.

Harvey, D. (1990), "Between Space and Time: Reflections on the Geographical Imagination," *Annals of the Association of American Geographers*, 80, pp. 418–34.

Harvey, D. (1996), *Justice, Nature, and the Geography of Difference*, Oxford: Blackwell.

Huston, J. (1998), *Securing the Fruits of Labor: The American Concept of Wealth Distribution, 1765–1900*, Baton Rouge: Louisiana State University Press.

Jencks, C. (1992), *Rethinking Social Policy: Race, Poverty and the Underclass*, New York: HarperCollins.

Jones, A. (1980), *Wealth of a Nation To Be: The American Colonies on the Eve of the American Revolution*, New York: Random.

Kairys, D. (1993), *With Liberty and Justice for Some: A Critique of the Conservative Supreme Court*, New York: New Press.

Knox, P., and J. Agnew (1989), *The Geography of the World Economy*, London: Edward Arnold.

Kodras, J. (1997a), "The Changing Map of American Poverty in an Era of Economic Restructuring and Political Realignment," *Economic Geography*, 72, pp. 67–93.

Kodras, J. (1997b), "Globalization and Social Restructuring of the American People: Geographies of Exclusion and Vulnerability," in L. Staeheli, J. Kodras, and C. Flint (eds.), *State Devolution in America: Implications for a Diverse Society*, Thousand Oaks, CA: Sage, pp. 41–60.

Kodras, J. (1997c), "Restructuring the State: Devolution, Privatization and the Geographic Redistribution of Power and Capacity in Governance," in L. Staeheli, J. Kodras, and C. Flint (eds.), *State Devolution in America: Implications for a Diverse Society*, Thousand Oaks, CA: Sage, pp. 79–96.

Kolko, J. (1988), *Restructuring the World Economy*, New York: Pantheon.

Lo, C., and M. Schwartz (1998), *Social Policy and the Conservative Agenda*, Oxford: Blackwell.

Lobao, L., J. Rulli, and L. A. Brown (1999), "Macro-level Theory and Local-Level Inequality: Industrial Structure, Institutional Arrangements, and the Political Economy of Redistribution, 1970 and 1990," *Annals of the Association of American Geographers*, 89, pp. 571–601.

Markusen, A., P. Hall, S. Campbell, and S. Deitrick (1991), *The Rise of the Gunbelt: The Military Remapping of Industrial America*, Oxford: Oxford University Press.

Massey, D. (1984), *Spatial Divisions of Labor: Social Structures and the Geography of Production*, London: Macmillan.

Massey, D. (1994), *Space, Place, and Gender*, Minneapolis: University of Minnesota Press.

Meinig, D. (1986), *The Shaping of America: A Geographical Perspective on 500 Years of History*, New Haven: Yale University Press.

Mitchell, D. (1996), *The Lie of the Land: Migrant Workres and the California Landscape*, Minneapolis: University of Minnesota Press.

Murray, C. (1984), *Losing Ground*, New York: Basic Books.

Nelson, J. (1995), *Post-Industrial Capatialism: Exploring Economic Inequality in America*, Thousand Oaks, CA: Sage.

Newman, K. (1992), *Falling from Grace: The Experience of Downward Mobility in the American Middle Class*, New York: Free Press.

O'Loughlin, J. (1997), "Economic Globalization and Income Inequality in the United States," in L. Staeheli, J. Kodras, and C. Flint (eds.), *State Devolution in America: Implications for a Diverse Society*, Thousand Oaks, CA: Sage, pp. 21–40.

Peck, J. (1996), *WorkPlace: The Social Regulation of Labor Markets*, New York: Guilford.

Phillips, K. (1990), *The Politics of Rich and Poor: Wealth and the American Electorate in the Reagan Aftermath*, New York: HarperCollins.

Phillips, K. (1993), *Boiling Point: Democrats, Republicans, and the Decline of Middle Class Prosperity*, New York: HarperCollins.

Pierson, C. (1991), *Beyond the Welfare State?* Cambridge: Polity.

Pinch, S. (1997), *Worlds of Welfare: Understanding the Changing Geographies of Social Welfare Provision*, London: Routledge.

RSS (Rural Sociological Society Task Force on Persistent Rural Poverty) (1993), *Persistent Poverty in Rural America*, Boulder, CO: Westview.

Schwartz, J., and T. Volgy (1992), *The Forgotten Americans*, New York: Norton.

Sen, A. (1999), *Development as Freedom*, New York: Knopf.

Sibley, D. (1995), *Geographies of Exclusion: Society and Difference in the West*, London: Routledge.

Silvern, S. (1999), "Scales of Justice: Law, American Indian Treaty Rights and the Political Construction of Scale," *Political Geography*, 18, pp. 639–68.

UNDP (1999), *Globalization with a Human Face*, United Nations Human Development Report (http://www.undp.org/hdro/).

United States Bureau of the Census (1970), *Census of the United States Population Summary Tape Files*, Washington, DC: Government Printing Office.

United States Bureau of the Census (1980), *Census of the United States Population Summary Tape Files*, Washington, DC: Government Printing Office.

United States Bureau of the Census (1990), *Census of the United States Population Summary Tape Files*, Washington, DC: Government Printing Office.

United States Bureau of the Census (1991a), *Poverty in the United States: 1990*, Current Population Reports, Series P-60, no. 175, Washington, DC: Government Printing Office.

United States Bureau of the Census (1991b), *Trends in Relative Income, 1964–1989*, Current Population Reports, Series P-60, no. 177, Washington, D.C.: Government Printing Office.

Washington Times (March 20, 1997), "Millions Spent to Rebuild Churches: Religious Leaders Give Arson Update."

Watkins, K. (1997), *Globalization and Liberalisation: Implications for Poverty, Distribution, and Inequality*, United Nations Development Program (UNDP) Occasional Paper 32 (http://www.undp.org/undp/hdro/oc32a.html).

White, S. K. (1991), *Political Theory and Postmodernism*, Cambridge: Cambridge University Press.

Williams, F. (1989), *Social Policy: A Critical Introduction*, Oxford: Blackwell.

Wolch, J., and M. Dear (1993), *Malign Neglect: Homelessness in an American City*, San Francisco: Jossey-Bass.

Yapa, L. (1996), "What Causes Poverty? A Postmodern View," *Annals of the Association of American Geographers*, 86(4), pp. 707–28.

Zukin, Sharon (1991), *Landscapes of Power*, Berkeley: University of California Press.

CHAPTER 8

A new geography of identity? Race, ethnicity, and American citizenship

Benjamin Forest

From the beginning, a major challenge to the image of a unified American space has been the treatment of racial and ethnic minorities with respect to social, legal, and political rights. Above all, "whiteness" has had a privileged status within the practices and ideology of American society. It is only since the 1950s that dominant American institutions such as the federal Supreme Court and the presidency have paid sustained and positive attention to the claims for equal treatment by racial minorities. As a result of their passage to America as slaves, African-Americans have endured a particularly long history of discrimination and exclusion. Since the Civil War in which slavery was formally abolished it has been largely as a result of their own efforts, particularly by means of the Civil Rights Movement in the 1950s and 1960s, that African-Americans have achieved even nominal political equality in the United States. Persisting high economic and social disparities between white and black Americans, however, make the promise of political equality something of a hollow one. Yet, there is a continuing tension between the need to right the historic wrong of systematic discrimination and exclusion and the American ideal of a "color blind" national identity in which people appear as individuals before the courts and as voters. This now erupts in disputes over government programs to make up for past discrimination through affirmative action programs (diluted perhaps by the extension of such programs to cover large numbers of groups, such as Hispanics, for example, that are neither racial groups in any meaningful sense nor subject to the systematic discrimination afflicted on African-Americans), over disparate prison sentences for similar offenses to those committed by white defendants that now lead large numbers of black men to spend more years in prison than they do in school, and over the drawing of electoral boundaries to try and guarantee group representation in political institutions. Political geographer Benjamin Forest takes up the difficult issue of race and identity in the United States through the question of electoral redistricting. First, however, he offers a useful overview of debates over racial and ethnic identity in the United States, pointing out how categories such as "black" and "white" are widely used socially yet are also regarded with suspicion when used academically or with respect to political debate. The recent rise of various "symbolic ethnicities" based on personal choice is distinguished from the persisting importance of black/white racial identity, suggesting the degree to which judgments about physical differences are actually important in motivating discriminatory behavior. A second section explores the history of racial identity in the United States, using a series of maps (Figures 8.1–8.6) to show how highly regionally- and locally-concentrated the various racial groupings identified by the United States Census actually are. Forest points out how racial categories themselves are subject to considerable contestation. The one permanent feature has been the continuing attempt to distinguish "whites" from "nonwhites." Much of the chapter, however, examines the disputes since the 1960s over race, segregation, and political representation and how these relate to the ongoing American difficulty of dealing honestly with race while also remaining true to the claim of allowing for distinction without domination. Forest suggests that regarding racial identities as akin to religious ones may allow Americans to finally come to terms with what has been arguably their greatest challenge.

Difference, equality, and identity

At the end of the nineteenth century, the Supreme Court issued one of its most infamous decisions, *Plessy v Ferguson* (1896), approving a Louisiana law requiring "separate but equal" railcars for white and African-American passengers. Most Americans today, however, would be far more inclined to agree with the Court's now widely quoted dissenting opinion, written by Justice John Marshall Harlan, which declared that the "Constitution is color-blind, and neither knows nor tolerates classes among citizens." That is, laws requiring separation by race create inherently unequal relationships. Yet most of us would be shocked by the passage that precedes Harlan's famous declaration. The legal enforcement of segregation in the United States is unnecessary, he argues, because in the United States the "white race" is dominant "in prestige, in achievements, in education, in wealth and in power... [and] will continue to be for all time." The shift in the Supreme Court's view of legally enforced segregation during the twentieth century, exemplified by its 1954 desegregation decision in *Brown v the Board of Education*, reflects a general sea-change in American attitudes toward race. Indeed, I can confidently write in terms like "we," "us," and "most Americans" because our society has a relatively broad consensus on the opinions we will publicly express about race. This is not the same, of course, as saying that all Americans believe that whites, African-Americans, Asian-Americans, Hispanics, and other groups are equal, or that different racial and ethnic groups perceive race relations in the same way. The point is that in public, at least, Americans generally profess a belief in the equality of all racial groups and expect the law to reflect this equality. At the end of the twentieth century, we are all formally equal.

At the same time, Harlan's observation about the economic and social inequality between whites and nonwhites also remains true. Differences among racial and ethnic groups in income, poverty and other important socioeconomic measures remain staggeringly large (See Tables 8.1 and 8.2). The statistical profile of minority groups is by

Table 8.1 Median income by race and ethnicity in the United States, 1950–98

Year	White	Black	Asian and Pacific Islander	Hispanic
1950	13,059	5661	–	–
1960	14,533	6819	–	–
1970	17,279	11,943	–	–
1980	16,302	11,570	–	13,286
1990	18,751	12,880	18,480	13,323
1998	20,603	15,509	20,037	14,235

Note: Figures are in 1998 dollars.
Source: United States Census Bureau, "Race and Hispanic Origin of People (Both Sexes Combined) by Median Income: 1947–1998." Revised 10 November 1999.
<http://www.census.gov/hhes/income/histinc/p04.html>

Table 8.2 Percent of children under 18 below poverty level

Year	White	Black	Asian and Pacific Islander	Hispanic
1959	20.6	65.6	–	–
1970	10.5	41.5	–	–
1980	13.4	42.1	–	33.0
1990	15.1	44.2	17.0	37.7
1998	14.4	36.4	17.5	33.6

Source: United States Census Bureau, "Table 3: Poverty Status of People, by Age, Race and Hispanic Origin: 1959–1998." Revised September 30 1999.
<http://www.census.gov/hhes/poverty/histpov/histpov3.html>

no means simple or uniform (and has become especially complex in the last 20 years), but it is clear that, during the past 100 years, racial and ethnic minorities have been far less successful in achieving economic and social parity with whites than in acquiring legal equality.

This difference between legal equality and socioeconomic parity has become singularly important at the end of the twentieth century. A number of political controversies since 1985 have centered on the tension between a universalistic ideal of American citizenship – exemplified by the concept of legal equality – and the particular experience of socioeconomic disparities faced by racial and ethnic minorities. This contradiction of racial identity is one of the most important reflections of the difference between the American ideology of spatial uniformity and the reality of local variation and inequality.

Controversies over racial and ethnic identity in the United States can be traced to the persistence of rigid racial categories and residential segregation, two legacies of legal separatism that have endured in the face of legal equality and a decline in personal racial animosity. Although the segregation of certain ethnic groups has sometimes been the basis of economic advancement for new immigrants by providing a base for small business ownership (Light and Bonacich 1988; Light and Gold 2000), residential segregation by race presents one of the most significant obstacles to achieving socioeconomic parity (Kaplan and Holloway 1998; Massey and Denton 1993; Wilson 1996). I discuss the different effects of racial and ethnic segregation below, but most of my discussion will focus on the issue of political power as manifested in conflicts over electoral redistricting.

The allocation of political power to racial minorities by redrawing electoral districts rests on the premise they are only entitled to political representation if they are clustered together in relatively large groups, for example in a regional community. In political redistricting, Federal courts have ruled that legislatures cannot create "bizarrely" shaped electoral districts with African-American or Hispanic majorities. Jurists and politicians assert that racial identity is an overriding concern in such "bizarre" districts and that this emphasis on the role of racial identity in political representation is both divisive and unconstitutional. Consequently, courts rule against districting plans that group together distant voters of the same race or that separate neighboring voters of different races. Using the same logic of community representation, courts argue that "compact" communities of racial minorities are entitled to

special consideration in redistricting, and that plans must not divide
them among different districts. Courts have tried to balance the idea
of purely individual identity inherent in an individual's right to vote
with the role of group identity inherent in political representation by
relying on the geographic segregation of racial groups to define "fair"
redistricting plans.

Before discussing these issues in detail, I will discuss why American
political and legal systems generally accept and support "symbolic" ethnic
identity and distinctiveness based on voluntarism and choice while
simultaneously rejecting the more rigid distinctions of race as dangerous and divisive. This difference is based on the history of racial categorization in the United States, a history that now constrains both
how Americans think about identity and the solutions for reducing
racial inequalities.

Identity in the United States

What is identity? The word itself has taken on contradictory meanings
in American culture, connoting both sameness and difference. In its
original sense, the word expressed exact similarity. In mathematics and
geometry, for example, "an identity" describes two expressions that
appear to be different, or which have different forms, but are actually
the same. Yet Americans typically describe their own identity in terms
of the qualities and experiences that they believe make them different
from others. Moreover, American culture tends to portray such "differences" as products of free, voluntaristic choices. This emphasis on the
flexible, voluntary nature of identity ignores the fact that many individuals are highly constrained by historical circumstance, social
structures, and geographic context. Indeed, particularly for African-
Americans, the difference between the ideology of free, unconstrained
choice and actual circumstances of constraint marks one of the most
important distinctions between race and other forms of identity. In
short, there are often contradictions between the way Americans talk
about identity and the way in which they act (or are able to act) based
on their identities. Such contradictions between talk and action suggest
that one can best describe the concept of identity in the United States
as an ideology.

The idea of a "personal identity" suggests that one has some quality
or condition that remains constant throughout life, yet in American

culture individuals are also seen to be largely free to create an identity through preferences and consumption. Indeed, much consumer advertising is based on the idea that one can (and should!) buy products that establish one's "unique" identity. (For example, see Williamson 1978; Sack 1992; and Jackson and Taylor 1996.) It probably matters little to you if your neighbor drives a Chevrolet or a Ford, or if your lunch companion orders Coca-Cola rather than Pepsi, but advertisers spend enormous sums to convince us that there are significant differences between such products and that the choice of one or the other reflects a particular identity. More broadly, the rise of "symbolic ethnicity" in the past thirty years represents a kind of "group" identity that is actually based in individual choice, and thus has relatively little impact on issues of inequality.

The difference between an ideology of individuals acting freely to fulfill their preferences and the reality of constraint does much to explain the current differences between "ethnic" and "racial" identity in the United States. Although both ethnicity and race were treated as fixed, biological categories at the start of the twentieth century, ethnicity has become a largely voluntaristic identity while race has remained a highly constrained one.

Symbolic ethnicity

The ambiguous nature of modern American identity is perhaps most obvious in the clichéd "hyphenated-American" of ethnic identity. A wonderfully tongue-in-cheek guidebook to the United States, *The Xenophobe's Guide to the Americas*, observes,

> Americans are proud to be American ... but each individual will explain that he, personally, is not like the other Americans ... There's no such thing as a plain American, anyway. Every American is a hyphenated-American. The original "melting pot" has crystallized out into a zillion ethnic splinters: Croatian-Americans, Irish-Americans, Japanese-Americans, Mexican-Americans, and so on. (Faul 1994: 6)

Such a cheerful assessment of hyphenated identity may overstate the current acceptance of ethnic differences in the United States. Nonetheless, the tolerance of such diversity is higher now than in the early twentieth century when Theodore Roosevelt denounced hyphenated identities and the First World War heightened anxiety over "foreign" Americans (Bourne 1916). The fear of un-American "aliens" based on both religious difference (i.e. Catholicism rather than Protestantism) and ethnic difference was a pervasive theme in nineteenth-century politics, a pattern that has continued in one form or another since then (Bennett 1988). Although such suspicion of hyphenated ethnic identities seems strange now, discrimination and animosity based on "race" and "ethnicity" were closely intertwined for much of American history.

During the period of high immigration before 1920, race and ethnicity were not clearly distinguished as forms of identity. Differences between blacks, "new" immigrants from Ireland and southern Europe, and descendents of northern Europeans originating in England and Germany were imagined to be essentialistic, biological differences (Ignatiev 1995; Jacobson 1998). During this period it was not clear if these "new" immigrant groups would be classified racially with "old" immigrant groups, with blacks or with neither. The eventual social and economic assimilation of these groups depended on their reclassification as "white," a struggle that was carried out in both political and legal arenas. Ethnicity became a more fluid form of identity at the same time as racial distinctions became more firmly entrenched.

Hyphenated identities – seeking both similarity and difference – reflect the voluntaristic, constructed character of identity in contemporary American culture. The immigrant origins of a hyphenated identity can often be quite remote; an American may claim an ethnic identity even if s/he is three or four generations removed from immigrant status. Indeed, the remoteness of these immigrant origins plays an important role in reducing anxiety over social fragmentation. Political rhetoric about the dangers of cultural and linguistic differences has generally focused on recent immigrants, particularly those from Mexico, Central and South America (Ellis and Wright 1998; Rumbaut 1991). Similarly, the rise of the term "African-American," replacing "black," since 1985 reflects a similar attempt to define an identity that is different, but not too different. Bringing "black" identity into line with immigrant groups also has at least one other important consequence: it blurs the distinction between the nominally voluntary act of immigration and the forced migration of Africans as slaves.

Identifying oneself as Italian-American or Jewish-American or Japanese-American, etc., means that a person has selected some portion of his

or her ancestry as the basis of identity even if the actual relationship
is relatively remote (Waters 1990). A person may further construct an
identity by adopting certain styles of dress, cuisine, customs, and language. Moreover, a person may adopt different ethnic identification at
different points in their life. Gans (1979) characterizes this phenomenon as "symbolic ethnicity," in which one can adopt elements of an
ethnic culture that do not fundamentally affect everyday behavior. In
short, the ability to claim an identity based on historically remote
immigration fits comfortably with American culture's emphasis on
individual choice and voluntarism.

Yet this account of identity is clearly at odds with how many people,
particularly racial minorities, experience their own identity. In many
respects, racial identity is not a self-consciously constructed collection
of characteristics, but a condition which is imposed by a set of external
social and historical constraints. Residential segregation has been
among the most important factors shaping these constraints during the
twentieth century.

Racial identity in the United States

In many ways, the history of the United States is a story of racial identity. As a country settled by colonizers and immigrants, the population
of the United States is a complex amalgamation of the world's people,
including of course the original inhabitants of North America. The
racial and ethnic diversity of the United States has increased through
the twentieth century, a trend that is predicted to continue through
the next 50 years (Table 8.3). Indeed, by 2050, non-Hispanic whites
will constitute just over half of the United States population, down
from nearly 90 percent in 1900. Hispanics (classified by the Census as
an ethnic rather than a racial category) will probably surpass blacks as
the largest minority group in 2010, a significant demographic shift for
a group that accounted for less than 2 percent of the population in
1940.

The relative concentrations of racial and ethnic groups still largely
reflect the historical geography of an immigrant population (Figures
8.1–8.5). Although whites (i.e., European-Americans) are a majority in
most areas of the country, counties with the highest percentage of whites
are concentrated in the Midwest, northeast and northwest (Figure 8.1).
Counties with a high proportion of blacks are concentrated in the

urban and rural southeast and urban north (Figure 8.2), while counties with relatively high proportions of Asians are on the Pacific coast and urban areas of the northeast (Figure 8.3). American Indians, Eskimos, and Aleuts generally account for high proportions of the population only in rural areas of the west and southwest, and of course in Alaska (Figure 8.4). There are, however, also scattered pockets of relative concentration east of the Mississippi. Hispanics are an especially diverse category, and their distribution in the southwest, Florida, and the urban northeast reflects the different settlement patterns of Mexican, Cuban, and Puerto Rican migrants (Figure 8.5).

Table 8.3 United States population by percentage race and ethnicity, 1900–2050

Year	White, non-Hispanic	White	Black	American Indian, Eskimo, and Aleut	Asian	Hispanic
1900	–	87.9	11.6	0.3	0.2	–
1910	–	88.9	10.7	0.3	0.2	–
1920	–	89.7	9.9	0.2	0.2	–
1930	–	89.8	9.7	0.3	0.2	–
1940	88.4	89.8	9.8	0.3	0.2	1.4
1950	–	89.5	10.0	0.2	0.2	–
1960	–	88.6	10.5	0.3	0.5	–
1970	83.5	87.7	11.1	0.4	0.8	4.5
1980	79.7	83.4	11.7	0.7	1.6	6.4
1990	75.8	80.3	12.0	0.8	2.9	9.0
2000	71.8	82.1	12.9	0.9	4.1	11.4
2010	68.0	80.5	13.5	0.9	5.1	13.8
2020	64.3	79.0	14.0	1.0	6.1	16.3
2030	60.5	77.6	14.4	1.0	7.0	18.9
2040	56.7	76.1	14.9	1.1	7.9	21.7
2050	52.8	74.8	15.4	1.1	8.7	24.5

Note: Data for 2000–50 are projections. Persons of Hispanic origin may be of any race. The Census has not asked about Hispanic ethnicity consistently.

Sources: Data for 1900–90 calculated from Gibson, Campbell J., and Emily Lennon (March 1999), "Historical Census Statistics on the Foreign-born Population of the United States: 1850–1990," Table 8, United States Census Bureau, *Population Division Working Paper*, No. 29, Revised March 26, 1999. <http://www.census.gov/population/www.documentation/twps0029/twps0029.html>

Data for 2000–50 from Day, Jennifer Cheeseman (1996), *Population Projections of the United States by Age, Sex, Race and Hispanic Origins: 1995–2050*, Table 1, Middle Series, United States Bureau of the Census, *Current Population Reports*, P25–1130, United States Government Printing Office, Washington, DC.

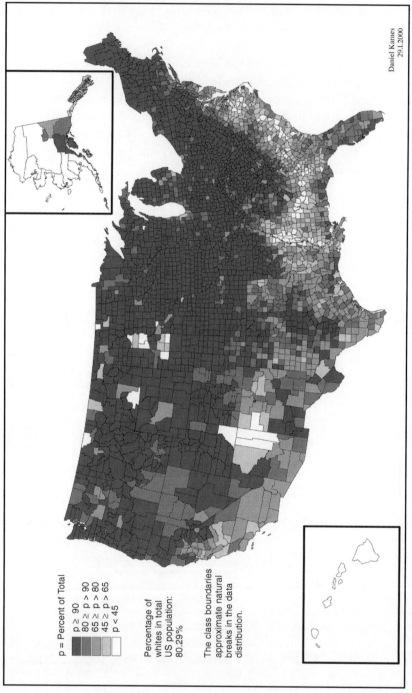

Figure 8.1 Whites, 1990 Census.

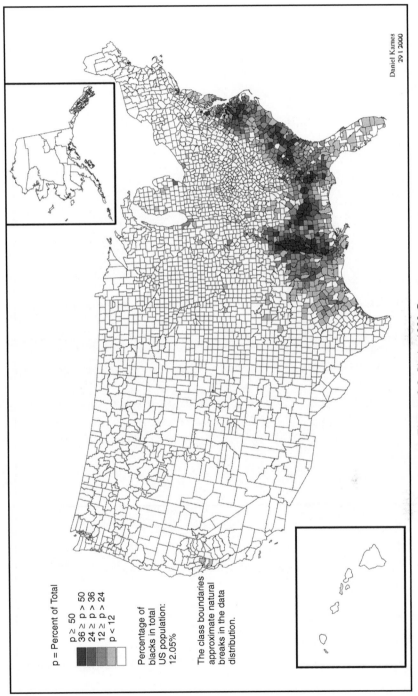

Figure 8.2 Blacks, 1990 Census.

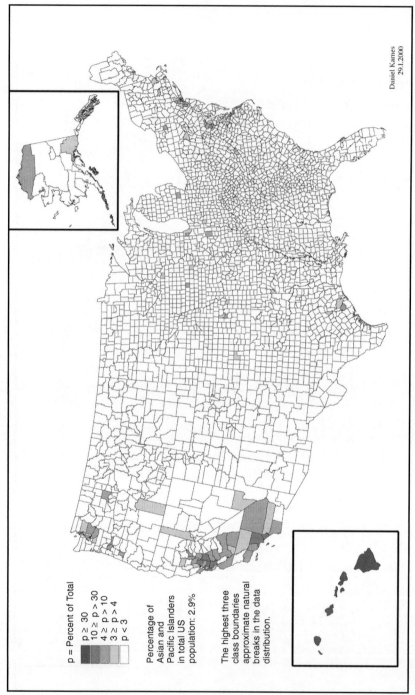

Figure 8.3 Asian and Pacific Islanders, 1990 Census.

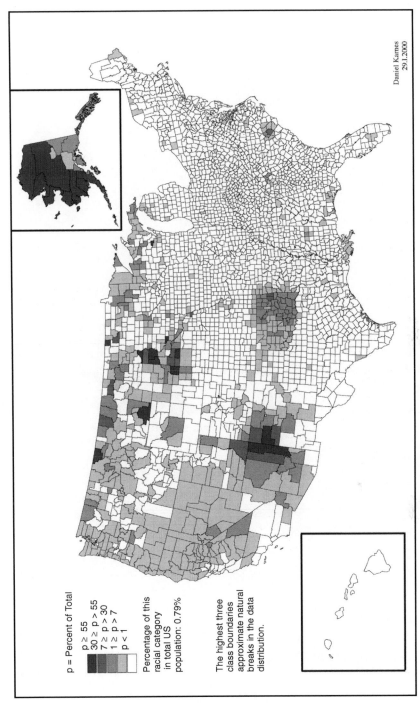

Figure 8.4 American Indian, Eskimo, and Aleut, 1990 Census.

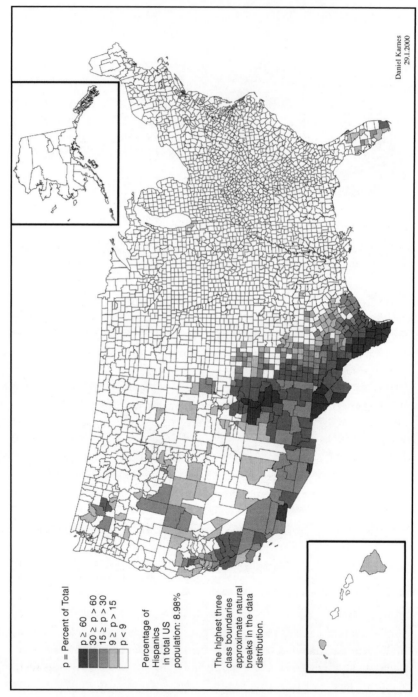

Figure 8.5 Hispanics, 1990 Census.

The patterns on such maps can reveal much about the historical geography of racial identity. (For example, the relatively high proportions of American Indians in Oklahoma counties on Figure 8.4 reflect that area's former designation as a reservation.) However, some of the most important geographies of race concern the definition and manipulation of racial categories rather than the spatial distribution of particular groups. For example, the four "racial" categories used by on the 1990 Census, White, Black, American Indian and Asian, and the "ethnic" distinction between Hispanics and non-Hispanics offers only the most basic representation of the diversity of the United States population. Indeed, after considerable debate, the 2000 Census permitted individuals to identify themselves in multiple racial categories, acknowledging the partial and inadequate basis of these classifications (Anderson and Feinberg 1999).

The political conflict over the racial and ethnic categories on the Census is merely one manifestation of the singularly important role that race has played in debates over equality, citizenship, and the definition of political community. The history of racism in the United States is often portrayed as a smooth progression toward equality, beginning with the abolition movement in the early nineteenth century, moving through the Civil War and civil rights guarantees of the 13th, 14th and 15th Amendments, to the integration of the armed services in the late 1940s, and culminating in the civil rights movement of the 1950s and 1960s. Indeed, those who now advocate the elimination of race-based affirmative action policies often claim to be working within this legacy of progressive racial emancipation. The actual story of race relations is, of course, a good deal more complex and it is more appropriate to think of racial equality as a series of ebbs and flows, rather than a smooth upwards progression. Racial equality in the United States has experienced periods of significant contraction whose effects cannot be easily shaken off.

The single most basic feature of American racial identity has been efforts to distinguish whites from nonwhites. The central importance of slavery in American political and social conflicts during the nineteenth century and the subsequent social realignments after the Civil War has meant that the distinction between whites and African-Americans has been the most important dimension of racial distinctiveness. There are, however, significant geographic variations in racial relations even within the United States. Variation in the relative concentration of racial and ethnic groups on the West coast and in the southwest meant, for example, that the distinction between Asians, Native Americans or Mexicans and Anglo-Americans played a central role in racial discourse (Almaguer 1994; Salyer 1995; Takaki 1979). Nonetheless, the division between whites and blacks has fundamentally shaped American racial consciousness.

Before 1865, of course, the division between whites and blacks corresponded closely to the rigid distinction between free and slave. Following emancipation, and particularly after the end of Reconstruction, whites reinscribed this rigid social and racial distinction with Jim Crow segregation. Indeed, Jim Crow laws were enforced more harshly and with more zeal than the "Black Codes" that had regulated the lives of slaves (Woodward 1974). In this manner, the fundamental social inequalities associated with slavery were attached to the racial distinction between whites and African-Americans.

Although racism is common in many societies, the particular system of racial classification used in the United States is largely unique. The principal "rule" for determining race in the United States is hypodescent, or the so-called "one-drop rule" (Davis 1991). A person would be defined – legally and socially – as nonwhite if they had a single non-white ancestor. To put this more simply, according to the ideology of hypodescent, a "white" parent can have a "black" child, but a "black" parent cannot have a "white" one (Jacobson 1998: 1–2). Clearly, of course, the application of this rule was not always simple or straightforward. Many Southern states and the Census had elaborate rules for classifying individuals based on the proportion of their African-American ancestry ("quadroons," "octoroons," etc.), although by 1920 the Census bureau adopted a simple "one-drop rule" to classify any person with black ancestry as "black" (Davis 1991: 11–12). There is little need to belabor the capricious nature of hypodescent, or the fact that it refers to a social rather than a biological system of classification.

It is useful, however, to illustrate the arbitrariness of the racial classification system in the United States with several counter-examples. Even within the United States, an individual's racial classification often depended on his or her geographic location. For example, people moving from the deep South to the North could find themselves "reclassified" from white to black because the norms governing racial identity (skin color, ancestry, etc.) were applied differently (Williams 1995). Contrasts with other countries and cultures can seem even more startling to Americans. In Britain, the term "black" refers not only to Afro-Caribbeans and Africans, but also to individuals from the Indian subcontinent (Jackson 1989: 146–8). In Russia the term "black" is used to describe "Caucasians," that is, people such as Chechens from the Caucasus region (Filipov 1999). In many parts of Latin America, particularly Brazil, "racial" classification is really a kind of class placement, in which members of the wealthy upper class are generally considered as "white," members of the middle class as mixed race or Mestizo, and members of the lower class as "black" (Davis 1991: 99–105). Indeed, because racial classifications are based on class standing and physical appearance rather than ancestry, "the designation of one's racial identity need not be the same as that of the parents, and siblings are often classified differently than one another" (Davis 1991: 101).

Although these examples illustrate alternative systems of racial classification, race – particularly in the United States – has long been a socially, legally, and politically imposed identity rather than one that has been freely adopted or chosen. While the vast majority of legally imposed racial classifications were overturned in the 1960s and 1970s, Louisiana continued to mark racial classification on birth certificates as late as the 1980s (Omi and Winant 1994: 53). One may fairly ask, however, why race has persisted as a form of social classification and source of group identity after such rigid racial classifications have been written out of the law and when African-Americans are routinely lauded as celebrities, military heroes, academics, and sports stars (Landry 1991)? In contrast to symbolic ethnicity, race can so profoundly influence an individual's experience and life-chances that it acquires the characteristics of a fixed, essential identity. Indeed, African-American intellectuals throughout the twentieth century have argued that racism is so deeply woven into American culture that blacks inhabit a world largely unrecognizable to whites (DuBois 1990; hooks 1990). In short, local geographies of race have served to reproduce and maintain rigid racial distinctions.

Inequality and the legacy of segregation

Racial inequality in the United States can be traced to the legacy of segregation established during the Jim Crow era. The residential segregation of whites from blacks in the first half of the twentieth century isolated African-Americans both socially and economically. This separation both reflected and reinforced the "social distance" between whites and blacks, and excluded African-Americans from the most dynamic sectors of the economy. In the late nineteenth century American cities were relatively integrated, yet by the middle of the twentieth century urban areas were characterized by high levels of racial segregation. Legal and social restrictions guided the creation of black urban ghettos during the "Great Migration" of African- Americans from the rural South to the urban North during the first half of the twentieth century (Grossman 1989; Lemann 1991). This profound change in residential patterns was perhaps the most fundamental factor influencing black social and economic development (Massey and Denton 1993). Indeed, the general geographic distribution of African-Americans can still be characterized as a split between the urban Northeast and the rural South (Figure 8.2).

As early as the 1920s, urban sociologists working in Chicago noted that the physical distance between ethnic and racial groups often corresponded to the "social distance" between them (Burgess 1967). That is, groups with high social status tended to live relatively far from groups with low social status, and this separation was particularly acute for blacks. Although immigration centers like Chicago were characterized by ethnic neighborhoods, even the most concentrated ethnic groups were less segregated than African-Americans (Massey and Denton 1993). This suggests that the "social distance" between blacks and nonblacks was greater than the distance between groups of ethnic whites.

The high degree of segregation by race was hardly accidental, but was rather the culmination of a vigorous effort to create separate racial residential zones (Delaney 1998). Indeed, this effort began with attempts to create a true system of apartheid in which certain urban and rural areas (qua homelands?) would be designated as white-only or black-only. When such segregation ordinances were overturned by the Supreme Court in 1917 (as a violation of the property rights of white landowners!), whites turned to restrictive covenants – private agreements that forbade the sale of property to nonwhites. The Court ruled that restrictive covenants were unenforceable in 1946, but by that time the pattern of racial segregation was already in place. Subsequent legislation such as the Fair Housing Act of 1968 has either been ineffective or weakly enforced, leaving racial segregation to its self-reinforcing cycle (Massey and Denton 1993). Consequently, the difference in social and legal status between freemen and slaves established during the nineteenth century became geographically inscribed as a racial difference during the twentieth century.

The economic effects of the segregation are at least as profound as the social effects. There is considerable debate over the exact nature and extent of these effects, but in general terms the residential isolation of African-Americans in older urban areas has tended to limit their employment opportunities and to isolate them from the benefits of industrial and suburban residential investment (Massey and Denton 1993; Wilson 1996). Since the 1960s, the low-skill industrial jobs that traditionally provided immigrants with middle-class opportunities have either moved overseas or have moved into suburban areas not accessible to African-Americans. Likewise, the explosive growth in suburban residential areas after 1945 benefited new white homeowners disproportionally and drained investment capital from inner-city areas populated by African-Americans.

In one of the bitterest ironies of segregation, the ability of upper- and middle-class blacks to move out of ghettos after the 1960s created "hyperghettos" of concentrated black poverty, without creating stable, integrated neighborhoods elsewhere (Wilson 1987). Social, legal, and economic opportunities have changed considerably since 1950, but racial residential segregation has persisted and consistently evolved to minimize the interaction and contact between whites and blacks (Massey and Hajnal 1995).

Racial identity and political representation

The residential segregation of African-Americans has maintained both racial inequalities and the idea that race is a fixed, essential identity, but this geographic concentration has simultaneously provided an opportunity for political empowerment. Given the opportunity to vote, segregated racial minorities can elect representatives because they form local political majorities in electoral districts. In the final section of this chapter, I will discuss the successes and limitations of this approach to minority political empowerment. This strategy relies on the spatially uneven distribution of racial minorities, but it is effective only because the United States uses an electoral system of simple-majority, single-member districts. Since the late 1960s, the Federal court system has enforced the individual right to vote strongly because it corresponds quite well with ideas of individual volunteerism and choice. The court system has been far less comfortable, however, with electoral districts that are deliberately constructed to create nonwhite majorities.

American political representation and single-member districts

One of the distinguishing features of American democratic practice is the use of single-member districts as the basic unit of political representation. Unlike party-lists or forms of proportional representation, a single representative is elected from a particular district, and under the dominant two-party system a candidate needs only a simple majority (50 percent + 1) of votes to win. This strong territorial basis for political representation was a revolutionary eighteenth-century response to the "virtual representation" of the American colonies in the British Parliament (Pole 1966). For purposes of this discussion, the idea of district representation includes two fundamental principles: (1) legislators should live in the districts they represent; and (2) legislators represent constituents in a specific area. Both of these requirements were meant to ensure that local interests would be represented and protected in higher levels of government.

During Constitutional debates, Federalists like James Madison justified election by district for precisely the opposite reason (Madison 1996). For Madison, single-member districts were a pragmatic way to limit the power of political factions because, in his view, districts would always contain constituents with a variety of political claims. Voters would need to compromise their conflicting interests in order to elect a candidate, and would thereby need to moderate their political views.

In both cases, however, American political representation was based on assumptions about local variation. For the radical revolutionaries, single-member districts provided a means to express local variation, while for the Federalists single-member districts provided a way to limit the expression of local variation.

These two themes have existed uneasily for much of American history, and this has been particularly true since the 1960s, as Federal courts have attempted to find a principled basis for allocating political representation to racial minorities. In the past ten years, however, courts have become more sympathetic to Madisonian arguments that emphasize uniform, universalistic rights and political compromise than to arguments emphasizing the expression of local variation and interests.

Consequently, the spatial segregation of racial minorities has provided some basis for political empowerment, but one that is simultaneously limited by the Madisonian interpretation of single-member districts.

Voting rights and political representation

Every ten years, the 435 United States Congressional representatives are reapportioned among the fifty states based on population as measured by the Census. In jurisdictions with more than one Representative, state legislatures are required to draw new Congressional districts following reapportionment. During the 1990 round of redistricting, racial identity became a central issue in this process.

Under the auspices of the Voting Rights Act, a number of states drew Congressional districts with irregular boundaries containing African-American or Hispanic majorities in an explicit effort to increase the political representation of these groups. Redistricting plans in North Carolina, Georgia, Louisiana, and Texas were challenged successfully in Federal courts on the grounds that such unusually shaped districts were a form of racial classification and therefore unconstitutional. In North Carolina, for example, the state assembly created a redistricting plan that included one black-majority district, the 12th, that stretched over 160 miles from Charlotte to Raleigh (see Figure 8.6). The district created an African-American majority by linking urban neighborhoods in different cities with narrow, unpopulated "bridges," including one infamous stretch along Interstate 85.

Federal courts held that such complex or "bizarre" boundaries proved that state legislators allocated voters by race rather than by permissible criteria such as political party. The results of the 1990s voting rights cases as well as the legal reasoning used by courts to decide them illustrate the deeply contradictory nature of racial identity in the United States (Forest forthcoming). I will first briefly review the historical background of political representation and voting rights before discussing more recent cases.

Equality in representation

The Voting Rights Act of 1965 established the principle that racial minorities are entitled to special consideration in the electoral system because they have been historically targeted for disenfranchisement.

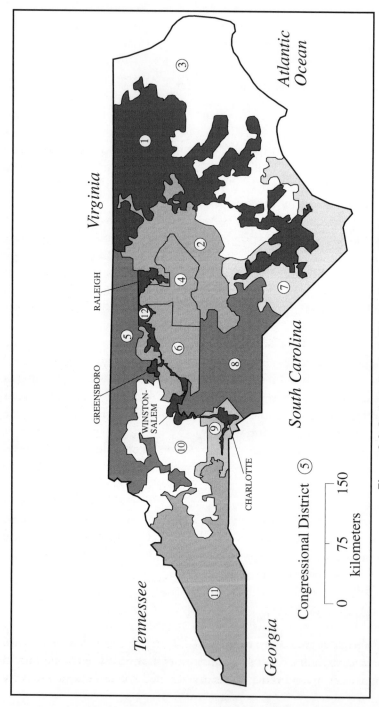

Figure 8.6 Redistricting plan of North Carolina (1991).

Under the Voting Rights Act, African-Americans gained access to the ballot box and to political power for the first time in many Southern states (Davidson and Grofman 1990).

The consequences of the Voting Rights Act have been complicated, in part because the Act is an intricate piece of legislation that was renewed and amended three times (in 1970, 1975, and 1982). Courts have interpreted the Voting Rights Act in two distinct ways. A relatively narrow reading of the Act, generally adopted by political conservatives, suggests that the law only guarantees access to the ballot box. That is, equal participation in the political process means the physical ability to cast a vote and to campaign for political office free from government interference (Thernstrom 1987). A broader interpretation, one generally adopted by political liberals, asserts that the concept of equal participation must include conditions under which racial minorities can actually win elections. Equality in this view refers to a "fair" share of political power, and not simply the ability of each voter to cast a ballot individually. The best-known, although often misunderstood, explanation of this perspective is Lani Guinier's *The Tyranny of the Majority* (1994).

Why is the equal ability to cast a vote not the same as an equal share of political power? Almost half the voters in a district may "waste" their votes by selecting a losing candidate because Congressional elections use single-member districts. Consequently, one can gerrymander, or manipulate, the results of an election by changing the boundaries of a district to alter the composition of voters in that district. The most common strategy is "cracking," in which a group of minority voters is split between two or more districts. In areas with sufficiently large minority populations, legislatures may resort to "packing," in which all or most minority voters are concentrated into a single district. They are guaranteed to win that seat, but will have no influence in other districts. Such strategies can be used against racial minorities only under conditions of segregation.

After passage of the Voting Rights Act, many Southern state legislatures turned to gerrymandering strategies to maintain white political control. African-Americans were free to vote and to run for office, but seldom won because most districts were majority white and, at least at that time, very few whites would vote for African-American candidates. Courts were thus faced with a difficult question. If the law permitted gerrymandering, minority votes would not translate into minority political power, and the Voting Rights Act would become largely symbolic, or another "broken promise" to racial minorities. Alternatively, if the law forbade gerrymandering, it was not clear how legislatures and courts could judge the difference between legal redistricting and illegal gerrymandering. Courts chose the latter path, and began a thirty-year struggle to identify illegal racial gerrymandering. The evolution of the Voting Rights Act illustrates the tension in the American concept of identity. Although voting is perhaps the epitome of an individual, voluntaristic act, political representation always involves the definition and recognition of group interests and values.

Segregation and political representation

The interplay between Federal courts and Congress from 1965 to the 1980s left the standard for redistricting rather confused. A redistricting plan could not "dilute" minority voting strength, nor could courts require proportional representation by race. The Supreme Court attempted to resolve this question definitively in a case from North Carolina, *Thornburg v Gingles* (1986) by turning to the idea of geographic compactness: essentially, minority groups were entitled to representation to the extent that they were segregated from whites.

In *Thornburg*, plaintiffs challenged the apportionment plan for North Carolina's general assembly, arguing that the electoral system in the state diluted the political strength of nonwhite voters. The basic question in the case was whether a legislature could have reasonably drawn districts so that more of them would contain African-American majorities. In an effort to answer what "reasonably drawn" might mean, the Supreme Court used a three-part test to evaluate the claim of vote dilution, including two basic measures of political polarization (the extent to which whites and nonwhites have different political interests and preferences). The third criterion held, however, that a minority group must be relatively large and geographically compact (*Thornburg v Gingles* 1986). In short, each distinct geographic community of racial minorities must correspond to a distinct district. The Court thus treated geographically defined communities as the basic unit of political identity by recognizing minorities only if they were concentrated in a compact area.

The standard adopted by the Court in *Thornburg* thus seemed to solve a number of political and legal dilemmas by recognizing that the ability to win elections is a critical element to minority political participation, and by placing limits on that ability. In short, the decision neither excluded minorities from power, nor appeared to treat race as an essential category. This "solution," however, rests on the assumption that racial minorities are spatially segregated from whites. Moreover, despite this apparent resolution, minority voting rights and redistricting became one of the most bitterly contested legal and political conflicts in the 1990s. This arose largely from the Court's failure to define what it meant by "compact."

Representing individuals

In the 1990s' voting rights cases, courts ruled against irregularly shaped, non-white-majority districts on the grounds that they classified voters based on race. Courts based these decisions on the general principle that states and government bodies should not categorize citizens according to an essentialistic form of identity. While redistricting always involves some form of classification, the only permissible categories are those that involve voluntaristic categories, such as political party.

The view of the self as an autonomous individual acting on personal preference is a powerful ideal for systems of political representation. From this perspective, the right to vote inheres only in the individual, and the contemporary act of voting is an almost perfect exemplar of this view, with the anonymity and privacy of the voting booth replicating an atmosphere of atomistic, equal individuals. This emphasis on individual choice reflects the preference-based theory of identity underlying symbolic ethnicity. In short, courts feel that redistricting as well as voting should reflect individual choice. It is clear, of course, that jurists do not necessarily believe that this is how people actually make decisions or how they identify themselves. Rather this idea supports a set of assumptions and beliefs about desirable social and political behavior: the reduction or elimination of racial identity as a meaningful political and social category.

The effort to eliminate explicit racial considerations from redistricting became quite clear in the Supreme Court's first major voting rights decision in the 1990s, *Shaw v Reno* (North Carolina). In this case, the court overturned the state's plan, comparing it to the South African system of apartheid:

> A reapportionment plan that includes in one district individuals . . .
> who may have little in common with one another but the color of
> their skin, bears an uncomfortable resemblance to political apartheid.
> (*Shaw v Reno* 1993: 529)

The elongated, irregular districts like those found in North Carolina
are unconstitutional because they are a way to place racial groups into
separate political constituencies. In particular, the Court saw the extraordinary convolutions of North Carolina's plan as clear evidence that
the state believed a common racial identity to be equivalent to common
political interests.

One statement that makes the *Reno* decision so revealing is the
Supreme Court's assertion that the residents of the 12th District had
nothing in common but "the color of their skin." Among other defenses,
North Carolina argued that the district linked minority urban neighborhoods from Charlotte to Raleigh, and thus reflected the common
interests of segregated, inner-city minorities. In rejecting this argument,
the Court rejected the theory that racial segregation itself creates
common identity. By using an individualistic model of identity, the
decision suggests that the social and political consequences of racial
segregation are not an appropriate basis for political values and interests. To put it another way, the Court argues that such districts reflect
a rigid form of racial categorization, rather than a flexible, voluntaristic
form of identity. It is furthermore unwilling to acknowledge that the
history of racial categorization and segregation may have created a
unique, racially defined political community.

The role of nonracial characteristics and identities in political representation has been emphasized in a number of recent works. These
studies argue that the interests of racial minorities (particularly
African-Americans) are better represented with districts that are likely
to elect (white) Democrats rather than minority candidates (Swain
1993; Cameron, Epstein, and O'Halloran 1996; Lubin 1997). Clearly,
white and minority voters indeed often share common interests that
can be advanced more effectively in political coalitions (Clark and
Morrison 1995). Furthermore, the ability to create such coalitions
clearly indicates an important change in American attitudes towards
race. Nonetheless, there are still circumstances – perhaps more often
at the local level – when racial identity defines a significant political
division. In these cases, the representation of minority groups as

minority groups may reflect a unique set of political interests based on racial identity. In short, to the extent that different racial groups continue to have different political interests and continue to vote for different candidates, these voting rights decisions have at least one very practical consequence: racial minority groups will achieve political representation to the degree that they are segregated from whites.

Race, politics, and the possibilities of identity

The controversies over voting rights during the 1990s illustrate the contradictory nature of identity in the United States. Courts moved away from the explicit recognition of racial identity – even in instances that would provide minorities with greater political power – toward more individualistic, or "colorblind" policies. In these cases, the only legally recognizable form of identity is an individualistic, constructed one. In both politics and law, the only legitimate basis for action is an identity that an individual has chosen or constructed.

As a result, during the 1990s the legal system has increasingly presented racial and ethnic minorities with a Faustian bargain. Courts will protect a right to political representation for minority groups only if they remain in distinct and compact geographic communities. Consequently, the same decisions and policies that purportedly seek to eliminate the recognition of group identity in fact rely on – and perhaps even encourage – racial distinctions rooted in segregation. The law's explicit rejection and implicit acceptance of racial difference tends to reinforce the social and economic disadvantages of racial minorities.

Alternative political approaches to racial segregation

What will be the outcome to the paradox posed by the racial segregation of African-Americans? One can imagine at least three different possibilities that could reduce the significance of racial identity.

First, some argue that the "Faustian" bargain of African-Americans is really no dilemma at all. As racial categories continue to lose their rigidity, as more African-Americans enter the middle class and as discrimination and segregation in the housing market declines, racial identity, like ethnicity, will become increasingly symbolic and less closely tied to physical appearance. In short, the 500-year experiment of European racism is nearly over, and minorities should embrace the emancipatory possibilities of a world without racial identity. From this perspective, as racial segregation breaks down, political cartographers will no longer be able to create nonwhite-majority districts but African-Americans will also no longer have meaningful political interests distinct from whites. In short, a racial identity will become no more important than a symbolic ethnicity.

The second possibility is a more limited version of the first. If upper- and middle-class African-Americans become significantly less segregated than lower-class blacks, this latter group will become increasing isolated politically by both race and class. (It is important to note, however, that Massey and Denton (1993) found little evidence that upper- and middle-class African-Americans are in fact becoming less segregated from whites.) Under such circumstances, the racial system in the United State could evolve into one similar to Brazil, where "racial" identity is a marker of class status. For example, a relatively wealthy, dark-skinned American of African origin might be considered "white" while a relatively poor person of similar physical appearance and ancestry would be considered "black." Indeed, one can see the potential for this to the extent that popular African-American figures like Michael Jordan or Colin Powell have achieved positions of power and privilege and can move freely in the "white" world. If this phenomenon were to extend to middle-class African-Americans as well, black-majority districts could only claim to represent the political interests of lower-class blacks rather than the pan-racial interests of all blacks. To think of this another way, upper- and middle-class blacks could "opt out" of racial identity.

Third, a number of scholars, notably Lani Guinier, suggest that the most reasonable path for resolving the dilemmas of racial identity and political representation involve changes to the electoral system (Guinier 1994; Forest 1996). There are, of course, many alternatives to the American system of simple majority, single-member districts, including party-list systems popular in most other democracies. Guinier proposes a combination of multimember districts with a cumulative voting system. Under such a plan, an electoral district elects two or more representatives and each voter is entitled to a number of votes equal to the number of representatives. For example, a district might elect three representatives and each voter could cast three votes. However, a voter could allocate all three of his or her votes for a single candidate, two for one candidate and one for another, etc. Such an electoral design lowers the "threshold of exclusion" and permits a minority of voters who cast all of their votes for a single person to elect that candidate. In this example, as few as 25 percent of the voters could guarantee the election of their candidate. All other things equal, a politically cohesive minority group could more easily elect candidates because they would only need to constitute one-quarter rather than one-half of the electorate in a particular district.

The effect of such a system is difficult to predict. On the one hand – as Guinier argues – it reduces the emphasis on racial identity because a citizen can allocate votes according to a number of different criteria. For example, a voter might cast two votes for one candidate based on political party loyalty, and one vote for a different candidate based on racial identity. Like the previous two scenarios, this would (potentially) weaken the tie between racial identity and political interest because (1) citizens could express their identity along a number of different dimensions (race, class, party, gender, region, etc.), and (2) it would reduce the incentive to draw electoral districts that reflect segregated communities of racial minorities.

On the other hand, such electoral designs increase the power of any political minority. Minority parties in European democracies using party-list systems, for example, typically hold far more power than third parties in the United States. This raises the potential for the rise of radical political parties based on single issues like abortion or school prayer. Such minority political parties could just as easily form around invocations of racial solidarity – black power, white supremacy, etc. – because such parties only need to appeal to a relatively narrow set of voters (Forest 1996). Thus Guinier's approach reveals yet another set of paradoxes. A proposal that (arguably) embraces the ideology of universalism and uniformity in politics by de-emphasizing the use of regionally defined political interests (and consequently reliance on racial segregation as a basis for minority political power) could lead to an even greater emphasis on racial identity and difference.

Conclusion: social privilege, race, and the politics of identity

By way of conclusion, I would like to address a theme that runs through the forgoing discussions of racial identity, segregation, and political representation: the relationship between social privilege and identity. The ability to "choose" an identity – or indeed even to contemplate the nature of identity – rests on socioeconomic advantages that are themselves distributed unevenly along racial lines. This relationship is implicit in my discussion of symbolic ethnicity and rather more explicit in the preceding section. To say this more simply, when compared to minorities, whites in general have access to resources, privileges, and rights that make it easier to "choose" an identity. Likewise, elite African-Americans have an advantage over lower-class blacks. Golfer Tiger Woods' insistence that he is mixed race rather than "black" is a recent example of this phenomenon. One may, of course, strongly support his right to identify himself as he sees fit, while at the same time acknowledging that most mixed-race individuals do not have the ability to make this choice effectively. Indeed, the ability to select multiracial identities on the 2000 Census raises a similar issue because this choice may limit the government's ability to monitor and correct racial discrimination against minority groups (Cohn 2000). More broadly, the American ideology of identity embodied by symbolic ethnicity – individuals in a uniform space of rights, preferences, and choices – stands in sharp contrast to the reality of segregation, local variation, and constraint.

Similarly, my own position of relative privilege and authority raises questions about my ability to comment on issues of identity. To paraphrase an editorial comment on an earlier version of this chapter, it is troubling to rely on a white, Ivy League college professor to explain what segregation means to blacks. To put this another way, why do I have the freedom to speculate about a "raceless" world, to hold an ambivalent position about "colorblindness," or to write with the "confidence" I mention in the first paragraph of this chapter? Such concerns are legitimate insofar as my freedom to do so is tied to the social privileges and advantages I enjoy as a white person in the United States. I believe these are serious issues, but I would also argue that the intellectual activity of academic research inevitably requires one to step outside one's own particular, subjective frame of reference. Indeed, the ability to step outside oneself can serve, as in this case, to shift attention from the issue of minority identity per se to the issue of white privilege.

In an important sense, this shift from identity to privilege recasts the terms of the political debate over racial identity. The ideology of spatial uniformity is often used to argue that racial minorities should give up race as a basis of social solidarity and political power. Yet a focus on white social privilege suggests how the difference between this ideology and reality has served to reinforce the power and status of whites. In this manner, the model of voluntaristic identity actually serves to maintain racial differences in a way that reproduces the advantages already enjoyed by whites.

References

Almaguer, Tomás (1994), *Racial Fault Lines: The Historical Origins of White Supremacy in California*, Berkeley: University of California Press.

Anderson, Margo, and Stephen Feinberg (1999), *Who Counts?: The Politics of Census Taking in Contemporary America*, New York: Russell Sage Foundation.

Bennett, David N. (1988), *The Party of Fear: From Nativist Movements to the New Right in American History*, Chapel Hill: The University of North Carolina Press.

Bourne, Randolph S. (1916), "Trans-National America," *Atlantic Monthly*, 118, July, pp. 86–97. Reprinted in Werner Sollors (1996) (ed.), *Theories of Ethnicity: A Classical Reader*, New York: New York University Press, pp. 93–108.

Burgess, Ernest (1967), "The Growth of the City: An Introduction to a Research Project," in Robert E. Park, Ernest W. Burgess, and Roderick D. McKenzie (eds.), *The City*, Chicago: University of Chicago Press. Article originally published 1925.

Cameron, C., D. Epstein, and S. O'Halloran (1996), "Do Majority-Minority Districts Maximize Substantive Black Representation in Congress?" *American Political Science Review*, 90(4), pp. 794–812.

Clark, William A. V., and Peter Morrison (1995), "Demographic Foundations of Political Empowerment in Multiminority Cities," *Demography*, 32(2), pp. 183–201.

Cohn, D'Vera (2000), "A Racial Tug of War over Census," *Washington Post*, March 3.

Davidson, Chandler, and Bernard Grofman (eds.) (1990), *Quiet Revolution in the South: The Impact of the Voting Rights Act, 1965–1990*, Princeton: Princeton University Press.

Davis, F. James (1991), *Who Is Black? One Nation's Definition*, University Park: The Pennsylvania State University Press.

Delaney, David (1998), *Race, Place and the Law 1836–1948*, Austin: University of Texas Press.

DuBois, W. E. B. (1990), *The Souls of Black Folk*, New York: Vintage Books. Originally published 1903.

Ellis, Mark and Richard Wright (1998), "The Balkanization Metaphor in the Analysis of United States Immigration," *Annals of the Association of American Geographers*, 88(4), pp. 686–98.

Faul, Stephanie (1994), *The Xenophobe's Guide to the Americas*, West Sussex: Ravette Publishing Limited.

Filipov, David (1999), "Eyeing Chechnya, Moscow Police Wage Racist War," *Boston Globe*, October 6.

Forest, Benjamin (1996), "Where Should Democratic Compromise Take Place? (Review essay of *The Tyranny of the Majority* [1994] by Lani Guinier)," *Social Science Quarterly*, 77(1), pp. 6–13.

Forest, Benjamin (Forthcoming), "Mapping Democracy: Racial Identity and the Quandary of Political Representation."

Gans, Herbert J. (1979), "Symbolic Ethnicity: The Future of Ethnic Groups and Cultures in America," *Ethnic and Racial Studies*, 2(1), pp. 1–20.

Grossman, James R. (1989), *Land of Hope: Chicago, Black Southerners, and the Great Migration*, Chicago: University of Chicago Press.

Guinier, Lani (1994), *The Tyranny of the Majority: Fundamental Fairness in Representative Democracy*, New York: The Free Press (Macmillan).

hooks, bell (1990), *Yearnings: Race, Gender, and Cultural Politics*, Boston: South End Press.

Ignatiev, Noel (1995), *How the Irish Became White*, New York: Routledge.

Jackson, P., and J. Taylor (1996), "Geography and the Cultural Politics of Advertising," *Progress in Human Geography*, 30(3), pp. 356–71.

Jacobson, Matthew Frye (1998), *Whiteness of a Different Color: European Immigrants and the Alchemy of Race*, Cambridge: Harvard University Press.

Jackson, Peter (1989), *Maps of Meaning*, London: Unwin Hyman.

Kaplan, David H., and Steven R. Holloway (1998), *Segregation in Cities*, Washington, DC: Association of American Geographers.

Landry, Bart (1991), "The Enduring Dilemma of Race in America," in Alan Wolfe (ed.), *America at Century's End*, Berkeley: University of California Press, pp. 185–207.

Lemann, Nicholas (1991), *The Promised Land: The Great Black Migration and How It Changed America*, New York: A. A. Knopf.

Light, Ivan Hubert, and Edna Bonacich (1988), *Immigrant Entrepreneurs: Koreans in Los Angeles, 1965–1982*, Berkeley: University of California Press.

Light, Ivan Hubert, and Steven J. Gold (2000), *Ethnic Economies*, San Diego: Academic Press.

Lubin, David (1997), *The Paradox of Representation: Racial Gerrymandering and Minority Interests in Congress*, Princeton: Princeton University Press.

Madison, James (1996), "The Federalist, Number Ten," in Alexander Hamilton, John Jay, and James Madison, *The Federalist: Or, The New Constitution*, ed. William R. Brock, London: J. M. Dent, and Rutland, VT: Charles E. Tuttle Co., pp. 41–8.

Massey, Douglas S., and Nancy A. Denton (1993), *American Apartheid: Segregation and the Making of the Underclass*, Cambridge, MA: Harvard University Press.

Massey, Douglas S., and Zoltan L. Hajnal (1995), "The Changing Structure of Black-White Segregation in the United States," *Social Science Quarterly*, 76(3), pp. 527–42.

Pole, J. R. (1966), *Political Representation in England and the Origins of the American Republic*, Berkeley: University of California Press.

Omi, Michael, and Howard Winant (1994), *Racial Formation in the United States from the 1960s to the 1990s*, 2nd ed., New York: Routledge.

Rumbaut, Rubén G. (1991), "Passages to America: Perspectives on the New Immigration," in Alan Wolfe (ed.), *America at Century's End*, Berkeley: University of California Press, pp. 208–44.

Sack, Robert (1992), *Place, Modernity, and the Consumer's World: A Relational Framework for Geographical Analysis*, Baltimore: Johns Hopkins University Press.

Salyer, Lucy E. (1995), *Laws Harsh as Tigers: Chinese Immigrants and the Shaping of Modern Immigration Law*, Chapel Hill: University of North Carolina Press.

Swain, Carol M. (1993), *Black Faces, Black Interests: The Representation of African Americans in Congress*, Cambridge: Harvard University Press.

Takaki, Ronald T. (1979), *Iron Cages: Race and Culture in 19th Century America*, Seattle: University of Washington Press.

Thernstrom, Abigail (1987), *Whose Votes Count? Affirmative Action and Minority Voting Rights*, Cambridge: Harvard University Press.

Waters, Mary C. (1990), *Ethnic Options: Choosing Identities in America*, Berkeley: University of California Press.

Williams, Gregory Howard (1995), *Life on the Color Line: The True Story of a White Boy Who Discovered He Was Black*, New York: Dutton.

Williamson, Judith (1978), *Decoding Advertisements: Ideology and Meaning in Advertising*, London: Marion Boyars.

Wilson, William Julius (1987), *The Truly Disadvantaged: The Inner City, the Underclass, and Public Policy*, Chicago: The University of Chicago Press.

Wilson, William Julius (1996), *When Work Disappears: The World of the New Urban Poor*, New York: Vintage Books.

Woodward, C. Vann (1974), *The Strange Career of Jim Crow*, 3rd rev. ed., New York: Oxford University Press.

Law Cases

Brown v Board of Education, 347 United States 483 (1954).

Plessy v Ferguson, 163 US 537 (1896).

Shaw v Reno, 125 L. Ed. 2d 511 (1993).

Thornburg v Gingles, 106 S. Ct. 2752 (1986).

Legislation

Voting Rights Act, 42 United States Code § 1973.

CHAPTER 9

Landscape, aesthetics, and power

James S. Duncan and David R. Lambert

The idealized American identity that took shape in the aftermath of independence was closely tied to the idea of the settlement of a pristine continent wrested with difficulty, sacrifice, and hard work from the grip of Nature. A commitment to pastoral romanticism represented by a rural landscape molded by human hand and inhabited by equal, independent, yeoman farmers became an important part of the national story. As America urbanized in the late nineteenth century this romantic vision was increasingly realized in the form of the suburb, a settlement oriented to the city because that was the location of the workplaces of many of its residents yet modeled on the ideal of a self-contained, secure, and pastoral community. The cultural geographers James S. Duncan and David R. Lambert focus on what has happened to this ideal in the twentieth century, particularly in the years since World War II when suburban living has become the norm for most Americans. They show the disintegration of a single model and the emergence of several distinctive types of suburban landscape that they associate with different places in different American regions: an Anglophile garden landscape in an upper-class suburb of New York City, the "militarized" landscape found in some suburbs of Los Angeles; and the coastal resort of Seaside, Florida, a community planned to fit a stereotypical model of the nineteenth-century American small town. What unites these different expressions of a suburban ideal is a social exclusivity that relies on a wide range of mechanisms, from house prices to walls, armed guards, and enforcement of aesthetic regulations, to produce elite social identities sustained by segregated living spaces. The official denial of class inequality and social privilege in the original story, therefore, is belied by the creation of privileged places that represent an America seriously divided with respect to access to superior public resources, such as public education, housing, and the very landscapes that reveal the American promise.

Introduction

This chapter will focus on suburbia as a type of residential landscape because that is where most Americans live as we enter the twenty-first century. The growth of suburbia has been inexorable throughout the twentieth century. The 1992 federal election was the first in which suburbanites constituted the majority of the voters. America has become, in the words of William Schneider (1992: 33), "a suburban nation with an urban fringe and a rural fringe." Kasinitz (1995) concurs, arguing that for most middle-class Americans suburbia is the norm and the city is thought of as the locus of the poor and of social breakdown. Such images, however, are far from new. One can trace them back beyond the writings of the Chicago School of urban sociology in the 1920s and 1930s. But they seem to resonate even more strongly at present as more and more Americans distance themselves both residentially and occupationally from cities. Today the image of the city as a "frontier" to be resettled in certain gentrifying zones by "urban pioneers" is a familiar one. Smith (1996) argues that such gentrification does not mark a major turning away from the suburbs. Rather it supplements it and is driven by the same aestheticizing mind set.

While America has always been more suburbanized than Europe or Asia (Kasinitz 1995) for a number of cultural and economic reasons, massive suburbanization in America is a twentieth-century phenomenon. As late as the 1920s large cities were still draining the countryside of people, but powerful forces were pressing for suburbanization (Fishman 1995: 395). Authors like Harvey (1989; 2000), Smith (1996), Walker (1981; 1995), and Zukin (1991) argue that suburbanization has offered a macroeconomic solution to problems of underconsumption. The argument is that suburbanization provided an alternative locus of capital investment to the cities and consequently cities declined relative to suburbs. As Harvey (1989) points out, although suburbs were privately developed, they profited from massive government subsidies in the form of government-backed housing finance and public investment in highway construction and other infrastructure. This massive building program has changed the residential landscape of America. Since the end of World War I, 85 percent of all new housing has been built in the suburbs (Zukin 1991: 140). The result is that by 1950 one-quarter of all Americans lived in suburbs. Fifty years later, over half of the population live in suburbs, only a third live in cities, and the rest live in the country (Kasinitz 1995: 387). So far we have argued that suburbs have become the dominant residential landscape in the United States and that powerful economic interests have been served by this development. We have to look elsewhere, however, to find the reasons why

Americans in increasing numbers have made suburbia their residential landscape of choice.

The model of landscape that underpins suburbia is English pastoralism. Pastoralism began as a literary movement and school of landscape architecture in England in the eighteenth century and rapidly spread to America. Thomas Jefferson was perhaps its most important popularizer in the United States. While Minister to France from 1785 to 1789, he spent time in England and was greatly influenced by the great aristocratic estates. He read English books on gardens and made Montecello a model English pastoral estate. As the best-known garden designer in the United States, he diffused English landscape tastes to an elite post-revolutionary population (Jenkins 1994: 16). Leo Marx (1964: 73–5, 88) has argued that a fully articulated pastoral ideal in America emerged by the end of the eighteenth century. Jefferson's *Notes on Virginia* written in 1785 applied the pastoral ideal long found in literature to American society. The idea he promoted was that America was the site of a New Golden Age based upon Virgilian pastoralism. Jefferson also drew upon Enlightenment beliefs about radical primitivism, perfectibility, progress, and the condition of man in the state of nature. A middle-state between the wild and tame conceived of as a pastoral economy was seen as the best attainable human condition.

The Jeffersonian model of rural life is, at its core, a literary model that was transformed into a guide for life. This pastoral model was also, of course, a political model, for Jefferson and others such as Franklin saw the independent farmer as the building block of American democracy. The sturdy yeoman farmer shielded from the artifice of city life and civilization (Schmitt 1990: xvii) was to be the foundation of a truly virtuous society.

Most urban Americans during the second quarter of the nineteenth century held a romantic view of the rural as people living in harmony with each other and the land. Such images were fostered by a continuing literary tradition of pastoral romanticism. Bunce (1994: 101) argues that,

> Although the idealization of agrarian society is associated most directly with Jefferson, much of the persistence of the agrarian myth in the American mind can be attributed to fictional literature and, more recently, to the portrayal of farm and country life in film and television.

Although Thoreau is often thought of as a philosopher of wilderness, he also greatly reinforced the pastoral impulse in American thought at mid-century. Before him, the pastoral was seen as a release from wilderness and civilization. His insight was to see it as a combination of the two: a middle landscape or point of equilibrium between the poles (Nash 1982: 94–5). In this sense, Thoreau theorizes a landscape that contains both cultivated fields and forest and yet is within the orbit of the city. As such, he is an early theorist of suburban develop-ment. The pastoral could operate at a variety of scales. While larger lots could reproduce an estate landscape of lawns, copses, waterways, and vistas, developers of small lots symbolized the estate through the use of a lawn and small clumps of trees (Jenkins 1994: 27).

From the latter part of the nineteenth century on, country life mag-azines aimed specifically at suburbanites proliferated. Such magazines had little to do with farming, and everything to do with the pleasures of the "the simple life" in the country (Schmitt 1990: 16; Jackson 1985: 72). At the end of the nineteenth century, one increasingly found gardening advice published in newspapers for the new suburban class. Essentially, the pastoral impulse in the Eastern United States was set by the beginning of the twentieth century. The model continued to be miniaturized down to a square of lawn and clump of trees. By 1930 the American elite preference for the lawn had been transmitted to the larger society through estates, parks, garden clubs, golf courses, and magazine articles (Jenkins 1994: 91). The celebration of pastoralism, understood as the value of country living, continues to be reinforced in magazines, gardening catalogues, television programs, movies, nov-els, and coffee table books. It is the basis of all suburban development.

In this chapter we will examine three different types of suburban landscapes, each representing a superimposition of what Meinig (1979) has termed a "symbolic landscape" upon the pastoral base that we have outlined above. Each type also relates to slightly different versions of the good life as conceived by middle- and upper-middle-class Americans. Suburbia itself, and the landscape models which cross-cut it, embody some of the tensions and contradictions between the American ideals of individualism, democracy, and equality of access on the one hand, and the realities of structured inequality and social exclusion on the other. Meinig singles out three landscape types that are of particular symbolic significance to Americans: the New England Village, California Suburbia, and Main Street of Middle America. We examine each of these in turn arguing that all three have become types of suburbs. Suburbia is no longer a type of symbolic landscape but rather the dominant landscape which sustains and increases its appeal by becoming a series of other American symbolic landscapes, such as the New England village and the small town.

The first place we consider is Bedford, New York, an upper-middle-class suburb of New York City. This landscape resonates with highly aestheticised notions of pastoralism, Anglophilia, rurality, and the history of the New England village, all culturally powerful images in the Eastern United States. The landscape is maintained by exclusionary mechanisms, few of which are clearly visible, that give places like Bedford an aura (Benjamin 1973) and turn it into a positional good (Hirsch 1976), a place which creates and maintains valued identities precisely because few can afford to live there. The second place we consider is middle-class suburban Los Angeles. This landscape is based on an historical model of an Hispanic, California culture that was swept away by Anglos in the nineteenth century, only to be reconstructed as a simulation for Anglo-Americans to enjoy behind gated neighborhoods in the late twentieth century. The third place is Seaside, in Florida, a landscape designed to signify small-town America, a neo-traditional community which is envisioned by some as the future of American suburban planning. Yet, its evocation of a nostalgic mythic past of Southern small-town life is exclusionary even as it simulates an idealized inclusive community. In each case we will argue that, contrary to the ideal of inclusion, the aestheticization and simulation of cultural heritage, nature, and distinction, through landscape is dependent on economic inequality, often virulent identity politics, and social exclusion.

Much has been made of the geographical mobility of late-twentieth-century Americans and their consequent lack of attachment to a long-term home place (Relph 1976; Tuan 1974; Seamon and Mugerauer 1985; Porteous 1988). But perhaps identities based on long-term geographical rootedness have, if not been replaced, then at least been supplemented by a different form of attachment, attachment to idealized places or landscape models. These are organizing models through which individuals and groups attempt to ground their fluid and mobile identities, differentiating themselves via attachments to singular places or place imagery and myths. This attachment, which is prevalent among the more affluent classes, is based on aestheticized lifestyles and the conspicuous and self -conscious consumption of symbolic objects. Landscapes are constellations of such symbolic objects linked to places and social identities through values such as "distinction," "authenticity," "community," and "heritage." Precisely because identities are linked to place-based constellations of symbolic objects, those with incompatible identities or aesthetic practices are denied access to certain places.

Landscape, aesthetics, and power

Middle- and upper-middle-class residential landscapes, such as the ones we are considering here, have exclusionary power; power to assimilate, erase, or expel, that which is alien or abject. They offer seemingly indisputable material evidence of the affluence, distinction, and political power that shapes them. Residential landscapes tend to be taken-for-granted by the majority of people as evidence of social value. People, including both the poor and the affluent, thus become complicit in perpetuating social hierarchies through their acceptance of the role of landscapes in confirming prestige.

In America, where social class is an important, but often denied, aspect of social identity, it is usually reduced to social status based on money, education, occupation, ethnicity, values, manners, and in many communities, such as the ones we are considering, landscape taste. Class, in the sense of structured or conflictual relations of power, authority, and production, is thus ignored or obscured by being translated into aestheticized categories of lifestyle, taste, and patterns of more or less conspicuous consumption. The spatial and visual separation of the realms of reproduction and consumption (residential landscapes) from those of production has proven to be an important element in sustaining such poorly articulated social relations. For example, suburbanites who are often totally dependent on the city and contemporary capitalism, profess strong anti-urban, anti-modern sentiments. The production of segregated living spaces (separation of the rich from the poor) further mystifies conflictual social relations, another example of Ed Soja's (1989, following John Berger's 1974) dictum that "space hides the consequences [of our exclusionary actions] from us."

The types of privileged places considered here have highly restrictive zoning codes, producing closely guarded boundaries. Such places are especially well insulated from unpleasant visual reminders of the

class basis of American capitalism. Here elite social identities are performed and maintained in relation to the identities of others. Upward
mobility is often achieved through association with particular places.
Place-based identity is a type of identity that Americans are relatively
comfortable with, as it doesn't appear to contradict the deeply embedded American cultural value of a classless society. It is, in this sense,
that aestheticized landscapes mystify social relations (Daniels 1989;
Mitchell 1996).

The aesthetic is thus the basis of a social taxonomy that effectively
depoliticizes the notion of economic class relations and mystifies economic inequalities (Eagleton 1990; Harvey 1989; Mitchell 1996). The
aestheticizing of local places, local histories and the "natural" landscape, seen as valuable but threatened heritage to be conserved, has
other, often unacknowledged consequences. It tends to obscure the
uneven and often inequitable spatial arrangements of populations and
resources between towns within a region (Duncan and Duncan 1997).
Distinction, as Bourdieu (1984) in his study of bourgeois consumption
in France tells us, is the aesthetic ideology applied to class as social status.
Because landscape taste functions as a marker of status and group
membership, the aesthetic serves to legitimate social differentiation and
segregation. This happens because class distinctions are quite literally
concretized in the landscape. Let us now turn to three examples of the
interweaving of landscapes, aesthetics, and power.

Bedford Village*

Bedford was the name given to a twenty-square-mile parcel of land
purchased from the Mohicans by settlers from the neighboring town
of Stamford, Connecticut, three hundred years ago (Figures 9.1 and
9.2). It remained a farming village until the mid-nineteenth century
when it participated in the first wave of suburbanization. As it was not
on the suburban railroad line, it became an elite romantic suburb
where dying farms were converted into "gentleman farms."[1] Members
of New York City's elite established weekend and summer places there,
and by the turn of century Bedford was becoming a commuter's town.

---

* The material for this section is drawn from a long-term study of the town by James and Nancy
Duncan (see Duncan 1973, 1986; Duncan and Duncan 1984, 1997, forthcoming).

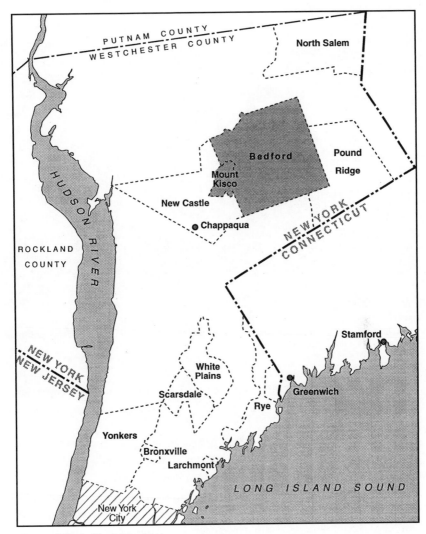

Figure 9.1 Bedford, New York.

In the 1920s in order to slow growth, the residents instituted one of the earliest and most restrictive residential and commercial zoning codes in the United States. To this day, 80 percent of the town is still restricted to a minimum of four acres per house. By the 1970s, although still a prestigious address (see Higley 1995), many of the old properties had fallen into disrepair and some of the largest properties had been subdivided. But in the 1980s and 1990s wealth from Wall Street and Hollywood (West 1997) was poured into the town and not

Figure 9.2 Colonial houses, Bedford, New York.

only was there a building boom, but also a number of new properties
of several hundred acres were formed out of smaller lots, and many
great estates were revitalized.

At the time of writing, Bedford, prized by many for the beauty of its
pastoral and wooded landscapes, is the site of a highly aestheticized
quest for social identity and a propertied way of life which draws upon
the discourses of good taste, heritage, tradition, distinction, and environmental conservation. Certain cherished ideas are inscribed in the
landscape, concretizing and naturalizing elite Anglophile landscape taste
as a commodity, a consumable good, and a marker of social identity
and mobility. In Bedford one can find many examples of landscape
elements standing as signifiers for a whole constellation of cultural
ideas based primarily in Anglophilia and class-based aesthetic values,
such as elite romanticism of Nature and History touted as elements
of "good taste." Here the concept of "History" stands as a synecdoche
for such ideas as "Old Bedford" family genealogies, "imposing" or
"charming" architecture, a simpler, and allegedly morally superior anti-
modern, anti-urban, and anti-immigrant community ideal, and more

generally a cultural aesthetic. Discourses of Anglo-American heritage are thus inscribed into a museum-like landscape, civic rituals, and local history lessons that celebrate "our English ancestors." A class and ethnically biased (upper-middle-class and Anglophile) history has become keenly sought-after as a marker of social distinction. In Bedford, class as an aestheticized category includes those who conform to certain aesthetic practices and sensibilities which although derived from a particular social background (old money, WASP) are taken up by many others as they become incorporated into the local culture. The landscape in this case serves to assimilate some differences thereby erasing other ethnic and class heritages. Those who can not afford to, or will not conform aesthetically are largely excluded.

Bedford has experienced relatively little contestation over the dominant interpretation of its landscape. Bedford's landscape is interesting for the remarkable consensus within and outside the town surrounding its preservation. Those who suffer the consequences of a housing crisis in the region, the middle and working classes, appear to fully support the preservation of open spaces (in the form of large lot zoning and nature preserves) in towns like Bedford. They do so in the name of the individualism, the American Dream, and the unquestioned goodness of heritage, community, and nature. There is a price to pay for these ideologies of the goodness of capitalism and nature. The American ideology of individualism obscures structural connections between one locality and the next. People fail to appreciate that large lot zoning in Bedford affects the rest of the county. We would argue that the aestheticization of power through landscape in Bedford serves as a good example of what is a close relationship between the logic of aesthetics and that of hegemony (Eagleton 1990). Through a focus on the landscape, one can show how dominant ideologies, such as individualism and consumer sovereignty, are made material, concretized, naturalized, and unquestioned, and how, consequently, they become hegemonic. Landscape taste and the appreciation of the visual are seen as freely chosen and without social consequences. The hegemony of the dominant classes in Bedford is achieved through the aestheticization of its landscapes, which, being celebrated as unique, acquire an "aura" of distinction.

A pastoral landscape such as Bedford's is expensive to maintain. Increasingly much of the gardening has been done by Central American immigrants. The number of Hispanics has more than doubled in

Westchester County in the 1990s. These laborers are paid at the minimum wage and are consequently forced to live in grossly overcrowded housing in towns around Bedford. The majority of those who work in Bedford are housed in the adjacent town of Mt. Kisco. Here they socialize in groups on the streets and congregate on certain corners waiting to be picked up by contractors and homeowners looking for laborers. In the 1990s a controversy has developed over these workers, which has centered on what locals have termed "the quality of life" issue (Berger 1993; Dugger 1996). The term "quality of life" is clearly code for different Hispanic uses of public space and the "threat" this poses to the Anglophile residents' image of the Town (Duncan and Duncan forthcoming). In fact a flyer was supplied throughout Westchester County explaining cultural differences between Anglo-Americans and Hispanics, instructing the latter in the so-called "proper" use of space.

The Town felt that it was receiving negative externalities of Bedford's desire for cheap labor and decided to try and drive the Hispanics from the town by forbidding them to solicit work on the road sides, harassing them for congregating on sidewalks and by staging midnight raids on illegally overcrowded houses and then prosecuting Hispanic renters as well as landlords. Many of the residents of Bedford and Mt. Kisco objected to the presence of working-class, Hispanic males gathering on the sidewalks and to Spanish being spoken in town. The Hispanic labourers changed the look of the town, and lowered the quality of life, they claimed.

The Hispanics argued that they were hard working and didn't cause trouble. They seemed to have little sense that it was their look and deportment that was objected to. Hispanic workers were needed to work in the area, but those same people, when they were not working, were seen as foreign and urban and working class and thus they undermined the image of the Anglo-American suburb, which has managed in large part to exclude people of color. Difference was cast in cultural terms. As one person from Bedford said, "When you step across the border into Mt. Kisco, it's like a frontier, like crossing into a different country." Another said, "I don't go to Mt. Kisco to shop any more because of all the 'Guatemalans' hanging around on the streets. It's like going to the Bronx to shop. It looks dangerous." For the Anglophiles of Bedford, the Hispanics cannot be visibly assimilated. In fact, they can be seen as a local manifestation of precisely what Bedford residents wish to retreat from: an increasingly multi-ethnic America.

Although Bedford is an elite, exclusionary community, many of its symbolic qualities are more broadly diffused. For example, Ralph Lauren, one of the masters of lifestyle marketing, moved to Bedford a number of years ago and bought a 250-acre estate. He has made his money marketing Anglophilia to Americans and now uses his estate in Bedford as an advertising backdrop to sell his Polo line. There is a cover of a fashion magazine showing Lauren standing beside a great oak on his property, his dog Rugby at his feet (Reginato 1993). The Caption reads "The Duke of Bedford." There is a certain constitutive or iterative circularity here in Lauren using Bedford to sell his lifestyle advertising and people wanting to live in Bedford because it embodies that marketed style. In an age of "themeing" and lifestyle advertising, where nature and heritage, even ancestors it seems, become commodities, it is a "look" that is marketed. Inclusion and exclusion are seen as based on apolitical personal taste and choices rather than as structured exclusion and inequality.

Los Angeles: suburban fortresses

Los Angeles is the fastest growing metropolis in the advanced industrialized world (Figure 9.3).

Most of the new inhabitants of Los Angeles in the twenty-first century will be non-Anglos, either migrants from beyond the United States of America's borders, or the children of its current Latino, Asian, and Black populations. Anglos – those of Anglo-Saxon ethnic origins – have already become a minority in the city and county of Los Angeles, and are expected to become so in the state as a whole before 2010 (Davis 1990: 7). In addition to a phenomenal shift in the structure of its population, Los Angeles has also become an increasingly polarized place, with the income gap between the rich and poor continuing to widen. It is partly because of the demographic changes and increasing social polarization that Los Angeles has been dubbed the "capital of the third world" (Rieff 1991; see also Soja 1989). Amongst the responses to such shifts has been an ever-more defensive process of Anglo suburbanization (Fulton 1997). Years of chronic under-investment in housing and the urban infrastructure have seen a dramatic fall in the quality of inner-city life (Fishman 1987), and this has been both encouraged and exacerbated by the occurrence of "white flight" (and that of other upwardly mobile groups) to the new suburbs (Figures 9.4a

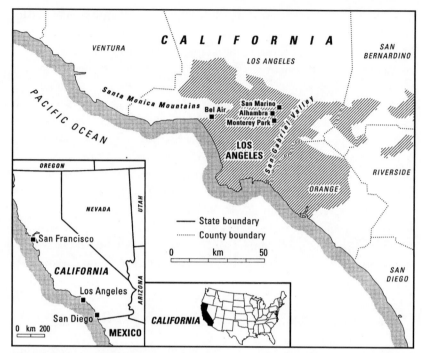

Figure 9.3 Los Angeles.

and b). The accompanying fall in tax revenue robs those areas most in need of financial support. This exodus is a defensive response to the social polarization, poverty, and crime which are seen as characterizing inner-city life, and is accompanied by a search for a "better" residential place (and time).

From its early growth, Los Angeles was marketed as "the anti-city" (Fulton 1997: 13) – a decentered metropolis occupying an interstitial place between the rural and urban. Many of the migrants who moved to Los Angeles were attracted by the hopes of a subsistence agricultural existence and of escaping the racial politics and tensions of other urban centers:

> All these components of L.A.'s allure – hobby farms, an anti-urban bias, the small-town atmosphere, localized governments – represent the American suburban ideal. (Fulton 1997: 14)

This California suburbia was an idealized landscape of safety and consumption. Encoded with a particular aesthetic – the red tile roofs and

Figure 9.4 Gated housing in Los Angeles, a: close up; b: further out.
(*Photographs: Carol Medlicott.*)

sprawling, low-rise form of Spanish colonial architecture – the suburb was a manifestation of a peaceful, pastoral former period of time. Indicative of the anti-urbanism which remains strong in Los Angeles (Fulton 1997), this suburban form is still sought by many today. Yet, this anti-urban ideal has always been predicated upon the thoroughly urban reality of phenomenal growth. For example, if – as Frank Donovan argued – the automobile was "the greatest single factor" in the trans-formation of the United States of America in the twentieth century (in Meinig 1979: 170), then California suburbia was the greatest spatial manifestation of this process:

> Low, wide-spreading, single-story houses standing on broad lots fronted by open, perfect green lawns; the most prominent feature of the house is the two-car garage opening onto a broad driveway, connecting to the broad curving street (with no sidewalks, for pedestrians are unknown and unwanted) which leads to the great freeways. (Meinig 1979: 169)

The tension between the anti-urban aspirations of those who settled in Los Angeles and the phenomenal growth which generated and was a result of Southern California's prosperity could be maintained as long as inhabitants could live in pseudo-rural suburbs. Yet, problems of met-ropolitan growth – pollution, traffic jams, urban sprawl, environmental destruction – began to impinge on the Los Angeles dream from the 1960s. The response – defensive suburbanization – was typically anti-urban: "Instead of trying to fix Los Angeles, we all simply decided that we live somewhere else" (Fulton 1997: 6). Much of this defensive sub-urbanization is organized through a whole series of homeowners' groups. Such associations were organized in a spatially coherent way, and reflected the common concerns of the homeowners within a particular place. They sought to promote their members' interests as property holders, particularly in terms of the maintenance of property values (McKenzie 1994), and some did so in particularly hostile ways. For example, the Anti-African Homeowners' Association was politically active in the 1920s in attempting to prevent blacks from purchasing homes outside the ghetto, as this was seen as a direct threat to home prices and to the "character" of white areas more generally.

After their initial emergence, the number of homeowners' associa-tions in Los Angeles rose dramatically. Since the 1960s, their activities have increasingly focused on the need to defend their various "bour-geois utopias" (Fishman 1987; Soja 1989), and to this end, zoning laws have been evoked as "barbed-wire social fencing around home values" (Davis 1990: 165). Such attempts at spatial manipulation revolve around the twin processes of inclusion and exclusion: homeowners' associa-tions seek to have their own residential areas designated as coherent "places," whilst excluding other areas. Such centrifugal and centripetal efforts at politico-legal inscription are founded on the identification of a sharp spatial gradient in property values which marks the "border" between those to be incorporated and those to be expelled. Such economic grounds for inclusion/exclusion are often supported by the definition of "communal" lifestyles, shared histories, or access to (semi) private amenities – such as golf courses, beaches, and country clubs – all of which are seen as contributing to the character of a place. This aestheticization of the insulation of home values amounts to an attempt at "suburban separatism" (Davis 1990: 165), which, whilst predicated on notions of internal identity, sovereignty, and equality, undermines such ideals across the constructed borders.

Forming a strategic backdrop to the defensive communalism of Los Angeles homeowners' associations is the promotion of "slow growth" (Soja 1989). Such a political stance is fundamentally anti-urban develop-ment and focuses on the maintenance of the spatial status quo. The homeowners seek to defend the exclusiveness (and hence value) of their own racially and economically homogeneous residential enclaves by opposing both further development and the in-migration of unwanted groups of people. These two external threats to suburban bliss are brought together in the phantom figure of "affordable housing," a landscape form which is read as code for the mindless violence and numbing poverty seen as (best) residing in the inner-cities (Till 1993), and from which the Anglo suburbanites wish to insulate themselves.

In their fight against any form of development that might threaten the exclusiveness and value of their property, many homeowners' asso-ciations have adopted the rhetoric of environmentalism. This slow-growth strategy has been deployed very successfully by the Hillside Federation, which was founded in Bel Air in the 1950s. It has emerged as the most powerful coalition of homeowners' associations in the United States of America, having fifty affiliated groups in 1990 (Davis 1990: 171). Representing one of the largest concentrations of wealth on the planet, the Hillside Federation has been highly successful in promoting "slow growth" by emphasizing the need to "protect" and "save" the Santa Monica Mountains.

Environmental protection is not the only rhetoric that has been adopted by homeowner's associations, however, and slow-growth issues have also become dangerously entangled with a virulent racial back-lash (McKenzie 1994). One of the most striking examples of this has occurred in Monterey Park, a San Gabriel Valley city, some eight miles east of Downtown Los Angeles. The valley was once predominantly Anglo (with some Mexican migrant workers) but has become a major destination for upwardly mobile Latinos and Chinese. Monterey Park itself has shifted from being a 90 percent Anglo single-family suburb in 1960 to being North America's first Chinese majority suburb by 1985, following large-scale immigration from Taiwan and Hong Kong.

In the context of the city's changing population structure, there emerged an Anglo backlash spearheaded by the Residents Association of Monterey Park (RAMP), which has espoused slow growth and the restriction of commercial development. Such slow-growth strategies have been articulated to the claim that RAMP is attempting to prevent a "Chinese take-over" and the organization deploys a rhetoric of "English Only." The virulent racism of RAMP and its supporters is chillingly described by the city's former president of the Chamber of Commerce, who suggests what the effort to "recover the lost Eden" of California suburbia entails: "[RAMP] would like to turn the clock back to 1950 and hang a Chinese from every lamppost" (in Rieff 1991: 189).[2] In pursuit of such exclusionary aims, RAMP was able to install supporters on the City Council after the 1986 elections. A resolution was passed by the new Council that affirmed English as the "official language" of Monterey Park, and made Chinese businesses produce English trans-lations on all their signs. Groups similar to RAMP have been formed in Alhambra, San Marino, and other San Gabriel Valley cities, all seeking to prevent what former Mayor Barry Hatch of Monterey Park termed the spread of the "Yellow Peril."

Although there is no denying the exclusionary way in which space is manipulated by homeowner's associations, the suburban places of Los Angeles are also home to much more overt forms of exclusion. Not only luxury developments, but also increasingly even more modest neigh-borhoods, have been transformed into "fortress cities, complete with encompassing walls, restricted entry points with guard posts, overlap-ping private and public police services, and even privatized roadways"

(Davis 1990: 244; see also McKenzie 1994). The strategies employed in this process of suburban fortification, bolstered by the "unending eyes" of surveillance technology (Soja 1996: 448), are numerous. San Marino restricts access to "public" amenities by closing its parks on weekends to Latino and Asian families from neighboring districts. Hidden Hills has walls and security fences, and local ordinances restrict parking to residents only. In Bel Air, private security firms promise residents rapid armed response. Such suburban militarization is organized through many of the same homeowners' associations which promote slow growth, and the two activities can clearly be seen as complementary: suburban fortification is a micro-strategy which seeks to exclude individual, unwanted bodies; slow growth is a macro-strategy aimed at excluding unwanted groups in general. Both rely on an intimate integration of landscape and power, and result in and draw upon a specific aesthetics.

The politico-legal suburban separatism of many Los Angeles homeowners' associations clearly amounts to an attempt to maintain or restore Anglo cultural, economic, and political hegemony, while invoking an aesthetics of exclusion which evokes a "lost Eden" of lily-white 1950s suburbia. Nevertheless, it also gestures towards an aesthetics of inclusion that serves to mystify underlying exclusionary practices. The idealized architectural aesthetic is a multicultural, heterogeneous, inclusive one based on a mix of styles, including prominently Mexican and California Mission style houses with red-tile roofs.[3] Here the reality of exclusion is obscured by an inclusive aesthetics, albeit sanitized and protected by gates and guards. In this sense, Los Angeles presents a contrast to Bedford with its homogeneously WASP landscape obscuring through aesthetic assimilation a more ethnically diverse population.

Seaside: the future of American planning?

The coastal resort of Seaside is situated between Fort Walton Beach and Panama City on the north Florida panhandle and has been described as "the most celebrated small town in the world," and by others as the "future" of American urban planning (Figure 9.5). It is the best-known example of the "neotraditional" urban form which emerged on the East and West coasts of America in the 1980s, and other such settlements include Tannin, in Orange Beach, Alabama;

Figure 9.5 Seaside, Florida.

Kentlands, in Gaithersburg, Maryland; and Rancho Santa Margarita, in
Orange County, California (McCann 1995; Till 1993). These developments have gained a great deal of publicity and praise in papers,
magazines, and architectural journals because proponents of neotraditionalism have claimed that their innovative designs are critical to
reshaping the contemporary American urban structure. As the most
famous neotraditional form and the first to be designed by Andres Duany
and Elizabeth Plater-Zyberk – two architects who have been critical to
the development and promotion of neotraditionalism – Seaside is an
extremely important site for study in our analysis of American space
and place at the turn of the century (Figure 9.6). Before turning to
consider Seaside itself, however, we must first examine the precepts of
neotraditionalism in order to understand how its idealized aesthetics
relate to notions of identity, sovereignty and equality.

Neotraditionalism has been proclaimed as the solution to America's
urban problems, from crime to community disintegration, pollution
to anomie. It is conceived of in opposition to socially alienating,
geographically dispersed, and environmentally harmful forms of urban

Figure 9.6 Seaside, Florida looking towards the sea. (*Photograph: Steven Brooke.*)

development (Till 1993: 709). Such development is seen as typified by the post-World War II growth of the suburb, and in many ways it is the image of the suburb that is the main target for neotraditionalists:

> The classic suburb is less a community than an agglomeration of houses, shops, and offices connected to one another by cars, not by the fabric of human life . . . The structure of the suburb tends to confine most people to their houses and cars; it discourages strolling, walking, mingling with neighbors. The suburb is the last word in privatization, perhaps even its lethal consummation, and it spells the end of authentic civil life. (Duany and Plater-Zyberk 1992: 21)

In contrast to the supposedly empty, lifeless suburb which "spells the end of authentic civil life," the proponents of neotraditionalism proclaim a message of salvation and resurrection in the form of the "second coming of the American small town" and go so far as to claim that they have "rediscovered" the village (Duany and Plater-Zyberk 1992). By simulating the physical structure of the small town, drawing on local histories and identities, and paying attention to vernacular styles and folk wisdom, proponents claim that neotraditionalism serves to foster – and repair – the traditional bonds of the authentic American community.

The neotraditional urban form represents the selective convergence of two planning traditions – urban aesthetics and social utopianism (McCann 1995). The former holds that some existing urban forms facilitate social life to a greater extent than others, whereas the latter sees the construction of certain new types of urban settlement as conducive to the creation of community spirit (McCann 1995: 211). At the core of neotraditionalism is the urban aesthetic belief that developments should emulate the spatial form of 1900s' small town, and the social utopian view that communities should be planned as small towns in their own right – as new forms – rather than as appendages to existing towns and cities (Falconer Al-Hindi and Staddon 1997). In this way, neotraditional developments are predicated upon ideas of small-scale, ecological sustainability, historical identification, and community building, and these themes are strongly interconnected. With this in mind, we can begin to see how the neotraditional ideal relates to particular notions of identity, sovereignty, and equality. Through their evocation of traditional historical landscapes, neotraditional developments seek to promote a sense of social communitarianism based on local participation, self-governance, authenticity, and the equality of shared residence.

Such neotraditional ideals are well exemplified by the development of Seaside. Having inherited eighty acres of north Florida property, the developer, Robert Davis, sought to create a new form of residential landscape that was radically different from the archetypal suburban development. He brought in the husband-and-wife architectural team Andres Duany and Elizabeth Plater-Zyberk who eventually found inspiration for the form they were seeking in cities such as Savannah, Georgia, Charleston, South Carolina, and Natchez, Mississippi. By drawing on such landscape forms, Duany and Plater-Zyberk sought to connect their new development to an idealized, mythical past that was seen as characterized by a greater sense of community.

The construction of Seaside began in 1982. The eighty-acre site is now mainly filled and the development has been incredibly commercially successful, with lot prices rising more than ten-fold. Duany and Plater-Zyberk's project of historical evocation is reflected in the beach and street names – Savannah Beach, Natchez Street – which form part of a more general but no less explicit attempt to (re)create the "feel" of a 1900s' Southern town (Falconer Al-Hindi and Staddon 1997: 351). In addition, the actual spatial organization of the built landscape attempts to engender social interaction and community-building by blending public and private space – with porches and picket fences, for example – again through the stylistic medium of an idealized Southern town. In this way, the architectural styles which are utilized – from the dogtrot to the antebellum mansion – are seen as both symbolically reflective of (and therefore evocative of) a historical sense of community, and as promoting this social interaction through their particular spatial forms.

Seaside's position at the forefront of a neotraditionalist attempt to reform the American urban form has created great interest, something reflected in its description as "the future of community planning in America" (Langdon 1988; cited in Falconer Al-Hindi and Staddon 1997: 349). It is to the accuracy of such claims and the question of whether the neotraditional ideology has been realized that we will now turn. Seaside is envisaged and celebrated as the future of American urban planning, yet when one moves from the rhetoric of its designers and advocates, and instead considers how it is sold and promoted by developers, a clear gap appears between discourse and practice. Although neotraditionalists claim that the urban forms they plan and design can serve as a solution to America's urban problems, this emancipatory impulse is undermined by the need to promote the landscapes in a way which is attractive to developers and potential home-buyers alike – as McCann puts it bluntly: "[C]ommunity is a selling point as well as an ideal" (1995: 217, emphasis in original). The myths associated with historical, authentic modes of community life and their emulation in the built form may appeal to particular sets of investors and buyers:

By buying a unit in a neotraditional town or urban village, a homeowner will inherit . . . the exclusive membership rights of an "authentic" planned residential community. (Till 1993: 719)

It is the reference to "exclusive membership" which is important here, and it is critical that we understand the connections between the notions of exclusiveness (a basis for cultural capital) and exclusion (a form of spatial and social othering): exclusiveness is predicated upon exclusion, and exclusion is absolutely necessary for something to be exclusive. Landscape is an important medium for the connections between these two – and hence for the power relations involved – and yet this does not simply involve physical exclusion. Seaside's lack of gates, guards, and other physical means of exclusion is celebrated as another feature of its visionary nature and is contrasted favorably with the gated enclaves of some cities. Yet despite this apparent openness, it is clear that such overt mechanisms are unnecessary (Falconer Al-Hindi and Staddon 1997: 363). The most obvious form of exclusion is the price of property – the cheapest homes cost $250,000 – yet many other more subtle forms are also in operation. The landscape of Seaside is encoded with a variety of symbolic meanings that emphasize its exclusiveness through reference to a variety of exclusions. This link between exclusiveness and exclusion is critical to understanding the contrast between the ideal "space" and the actual "place" of Seaside.

In terms of the promotion of Seaside, it can be seen that the manipulation of social divisions – both historical and contemporary – is central to its promotion and appeal. In historical terms, this occurs through the evocation of certain white elitist aspects of the antebellum South which are simultaneously "neutralized" through the process of aestheticization. Yet, far from challenging the racist and classist aspects of this society, this aestheticization serves to obscure the power relations that characterized the antebellum South. In this way, dogtrots are no longer cheap housing for blacks on the margins of nineteenth-century Southern cities (Falconer Al-Hindi and Staddon 1997: 355), and mansions are no longer the products of slavery-derived wealth. Rather, stripped of its original contextual meaning, the landscape of the South becomes a collection of objects of desire for consumable distinction, which appeal to a particular set of bourgeois and petty-bourgeois potential home-buyers (McCann 1995).

This subtle encoding of systems of racial and class domination in the landscape of Seaside involves the elision of historical power relations through an aestheticization that nevertheless leaves traces to be consumed and read. This is critical for the contemporary manipulation of social divisions in American society by Seaside's promoters: Seaside is portrayed as both a safe, "family" place in an area far removed from the racial tension, class violence, and sexual deviance of the pathological inner-city street, and as an exclusive place of distinction for those seeking to escape the non-descript suburb. In short, Seaside appeals to both the fears and desires of middle-class Anglos. It is precisely this interconnectedness of exclusiveness and exclusion which is reflected in letters to the *Seaside Times* which argue that attracting the "right kinds" of people to Seaside is important (in Falconer Al-Hindi and Staddon 1997). From this perspective then, far from serving as the basis of new and liberating social environments, Seaside's neotraditional urban form is mobilized to support existing structures of class, race, and gender domination (compare Duncan 1992). Hence, neotraditionalism may actually serve as an exclusionary urban vision which functions to (re)produce certain hegemonic class fractions.

Here we have tried to argue that the neotraditional form is portrayed as an antidote to the failings of American urban planning. By celebrating notions of authenticity, heritage, and community, neotraditional spaces are envisioned as promoting certain lost American ideals. Yet, in places such as Seaside, such forms of historical identification and community building can serve to maintain and exacerbate social divisions. The promotion of neotraditional places as exclusive relies on a series of aesthetically-encoded exclusions in the landscape. This serves to remind us that – even in the context of the "future" of American planning – the notion of "community" is always predicated as the expulsion of those not deemed to fit in.

Conclusion

David Harvey (2000) and others have noted that suburbs, such as the ones we have examined here, are not simply an alternative to the city but rather positively undermine it. Contemporary suburbanization, Harvey writes (2000: 138–9), is driven by a mix of fear of the city, racism and class prejudice, collapsing urban infrastructures, and a desire for the pastoral utopia. As Kasinitz (1995: 391) points out, the separation of middle- and upper-middle-class suburbanites from the urban poor erodes the fiscal will to provide many public services. It also, as Schneider (1992) argues, has an enormous impact on electoral politics because of the "privatization of public life in the suburbs."

We have argued that residential landscapes when they are highly aestheticized become, in Daniels' (1989) words, duplicitous. That is, they play a central role in depoliticizing class relations by turning them into matters of cultivated tastes, education, stewardship, and cultural capital. Place-based identity and the celebration of the uniqueness of a local landscape diverts attention away from the interrelatedness of issues of landscape aesthetics, cultural identity, and social justice. Exclusion, which lies at the heart of suburban form, rather than being recognized as anti-democratic acquires the aura of scarcity and thus becomes a form of cultural capital. The negatively charged words "exclusion" and "exclusionary" are replaced by the positively charged term "exclusive." An exclusive neighborhood thus is a positional good, one that plays an active role in the constitution of middle- and upper-middle-class social identities.

Such aestheticizing moves maintain an illusion of disconnection from other social groups through spatial separation of the home realm from the work realm and through an aestheticized attitude which create simulacra of such things as the New England village, rurality, multicultural California culture, and the Southern, small town community. Self-assured in the virtues of local sovereignty, heritage, and the preservation of green space, the residents of these places spatially and visually isolate themselves from the more uncomfortable questions of racial relations and poverty that are in actual fact exacerbated by exclusionary practices which keep out of sight any reminders of the social consequences of what has been called "painless privilege" (Pile 1994).

Endnotes

1. For a discussion of the transformation of such towns see (Wood 1991). For material on elite residential landscapes, see Breen 1989; Dorst 1990; Higley 1995; Hugill 1986, 1989, 1995; Ley 1993, 1995; Wyckoff 1990.
2. For a discussion of Anglo-Canadian reactions to wealthy Chinese immigrants to elite Vancouver neighborhoods, see Ley 1995.
3. On this idea of a "play" of cultural difference that produces no meaningful politics of inclusion, see Harvey 1989: 88–9; but also see Jane Jacobs's (1998) critique of the uncritical acceptance of the depoliticizing force of aestheticization.

References

Benjamin, W. (1973), "The Work of Art in the Age of Mechanical Reproduction," in H. Arendt (ed.), *Illuminations*, New York: Schocken, pp. 217–52.
Berger, J. (1974), *The Look of Things*, New York: Viking Press.

Berger, J. (1993), "Bienvenidos a los suburbios: Increasingly, New York's Outskirts Take on a Latin Accent," *New York Times*, July 29.

Bourdieu, P. (1984), *Distinction: A Social Critique of the Judgement of Taste*, trans. R. Nice, Cambridge, MA: Harvard University Press.

Breen, T. H. (1989), *Imagining the Past: East Hampton Histories*, Reading, MA: Addison-Wesley.

Bunce, M. (1994), *The Countryside Ideal: Anglo-American Images of Landscape*, London: Routledge

Daniels, S. (1989), "Marxism and the Duplicity of Landscape," in R. Peet and N. Thrift (eds.), *New models in geography*, Vol. 2, London: Unwin-Hyman, pp. 196–220.

Davis, M. (1990), *City of Quartz: Excavating the Future in Los Angeles*, London: Verso.

Dorst, J. (1990), *The Written Suburb*, Philadelphia: University of Pennsylvania Press.

Duany, A., and E. Plater-Zyberk (1992), "The Second Coming of the American Small Town," *Wilson Quarterly*, 16, pp. 19–50.

Dugger, C. W. (1996), "Immigrants and Suburbia Square Off: Hispanic Residents of Mt. Kisco Say They're Being Harassed," *New York Times*, December 1.

Duncan, James Stuart (1973), "Landscape Taste as a Symbol of a Group Identity: A Westchester County Village," *Geographical Review*, 63, pp. 334–55.

Duncan, James Stuart (1992), "Elite Landscapes as Cultural (Re)productions: The Case of Shaughnessy Heights," in K. Anderson and F. Gale (eds.), *Inventing Places: Studies in Cultural Geography*, Melbourne: Longman, pp. 37–51.

Duncan, James Stuart, and Nancy Ginnel Duncan (1984), "A Cultural Analysis of Urban Residential Landscapes in North America: The Case of the Anglophile Elite," in *The City in Cultural Context*, ed. John A. Agnew, John Mercer, and David E. Sopher, Boston: Unwin Hyman, pp. 255–76.

Duncan, James Stuart, and Nancy Ginnel Duncan (forthcoming), *American Beauty: Living the Aestheticized Life in an Affluent New York Suburb*, Baltimore: Johns Hopkins University Press.

Duncan, Nancy Ginnel (1986), "Suburban Landscapes and Suburbanites: A Structurationist Perspective on Residential Land Use in Northern Westchester County," New York Ph.D. dissertation, Syracuse University, Department of Geography.

Duncan, Nancy Ginnel, and James Stuart Duncan (1997), "Deep Suburban Irony: The Perils of Democracy in Westchester County, New York," in Roger Silverstons (ed.), *Visions of Suburbia*, London: Routledge, pp. 161–79.

Eagleton, T. (1990), *The Ideology of the Aesthetic*, Oxford: Blackwell Publishers.

Falconer Al-Hindi, K., and C. Staddon, (1997), "The Hidden Histories and Geographies of Neotraditional Town Planning: The Case of Seaside, Florida," *Environment and Planning D: Society and Space*, 15, pp. 349–72.

Fishman, R. (1987), *Bourgeois Utopias: Rise and Fall of Suburbia*, New York: Basic Books.

Fishman, R. (1995), "Metropolis Unbound," in P. Kasinitz (ed.), *Metropolis: Center and Symbol of Our Times*, New York: New York University Press, pp. 395–417.

Fulton, W. B. (1997), *The Reluctant Metropolis: The Politics of Urban Growth in Los Angeles*, Point Arena, CA: Solano Press Books.

Harvey, D. (1989), *The Condition of Postmodernity*, Oxford: Blackwell.

Harvey, D. (2000), *Spaces of Hope*, Edinburgh: Edinburgh University Press.

Higley, S. R. (1995), *Privilege, Power and Place: The Geography of the American Upper Class*, Lanham: Rowman and Littlefield.

Hirsch, F. (1976), *Social Limits to Growth*, Cambridge: Harvard University Press.

Hugill, Peter (1986), "English Landscape Tastes in the United States," *Geographical Review*, 76, pp. 408–23.

Hugill, Peter (1989), "Home and Class among an American Landed Elite," in J. Agnew and J. Duncan (eds.), *The Power of Place: Bringing Together Geographical and Sociological Imaginations*, Boston: Unwin Hyman, pp. 66–80.

Hugill, P. J. (1995), *Upstate Arcadia: Landscape, Aesthetics, and the Triumph of Social Differentiation in America*, Lanham, MD: Rowman and Littlefield.

Jackson, K. T. (1985), *The Crabgrass Frontier*, New York: Oxford University Press.

Jacobs, J. (1998), "Staging Difference: Aestheticisation and the Politics of Difference in Contemporary Cities," R. Fincher and J. Jacobs (eds.), *Cities of Difference*, New York: Guilford.

Jenkins, V. S. (1994), *The Lawn: A History of an American Obsession*, Washington, DC: Smithsonian Institution Press.

Kasinitz, P. (ed.) (1995), *Metropolis: Center and Symbol of Our Times*, New York: New York University Press.

Langdon, P. (1988), "A Good Place to Live," *Atlantic Monthly*, 261, pp. 39–60.

Ley, David (1993), "Past Elites, Present Gentry: Neighbourhood of Privilege in Canadian Cities," in L. Bourne and D. Leys (eds.), *The Changing Social Geography of Canadian Cities*, Montreal: McGill-Queens University Press, pp. 214–33.

Ley, David (1995), "Between Europe and Asia: The Case of the Missing Sequoias," *Ecumene*, 2, pp. 185–210.

McCann, E. J. (1995), "Neotraditional Developments: The Anatomy of a New Urban Form," *Urban Geography*, 16(3), pp. 210–33.

McKenzie, E. (1994), *Privatopia: Homeowner Associations and the Rise of Residential Government*, New Haven: Yale University.

Marx, L. (1964), *The Machine in the Garden: Technology and the Pastoral Ideal in America*, Oxford: Oxford University Press.

Meinig, D. W. (ed.) (1979), *The Interpretation of Ordinary Landscapes*, Oxford: Oxford University Press.

Mitchell, D. (1996), *The Lie of the Land*, Minneapolis: University of Minnesota.

Nash, R. (1982), *Wilderness and the American Mind*, New Haven: Yale University Press.

Pile, S. (1994), "Masculism, the Use of Dualistic Epistemologies, and Third Spaces," *Antipode*, 26, pp. 255–77.

Porteous, J. D. (1988), "Topicide: The Annihilation of Place," in J. Eyles, and D. M. Smith (eds.), *Qualitative Methods in Human Geography*, Cambridge: Polity, pp. 75–93.

Reginato, J. (1993), "The Duke of Bedford: Ralph Lauren Gives WH an Exclusive Tour through His Just-Completed Country Estate," *WH*, March 29-April 5, pp. 1–8.

Relph, E. (1976), *Place and Placelessness*, London: Pion.

Rieff, D. (1991), *Los Angeles: Capital of the Third World*, New York: Simon & Schuster.

Schmitt, P. J. (1990), *Back to Nature: The Arcadian Myth in Urban America*, Baltimore: Johns Hopkins University Press.

Schneider, W. (1992), "The Suburban Century Begins," *The Atlantic*, July, pp. 31–8.

Seamon, D., and R. Mugerauer (eds.) (1985), *Dwelling, Place and Environment: Towards a Phenomenology of Person and World*, Dordrecht: Martinus Nijhoff.

Smith, N. (1996), *The New Urban Frontier and the Revanchist City*, London: Routledge.

Soja, E. (1989), *Postmodern Geographies: The Reassertion of Space in Critical Social Theory*, London: Verso.

Soja E. (1996), "Los Angeles, 1965–1992: From Crisis-Generating Restructuring to Restructuring-Generated Crisis," in A. J. Scott and E. Soja (eds), *The City: Los Angeles and Urban Theory at the End of the Twentieth Century*, London: University of California Press, pp. 426–62.

Till, K. (1993), "Neotraditional Towns and Urban Villages: The Cultural Production of a Geography of 'Otherness,'" *Environment and Planning D: Society and Space*, 11, pp. 709–32.

Tuan, Y.-F. (1974), *Topophilia: A Study of Environmental Perception, Attitudes, and Values*, Englewood Cliff, NJ: Prentice Hall.

Walker, D. (1981), "A Theory of Suburbanisation: Capitalism and the Construction of Urban Space in the United States," in M. Dear and A. J. Scott (eds.), *Urbanisation and Urban Planning in Capitalist Societies*, London: Methuen.

Walker, D. (1995), "Landscape and City Life: Four Ecologies of Residence in the San Francisco Bay Area," *Ecumene*, 2, pp. 33–64.

West, D. (1997), "Who Needs a House in Beverly Hills? Stars Now Flock to Wealthy But Unassuming Bedford, N.Y.," *New York Times*, May.

Wood, Joseph (1991), "Build Therefore, Your Own World: The New England village as Settlement Ideal," *Annals, Association of American Geographers*, 81, pp. 32–50.

Wyckoff, William (1990), "Landscapes of Private Power and Wealth," in M. P. Conzen (ed.), *The Making of the American Landscape*, London: Unwin Hyman, pp. 335–54.

Zukin, S. (1991), *Landscapes of power*, Berkeley: University of California Press.

CHAPTER 10

Mediascapes

Paul C. Adams

Americans have long been among the most geographically mobile people in the modern world. Their seeming geographical rootlessness has been the inspiration for the development of many transportation and communication technologies to join them back together, from the telephone and the car to television, the jet airliner, and the Internet. While privacy and autonomy are long-cherished elements of the American story, they have always been buttressed by the claim of active social participation as a chosen activity. At the same time, the space-shrinking technologies have allowed for an intense privatization of life. In particular, the media of communication make possible a distancing of self from active social involvement in public spaces through the creation of private worlds dependent on technology. These trends would seem to undermine the celebration of active community participation and social engagement upon which dominant stories about American identity rely. Television is the most important of the media technologies both in its everyday impact on most people and in the way it encourages passive spectatorship rather than active participation in everyday life. Cultural geographer Paul Adams uses examples from film, science fiction writing, and, above all, network television, to draw attention to both the fragmentary character of the experience of watching television and the strange way in which television programs signify both avoidance of community and the quest for it through vicarious identification with the personalities and plots of favorite shows. The downside is evidence that television community is not an adequate substitute for the real thing, revealed by, among other events, school shootings by intensely private, troubled, televisually obsessed teenage boys. With the explosion of Information Technology or IT, the tension between physical and virtual realities has become intensified, challenging the conception of stable personal identities or selves and understandings of privacy and community upon which both American space and American place have been built.

A stay-at-home mother in Albany, New York, surfs the Web while assembling the components of a product that will be sold in Eugene,

Oregon. The Web page she explores is physically located in Dallas, but provides news of events in Africa and Asia, along with hypertext links to sites elsewhere in the United States, including (almost incidentally) her home state. While she surfs, she listens to an "oldies" radio station playing a Beatles song that was recorded in the 1960s in England and is broadcast on this day in the 1990s over a several hundred square mile area of upstate New York, and, coincidentally, in Boise, Idaho. Meanwhile her boss does business with a client in California, using his cellular phone, as he drives across Schenectady, New York, in a car made in Alabama by a German company. The activity patterns, social networks, and experiential ranges of Americans are scattered through space and time in a pattern of dizzying complexity.

Transportation and communication technologies permit this scattering and also tie together economic, political, and cultural processes. Communications media link places with other places even as they split apart the stream of sensation into experiences from various places catering to different senses. Sight is separated from hearing, smell, and touch, so that each sense links up with its own geography of connections.

Communication media do not become involved in geography just by disseminating place images. The media actually disassemble and reassemble people's frameworks of knowledge and action in space and time. This helps Americans build a lifestyle that is unique and "custom tailored" to their interests and abilities. As Tuan (1982: 11) argues, modernity brings a "progressive partitioning of space that clearly reflects . . . people's growing sense of self." But this sense of self is also increasingly threatened by internal segmentation, fear, and hostility as experiences from so many different places are jumbled together and life becomes decentered and disjointed. It is threatened above all by the withdrawal from public space to private space. As private space links up with an increasing number of virtual places "in" the media and public spaces are quietly replaced by "quasi-public" spaces that look public but aren't, the opportunity for privacy and hence the meaning of self undergo strange transformations.

Media dependency and American culture

While media dependency is manifested in all of the wealthy countries, nowhere is this process as pervasive as in the United States. To understand why this is the case we must look at American culture. According to geographer Wilbur Zelinsky (1973: 40), American culture can be characterized by:

1. an intense, almost anarchistic individualism;
2. a high valuation placed upon mobility and change;
3. a mechanistic vision of the world;
4. a messianic perfectionism.

Zelinsky's last two factors, a mechanistic world-view and messianic perfectionism, are certainly sufficient to explain the American infatuation with communication technologies, since the evolution from the horse-drawn cart, to the streetcar and train, to the car, to the Internet is a quest to live life without boundaries, to perfect our accessibility to distant places. If time and distance are seen as obstacles (rather than, for example, essential elements of experience), or as costs, or inefficiencies, then the perfection of life appears to require instantaneous interaction. Communication media also help concretize a mechanistic vision of the world. Alphabetic writing, for example, breaks down speech into its component sounds then reassembles these sounds to form words. Words become objects rather than events, frozen in time and space on a page, billboard, or other surface. By capturing words, the invention of writing and printing and their use in recording transactions, commands, and so on, facilitated the formation of empires and nations because every message from trading contracts to military orders could be disseminated within a wide territory, facilitating political, economic, and cultural coordination. Modern countries are similar to the earliest empires in this regard; despite the radical change in the degree to which their technologies overcome temporal and spatial limitations. Communication media assist in transforming human collectives into great and complex machines. A culture obsessed with a mechanistic world-view, then, is a culture that is likely to embrace new communication technologies and use them to expand the scale and complexity of its own organization.

The American valuation of mobility and change also accounts for the popularity of communication. Media can be used to promote a sense of visiting and participating in diverse sites around the world, a kind of virtual mobility. Communication also complements physical mobility when it helps to maintain far-flung business, academic, and social linkages, or when a book, magazine, television program, or Web page is used to gather information that directs subsequent tourism or business investment in distant places.

But the most subtle and interesting link can be found between Zelinsky's first observation, the intense individualism of American society, and the American passion for new communication technologies. Since the 1950s, American entertainment and advertising industries have turned individualism into profit, and accentuated aspects of individualism (such as insecurity, ambition, and aggression). Advertisements and programs in various media focus on the personal insecurities and inadequacies, and alternatively on the accomplishments and victories, of the lone, isolated individual (Marchand 1985). Such media content, when successful, promotes the habit of forging an identity through the products one buys. Since this habit subjugates personal identity to the rationality of the market and maximization of personal benefits, it creates a limitless desire for goods.

As American lifestyles have shifted from the one-story bungalow of the 1950s to the dream house of the 1990s (at least $200,000, at least 2,500 square feet in size, with private swimming pool, home-entertainment system, and automatic alarm system), consumption to meet the self-image associated with this domestic environment has continued apace. New houses feature built-in offices and exercise rooms. Individualism is often interpreted to mean the pursuit of convenience, epitomized by the remote control device for virtually everything. Private space becomes a realm of immobility where monotonous rituals of leisure and consumption substitute for the diversity and sensory stimulation of public life and public space. Computer games, television programs, videos, CD musical recordings, and the Internet, all can exceed the sensory richness and interest of the remaining public spaces of the American city: sidewalk-less streets with endless traffic, fast-food outlets, and look-alike shopping malls. In comparison to real American landscapes, the mediascapes constituted in new media such as the Internet and "virtual reality" may seem more real, leading to what Baudrillard (1983) calls "hyperreality." But this is best seen as a symptom of the segmentation of society, the loss of stable communities in which to constitute personal identity, and the loss of a coherent sense of place.

Consumption is no longer conspicuous, except in the form of the private vehicle, which in America is much more than merely transportation; vehicles of absurd size and/or power continue to gain in popularity (more than 50 percent of new vehicle sales in the United States are vans, sport utility vehicles, and light trucks). The destruction of public space and obsession with personal identity drive a private life of consumption, where one becomes one's own audience. And behind consumption lie the materialistic images – the movies, television programs, and advertisements – of an affluent society. Privatization is evident in the vast array of products designed to encapsulate all activities within the confines of the vehicle or the home: shopping, eating, working, exercising, even socializing.

Richard Sennett observed over thirty years ago (Sennett 1970) that suburban Americans had built for themselves a "purified identity" based on an ideal image of community. Implicit in the postwar flight of the white, middle classes to the suburbs were classist and racist attitudes of avoidance. The "we" constructed in suburban spaces was based not on interaction, as in real community, but on an imagined image of community and an outward conformity. Fitting into suburban society involved keeping up with fashions and having the right appearance. If we understand community as a product of interdependence and communication among a group of people, then the suburbanites actually avoided community even as they sought an elusive and illusory image of perfect social unity.

Jane Jacobs, in her classic work, *The Death and Life of the Great American Cities* (1961), argued that the dangers of city life from which the suburbanites fled were often mythical. She examined older urban neighborhoods where private and public spaces were mixed, where homes, shops, and service establishments were in close proximity. In the chaotic activity of these densely populated mixed-use areas of the city she found little opportunity for crime. In contrast, the housing projects that were constructed to "solve" the urban problem through the separation of purified residential spaces from the rest of the city's activities actually encouraged crime to proliferate. All too often, the image of perfect community replaced the reality.

American suburbs are distinguished from each other by ever finer income gradations (Davis 1990) and many suburbs are indeed fairly safe, but entirely lacking in a positive sense of public space or community. When problems arise in suburban life, such as depression or random violence, they reflect this absense. "Community" values become synonymous with protection of private property, property values, and the freedom to stay inside and undisturbed with one's "toys." In place of the shopping district, people spend out-of-home leisure time in the pseudo-public space of the shopping mall – a place divorced from its political and social context, a purified space where people can purchase a part of the idealized world they see every day on the mass media, thereby conferring a certain fugitive reality on the illusory public world (Goss 1999, 1993). This constitution of "the public" occurs without actually talking to strangers and thereby constituting a real public realm. Mall space, functionally limited as it is, can generally be reached only by automobile, so even this simulation of public life is often inaccessible to children, adolescents, seniors, and others who cannot drive.

The media are central to the construction of this privatized lifestyle, as means of involvement in society and as means of distancing oneself from society, as the spur to private ownership through advertisements, and as the framework giving meaning to such ownership. Media create a social context that is not physically occupied, consisting of the symbolism and infrastructure for constructing identity and the means of interacting at a distance. Meanwhile, media act in synergy with the physical layout and composition of cities to reduce the activity level in real (physical) gathering places such as parks and shopping districts. Privatization of lifestyles is greatest in sunbelt states where the "needs" of the car have been allowed to shape virtually all of the urban fabric. Two kinds of place – virtual and physical – therefore work together to create and fortify privatization in America.

Privatization and paranoia

The retreat to private space lends an odd kind of reality to virtual places. At the same time, it confers a sense of unreality on the "Real World." Privatization makes the virtual world seem more real (since it is more accessible and more interesting) than the physical, material, and tangible world. Behind this inversion of the real and the unreal, one senses a fear for the integrity of personal identity in the emerging technologically dependent world. Retreat, including the retreat to private spaces of large homes and automobiles, is most likely a sign of fear.

The film called *The Matrix* embodies these peculiar twists. A man who seems to be living in twentieth-century America is really, it turns out, inhabiting a computer simulation built in the twenty-first or twenty-second century. He and all the people he encounters are in fact dreaming the twentieth century, and their dreams are coordinated electronically in "the Matrix," a computer network that has been connected directly to their brains by an evil empire of machines (which has taken over the earth as a result of twentieth-century artificial intelligence experiments gone awry). The shared hallucination of the world, complete with streets, buildings, moving people, and so on, serves to occupy and pacify the human population which is kept asleep in endless banks of sleeping pods; their purpose is to serve the machines as a source of electricity (there is no explanation in the film of why people are better for this purpose than, say cows, or more to the point why their brains have not simply been removed when they are installed in the generator!). A man named "Neo" finds himself (literally) awakened and adopted by a band of resistance fighters. He eventually learns to fight the Matrix by redefining its reality subjectively, that is, mentally. He is a slow learner, however, and the movie provides lots of spectacular machine-gun fire and even some heavy artillery before Neo learns that it is more effective to stop bullets with his mind rather than returning fire. The movie is, of course, a kind of shared hallucination in its own right, manufactured for the immobilized, sensorially deprived movie audience of the late twentieth century. It is a manifestation of real societal dependence on machines such as guns, cars, and mass media, not to mention the fact that animals are presently immobilized in giant factories like the ones made for people in *The Matrix*, in order to maximize meat production, but these ironies are not explored.

Part of the difficulty in Neo's situation is that the only way to fight the Matrix is from within, that is, as one of the dreamers in the collective hallucination. This space is where the reality of the Matrix resides and where it can best be threatened, but whichever way Neo goes in the Matrix, the agents (artificial intelligence programs designed to prevent people from being awakened) know exactly "where" he is. His every "move" is in fact an electronic signal emanating from his (real, immobilized) brain and monitored by the (networked machine) enemy; the agents know everything he does even as he does it. This is, in short, a world where privacy is nonexistent because technology has run rampant.

Similar themes are explored in *Blade Runner*. While David Harvey (1989: 308–23) finds in this film a sublimation of class conflict, it deals more obviously with the paradoxes of privatization, personal identity, and technology. The story focuses on a band of "replicants," synthetic people designed for space exploration and settlement. Although superior to human beings in strength, dexterity, and even intelligence, the replicants are given a lifespan of only four years in order to reduce the possibility that they might return to earth and endanger human beings. The replicants are also implanted with synthetic memories of a full human past, and are given "old" photographs to validate this fictive past to themselves and others and prevent them from discovering their real identity as disposable products. The plot concerns some replicants that are trying to track down their maker and bargain or bully him into giving them a longer life. There is a hint that the man hired to track and destroy these renegade replicants is himself a replicant. In a world where memories can be manufactured, identity is necessarily unstable and one's "own" thoughts are never incontrovertibly one's own. Again, the story works through a deep-seated fear of a high-tech world where privacy is nonexistent because identity is reduced to data. Harvey is correct to argue that this situation mirrors the modern world, since identity is constructed in and around the images of advertising and the media. To buy a certain brand of beer is to identify oneself as a rebel, a "high-brow," or some other stereotype promulgated by the media. You are what you consume and personal identity is almost a kind of implant.

Modern American science fiction returns obsessively to these themes of privacy, identity, and technology. Neil Stephenson's *Snow Crash* (1992) and William Gibson's *Neuromancer* (1984) are two of the most influential novels in the "cyberpunk" sub-genre, both of which also address the erosion of privacy through the proliferation of technology. In *Snow Crash* the wryly named Hiro Protagonist discovers the secret of a new drug which is also a computer virus. The barriers between mind and computer have been so eroded that the forces of social disorder propagate a new weapon in the form of a mental virus. In *Neuromancer* we encounter an artificial intelligence called Wintermute that knows enough about people to replicate their physical images and thought patterns, impersonating them at will. Again we find the technological erosion of the boundary between self and other, and the chronic loss of the possibility of a private life, because of technologies of replication.

Many more examples could be listed. The point is to suggest that

American culture is exploring the nightmarish idea of a technologically-compromised privacy even as it is in the process of mediating all of life and thereby constructing this reality. With a vocabulary of identity derived from science fiction, in particular, Americans are exploring their own identity transformations in this mediated social environment. Where privacy is already eroded by technological (and economic) intrusions, people go home to dream about cyborgs and replicants. In effect, the theme of technologically-reconstructed identity is well-grounded, even if the plot lines are fantastic.

Privatization and the virtual friend

Despite the popular excitement at a wide range of new media, including the Internet, Americans still primarily "gather" in the virtual space of television (Adams 1992). At the time of this writing, the most-watched show, *E.R.*, is seen on over 18 million American television sets each week (not counting those households where re-runs from previous seasons are viewed). The ten most-watched TV shows play on over 10 million American television sets each week. This would count as a significant "shared" activity in any society. What is peculiar about this sharing is its fragmentary, atomized quality. Aside from the physical gathering of household members who watch together, viewing is basically solitary and most immediate responses are not shared with other viewers (this is particularly true of male viewers, Morley 1986). Television is not like a physical gathering space, such as a stadium or arena where all of the congregants are co-present to each other and sense each others' responses. Broadcast television creates a radial, one-way topology of connection, as indicated in Debord's (1990) term "society of the spectacle."

In America, television viewing occupies more free time than any other activity. A 1985 study of average time use in the United States found that TV-viewing as a primary activity consumes 37.9 percent of free time, 15 hours out of a total of 39.6 free-time hours per week (Robinson and Godbey 1997: 125). This is more time than the following activities combined: hobbies, recreation, sports, outdoor activities, reading, listening to music, adult education, religion, participation in social organizations, and attending cultural events. The closest contender for the focus of free time in America is person-to-person communication. Including both socializing and communication with household members, this consumes only 11.1 hours per week, on average. Americans therefore appear to spend 35 percent more time watching television than chatting with family and friends. Furthermore, television viewing in the average American household increased from 10.4 hours per week in the 1960s to more than 15 hours per week at the time of writing, a greater increase in total time use than that of any other medium.

What, then, does the audience obtain from television that accounts for this popularity? To a large extent, we can answer this question by looking at American social space, in the course of privatization, and the form of the programs that have become the most popular. These programs, such as *E.R.*, *Friends*, *Frasier*, *Veronica's Closet*, *Jesse*, and the *X-Files*, combine the serial format traditionally associated with the soap opera (a running plot that continues from show to show) with the comic or dramatic conventions of several other genres such as the situation comedy, the drama, and the science fiction thriller. There are other kinds of shows among the top twenty, such as investigative news programs (*60 Minutes*, *Dateline*), standard format sit-coms (*Will and Grace*, *The Drew Carey Show*, *Just Shoot Me*, and *Becker*), sports programs, and a rather unusual cartoon (*The Simpsons*), but the "prime-time soaps" most clearly indicate the search for community and hence the impoverished social life that necessitates such a search. A facsimile of community is experienced through personal identification and bonding with television characters. The characters usually are more realistic than the characters of popular shows in earlier generations (and other kinds of contemporary shows), displaying both good and bad qualities, weaknesses and strengths, and essentially normal patterns of social interaction (except, of course, in *X-Files*). The plots of prime-time serials include experiences that are familiar (such as adults coping with visits of their parents) even if the details of such situations are exaggerated. Moreover, the most bizarre and unpredictable characters (often neighbors of the main characters) are balanced by the main characters' predictability. Despite plot development from episode to episode, enough remains the same in the overall situation to preserve personal attachments between audience members and characters.

NBC's *Friends*, for example, uses the audience's fear of a major change in the characters' situation (a group of six singles in their twenties who remarkably remain single and closely tied to each other) to build suspense at the end of each season: will the group split up? But outrageous twists of fate always restore equilibrium to this group, drawing each of them back into the fold, away from outside competition, and thereby retaining the audience segments most closely attached to each character.

A serial must be watched regularly in order to make sense to the viewers and provide the most pleasure, a fact which encourages people to incorporate the program as a ritual in their lives. The "television ritual" has a weekly periodicity not unlike going to church, but whereas the community one bonded with at church was a congregation of real people, the community on a television show is the cast, with which the audience is invited to share good and bad times, and in essence become "friends" (Figure 10.1). Intertextual association (Fiske 1987: 108–27) with other media helps build a sense of the reality of the characters, as well as provoking curiosity about the actor's real personality and life. For example, a search on the Yahoo search engine, April 29, 1999, turned up eighty-three web sites dedicated to individual actors and actresses on *Friends*, and another sixty-six dedicated to the show in general. Picture galleries on these sites (not all of which were in English) featured the stars in various moods, settings, outfits, and stages of undress. In addition, one could chat with other *Friends* fans in at least three different online chat rooms – making friends with other friends of *Friends*.

While *Friends* overtly draws in the viewer as a virtual friend, other shows situate the viewer somewhat differently. *E.R.* constructs a "human" side of doctors, which is inaccessible in real life from the patient relationship. The viewer is a fly on the wall rather than a friend, and is favored with what seems to be a realistic view of every aspect of doctors' lives. Why should people want to see doctors as people, with the full array of human qualities including dishonesty, ambition, fears, failures, love interests, and sexuality (Figure 10.2)? Why should they find it pleasurable to do so, even when the doctors in question are not real doctors? In a society of narrow specializations, where people generally know each other only in a professional capacity, people live in "segmented worlds" (Tuan 1982). There is a desire to overcome these segmented worlds and the isolation they imply, and one way to overcome segmentation is to learn about people whose role might be very important, indeed life-preserving, in one's own life. These important-but-unknown-others include police officers, doctors, and other public figures such as radio station personalities. While a well-rounded

Figure 10.1 The cast of *Friends*, a serial-sitcom aimed at the "twenty-something" audience. This magazine cover promotes the idea that these actors and actresses are friends in real-life as well as on in the make-believe world of the sitcom, blurring the line between fantasy and reality, private and public. Cover, *People* January 24, 2000; 'People' Weekly is a registered trademark of Time Inc., used with permission.

image of others is often out of reach in a society with little public life, the desire for community may be satisfied by a fantasy vision of others'

Figure 10.2 George Clooney, who played Dr. Douglas Ross on *ER*, is presented here as one of America's 100 most eligible bachelors. Mass-media audiences are encouraged to fantasize about romantic involvement with a doctor and a famous actor at the same time, satisfying private desires with a public icon. Cover, *People*, July 10, 2000; 'People' Weekly is a registered trademark of Time Inc., used with permission.

private lives. A virtual friend stands in for a real friend, and a virtual doctor makes one's real doctor seem a bit more human.

Television characters make unique friends and virtual lovers: they have no privacy and at the same time they do not intrude on the viewer's privacy. They are easy to "deliver" to millions of separate living rooms and can be custom-tailored to fit different age groups from children to the elderly. If, as Lull argues (1988), television extends the rituals of a society, then the American withdrawal from public space is extended even further by such virtual friendships, and it is enabled by them in its drift toward fragmentation. Virtual friends substitute for community in many ways while allowing people to purify their lives of outside influences that are too disturbing or challenging with regard to their personal values. A doctor can be sexy and loveable (*E.R*); a gay man can be cute, funny, and non-threatening (*Will and Grace*); indeed it appears that all social differences can be leveled, but the leveling occurs on screen and is not the same as acceptance of difference in real life.

The newest genre to appear on American television in a serious way is the real-life drama like CBS's *Survivor* and *Big Brother*. Here, audiences can form attachments in virtual space to characters who are real, not just actors. The feelings are likely to be even stronger in this case, and antipathy towards certain persons (such as *Survivor*'s conniving Susan or the smug exhibitionist, Rich) may be stronger than any particular attachment. This newfound ability to truly hate a TV character perhaps explains the particular emotional niche filled by the program and why it is so successful. The real life characters give up their privacy so that viewers can accentuate their own privacy.

In short, the popularity of many television programs demonstrates the quest for community and the simultaneous avoidance of community in American society. Furthermore, television's dominant role in American free time indicates that American community is now developing as a hybrid of in-person and virtual forms of interaction.

Privatization and the virtual enemy

On April 20, 1999, in Littleton, Colorado, two students entered Columbine High School with sawed-off shotguns, a 9-mm semiautomatic carbine, a TEC-DC9 semiautomatic handgun, dozens of pipe bombs and a large home-made bomb (Gibbs 1999: 34). Dylan Klebold, 17, and Eric Harris, 18, proceeded to kill twelve of their classmates, one of their teachers, and themselves. Although violent crime appears

to be declining overall in American schools, the occurrence of imper-
sonal, rampage-style killing by children bearing automatic weapons is
on the rise. There were three such incidents with fatalities in the 1997–8
school year. In one an 11-year-old and a 13-year-old in Jonesboro, Arkansas, set off the school fire alarm and shot fifteen people as they left the
school, killing four students and a teacher. In another, a 14-year-old in
West Paducah, Kentucky, shot eight members of a school-based prayer
group, killing three. In a third incident, a 15-year-old in Springfield,
Oregon, shot and killed both his parents then went to school, ultimately killing two of his classmates and wounding twenty-two other
persons (NSSC 1999). This type of violence differs from the gang
warfare of the 1980s and early 1990s in that it is a private savagery,
perpetrated by pairs or individuals who become so thoroughly alienated
from classmates and family that they act out the bloody pyrotechnic
scenes they have seen in video games and adventure movies. This
type of crime is symptomatic of a society with little real public space,
virtually none of which allows children to see adult role models in an
ordinary work environment. What remains is a virtual public space –
the media – that is saturated with violence.

An article in *Time* magazine (Corliss 1999: 50) defends the American
media with a hip version of the "guns don't kill people" argument:
"Flash: movies don't kill people. Guns kill people." But the killers in
the Columbine High massacre were avid fans of *Doom*, a video game in
which "players wander through claustophobic corridors in a terrifyingly
real first-person perspective, blasting the guts out of their enemies with
a blistering array of weaponry" (Taylor 1999: 50). One of them, at least,
was fond of *Natural Born Killers* (Corliss 1999: 49), the same movie that
was reported to have inspired Barry Loukitas, 16, to go on a shooting
spree at his Moses Lake, Washington high school in 1996 (NSSC 1999).

Media also entered the equation in the aftermath of the Littleton
killings (as a blood-spattered high school provided the news media
with a diversion from the gore in Kosovo) and as inspiration for
bomb-making techniques. Media even formed the fragile mortar of the
perpetrator's sense of "community," as evident in their posting of a
Web page. In a more public society, the influence of media is not likely
to produce such a reaction, but in combination with a particular constitution of public and private space, that is, a highly privatized world,
it appears to have an effect on certain susceptible children. The garage
where Harris and Klebold built their bombs was located in a wealthy

suburb devoid of real public life. The boys' families, school, and neighbors all respected their privacy to the degree that no one was seriously
concerned about the death threats they had posted on the Internet or
the noise they made building armaments (Dickinson 1999). In the end,
even the killing was not so much a public action as a means of private
stimulation; witnesses report that the gunmen took delight in the aesthetic effects of close-range shotgun blasts, displaying an erotic sadism
like that at the heart of "action" movies. In the American suburb – an
intensely private place where the free-floating space of the mind meets
the virtual space of the media – loneliness can proliferate, and brutal
fantasies are allowed to grow and bear fruit.

IT and the United States' global situation

We turn now to what has been hailed as a technological fix, not only
for the problems indicated here (Rheingold 1993; Mitchell 1995; Rushkoff 1994; McLuhan and Fiore 1967) but for many others: Information
Techology or IT. We must regard any claims about this technology with
caution (not least because they are implicated in stories like the one
above), but if media-dependency and the American society are so
thoroughly enmeshed, then perhaps a change of media will facilitate a
change of social relations. While no environment – physical or virtual
– can determine behavior, an environment can support or discourage
the formation of social relations that in turn shape behavior. In particular, if America suffers from a truncated public life, then perhaps a
medium that expands the opportunities to interact with others (rather
than passively receiving a "program") is a step in the right direction.

IT generally denotes a convergence of various technologies including
the existing public switched telephone network, broadcast media such
as television, and the computer. Many other technologies such as pagers,
cell phones, satellite phones, fax machines, calculators, watches, electronic note pads, and GPS units are being drawn into this technological
vortex. In general, the challenge of imagining IT as a field of social
potentials – a virtual space – lies in the range of communication situations that IT can support: one-to-one, one-to-many, many-to-many, real
time, asynchronous, text, image, sound, moving picture clips. These
situations cover the range previously covered by a wide range of separate and completely distinct media, including newspaper, telephone,
television, radio, film, the magazine, and the humble cork bulletin

board. The emerging "information superhighway" is massively concentrated in the United States at the present time (Cukier 1998). This system has evolved from a wholly state-controlled project with military objectives into a fertile environment for private enterprise (Leiner et al. 1998). The trend of privatization is mirrored by increases in time spent using these media on the whole, which suggests a further physical retreat into private space. But the break from the "broadcasting" model of telecommunication which has dominated since 1950 holds out the promise of a livelier and somewhat more public virtual space, despite the violence implicit in some IT content.

The new pervasive and networked communication technologies support social segmentation in ways that diverge from the earlier techniques of spatial segregation. Instead of "a place for everything and everything in its place" Americans increasingly differentiate objects, social functions, and behaviors through different communication contexts and symbolic languages, that is, through different virtual places. This trend does not necessarily mean less travel. In some cases, communication becomes a "trade-off" for mobility while in other cases it becomes a stimulus to increased mobility. As Susan Hanson (1998) frames the issue, IT has applications both "on the road" and "off the road." Communication stimulates transportation when it becomes a mechanism for more responsive signaling and user information, through so-called "intelligent transportation systems" (Hanson 1998) or "smart roads" and when it encourages more distant contacts in business and socialization that in turn place higher demands on transportation. Communication substitutes for transportation in the classic (though still uncommon) case of telecommuting (Castells 1996: 395), and in certain market sectors such as book sales (Verhovek 1998). IT therefore offers an increasing range of alternative time–space routines, some more mobile and some less mobile.

Since the 1980s, the lines between communication and transportation appear to have bifurcated. Some people are bringing their workplace into the home, narrowing their range of daily movement, and spatially combining activities to create a new kind of situational segmentation, while others are using mobile telecommunications to become more mobile during work hours and overcome spatial segmentation (like the persons mentioned at the beginning of the chapter). Social norms and other factors of culture are changing to "fit" the new situations people have created and their virtual places. A home can take on qualities of an office, an office can take on qualities of a home, and one's means of transportation can take on qualities of either place. Being "at work" or "at home" may refer only to using a particular medium of communication or even variations in how a medium is used. These changes in the mixture of the three ingredients of place – nature, meaning, and social relations (Sack 1997) – imply shifts in personal identity and in world-views in general, including science, art, and religious/moral systems.

Through all of this complex change we can observe the continued "encapsulization" of lifeworlds to fit certain ideals, as observed critically by Sennett, Jacobs and Goss (see also Sorkin 1992), but there is something new. The invisibility and anonymity afforded to communicators on the Internet is a special kind of privacy. It therefore encourages unusual modes of interaction, and new constitutions of "the public." A psychologist, Sherry Turkle (1995), has discovered that computer chat rooms and virtual environments (often called MUDs after the archaic "Multi-User Dungeon") encourage experimentation with gender. Women may "pose" as men to feel more independent and autonomous, to avoid harrassment, to join in conversations where they would otherwise feel excluded, or to experiment with gender identity and sexual orientation in a "safe" context. Men may likewise adopt a female persona to experience the power of being an object of desire, to achieve a level of conversational intimacy that they have not previously experienced with women, to experiment with homosexual or transsexual interests, or simply out of curiosity (Turkle 1995: 210–32). In cyberspace, a man or woman may also relate to others from a neutral or ambiguous gender status, an experience that is hard to encounter otherwise. Age switching is also common. Turkle finds a 12-year-old girl who pretends she is 18 when she is meeting people online (1995: 227). The opposite type of age switching has led to the seduction of minors by older men posing as adolescents. Another axis of social differentiation that is disguised or transformed by the privacy of virtual interactions is social class. People with humdrum jobs and modest incomes can build elaborate "dwellings" in MUDs, and create sophisticated personas to inhabit those dwellings. The relation between real and artificial identity is not as stable or clear as it might seem. A man explains, "MUDs make me more what I really am. Off the MUD, I am not as much me," and a woman points to the paradox of virtual possession: "I feel like I have more stuff on the MUD than I have off it" (Turkle 1995: 240).

Ethnicity is yet another facet of self that becomes fluid when one converses online, as "race" can be hidden or falsified. Despite the different levels of access to computers based on factors of income, ethnicity, sex, and age, the participants operate within a social space that lacks visual indicators of one's biological nature and material situation, and a special kind of privacy that lets people partially transcend many axes of social stratification.

We should be aware that the notion of identity is, however, always a construction. Since identity is always constructed in a social context, and that context is dependent on all sorts of infrastructure including transportation networks, architecture, and media, we cannot isolate the interactions within a single medium (IT, for example) and call them "false." What we have is a new kind of space and a new segment of identity to somehow integrate into the rest of our segmented, highly privatized identity.

IT and the loss of privacy

Information Technologies extend a long cultural process of the differentiation and fragmentation of space. This, in turn, contributes to the trend of accentuation and fragmentation of individuality. Even as they carry society farther along this course, creating new forms of privacy, they paradoxically indicate the reversal of this entire current of change. Privacy, itself a product of communication technologies as we have seen, is fundamentally threatened by new developments in the technology of communication.

Judith Squires argues (1994: 387) that

> the condition of postmodernity is characterised by forces that would erode many of the spaces and places in which privacy was previously grounded. Where there was distance we witness time-space compression; where there were boundaries we perceive transparency; where there was confidentiality we find information flows.

Squires links this situation to a wide range of changes including "feminist theory and global information technologies" (1994: 395). The latter includes the surveillance cameras that are quietly proliferating in banks, stores, apartment buildings, public transit stations, and along many roads. It arises primarily from the accumulation and cross-tabulation of personal data in computer databases. These databases can be bought and sold, passing from state agencies into the hands of private entrepreneurs and vice versa. Measures to safeguard individuals from violations of privacy are potentially overcome by software "agents," virtual intelligence programs that assist with anything from the sorting of e-mail to the discovery of information on the World Wide Web. Aside from the use of agents to ferret out information about others, one's own agents "learn" from experience (Turkle 1995: 98–101), which means they contain information about one's habits, interests, and opinions, which can potentially be retrieved by others online.

IT not only supports a withdrawal into private space, it also creates an integrated system of surveillance and data sharing that makes privacy subject to technological obsolescence. Electronic copies are now made of all transactions and personal information from e-mail to DNA. The new "surveillance space" serves the needs of both legal and illegal espionage (Gandy 1989; Wade 1998; Shimomura and Markoff 1996). Some observers find hope in the possibility that surveillance will be democratized instead of remaining the exclusive province of the wealthy and powerful (Teitelbaum 1996), but they hold out little hope that privacy as we know it can be preserved. If this is not an attractive world, it may nonetheless be an economically productive one and hence assert itself as the environment of the future against our resistance (in a shift reminiscent of *The Matrix*). In a related vein, AnnaLee Saxenian (1996) has found that Silicon Valley's advantage over Route 128 in Massachusetts derives from the regional culture of Silicon Valley, which promotes the "open flow of information, technology, and know-how" among high-tech firms. Loss of privacy on the corporate level is apparently a requirement for success in high technology production.

Michael Curry applies the name "digital individual" to the collection of data associated with an individual. Digital individuals are collections of personal data derived from a wide range of sources and merged in comprehensive dossiers. Curry argues (1997: 689) that the laws limiting cross-tabulation of various sources of personal data have been ineffective, leading to more detailed profiles, which are now bought and sold in the private sector and combined with "geodemographic" databases, collections of spatially-aggregated data. A digital individual might include information regarding a person's health, credit rating, videotape and book borrowing preferences, and dozens of other personal facts, erroneous and valid, as well as census information from the block group scale attached hypothetically to an individual based on his or her address. The synthesis of such information raises the potential of the abuse of information in a discriminatory way. On what bases might one be judged dangerous, irresponsible, indecent, or otherwise suspect? An American can do little to prevent this invasion from occurring, and will seldom be informed when it does. Web sites already can monitor the "clickstreams" of users to provide targeted marketing. Engage Technology's website (www.accipiter.com) claims they provide "the ability to see the world through each visitor's eyes and to market to each individual's reality," through their anonymous user profiling technology. Redeye (www.redeye.com) similarly "keeps a record of lifetime value from each and every click through." Customers using the online bookstore Amazon.com already experience this kind of advertising as suggested purchases pop up on the screen based on their past purchases which are "remembered" by Amazon's Web server. In some grocery stores, customers receive coupons on the back of their receipts which are tailored to their purchasing patterns by on-the-spot computer analysis of their purchases based on the UPC codes of their groceries.   Most impressive of all is Acxiom, a company based in Conway, Arkansas, which has dossiers of information on 160 million Americans (90 percent of United States households) which is bought by telemarketers, retailers, store inventory managers, law enforcement agencies, lawyers, private investigators, and debt collectors – generating a billion dollars in sales annually (Elias 2001).

Relative to older types of privacy invasion like trespassing, this sort of surveillance is often harder to detect, harder to stop, and harder to clearly identify as an invasion of privacy. Furthermore, the practice of surveillance is decentralizing from state control to business firms and organizations of all kinds since all that is required is the money to buy access to databases (Castells 1997: 299–303).

A new sense of self?

We have at our disposal the perfect role model for the American of the future. As David Bolter (1984) argues in *Turing's Man*, people have repeatedly modeled their image of humanity on the technologies in their environment; humanity has evolved, in the mind's eye, from a clay sculpture to clockwork, to a kind of mobile computer, as technology has successively entered the ceramic, mechanical, and cybernetic phases. In the computer age, "By making a machine think as a man, man recreates himself, defines himself as a machine" (Bolter 1984: 13). Bolter calls this technologically-based self-image "Turing's man" in honor of A. M. Turing, who apparently was the first person to publish an argument that a machine could perfectly imitate human intelligence. In the unbounded flows of digital space, we not only have a post-private kind of social context, but also the model of the post-private individual. We can envision self in a new way, as the psychological equivalent of the Internet: a mind that is constantly "online," attached to diverse social situations professional and personal, and simultaneously involved in a number of different social "spaces." Self becomes a node.

Sherry Turkle finds that the windows format of the 1990s computer screen has "become a powerful metaphor for thinking about the self as a multiple, distributed system" (1995: 14). The disconnect between body and identity promotes a semi-serious masquerade that decenters the identity, since a digital persona can be changed or dropped at will (Nguyen and Alexander 1996: 104). This is more than the fragmentation of a modern assembly line, where each station performs a predefined function, or the modernist self mapped by the Freudian Id, Ego, and Super Ego. The self-knowledge valued in Freud's model becomes obsolete with "Turing's man" because the self can be reprogrammed, or operate several programs at once. There is no real self to know. Furthermore, self-knowledge is pointless because the basic rules that make information transfer possible, mathematics and logic, are known and do not change, and hence are not a mystery (Bolter 1984: 224). To be Turing's man is to "lock in" self at a fundamental level to a shared reality, to become transparent, and to advocate transparency as a social norm. Privacy, in the sense Americans have known it, would become obsolete. Accommodations would have to be made from the old world in which certain activities, like sex, are hidden by the clear separation of public and private, to a new world where such activities are still segregated (in different "areas" of virtual space) but no longer effectively hidden.

If this potential is latent in the technology, it runs counter to the trend of privatization evident in American lifestyles over the past 200 years. The conflict between trends is potentially explosive. Identities constructed through unbounded and fluid interactions in virtual spaces are likely to chafe at the limitations imposed by the highly segmented physical spaces created in the quest for privacy. Meanwhile, the commonly held and still central ideal of privacy is likely to be violated time and again by the potential invasions from the virtual space of IT. Dissatisfactions with one space (virtual or physical) may lead to activities in the other space that run counter to the previous construction of one's identity. This tension between virtual and physical spaces, and its effects in psychological and social processes, should be a source of considerable dynamism in American culture for some time to come.

References

Adams, Paul C. (1992), "Television as Gathering Place," *Annals of the Association of American Geographers*, 82(1), pp. 117–35.
Baudrillard, Jean (1983), *Simulations*, Foreign Agents Series, New York: Semiotext(e).
Bolter, J. David (1984), *Turing's Man: Western Culture in the Computer Age*, Chapel Hill: University of North Carolina Press.
Castells, Manuel (1996), *The Rise of the Network Society, The Information Age: Economy, Society and Culture*, Vol. 1, Malden, MA, and Oxford, United Kingdom: Blackwell Publishers.
Castells, Manuel (1997), *The Power of Identity, The Information Age: Economy, Society and Culture*, Vol. 2, Malden, MA, and Oxford, United Kingdom: Blackwell Publishers.
Corliss, Richard (1999), "Bang, You're Dead," *Time*, May 3, pp. 49–50.
Cukier, Kenneth (1998), "The Global Internet: A Primer," in Gregory C. Staple (ed.), *Telegeography 1999*, Washington, DC: Telegeography, Inc., pp. 112–49.
Curry, Michael (1997), "The Digital Individual and the Private Realm," *Annals of the Association of American Geographers*, 87(4), pp. 681–99.
Davis, Mike (1990), *City of Quartz: Excavating the Future in Los Angeles*, London and New York: Verso.
Debord, Guy (1990), *Comments on the Society of the Spectacle*, London and New York: Verso.
Dickinson, Amy (1999), "Where Were the Parents?" *Time*, May 3, p. 40.
Elias, Paul (2001), "Paid Informant," *Red Herring*, January 16, p. 51.
Fiske, John (1987), *Television Culture*, London and New York: Methuen.
Gandy, Oscar (1989), "The Surveillance Society: Information Technology and Bureaucratic Social Control," *Journal of Communication*, 39(3), pp. 61–76.
Gibbs, Nancy (1999), "Special Report: The Littleton Massacre," *Time*, May 3, pp. 20–36.
Gibson, William (1984), *Neuromancer*, New York: Ace Books.
Goss, Jon (1993), "The 'Magic of the Mall': An Analysis of Form, Function, and Meaning in the Contemporary Retail Built Environment," *Annals of the Association of American Geographers*, 83, pp. 18–47.
Goss, Jon (1999), "Once Upon a Time in the Commodity World: An Unofficial Guide to the Mall of America," *Annals of the Association of American Geographers*, 89, pp. 45–75.

Hanson, Susan (1998), "Off the Road? Reflections on Transportation Geography in the Information Age," *Journal of Transport Geography*, 6(4), pp. 241–9.

Harvey, David (1989), *The Condition of Postmodernity: An Enquiry into the Origins of Cultural Change*, Cambridge, MA, and Oxford, United Kingdom: Basil Blackwell.

Jacobs, Jane (1961), *The Death and Life of Great American Cities*, New York: Vintage Books/Random House.

Leiner, Barry, Vinton G. Cerf, David D. Clark, Robert E. Kahn, Leonard Kleinrock, Daniel C. Lynch, Jon Postel, Larry G. Roberts, and Stephen Wolff (1998), *A Brief History of the Internet* (revised February 20, 1998), online file at: http://www.isoc.org/internet-history/brief.html.

Lull, James (1988), "Constructing Rituals of Extension through Family Television Viewing," in James Lull (ed.), *World Families Watch Television*, Newbury Park, CA: Sage Publications, pp. 237–59.

McLuhan, Marshall, and Quentin Fiore (1967), *The Medium Is the Massage*, co-ordinated by Jerome Agel, New York: Random House.

Marchand, Roland (1985), *Advertising the American Dream: Making Way for Modernity, 1920–1940*, Berkeley and Los Angeles: University of California Press.

Mitchell, William (1995), *City of Bits: Space, Place, and the Infobahn*, Cambridge, MA: MIT Press.

Morley, David (1986), *Family Television: Cultural Power and Domestic Leisure*, London: Comedia.

Nguyen, Dan Thu, and Jon Alexander (1996), "The Coming of Cyberspacetime and the End of the Polity," in Rob Shields (ed.), *Cultures of Internet: Virtual Spaces, Real Histories, Living Bodies*, London and Thousand Oaks, CA: Sage Publications, pp. 99–124.

NSSC (National School Safety Center) (1999), *School Associated Violent Deaths*, online file at: www.nssc1.org.

Rheingold, Howard (1993), *The Virtual Community: Homesteading on the Electronic Frontier*, Reading, MA: Addison-Wesley Publishing Co.

Robinson, John, and Geoffrey Godbey (1997), *Time for Life: The Surprising Ways Americans Use Their Time*, University Park, PA: The Pennsylvania State University Press.

Rushkoff, Douglas (1994), *Cyberia: Life in the Trenches of Hyperspace*, New York: HarperCollins.

Sack, Robert D. (1997), *Homo Geographicus: A Framework for Action, Awareness, and Moral Concern*, Baltimore and London: The Johns Hopkins University Press.

Saxenian, AnnaLee (1996), "Inside-Out: Regional Networks and Industrial Adaptation in Silicon Valley and Route 128," *Cityscape: A Journal of Policy Development and Research*, 2(2), pp. 41–60.

Sennett, Richard (1970), *The Uses of Disorder*, New York: Knopf.

Shimomura, Tsutomu, and John Markoff (1996), "Catching Kevin," *Wired*, February, pp. 119–23, 172–6.

Sorkin, Michael (ed.) (1992), *Variations on a Theme Park: The New American City and the End of Public Space*, New York: Hill and Wang.

Squires, Judith (1994), "Private Lives, Secluded Places: Privacy as Political Possibility," *Environment and Planning D: Society and Space*, 12, pp. 387–401.

Stephenson, Neil (1992), *Snow Crash*, New York: Bantam.

Taylor, Chris (1999), "Digital Dungeons," *Time*, May 3, p. 50.

Teitelbaum, Sheldon (1996), "Privacy Is History, Get Over It," *Wired*, February, p. 125.

Tuan, Yi-Fu (1982), *Segmented Worlds and Self: Group Life and Individual Consciousness*, Minneapolis: University of Minnesota Press.

Turkle, Sherry (1995), *Life on the Screen: Identity in the Age of the Internet*, New York: Simon & Schuster.

Verhovek, Sam Howe (1998), "Where a Fingertip Click Meets the Elbow Grease," *New York Times* December 23, A14.

Wade, Nicholas (1998), "F.B.I. Set to Open Its DNA Database for Fighting Crime," *New York Times*, October 12, A1, A16.

Zelinsky, Wilbur (1973), *The Cultural Geography of the United States*, Foundations of Cultural Geography Series, ed. Philip Wagner, Englewood Cliffs, NJ: Prentice Hall.

Conclusion

CHAPTER 11

American geographical ironies: A conclusion

Jonathan M. Smith

The first general purpose of this book has been to dispute two theses of the popular American geographical imagination. The first of these is what we might call the thesis of American geographical equality. This states that the territory of the country is fundamentally homogeneous, with individual places no more than local variations on the national theme. Although this view has never had much appeal for geographers, it is necessary to such popular notions as the "American way of life" or the "American dream," and to the scholar's belief that it is possible to speak intelligently about such things as American culture or American history. Indeed one invokes the thesis of American geographical equality almost any time one uses the word American as an adjective. Although we readily concede that federal legislation, mass media, geographical mobility, and large corporations have worked to give much of the country an apparent uniformity – what the geographer Edward Relph called placelessness – we insist that the United States is nevertheless best understood as a congeries of unequal places, a confederation of unequal regional societies.

The second thesis of the popular American geographical imagination that we wish to dispute is often called the thesis of American exceptionalism. This states that the United States is fundamentally unlike other political, social, and cultural entities, largely because it always acts with benevolent intentions. It acts, in fact, for the good of mankind. (It should be noted that this thesis of American exceptionalism sometimes takes a negative form in which the United States is uniquely nefarious.) The origins of this idea are complex, but they clearly include biblical notions of a chosen people, the Enlightenment belief in social progress, and more than two hundred years of remarkably good fortune. At the heart of the thesis of American exceptionalism is the belief that the foundation of the United States marks a fundamental break with the past, so that American history cannot be expected to follow the patterns traced by other large and influential states. We do not for a moment dispute the fact that the United States is an extraordinary country, or even that it may be extraordinary to an extraordinary degree, but must observe that to be extraordinary is not to be exceptional. Extraordinary means unusual, exceptional means exempt from the common condition. We dispute the thesis of American exceptionalism, positive or negative, and insist that the United States is best viewed as a normal state; extraordinarily powerful, to be sure, but subject to the same strains and temptations as other states. The belief that the United States is a nation with a unique destiny to transform the world through its example has had numerous geographic and geopolitical consequences. The most remarkable of these are the ideological wars of the twentieth century, which the United States waged against rival messianic systems to ensure that the peoples of the world remained free to follow the American example in their political and economic arrangements. The domestic consequences of this belief in a unique destiny are not at first so obvious. They spring from the idea that if America is to serve as an example, it must be a clear example. Its example must not be clouded by the influence of foreign states or confused by contradictory complexities in American society itself. The desire to preserve a clear example, uncorrupted by foreign influence, has made the United States uniquely jealous of its own sovereignty. This is evident in the ambivalence that it feels toward the United Nations, in the insistence that its soldiers not serve under foreign commanders, in its reluctance to enter into international agreements, and in its determination to exempt itself from the World Court. It is evident in the surprised indignation Americans express when they discover that foreigners have, unsurprisingly, attempted to influence American elections. It is evident in the belief that the United States, unlike other states, can exercise self-restraint and therefore be trusted with atomic, chemical, and biological weapons (not to mention land mines).

There is at first glance a curious inconsistency between these two theses. The first suggests that the territory of the United States is homogeneous while the second suggests that the territory of the earth's surface is not homogeneous. The first states that all places within the borders of the United States play by the same rules, while the second states that all places on earth outside the United States play by rules different than those that govern the United States. It would appear from this that, in the popular geographical imagination, the United States border marks the most important geographical difference on earth. As geographers, we find such a notion highly implausible, largely because it maps the world's differences at the wrong scale. If one zooms in and views matters in detail, one sees that the greatest differences exist between places. States and macro-regions are by no means the same, of course, but they are in certain respects very similar to one another. There are, for instance, places in the United States that have more in common with places in Latin America, Africa, or Europe, than they do with other places in the United States.

Although these two theses are inconsistent, they are nevertheless closely related, for they together perform the important ideological function of promoting cohesion among what are, in fact, heterogeneous peoples living in some very heterogeneous places. They permit citizens of the United States to imagine themselves as a community without recourse to the sort of nationalistic myths that unify other peoples. It is, of course, impossible to pretend that the American people sprang from common ancestors, from a mythic tribe in the mists of antiquity, as so many other nations do, and so it is necessary to define the group by its relation to a common territory. Whereas other nations imagine that their common ancestry confers certain benefits on members of the national group, Americans imagine that benefits flow from habitation in a common territory. The phrase "land of liberty" captures this territorial mythology. We recognize that this territorial myth has a purpose, for the United States, like any social group, must achieve cohesion if it is to survive, but we believe that it clouds understanding of the actual geography of the country. We would add that the territorial myth of American space will likely become more important in the twenty-first century, when the percentage of Americans with hereditary ties to Europe will appreciably decline.

We believe that Americans, and others who are interested in the United States, must become much more conscious of the country's internal differences, and we believe that these differences are best understood as differences between one place and another. These are not only differences in regional dialects or foodways, but also, and more importantly, differences in power, opportunity, and national influence. These place differences have long been obscured by a preoccupation with inequalities between racial and ethnic groups in the United States, but it seems to us increasingly clear that these inequalities are best understood as inequalities between places. This is not to belittle the plight of marginalized social groups, but to underline the fact that the truly disadvantaged are those members of marginalized social groups who inhabit particular disadvantaged places. Inequality in the United States is primarily, although not entirely, a matter of geographic inequality.

We also believe that Americans, and others who are interested in the United States, must become much more conscious of the similarities between the United States and other countries. They must understand that the United States is subject to the same economic, political, and environmental forces that press upon other states. History ensures that the United States will attempt to cope with these pressures in a unique fashion, but history does not exempt the United States from these pressures. They must also understand that more and more countries now possess social characteristics, such as democracy, advanced technology, widespread prosperity, and social mobility, that were in the past supposedly unique to the United States. At the same time, the United States contains places that exhibit characteristics long believed foreign to the United States: political corruption, collapsing infrastructure, economic stagnation, and a solidifying class system. As other places in the world come to look more and more like the United States, the United States comes to look more and more like other places in the world.

It should be noted that internal geographic inequality appears to be growing, even as efforts to redress this inequality through federal policy and spending are decreasing. We believe that this trend will likely continue in the twenty-first century. Also growing are the similarities between the United States and much of the rest of the world. What this means to the geographer is that historical change requires us to change the scale at which we customarily think about geographical matters. We must move away from our longstanding preoccupation with the state and its territories, simultaneously moving down to the scale of places and up to the scale of the global networks and systems in which these places are involved. We must do this not because the state has ceased to be an important geographical actor, but because the geographical structure and strategies of states appear to be changing.

The second general purpose of this book is to draw attention to selected ironies of the contemporary United States. In *The Irony of American History* (1952), American theologian and political philosopher Reinhold Niebuhr defined irony this way:

An ironic situation is distinguished from a pathetic one by the fact that a person involved in it bears some responsibility for it. It is distinguished from a tragic one by the fact that the responsibility is not due to a conscious choice but to an unconscious weakness. (Niebuhr 1952: 166–7)

In other words a pathetic situation is an unfortunate accident, a tragic situation is a painful sacrifice, and an ironic situation is an exploded pretense. Like individuals, any human community can pass through these dramatic situations. It will elicit pity when, as in a natural disaster, it is the victim of circumstance. It will elicit admiration when, as in a just war, it sacrifices many lesser goods to a greater good. The feelings aroused when a human community passes through an ironic situation are, however, more uncertain, because irony is humbling and, Niebuhr notes, humbling situations are difficult to accept. If evidence is brought forward to suggest that I, as an individual, am not so kind, or so generous, or so intelligent, or so dexterous as I like to think I am, I may well feel hatred against those producing evidence of my weakness. I may dispute the items in their case that are unjust or inaccurate, and by so doing hope to discredit the valid and embarrassing remainder. I may, alternatively, sink into bitter despair, exchanging vain pretensions of power for exaggerated self-abasement. The salutary response to irony would be, of course, contrition and subsequent efforts to achieve closer conformity between my self-image and my actual performance. Like individuals, nations are subject to vain pretensions and ironic refutations, but Niebuhr insists that nations are for various reasons even less inclined than individuals to be chastened by irony. "Collective man always tends to be morally complacent, self-righteous, and lacking in a sense of humor," he writes, and "this tendency is accentuated in our own day by the humorless idealism of our [United States] culture with its simple moral distinctions between good and bad nations" (Niebuhr 1952: 169). Writing in the depths of the Cold War, Niebuhr was primarily concerned to warn that the struggle with the Soviet Union was morally hazardous for the United States because it stimulated the always-latent pretense that America is savior to the world. His concern was not simply topical, however, for

the progress of American culture toward hegemony in the world community as well as toward the ultimate in standards of living has brought us everywhere to limits where our ideals and norms are brought under ironic indictment. (Niebuhr 1952: 57)

Power and prosperity seemed to most Americans of the 1950s proof of the wisdom and virtue of American culture. To outside critics, however, this power and prosperity appeared to have other origins. Abundant natural resources, a fortuitous geopolitical situation, and the disasters of Europe between 1914 and 1945, all favored the United States. Other critics saw American power and prosperity as the illicit fruit of American injustices such as Native American expropriations, African-American slavery, and working class exploitation. These ironic indictments grew louder in the 1960s, and were increasingly compounded by indictments by critics who drew attention to ironic refutations of supposed American norms and ideals. The civil rights movement drew attention to ironic refutations of the pretense that the United States was a nation of civic equality; the environmental movement drew attention to ironic refutations of the pretense that technological innovation invariably improves human life; the peace movement drew attention to ironic refutation of the pretense that Americans are always a peace-loving people.

By the late 1960s, therefore, the United States found itself in a deeply ironic situation. As Niebuhr would have predicted, the responses of Americans to this humbling were mixed. Some, upon being told that the United States was not perfectly virtuous, immediately concluded that it must be devoid of virtue and irredeemable by anything short of radical change. Others reacted with anger and hostility to what they saw as unjust defamation of the United States, their apologetics made considerably easier by the excesses of their critics (who, after all, quickly developed the blinding pretensions typical of "humorless idealism"). A third group experienced something like contrition. In some cases they set their illusions about the United States aside; in others they initiated reforms that would bring American reality into line with American ideals. These responses to the ironic situation of the late 1960s continue to define American politics to this day.

The authors collected here are not politically or ideologically uniform, as any reader who reaches this point in the book can attest, but all agree that discrepancies remain between American myth and American reality, and that these discrepancies give rise to ironies. The thesis of American geographical uniformity is one such myth, ironically refuted by the reality of America's growing spatial diversity. The thesis of American exceptionalism is another such myth, ironically refuted by the global diffusion of supposedly American traits and the appearance in America of ills supposedly unique to foreigners. We draw attention to these and other ironies because, like Niebuhr, we believe that awareness of irony can lead to a salutary dissolution of pretense. We at the same time recognize that anger will be for some the automatic response.

The United States was founded in 1783 as an experiment that would test and, hopefully, demonstrate the political and economic ideas of the European Enlightenment. This intellectual movement had prospered over the course of the eighteenth century, espousing three general propositions that would become foundational to the American world-view. First, it regarded rational scientific inquiry as the only sure route to knowledge, and in so doing undermined the authority that had previously been granted to tradition. Second, it maintained that the scientific method could be used to study and understand social institutions such as governments and economies, as well as the natural world. Third, it believed that such study of the physical and social worlds would lead to progressive improvement in the human condition. While it is true that, in the early United States, several countercurrents of conservative thought mixed with this revolutionary program, and that many joined in the war for American Independence to preserve what they saw as traditional liberties, the core institutions of the United States were largely creatures of the Enlightenment.

American exceptionalism was grounded in the belief that here, as nowhere else, the promise of the Enlightenment was being daily realized. It is true that this combined with a messianic Protestantism that the French and Scottish philosophes would have found uncongenial, but the United States' principal claims to distinction have always been drawn from the Enlightenment. The thesis of American spatial uniformity is itself a product of this Enlightenment thought, since it supposes that there is a form of consciousness known as the American mind that is acceptable to, indeed irresistibly attractive to, all free and rational humans. This is why many have believed, and continue to believe, that to resist or repudiate American culture is as perverse as to deny the solution to a mathematical equation.

Nature was an extremely important concept for Enlightenment thinkers. Their knowledge was grounded in the observed truths of the natural world rather than the revealed truths of the Bible or the inherited truths of tradition. Their ethics, politics, and economics all were founded on a postulated state of nature, which was the way humans were supposed to have behaved before they entered into the social contract. It was, therefore, propitious that Enlightenment ideas could be tested in the New World, where a richly endowed but sparsely populated continent furnished the very conditions that Enlightenment social theory demanded. A rational society could begin in something very like the state of nature, without having first to pass through the violent and potentially self-destructive struggles that were in Europe necessary to clear away monarchy, aristocracy, and clergy. Thus nature, as Smith argues in Chapter 2, became a central idea in American thought, and iconic natural landscapes became symbols by which Americans were able to contemplate this idea. The pretense that the United States was uniquely nature's nation has, however, become increasingly difficult to sustain when the population is overwhelmingly urban and environmental degradation is clear. This is, indeed, part of the deeper irony that a society that expands its knowledge of nature will necessarily reduce its direct experience of nature (as defined by Enlightenment thinkers) and encase itself in a technological shell.

The application of science to practical problems was a central proposal of philosophes like Diderot, since this was one of the most obvious ways in which reason could contribute to human happiness. This too received pronounced expression in the United States, where opportunities for social mobility spurred widespread technological innovation. That much of this was accomplished by ordinary mechanics only served to confirm Enlightenment thinkers' high opinion of the potential of ordinary men and women when they are set free and given property. Thus Smith in Chapter 3 describes the process of place formation and destruction in the United States as a consequence of incessant technological innovation. Indeed he describes modern technocrats in terms that suggest that they are direct descendants of the philosophes. The pretense that technological innovation confers universal benefit is, however, impossible to sustain when we consider the ironic fate of people and places with depreciating value in the new technological complex. This is the irony encapsulated in the oxymoron "creative destruction."

Because they were grounded in nature, which was there for anyone to observe, and reason, which all men were presumed to possess, Enlightenment ideas always had a pretense of universality. Proponents believed that they demanded assent, and so in time would erode the errors and prejudices of individual cultures and cause the human race to be truly of one mind. Agnew and Sharpe detail the consequences of this pretense to universality in Chapter 4. For a hundred years the United States worked to create a space that was, at least in theory, open and attractive to all peoples of the world. The United States was not simply another culture, beloved by those raised in it but enigmatic to outsiders. It was a post-cultural melting pot. For much of the twentieth century the United States has worked to export these supposedly universal values. Yet this pretense too has come under ironic indictment, by growing multiculturalism at home and indigenization abroad. To view both of these movements as ironic indictments of the American pretense of universality is to understand the hatred they arouse in certain quarters.

A central promise of Enlightenment political thought was good government grounded in popular sovereignty, and this unsurprisingly became a basic ideal in the United States. Indeed it was long thought that popular government was what made the United States unique; government not only by the people, but also for the people. Government here was not to be institutionalized power of a family or class of families, to be ignored, evaded, and despised whenever this was prudently possible; it was a to be a universal benefactor. The great difficulty was to devise a form of government that was under popular control and responsive to popular needs, and yet at the same time extensible over a large territory. The solution to this difficulty was the complex federal system that Jonas describes in Chapter 5. In many respects this mix of universal guarantees and local autonomy has proven highly effective, yet the pretense that greater local autonomy will result in greater popular control and greater responsiveness to popular need is subject to numerous ironic refutations. Of these the most striking is that an increasingly autonomous local government is increasingly responsive not to its voters, but to economic investors whose decisions will affect its tax base and credit rating. A second irony is that a nation committed to local autonomy necessarily fosters a geographical diversity that can call into question the very idea of a unified nation.

The idea that economic activity can be scientifically analyzed and rationally managed is largely a legacy of the Enlightenment. At the heart of these discussions was the idea that total wealth could be increased by increased efficiency. This challenged the prevailing aristocratic view of the day, which held that total wealth was more or less fixed and an individual could increase his personal wealth only by taking the property of another. The way to increase efficiency was, in essence, to minimize government control over the economy. An end to mercantilism would permit the efficiency of free trade; an end to government charters and monopolies would stimulate individual initiative; minimal taxes would permit high rates of capital investment and mechanization. The government's role in the economy was, in theory, for the most part limited to enforcement of contracts and protection of property rights. Laissez-faire economics was embraced in the United States to an unusual degree, although the supposed degree has almost always been exaggerated. Ironic refutations of this pretense abound. Several can be found in Rigby's discussion, in Chapter 6, of American economic restructuring in the postwar period. Even more striking is his account of how the strength and dominance of American manufacturing in the 1950s and 1960s created the conditions for its decline in the 1970s and 1980s. Similarly ironic is the way in which the historic underdevelopment of the South created conditions that gave it a comparative economic advantage in the closing decades of the twentieth century. However the greatest irony in this forest of ironies was the emergence of growing pockets of poverty in a country committed to general prosperity. Critics who hold these up as ironic indictments of the pretense of the American Dream are, predictably, often subjected to angry scorn.

Enlightenment thought was not without its contradictions. Among these some of the most important emerged from John Locke's formulation of the universal human rights to life, liberty, and property. Depending on how these terms are defined, it is possible, for instance, that one man's claim to life may infringe upon another man's claim to property. To resolve such a conflict a society needs a more-or-less coherent theory of justice. In this instance it requires a theory of justice that defines the quality of life that the first man can reasonably expect and the quantity of property that the second man can reasonably withhold unto himself. Similar adjudication must balance conflicts between life and liberty, and liberty and property. Enlightenment thinkers believed that such justice could be objectively established, either by the free market or the opinions of impartial observers, and these beliefs were built in to the American economy and judicial system. This has not, however, ensured universal assent. Groups that have fared badly in the marketplace and the courts have always viewed American justice as a pretence ironically refuted by their own experience. Their successful efforts to receive redress have led thinkers such as Kodras, in Chapter 7, to insist that standards of justice are negotiated in local communities. The advantage in these negotiations invariably falls to those with established power, but temporal and geographical change in the definition of justice makes clear the degree to which justice is negotiable. This flexibility is indeed functional within the political economy of the United States, where the actual allocation of quality of life, degree of freedom, and quantity of property is subject to change. Without corresponding changes in the consensus view of justice, intolerably large ironies would invariably appear.

Individualism is yet another Enlightenment value that was incorporated into the culture and political institutions of the United States. This is particularly evident in the case of individual civil rights, which it is the responsibility of the Federal government to protect. In Chapter 8 Forest explains how individualism has given rise to an individualistic ideology of identity, so that most Americans conceive of identity as something personal and unique, the result of experiences and affiliations they themselves have chosen. This gives rise to a liberal political philosophy in which voters are expected to pursue individual interests. Little accommodation is made for groups, unless those groups are geographically concentrated. Thus Kansas farmers can elect a senator, and affluent suburbanites and poor inner-city residents can elect congressmen, but such dedicated political representation is impossible for spatially diffuse interest groups such as environmentalists. One effect of this is to encourage the spatial concentration of identity groups, who can hope to exercise power as a political minority only if they are a majority in a particular voting district. This leads to a deep irony for African-Americans in Forest's account, because the spatial strategy that leads to political success is also the spatial strategy that leads to economic failure. Economic success requires spatial desegregation, but spatial desegregation would virtually ensure the disappearance of African-Americans from political office.

The Enlightenment was, as we have seen, devoted to the idea that society should be far more egalitarian than it had been under the ancien régime, and its ideas were imported directly to the United States, where they helped to bolster a democratic culture. This was closely related to, but not the same as, universal male suffrage. Democratic culture, or what is sometimes called democratism, lead to an easy familiarity between persons of unequal social station that almost all nineteenth-century European travelers to the United States found remarkable. Although ordinary Americans were prepared to tolerate high levels of income disparity, they were generally not inclined to defer to the affluent as social superiors. Indeed one of the enduring curiosities of the United States is the way that it mixes extravagant conspicuous consumption with the rather inflexible enjoinder that no one should act as if he thinks he is better than anyone else. In Chapter 9 Duncan and Lambert describe the way in which democratism and economic inequality are reconciled by dressing the realities of class in the inoffensive garb of taste. This allows the common American pretense that the upper classes consist of ordinary folk who just happen to be very rich. They don't keep to themselves because they are snobs, but only because they prefer the company of those who share their tastes and pastimes. This pretense is, of course, quite easily brought under ironic indictment when members of some lower class act as if this bogus democratism were true. And little angers the American upper class more quickly than the suggestion that they are snobs.

Open communication of information was at the very heart of the Enlightenment, and this was imbedded in American culture as the principle of freedom of speech. Information was the means whereby individuals could transcend the limits of personal experience and community prejudice and enjoy the benefits of universal reason. This emancipation is well advanced today, as Adams argues in Chapter 10, when experience is increasingly detached from the nominal location of the body and one's senses are extended in space by the prostheses of broadcasting, cable, and the Internet. Vicarious experience is not new, of course; it is in a sense as old as language. What is new is the realism of vicarious experience, the range of vicarious experiences that Americans can choose from, and the large portion of total experience that Americans now choose to have vicariously. The attraction of vicarious experience is that it can be controlled to a degree that is seldom possible with direct experience. Here we encounter a second Enlightenment theme. The effort to exercise rational control over our environment today includes efforts to exercise rational control over our information environment. Discontented with the haphazard information that comes willy-nilly from our actual surroundings, we increasingly substitute refined, filtered, and synthetic information that comes by way of media. Inhabiting this new information environment, individual Americans work to manage the image they project by filtering and refining the information they divulge in personal communication. They at the same time work to manage the images they consume by filtering and critically evaluating the information they receive. This pretense of control over the information environment is, however, subject to repeated ironic refutation. We all know that our personal information is irresistibly extracted, assembled and stored to serve the interest of other people, and that our artificial experiences are always to some degree fashioned by other people, in the interest of other people. On top of this is the general irony that open communication has not brought us closer to the Enlightenment promise of universal reason, but has instead spawned philosophic pluralism.

It is exhilarating to debunk the myths of someone else's conventional wisdom, and to point out ironic refutations of someone else's pretensions. One might go so far as to say that it is intoxicating. In such an exercise opportunity for pretension is almost limitless, and along with this, opportunity for ironic refutation. Thus are ambitious faultfinders often caught and mangled in the gears of their own critical machinery. We claim no exemption from this hazard. We have, however, in our several ways assumed this risk in the hope that we will be able to describe the geography of the United States in terms that are unfamiliar, yet revealing. In doing so we have in various ways attempted a new form of regional geography. We have already noted how this places the geography of the United States in larger spatial, geopolitical, economic, and technological contexts. It also places the geography of the United States in a larger intellectual context, making concepts such as symbolism, identity, myth, ethics, aesthetics, and communication fundamental to the geographical imagination. A geography cannot be understood apart from the ideas entertained by the people who make that geography, even when these ideas are erroneous or their connections to the material world are not obvious.

Reference

Niebuhr, Reinhold (1952), *The Irony of American History*, New York: Charles Scribner's Sons.

Discussion questions

Chapter 1 Introduction

1. If place still matters in the United States why do some people think that it is being "destroyed"?
2. The terms "America" and "the United States" are often used interchangeably. What might this indicate about the geographical imagination of the user?
3. Space versus place is the conceptual opposition that is central to this book. For this to work, how are the terms defined?
4. The history of the United States is often seen as expressing an "exceptionalism." What does this mean? Can one accept the distinctiveness of the "American experience" without endorsing exceptionalism? How does this book propose doing so?

Chapter 2 The place of nature

1. In what ways do you directly interact with your local environment?
2. In what ways did your grandparents or great grandparents directly interact with their local environment?
3. Make a list of all the commodities you knowingly consumed in the past week. Where do you suppose they came from? What environmental impact likely resulted from their extraction?
4. What are the qualities that you expect to find in a "natural" landscape?
5. Do you tend to regard natural landscapes as settings for activity or as scenes for contemplation? Where did you learn to view natural landscapes in this fashion?
6. Is "the environment" the same thing as "nature"? If not, what is the difference?
7. Did the Cuyahoga River fire reveal something important about the general state of nature in the United States in the late 1960s?
8. Are we fortunate that technocratic environmentalism replaced frugal environmentalism as the dominant strategy of environmentalists in the last decades of the twentieth century?

Chapter 3 The place of value

1. What is the primary source of value in the place where you live?
2. Is this presently appreciating or depreciating?
3. What are the visible signs of appreciation or depreciation?
4. What are the principal causes of appreciation or depreciation?
5. Do you aspire to be a technocrat? Why or why not?
6. What would you find appealing about living in a technopolis?
7. Do humans guide technological development? Or are they guided by it?
8. In the year 2050, will places in the United States be more equal or unequal than they are today, in terms of value?

Chapter 4 America, frontier nation

1. The idea of the "frontier" has been an important one in explaining the historical geography of the United States. What does it mean? How is it used?
2. The characters played in many films by John Wayne were often associated with a dominant understanding of masculinity in mid-twentieth-century American culture. What were the traits of this masculinity? How did they relate to American foreign policy during the Cold War?
3. Globalization can be seen as a force that shrinks or stretches the world but that is without obvious origins in any particular part of the world. How might the argument of this chapter be used to counter this understanding of globalization?
4. How are the United States' origins as a country connected to its contemporary place in the world?

Chapter 5 Local territories of government

1. How much influence should the Federal Government have in local affairs?
2. What are the issues that really concern people in your home community? How do people, community groups, and business organizations in your locality get involved with politics?
3. How fragmented is local government? (Focus on one county or metropolitan area.)
4. What is the evidence for the persistence of interjurisdictional disparities in fiscal effort, social conditions, levels of service provision in your city or state?

5. Do you think that choice rather than equality has become the main principle informing the delivery of local services like education? What other principles appear to be important?
6. What evidence can you find for the impact of globalization in your community, city, or state? How have local residents responded to this impact?
7. In your experience, what have been the most notable local impacts of welfare reform, school desegregation, environmental regulation, or public service privatization?
8. How does your state or locality compete for economic activity? Has there been any conflict as a result? How does your city or locality like to present itself to the world outside it?
9. What support can you find for the idea that the United States is experiencing a crisis of government?
10. In your travels abroad or while watching TV, have you seen any evidence of American political values and institutions being copied elsewhere in the world?
11. What ideas from abroad have influenced or should inform American politics and government?

Chapter 6 Urban and regional restructuring in the second half of the twentieth century

1. Can the capitalist economy experience continuous, uninterrupted growth, or must it undergo phases of economic crisis and recession?
2. Is regional uneven development a necessary or an inevitable feature of the capitalist economy?
3. What is the division of labor? How has the spatial division of labor changed over the twentieth century?
4. Is trade beneficial to the United States economy? Are the gains/losses from trade equally shared among different people and places?
5. What is foreign direct investment? Why do firms internationalize?
6. What do we mean by income inequality? How might we measure income inequality? Has income inequality increased or decreased in the United States over the past fifty years?
7. Identify the snowbelt and sunbelt regions of the United States. Name some of the key cities in these regions. What factors encouraged the movement of people and jobs from the snowbelt to the sunbelt over the last half of the twentieth century?

Chapter 7 "With liberty and justice for all"

1. What forces shape the local social order of your town or city? What activities provide employment and incomes? Are they public (e.g. government) or private? What recent economic, political, or social changes have shaped the local social order? Were these changes related to broader regional, national, or global changes?

2. Where would you place your locale (town, city, county) in the regional/state economy? the national economy? the global economy?

3. Where would you position your immediate family within the income distribution of all families in your town/city?/state?/country?

4. Think about the well-being of your immediate family in relation to the market, state, and civil society. By what practices do you and your family members earn income (wages, salaries and/or dividends)? Does anyone in your family receive public (i.e. state) assistance such as Social Security payments, disability support, food stamps, or an education grant? Does your family receive or provide support and resources through social networks organized outside the market or state, such as the church, a charity concern, or extended family and friendship ties?

5. The principle of equal opportunity underlies popular notions of freedom and justice in America. Do you think the opportunities you or your family have to succeed are as good as anyone else's in America? Are they better? Worse? Why? Does your race, gender, age, or sexuality privilege or disadvantage you? What would you think about your opportunities if you were of another race, gender, age, or sexuality?

6. Assuming that each person in America has an equal opportunity to succeed, do you think that unequal outcomes are acceptable? What about those who do not have the resources to obtain food, health care, education? Is their deprivation justifiable as long as each person has had the same opportunity to succeed?

7. Do you agree or disagree with the following statements about freedom in America?
   All Americans, regardless of income, race, age, gender, and so on, have the freedom
   1. to vote in elections
   2. to speak their mind

3. to get an education
4. to obtain secure employment
5. to avoid being sick and unable to obtain health care
6. to avoid being hungry but unable to obtain food

Chapter 8 A new geography of identity?

1. What would be the major political and economic consequences of complete racial desegregation? Who would benefit the most from such a development? Who would benefit the least? Would such a development tend to limit or increase white racial privilege?
2. Is segregation inevitable if race remains an important social distinction? Do social distinctions always lead to segregation? Is this true for ethnicity? For gender?
3. What might be the major consequences of multiple-racial identification on the Census? (Keep in mind that this categorization is generally based on self-identification.) Does the use of multiple-racial identification suggest that racial categories are disappearing completely, or does it just suggest that new racial categories are forming?
4. Should the state only enforce formal legal equality? To what extent should the state address issues of social, economic, and political inequalities between different racial groups?
5. What are the consequences of single-member electoral districts as compared to other systems of political representation (such as those suggested by Lani Guinier)? Is one system always better than the other? If not, in what situations might one prefer alternative systems?
6. What are the major racial distinctions in your region? In what ways is this related to settlement and migration patterns? Do these racial distinction correspond closely to social distance?
7. How do you identify yourself in terms of race and ethnicity? How much control do you have over this classification? That is, do others "see" you as you "see" yourself? Is your identity more like a volunteristic symbolic ethnicity or like an imposed racial category?
8. How does your identity vary (if at all) in different geographic and social contexts? How much freedom do you have to move between these different contexts? Is this related to the level of segregation in your area?

Discussion questions   337

Chapter 9 Landscape, aesthetics, and power

1. It is claimed that neotraditionalism is the future of community planning in America. What is it reacting against? How does it differ from other forms of planning?
2. How do some residential landscapes maintain social inequalities by acting to include some people but exclude others? Consider both their aesthetics and material forms.
3. Some contemporary landscapes draw upon an aesthetics of historical places. In what ways are the social realities of these historical landscapes often hidden?

Chapter 10 Mediascapes

1. Why is American culture unusually receptive to the diffusion of new innovations, including communication technologies?
2. How have communication technologies assisted in the American quest for privacy?
3. How have communication technologies been represented in popular culture as destroyers of the possibility of privacy?
4. In what ways are the distinctions between public and private life blurred by media products such as television shows?
5. Does dependency on media appear to inhibit the socialization of children as safe and sane individuals?
6. How does the emergence of surveillance as an industry rather than a government monopoly relate to the proliferation of Information Technology (IT)?
7. If we accept Turing's hypothesis, what constitution of personal identity is encouraged by the diffusion of computers and IT?
8. What particular political and social events might arise from the fact that America's receptivity to technological innovations is not entirely compatible with America's passion for privacy and autonomy?

Further reading

Chapter 1 Introduction

Agnew, John, and James Duncan (eds.) (1989), *The Power of Place: Bringing Together Geographical and Sociological Imaginations*, London: Unwin Hyman. Surveys the case for seeing "place" as a useful concept for examining a range of problems in the social sciences and the humanities.

Burstein, Andrew (1999), *Sentimental Democracy: The Evolution of America's Romantic Self-Image*, New York: Hill and Wang. Critically engages with the tendency of late eighteenth- and early nineteenth-century Americans to romanticize themselves and their political "experiment."

Countryman, Edward (1996), *Americans: A Collision of Histories*, New York: Hill and Wang. Interprets American history as a "collision" between contested notions of the nation's origins and development rather than a single, simple narrative upon which all have agreed. What is clear, however, is that out of these various currents an American identity, though contested and changing, has emerged.

Greene, Jack P. (1993), *The Intellectual Construction of America: Exceptionalism and Identity from 1492 to 1800*, Chapel Hill, NC: University of North Carolina Press. Traces the history of ideas about "America" among European and American thinkers, particularly the idea of America (the United States) as a land apart, a morally separate and "exceptional" realm from that left "behind" in Europe.

Leach, William (1999), *Country of Exiles: The Destruction of Place in American Life*, New York: Pantheon. Claims that geographical mobility and cultural homogenization have destroyed the American experience of places as unique settings. Of course, Americans have always been highly mobile and subject to common pressures. The book nevertheless does capture a sense of an older America in which local places were more distinctive.

Meinig, Donald W. (1986), *The Shaping of America. Volume I: Atlantic America, 1492–1800*, New Haven, CT: Yale University Press. The first volume in a magisterial series on the conquest and settlement of North America by Europeans. This volume deals with the Atlantic world in which the United States originated as a separate political entity and the regional and local distinctions that marked and sometimes wracked the country from its origins.

Perret, Geoffrey (1989), *A Country Made by War: From the Revolution to Vietnam – the Story of America's Rise to Power*, New York: Random House. Sees the origins and rise of the United States as connected to the systematic use of violence to secure political and economic objectives. This is something of an antidote to those who see American history in an overly idealistic light.

Tuan, Yi-Fu (1974), "Space and Place: A Humanistic Perspective," *Progress in Geography*, 6, pp. 211–52. A classic statement of the difference between the concepts of "space" and "place" and why this matters.

Wolfe, Alan (ed.) (1991), *America at Century's End*, Berkeley and Los Angeles: University of California Press. A survey of the social, economic, demographic, and political condition of the United States towards the close of the twentieth century edited by a leading American sociologist.

Zelinsky, Wilbur (1973), *The Cultural Geography of the United States*, Englewood Cliffs, NJ: Prentice-Hall. An exhaustive cultural geography of the United States paying close attention to persisting regional and local differences down through the 1960s by the leading empirical cultural geographer of the United States of his day.

Chapter 2 The place of nature

Evernden, Neil (1992), *The Social Creation of Nature*, Baltimore: Johns Hopkins University Press. Several histories of the idea of nature have been written, those published in recent years most often stressing the "construction" of nature by the social imagination. This book is a good place to start in this literature.

McGreevy, Patrick (1994), *Imagining Niagara: The Meaning and Making of Niagara Falls*, Amherst: University of Massachusetts Press. Symbolic landscapes of nature have meaning because they are set in a larger context of cultural products – literature, philosophy, science, art – that describe and interpret that landscape. These relations are sometimes described as intertextuality. This book provides a brief, penetrating account of one very important example. It is theoretically sophisticated but at no point attempts to awe the reader with this accomplishment.

O'Brien, Raymond J. (1981), *American Sublime: Landscape and Scenery of the Lower Hudson Valley*, New York: Columbia University Press. Another useful work along lines similar to those followed by McGreevy, this is a historical geography of another very important nineteenth-century symbolic landscape.

Schama, Simon (1995), *Landscape and Memory*, New York: Alfred A. Knopf. Those interested in the cultural significance of natural landscapes should peruse this book, which is a model for cultural analysis of landscape icons and images, although only some of its chapters are devoted to North American examples.

Weaver, Richard M. (1964), *Visions of Order: The Cultural Crisis of Our Time*, Baton Rouge: Louisiana State University Press. Symbols both express certain dominant ideas in a culture and function to maintain the dominance of those ideas. Symbols also are an important source of cultural identity and cohesion. This book gives a cogent account of this.

Chapter 3 The place of value

Brooks, David (2000), *Bobos in Paradise: The New Upper Class and How They Got There*, New York: Simon & Schuster. Funny but serious, this book describes and reflects the habits and attitudes of the new technocratic, meritocratic elite. The thesis is that this new elite has reconciled the old opposition between the values of counter-cultural bohemians and those of the strait-laced bourgeoisie – hence the title Bobos. Acquisitive and fully adapted to the demands of the workplace, this group is at the same time tolerant of a very high level of cultural pluralism.

The ability of this class to absorb contradictions without feeling any resulting strain leads Brooks to conclude that they will remain in power for a very long time.

Garreau, Joel (1988), *Edge City: Life on the New Frontier*, New York: Doubleday. New places of value in the late-twentieth-century United States have sprung up almost exclusively in suburban locations at the edge of cities. Journalist Joel Garreau, who earlier revealed his geographical acumen in *The Nine Nations of North America* (New York: Doubleday, 1991), here provides a geographically-informed journalist's account of the people and decisions behind this new landscape.

Harrison, Lawrence E., and Samuel P. Huntington (eds.) (2000), *Culture Matters: How Values Shape Human Progress*, New York: Basic Books. Increasingly apparent inequality in the rates of development in various sectors of the developing world has led many to look to culture as a critical variable. The ability to create wealth is not simply a matter of access to necessary resources and a conducive regulatory environment, but also requires a particular attitude and orientation toward those resources and that environment. Places of value are, therefore, a result of a combination of favorable site, fortunate situation, and appropriate culture.

Hugill, Peter J. (1993), *World Trade since 1431: Geography, Technology, and Capitalism*, Baltimore: The Johns Hopkins University Press. This geographer combines Lewis Mumford and Immanuel Wallerstein with a vast knowledge of the history of technology to make an endlessly insightful account of the evolution of the modern world system. This book is highly readable and yet virtually alone among geographies in grasping the full geographical consequences of technological shifts.

Kaplan, Robert D. (1998), *An Empire Wilderness: Travels into America's Future*, New York: Random House. Kaplan is another serious journalist who thinks about geography, and listens to geographers. A record of journeys he has taken in various regions of the United States, this book describes the social, cultural, and geographical fracturing of the nation. Of particular note is his rather gloomy assessment of an emerging landscape in which islands of prosperity stud a sea of economic stagnation and decline. He is, perhaps, too ready to discover in the United States those same patterns of social disintegration he has famously described elsewhere (see, for instance, "The Coming Anarchy," *Atlantic* [February 1994], pp. 44–75), but one cannot view the American scene in quite the same light after reading his book.

Lasch, Christopher (1995), *The Revolt of the Elites and the Betrayal of Democracy*, New York: W. W. Norton. The rise of the technocratic meritocracy has alarmed some critics, but their criticisms often seem little more than a thin defense of inefficiency and incompetence. Lasch is original and interesting because in this and other works he reaches back to nineteenth-century populism for the idea that democracy requires a democratization of competence rather than a democratization of consumption. Particularly interesting to geographers will be his description of declining loyalty to place among the new meritocracy, and the disappearance of places for popular debate in an era of ideological enclaves and ghettos.

Meinig, D. W. (1986–), *The Shaping of America: A Geographical Perspective on 500 Years of History*, 4 vols., New Haven: Yale University Press. Three volumes of this monumental work are now in print and the release of the fourth is anticipated shortly. Meinig provides a detailed understanding of the United States as a dynamic geographical system of routes, regions, and places. Though long and highly learned, this work is eminently readable, and is indispensable to all who would understand why certain historical periods have produced certain places of value.

Reich, Robert (1991), *The Work of Nations: Preparing Ourselves for 21st Century Capitalism*, New York: Alfred A. Knopf. This is a highly readable if perhaps overly buoyant account of, among other things, symbolic analysts and the zones they inhabit. It has been highly influential in shaping public understanding of the origins and significance of what are sometimes called the "new class." Its author was Secretary of Labor in the Clinton administration, and so it carries some political baggage, but the work is for the most part a good example of popular scholarship.

Chapter 4 America, frontier nation

Agnew, John (1987), *The United States in the World Economy: A Regional Geography*, Cambridge: Cambridge University Press. Views the history of the United States economy as balanced between pressures towards national integration, on the one hand, and the long-term relationship of many regions and localities to foreign markets and sources of investment, on the other. Though the "globalization" of the American economy has increased significantly recently, the connections to a larger world economy were there from the start, if more for some regions than for others.

Agnew, John (1998), *Geopolitics: Re-Visioning World Politics*, London: Routledge. Describes the way in which a "modern geopolitical imagination" developed in Europe, spread to the rest of the world with colonialism, and still informs the making of foreign policy. This imagination sees the world as a whole with strategically ranked regions based on how "threatening" the states of a region are economically and culturally and the competitive pursuit of primacy by leading states as the driving force behind it.

Appy, Christian G. (ed.) (2000), *Cold War Constructions: The Political Culture of United States Imperialism, 1945–1966*, Amherst, MA: University of Massachusetts Press. Examines how American culture and society were negatively affected by the early Cold War and the effects that this had on other countries.

Perlmutter, Amos (1997), *Making the World Safe for Democracy: A Century of Wilsonianism and Its Totalitarian Challengers*, Chapel Hill, NC: University of North Carolina Press. Describes the conflict between an American "mission" to make over the world in its image, named "Wilsonianism" after President Woodrow Wilson, its first great proponent, and its major twentieth-century adversaries, German Nazism and Soviet Communism.

Sharp, Joanne P. (2000), *Condensing the Cold War: Reader's Digest and American Identity*, Minneapolis: University of Minnesota Press. Uses the popular American magazine *Reader's Digest* as a source of information about American popular attitudes towards the Soviet Union and the Cold War and how these helped to refine an American identity.

Turner, Frederick Jackson (1893), *The Significance of the Frontier in American History*, Washington, DC: American Historical Association. The classic statement of the impact of the American settlement frontier on the mores of American society and politics.

Williams, William Appleman (1972), *The Tragedy of American Diplomacy*, New York: Dell. A critical evaluation of the course of American foreign relations since the 1890s suggesting how the hubris of American foreign policy in the twentieth century owes much to the long-standing American hubris about the need for others to emulate America.

Wills, Garry (1997), *John Wayne's America*, New York: Simon & Schuster. A colorful portrayal of the American film icon John Wayne, carefully relating Wayne's screen persona to the evolving sense of American manhood and fears of foreign contamination over the years of his career, from the 1930s down to the 1970s.

Chapter 5 Local territories of government

Burns, Nancy (1994), *The Formation of American Local Governments: Private Values in Public Institutions*, New York: Oxford University Press. A useful short monograph on the importance of local government in the United States political system. Discusses different types of local government and the values that have shaped local political institutions. Argues that local public institutions are the result of collective action and tend to embody private values.

Donahue, John D. (1997), *Disunited States*, New York: Basic Books. An excellent summary of recent arguments for and against devolution in the United States. Provides empirical evidence that devolution and inter-territorial competition for capital have enhanced inter-state disparities in economic development and social well-being. One of the few books to focus explicitly on the state level of government.

Burrows, Nigel (1988), *Government and Politics of the United States*, 2nd. edn., Basingstoke and London: MacMillan Press. A fairly standard textbook summarizing processes and institutions of government in the United States. Although mainly focused on the federal level, it also has useful chapters on federalism and the politics of cities and suburbs.

Naylor, Thomas H., and William H. Willimon (1997), *Downsizing the U.S.A.*, Grand Rapids, MI: William B. Eerdmans Publishing Company. A very readable, albeit "over-the-top," analysis of contemporary American society and institutions. The authors argue that America's government, its corporations, cities, schools, and other institutions, have become too big and powerful. Makes the case for the peaceful dissolution of the United States through secession.

Ohmae, Kenichi (1995), *The Borderless World: Power and Strategy in the Interlinked Economy*, New York: Harper Business. Widely cited analysis of the disappearing nation state and the emerging global economy. Already a classic neo-liberal treatise on the new world economic and political order.

Staeheli, Lynn A., Janet E. Kodras, and Colin Flint (eds.) (1997), *State Devolution in America*, Urban Affairs Annual Reviews 48, Thousand Oaks, CA: Sage Publications. Theoretically aware and carefully edited collection of papers discussing different dimensions of political devolution in the United States. Most of the contributors are leading political geographers, making this a coherent and unique perspective on devolution. Especially useful chapters on citizenship, political rights, labor relations, welfare reform, education, and the environment.

Teaford, Jon C. (1997), *Post-Suburbia: Government and Politics in the Edge Cities*,

Baltimore, MD: Johns Hopkins University Press. A useful and straightforward discussion of the creeping privatization of public space in suburbia, written by one of the leading historians of local government in the United States.

Weiher, Gregory R. (1991), *The Fractured Metropolis: Political Fragmentation and Metropolitan Segregation*, Albany, NY: State University Press of New York. A rigorous statistical analysis of the effects of political fragmentation in American metropolitan areas. Provides useful summaries of public choice and liberal reformist approaches to local government organization. Some students may find the data analysis hard going.

Chapter 6 Urban and regional restructuring in the second half of the twentieth century

Armstrong, H., and J. Taylor (2000), *Regional Economics and Policy*, 3rd edn., Oxford: Blackwell. Comprehensive overview of methods of regional economic analysis. Brief reviews of different theoretical debates on regional economic development, careful exposition of methods of analysis and numerous, largely United Kingdom, applications. Extensive discussion of European regional policy.

Best, M. (1990), *The New Competition: Institutions of Industrial Restructuring*, Cambridge: Harvard University Press. Examines the causes of economic decline and prospects for growth. Failure of United States business linked to bureaucratic/hierarchical forms of organization and the inability of large firms to respond to new forms of competition. The new competitors are characterized by a commitment to continuous improvement in products and processes of production and by organizational forms that encourage flexibility and innovation – clusters and networks of small and medium-sized firms. Empirical studies of business organization in the United States, Japan, and parts of the Third World lend some support to the theoretical claims.

Bluestone, B., and B. Harrison (1982), *The Deindustrialization of America*, New York: Basic Books. Describes the decline of American "smokestack industries," such as steel and automobiles, and the consequences of this decline on individuals and communities across the United States. Attributes the collapse of these economic sectors to increased foreign competition and the willingness of American business to abandon industries and regions and reinvest capital in new industrial spaces, often outside the United States. In turn these tendencies are linked to public forms of corporate financing and the consequent exposure of United States economic activity to short-run fluctuations in financial markets. Various policy options to reindustrialize in a more stable fashion are contrasted with state efforts to liberalize the economy.

Dicken, P. (1998), *Global Shift*, 3rd edn., London: Paul Chapman. Comprehensive account of the global economy. Packed with an enormous amount of empirical information on international production, trade, and investment, along with detailed case studies of the global extent of select industries. Summarizes key debates over the meaning of globalization and reviews literature on firm organization, on why firms internationalize, on the costs and benefits of trans-national corporations (TNCs), and on relations between TNCs and nation states.

Levy, F. (1998), *The New Dollars and Dreams*, New York: Russell Sage Foundation.

Detailed account of economic growth and income inequality in the United States over the second-half of the twentieth century. A history of rapid economic growth and decline is outlined and tied to different forms of industrial development. The geography of growth and labor mobility are also explored at different spatial scales. These geographies and histories of growth are linked to the changing distribution of United States incomes. The claims are supported by a vast amount of empirical material.

Long, L. (1987), *Migration and Residential Mobility in the United States*, New York: Russell Sage Foundation. Main aim is to reveal the trends and patterns of geographical mobility within the United States since 1940. Analysis is based upon the decennial United States Census of Population and a number of related national surveys. Reviews current literature on migration and mobility and provides a broad overview of population movements in the United States at a variety of spatial and temporal scales. Excellent source of United States migration data with some international comparisons.

Madrick, J. (1995), *The End of Affluence: The Causes and Consequences of America's Economic Dilemma*, New York: Random House. Reviews the recent history of United States economic growth. Central argument is that productivity growth declined significantly from the 1970s and income growth followed. Prior to the 1970s the "American Dream" was based upon the combination of high rates of productivity growth and sustained income gains that saw wages doubling every thirty-five years or so. The end of affluence has also been marked by growing income inequality. The slowdown of United States economic growth is again linked to international competition and erosion of the efficiencies previously associated with mass production. A number of policy prescriptions to restore growth are examined, though no clear solution to the productivity slowdown is offered.

Massey, D. (1984), *Spatial Divisions of Labour*, London: Macmillan. Integrates Marxist theory with geography to understand recent patterns of uneven development in the British space-economy. Key methodological arguments linking abstract theory with concrete observation. The spatial organization of capitalist production in the United Kingdom is conceptually linked to the division of labor and to the creation of regional economies through the history of investment. Case studies of industrial and regional change and the geography of British employment.

Storper, M., and R. Walker (1989), *The Capitalist Imperative*, New York: Blackwell. Develops an explicitly geographical model of competition to explore the spatial dynamics of capitalist production. Focuses on competition and technology as motors of change and agues strenuously for a geographical understanding of the development and location of industry. Criticizes equilibrium arguments and offers an evolutionary account of political economics, industrial, and regional development in the United States.

Chapter 7 "With liberty and justice for all"

Galloway, R. (1991), *Justice for All? The Rich and Poor in Supreme Court History, 1790–1990*, Durham, NC: Carolina Academic Press. Demonstrates the considerable flexibility given to United States Supreme Court Justices in interpreting the body of law mediating economic interests.

Goldsmith, W., and E. Blakely (1992), *Separate Societies: Poverty and Inequality in U.S. Cities*, Philadelphia: Temple University Press. Documents how rising inequalities in American societies play out in distinct economic and political transformations of United States metropolitan areas.

Harrison, B., and B. Bluestone (1988), *The Great U-Turn: Corporate Restructuring and the Polarizing of America*, New York: Basic Books. The classic text articulating the linkage between recent restructurings in the United States' economy and income polarization within the American population.

Harvey, D. (1996), *Justice, Nature, and the Geography of Difference*, Oxford: Blackwell. Interrogates the processes whereby injustice is geographically produced.

Newman, K. (1992), *Falling from Grace: The Experience of Downward Mobility in the American Middle Class*, New York: Free Press. Documents varied personal experiences of middle-class failures, set in the context of larger transformations in the American political economy.

Smith, D. (1994), *Geography and Social Justice*, Oxford: Blackwell. How central geography is to questions of social justice.

Watkins, K. (1997), *Globalization and Liberalisation: Implications for Poverty, Distribution, and Inequality*, Occasional Paper 32, United Nations Development Program (UNDP). Demonstrates how globalization and neo-liberalization generate rising income disparities around the world.

Chapter 8 A new geography of identity?

Almaguer, Tomás (1994), *Racial Fault Lines: The Historical Origins of White Supremacy in California*, Berkeley: University of California Press. Almaguer's study of race relations explores the different racial ideologies applied to Mexicans, American Indians, and Asians in California. By addressing the construction of racial difference for these three groups, he argues that the study of racism must move beyond consideration of black–white relations.

Anderson, Margo, and Stephen Feinberg (1999), *Who Counts?: The Politics of Census Taking in Contemporary America*, New York: Russell Sage Foundation. This highly readable and accessible book discusses the social context of the Census and shows how seemingly technical questions have become the center of political conflict. Such conflicts affect both the balance and distribution of political power and the process of social science research.

Davis, F. James (1991), *Who is Black? One Nation's Definition*, University Park: The Pennsylvania State University Press. *Who is Black?* is a comprehensive study of the American system of hypodescent. Davis traces the origin, development, and consequences of the "one-drop rule" for racial identity in the United States.

Delaney, David (1998), *Race, Place and the Law 1836–1948*, Austin, TX: University of Texas Press. This book is a detailed geographic analysis of the origin and legal dimensions of racial segregation in the United States. Delaney traces various legal efforts to separate blacks and whites from the early nineteenth to the mid-twentieth century.

Jacobson, Matthew Frye (1998), *Whiteness of a Different Color: European Immigrants and the Alchemy of Race*, Cambridge: Harvard University Press. Jacobson joins a number of scholars exploring the construction of "whiteness" as a racial category.

This book analyzes the complex relationship between the "national" and "racial" identities of immigrants and how these categories were modified in respond to changing conceptions of American national identity.

Massey, Douglas S., and Nancy A. Denton (1993), *American Apartheid: Segregation and the Making of the Underclass*, Cambridge, MA: Harvard University Press. *American Apartheid* is the best, most comprehensive study of racial segregation in the twentieth century. Massey and Denton combine extensive empirical data on residential patterns in American cities with a carefully crafted analysis of poverty and economic inequality. It is an absolutely indispensable reference.

Wilson, William Julius (1996), *When Work Disappears: The World of the New Urban Poor*, New York: Vintage Books. This is the most recent in a series of books by Wilson exploring the relationships among urban segregation, race, and industrial restructuring. His focus on the role of blue-collar jobs leads Wilson to suggest that economic and class-based policies may be the best way to reduce racial inequalities.

Woodward, C. Vann (1974), *The Strange Career of Jim Crow*, 3rd rev. edn., New York: Oxford University Press. Originally published in 1955, this landmark book remains the classic study of the institutionalization of white supremacy in the South after 1877. This revised edition also discusses the consequences of the civil rights movement's successful struggle against this legalized racial order.

Chapter 9 Landscape, aesthetics, and power

Brooke, S. (1995), *Seaside*, La Gretna: Pelican.

Davis, M. (2000), *Magical Urbanism: Latinos Reinvent the US City*, New York: Verso.

Duncan, J. S., and N. G. Duncan (forthcoming), *American Beauty: Living the Aestheticized Life in an Affluent New York Suburb*, Baltimore: Johns Hopkins University Press.

Chapter 10 Mediascapes

Carey, James W. (1988), *Communication as Culture: Essays on Media and Society. Media and Popular Culture: I*, Boston: Unwin Hyman. A work in media theory quite often cited approvingly by geographers. The title expresses the basic premise that communication technologies and their appropriation by society are indicative of culture.

Castells, Manuel (1997), *The Power of Identity, the Information Age: Econ-omy, Society and Culture*, Vol. 2, Malden, MA and Oxford, United Kingdom: Blackwell Publishers. A study of the relationship between globalization and personal identity by one of the most influential voices in academia. Part of a three-volume set.

Light, Andrew, and Jonathan M. Smith (1998), *The Production of Public Space: Philosophy and Geography II*, Lanham, MD: Rowman and Little-field. Philosophers and geographers come together in this collection of essays to reflect on contemporary changes in the meaning and use of public spaces, and on the social and political processes that have caused these changes.

Meyrowitz, Joshua (1985), *No Sense of Place: The Impact of Electronic Media on Social Behavior*, New York: Oxford University Press. An extremely detailed argument to the effect that television reconfigures the boundaries between social situations, thereby altering power relations in society. Topics brought into the discussion include most notably gender relations, relations between adults and children, and the establishment of political authority and legitimacy.

Sorkin, Michael (ed.) (1992), *Variations on a Theme Park: The New American City and the End of Public Space*, New York: Hill and Wang. A collection of essays on the state of public space. In general, the authors attest to the weakening and decline, if not the actual "end" of public space.

Sennett, Richard (1970), *The Uses of Disorder: Personal Identity and City Life*, New York: Knopf. A classic work explaining some possible psychological motivations for living in the suburbs, particularly the flight from disorder and complexity in society and personal experience. This book dismantles the idea that a suburban neighborhood constitutes a community.

Tuan, Yi-Fu (1982), *Segmented Worlds and Self: Group Life and Individual Consciousness*, Minneapolis: University of Minnesota Press. Perhaps Tuan's most accessible book, it sets forth persuasive evidence that the historical changes we associate with modernization are linked to specific changes in the social construction of space. Theater spaces, domestic spaces, and even table settings garner Tuan's attention.

Some useful websites

Chapter 1 Introduction

American Studies Crossroads Project: www.georgetown.edu/crossroads/
Library of Congress, American Memory: Historical Collections for the National
Digital Library: http://memory.loc.gov
National Atlas of the United States: www-atlas.usgs.gov

Chapter 4 America, frontier nation

Columbia International Affairs Online: www.ciaonet.org
Council on Foreign Relations: www.cfr.org/p/
Foreign Affairs: www.foreignaffairs.org/
Radical History Review: http://chnm.gmu.edu/rhr/
US Census Bureau, Statistical Abstract of the United States:
www.census.gov/prod/www/statistical-abstract.us.html

Chapter 5 Local territories of government

Many states, counties, municipalities, and special districts in America publish
their own web sites, containing useful information, publications, and links to
other sites. For example, the Commonwealth of Massachusetts' web set can be
found at www.magnet.state.ma.us/, and the web site for the City of Charlotte and
Mecklenburg County, North Carolina, is at www.charmeck.nc.us/.
The United States Bureau of Labor Statistics publishes statistical data by United
States region at http://stats.bls.gov/regnhome.htm

Chapter 6 Urban and regional restructuring in the second half of the twentieth century

For world economic and social data (by country):
www.un.org/esa (economic and social development indicators, and related statistics)
www.unido.org (industrial development, technology, and economic data)
www.worldbank.org (development indicators and national economic statistics)

For comprehensive United States trade data:
www.ita.doc.gov (international trade statistics, state, and metropolitan trade data)

For United States national and regional economic data :
www.census.gov (general household and economic data)
www.bls.gov (employment, income, and related information)
www.nber.org (general economic data and reports)

Chapter 7 "With liberty and justice for all"

Center on Budget and Policy Priorities: www.cbpp.org/
Northwestern University and University of Chicago Joint Center for Poverty
Research: www.jcpr.org/
United Nations Development Program: www.undp.org/undp/
University of Michigan, Survey Research Center, Panel Survey of Income
Dynamics: www.isr.umich.edu/src/psid/
University of Wisconsin Institute for Research on Poverty: www.ssc.wisc.edu/irp/

Chapter 8 A new geography of identity?

The Census Bureau makes a wealth of information available from its web site:
www.census.gov/

Links of particular interest include:

- Congressional Apportionment:
  www.census.gov/population/www/censusdata/apportionment.html
- Income: www.census.gov/hhes/www/income.html
- Poverty: www.census.gov/hhes/www/poverty.html
- Ethnic and Racial Minorities:
  www.census.gov/pubinfo/www/hotlinks.html
  www.census.gov/population/www/socdemo/race.html
- Color Maps of Racial and Ethnic Distribution in the United States:
  www.census.gov:80/geo/www/mapGallery/RHOriginPD-1990.html

Legal materials:
Department of Justice, Civil Rights Division: www.usdoj.gov/crt/crt-home.html
Oyez Project: Supreme Court Multimedia Database: http://oyez.nwu.edu/
Segregation Simulator from the *New York Times*:
www.nytimes.com/library/cyber/week/012298segregate-sim2.html
Supreme Court Decisions: http://supct.law.cornell.edu/supct/

Chapter 9 Landscape, aesthetics, and power

www.bedfordny.com/
www.seasidefl.com/

Chapter 10 Mediascapes

The Annenberg Public Policy Center: http://appcpenn.org (for research on society and media)

Centers for Disease Control and Prevention, United States Department of Health and Human Services: www.cdc.gov/safeusa/youthviolence.htm (guidelines for preventing youth violence)

Educators for Social Responsibility: www.esrnational.org (organization advocating school-based instruction in conflict resolution)

Privacy International: www.privacyinternational.org (human rights group that monitors surveillance by corporations and governments worldwide)

Privacy Rights Clearinghouse: www.privacyrights.org (for information on the protection of personal privacy)

Index